CANADIAN CHILD WELFARE LAW

This book states the law as of
April 15, 1990

CANADIAN CHILD WELFARE LAW

Children, Families and the State

NICHOLAS BALA
Faculty of Law, Queen's University, Kingston, Ontario

JOSEPH P. HORNICK
*Executive Director, Canadian Research Institute
for Law and the Family, Calgary, Alberta*

ROBIN VOGL
*Former Senior Counsel, Metro Toronto Children's Aid Society,
Toronto, Ontario*

THOMPSON EDUCATIONAL PUBLISHING, INC.
TORONTO

Canadian Cataloguing in Publication Data

Bala, Nicholas C.
 Canadian child welfare law

Includes bibliographical references.
ISBN 1-55077-018-7

1. Parent and child (Law) - Canada. 2. Children - Legal status, laws, etc. -
Canada. 3. Social work with children - Law and legislation - Canada.
4. Child welfare - Canada. I. Hornick, Joseph P. (Joseph Phillip), 1946-   .
II. Vogl, Robin. III. Title.

KE3515.B35 1990   344.71'0327   C90-094915-5
KE3735.B35 1990   66917

ISBN 1–55077–018–7
Printed in Canada by T.H. Best Printing Company.
1 2 3 4 5 6   95 94 93 92 91 90

TABLE OF CONTENTS

ACKNOWLEDGEMENTS

Completion of *Canadian Child Welfare Law: Children, Families and the State* would not have been possible without the support of numerous organizations and individuals. The production of the text was the product of the energy, knowledge and skill of the contributing authors. We were fortunate to secure the expertise of numerous individuals whose experience and knowledge of Canadian child welfare legislation is so diverse and comprehensive. The authors each bring their own experiences and perspectives to their work and the analysis and interpretation in each chapter is that of the contributing authors alone.

The financial support provided by the Alberta Law Foundation to the Canadian Research Institute for Law and the Family (CRILF) is gratefully acknowledged. Thanks are also extended to the Ontario Law Foundation for providing support to Robin Vogl, making her contribution to this book possible.

We would also like to thank Ruellen Forsyth-Lawson, Joanne Paetsch and Marilyn Anderson for their diligent assistance in the preparation of the manuscript. Finally, thanks are due to Barbara Burrows and Donna Phillips for their patience and careful assistance in reviewing and researching the manuscript.

N. Bala
J.P. Hornick
R. Vogl

May, 1990

EDITORS AND CONTRIBUTORS

EDITORS

Nicholas Bala, Professor, Faculty of Law, Queen's University, Kingston, Ontario

Joseph P. Hornick, Executive Director, Canadian Research Institute for Law and the Family, Calgary, Alberta

Robin Vogl, Former Senior Counsel, Metro Toronto Children's Aid Society; now a lawyer in private practice, Toronto, Ontario

CONTRIBUTORS

Christopher Bagley, Professor, Faculty of Social Work, The University of Calgary, Calgary, Alberta

Richard F. Barnhorst, Executive Director, The Child, Youth and Family Policy Research Centre (Ontario), Toronto, Ontario

Jennifer A. Blishen, Senior Counsel, The Children's Aid Society of Ottawa-Carleton, Ottawa, Ontario

Barbara A. Burrows, Research Associate, Canadian Research Institute for Law and the Family, Calgary, Alberta

David A. Cruickshank, Visiting Professor, Faculty of Law, University of British Columbia and Director, Professional Legal Training Course, Continuing Legal Education Society of B.C.

James P. Felstiner, Judge, Provincial Court (Family Division), North York, Ontario

Anne Genereux, Manager of Accreditation and Legal Support, Ontario Association of Children's Aid Societies, Toronto, Ontario

Shelly Hallett, Court Reform Task Force, Ontario Ministry of the Attorney General, Toronto, Ontario

Wendy Harvey, Crown Counsel, Ministry of the Attorney General, Vancouver, British Columbia

Mary Jane Hatton, Judge, Provincial Court (Family Division), Toronto, Ontario

Susan G. Himel, Deputy Offical Guardian (Personal Rights), Ministry of the Attorney General, Toronto, Ontario

Heather Katarynych, Senior Counsel, Metropolitan Toronto Children's Aid Society, Toronto, Ontario

A. Peter Nasmith, Judge, Provincial Court (Family Division), Toronto, Ontario

Donna Phillips, Research Assistant, Canadian Research Institute for Law and the Family, Calgary, Alberta

Mary-Jo Maur Raycroft, Lawyer in private practice, Kingston, Ontario

Anne Russell, Judge, Provincial Court (Family and Youth Divisions), Edmonton, Alberta

Murray Sinclair, Associate Chief Judge, Provincial Court, and Co-Commissioner, Public Inquiry Into the Administration of Justice and Aboriginal People, Winnipeg, Manitoba

D.A. Rollie Thompson, Associate Professor, Dalhousie Law School, Halifax, Nova Scotia

Bernd Walter, Children's Advocate, Alberta Family and Social Services, Edmonton, Alberta

R. James Williams, Judge, The Family Court for the Province of Nova Scotia, Dartmouth, Nova Scotia

Carol Yaworski, Director, Henwood Homes, Oshawa, Ontario

PREFACE

George Thomson

This book provides readers with an easily accessible overview of child protection proceedings. It is a valuable addition to an extremely important field, one which has been too seldom addressed by Canadian authors. For the most part, the authors write from a legal perspective and have themselves played a major role in bringing about the substantial changes in child protection laws and procedures that have been introduced across Canada over the past 10 to 15 years. The book has been written expressly for those with less experience in the field, and for those from other disciplines who are required to function within the alien, confusing and sometimes hostile environment of the Family Court.

Much greater attention has traditionally been paid to juvenile delinquency (now young offender) proceedings than to child protection proceedings, despite the fact that many more Canadian children are removed from their homes pursuant to our child protection laws. Paradoxically, the major recent changes in child protection laws have been the result of two factors: on the one hand, a much greater recognition of how extensive and serious is the physical and sexual abuse of children and, on the other, a realization of how unregulated and unstructured has been the power granted to those who make major decisions about the welfare of children and their families. This book summarizes well the almost revolutionary changes in law and procedure that this new knowledge has produced.

The child protection field is truly multidisciplinary and yet much of the decision-making is legally constrained and must be justified within an increasingly legal framework. Professional survival within this area depends not only on an understanding of this legal framework and the reasons for its existence, but also on a knowledge of practical methods of overcoming the uncertainty, feelings of loss of control and fear that come from crossing professional boundaries and justifying one's approaches and decisions to lawyers and judges. The helpful information in this text should aid in bridging the professional gulf that often exists, whether that gulf is ideological or comes from obvious differences in vernacular and professional attitude.

The book is valuable for reasons that go beyond the fact that it explains well the law, the legal process and the perspectives of lawyers, legal analysts and judges. First, the material demonstrates how enormously complex child protection matters can be by including discussion of such issues as: when to grant access to biological parents after permanent orders; how to represent children, parents and child welfare authorities; the devastating impact of child welfare laws on aboriginal children and parents; and the confusion that comes from parallel civil and criminal proceedings. Particularly helpful is the chapter that compares child welfare laws from province to province, highlighting the ongoing debate over whether a best interests or a noninterventionist approach is the better one to take. It is always clear in these readings that this is a field beset with uncertainty stemming from our modest ability to predict human behaviour, the always limited funds for child welfare services and the fact that all proposed answers carry with them an element of risk.

Second, this book builds upon a firm understanding of how dependent the legal process is upon the expertise and commitment of those from other disciplines. The inevitable tension between legal and other professionals is acknowledged. The authors also seek to explain and justify the basic protections demanded by a concern for fairness and individual rights. This generally serves as a springboard for consideration of how the legal process must attempt to support those who work with children and families, while still ensuring their positions are justified, tested and given the appropriate weight. Much of the controversy in this field is apparent when one attempts to balance the competing perspectives of different disciplines. These authors understand this, and demonstrate only modest tendencies to see legal rules and principles as the sure guide to correct answers.

Third, the writings demonstrate the authors' commitment and dedication to child welfare. They also bring home the strong personal beliefs held by those who work in this field, and the healthy uncertainty and openness to new ideas that characterize those who practice successfully in an area where human tragedy and fallible decision-making are everyday events. Perhaps nowhere in the book is this more apparent than in the chapter where four judges explain their individual approaches to child protection cases and their efforts to cope with the enormous responsibility that is placed on their shoulders. It is also reflected in the chapter on representation in protection cases, where lawyers who regularly represent children, parents and protection agencies explain the dilemmas and challenges they face in presenting their cases in court.

In summary then, this book is a valuable addition to the literature in this field. It explains, in an easy-to-read manner, a complex, often unintelligible set of legal rules and procedures. It describes the ongoing debate over difficult questions, the answers to which can decide the fate of children and families who come before the Family Court. It also reinforces the human aspects of all decision-making in this field, where the role of the state is clearly at issue and the needs and interests of our most vulnerable citizens are at stake.

George Thomson
Deputy Minister
Province of Ontario

AN INTRODUCTION TO CHILD PROTECTION PROBLEMS

Nicholas Bala[*]

THE ROLE OF THE STATE IN THE RAISING OF CHILDREN

In our society there is much controversy over the "best" way to raise children. Appropriate parental practices concerning such matters as children's nutrition, discipline, toilet training, day care, schooling, sports, sex education, dating and recreation are all the subject of heated debate among experts and social commentators. However, parents are largely left to make their own decisions about the best way to care for their children, according to their own values, beliefs and experience. This includes the parental right to determine the extent to which their children will be involved in making decisions about their own lives, though inevitably as they grow older children begin to exercise more autonomy.

It is accepted that parents are human, and far from perfect. Even if parents know what is best for their children, they may be unwilling or unable to do it. Nevertheless, it is a fundamental premise of our society that coercive government interference in family life should be kept to a minimum.

Many government services and benefits are offered to assist parents on a voluntary basis. For example, Canadian governments support day care, as well as cultural activities and recreational programs for children, but it is for parents to decide whether their children will participate in them. Parents are required by law to ensure that their children receive an education, and the government spends billions of dollars supporting the public school system, but parents may choose to send their children to private or sectarian schools or to educate them at home.

There are, however, some situations in which the care parents provide is considered so inadequate that direct interference by the state is justified to protect children from their families. These include situations where parental care has fallen below the minimum standards our society will tolerate. Removal of a child from his or her home is not legally justified just because the child might have greater opportunities elsewhere; rather, it is necessary to prove that parental care poses significant risk to the child.

[*]   Professor, Faculty of Law, Queen's University, Kingston, Ontario.

This book examines the situations in which the state becomes involved in protecting children from their parents, with a particular emphasis on the role of the legal system. It considers the situations, processes and consequences of involuntary state intervention in the family.

THE HISTORY OF CHILD PROTECTION IN CANADA

It has not always been accepted that the state has a duty to protect children. The legal system of ancient Rome recognized the concept of *patria potestas*[1] which gave a father complete authority over his children, including the lawful authority to sell them into slavery or even put them to death. With the spread of Christianity, the harshest aspects of Roman law were tempered, and by the 6th century A.D. the father's power had been limited to the right of "reasonable chastisement."

The English common law adopted the principle of a parental right of reasonable chastisement, which in practice gave parents a licence to subject their children to harsh discipline, and even to sell them into apprenticeship. Through the Middle Ages there was little recognition of a concept of childhood as a time of special needs, and there was a tendency to treat children as miniature adults.[2] While gradually provision was made to care for orphans, first by religious bodies and later by municipal institutions, little was done to protect children in the care of a parent or guardian. The criminal law made it an offence to kill or maim a child, and it was an offence to fail to provide a child under one's care with necessities of life. In practice, however, these laws were sporadically enforced, and children were regularly beaten by parents, subjected to sexual exploitation and forced to work long hours under terrible conditions in mines and factories.

Prompted by the work of such social critics as Charles Dickens, who described the fate of children in institutions in *Oliver Twist*, the 19th century was a period of social reform in the United States, Great Britain and Canada. Many developments in this period improved the lot of children. The latter part of the century witnessed the establishment of a compulsory, publicly-funded school system, as well as special courts and corrections facilities to deal with juvenile offenders.

Private Children's Aid Societies were established in various Canadian municipalities in the last decade of the 19th century, with the objective of helping orphaned, abandoned and neglected children. In 1893, reformers persuaded the Ontario legislature to enact *The Children's Protection Act*,[3] which gave these

---

[1]   Latin for "the power of the father."

[2]   See L. de Mause, *The History of Childhood* (London: Souvenir Press, 1976). Generally, on the history of child abuse, see M.C. Olmesdahl, "Paternal Power and Child Abuse: An Historical and Cross-Cultural Study" in J. Eekelaar & S. Katz, eds, *Family Violence* (Toronto: Butterworths, 1978) 253.

[3]   S.O. 1893, c. 45.

Societies broad legal powers, including the right to remove neglected or abused children from their homes and become legal guardians for such children.

Child protection agencies were established throughout Canada by the early years of this century, and child protection legislation was enacted in each province. However, the enormous growth and the legalization of the field has really only occurred in the last 30 years.

Until the early 1960s, child protection agencies dealt largely with fairly obvious cases of abuse and neglect and with situations of adolescent unmanageability. Agencies also had responsibility for the placement and adoption of illegitimate children, (i.e., those born out of wedlock) and had considerable responsibility for dealing with delinquent youth as well. While the courts exercised a supervisory function over the removal of children from their homes and over the adoption process, in practice the system tended to operate informally. Historically, most of the judges who sat in the Family Courts and dealt with this type of case lacked legal training, and lawyers rarely appeared in these proceedings. Parents who were involved in the protection process were often poorly educated, low-income individuals who lacked the sophistication and resources to contest the actions of the agencies. There was no thought given to notions of children's rights, and children were not involved in court proceedings deciding their futures.

In the last 30 years, enormous changes have occurred in the child protection field in Canada. One development was the identification of the battered child syndrome in the early 1960s.[4] Until that time, doctors and social workers tended to suspect physical abuse only in cases where there was a witness to the abuse, or a child stated that an assault had occurred. Then researchers began to realize that parents often lied about abuse, describing injuries they inflicted as the result of accidents, and that children were often too frightened or too young to tell the truth to investigators during a single interview. Increased understanding of the problem led to changes in legislation to require professionals and members of the public to report suspected cases of child abuse. Child abuse registers were established in many North American jurisdictions in the mid–1960s to help keep track of abusers and abused children, and to facilitate research. Changes in reporting laws and growing professional awareness led to significant increases in the number of reports of physical abuse.

The late 1970s and early 1980s were marked by a "discovery" of child sexual abuse, similar to the earlier uncovering of physical abuse. Researchers learned that children were often too intimidated, guilty or ill-informed to report sexual abuse, and that parents and professionals often ignored reports or symptoms of abuse. Changes in public and professional awareness have resulted in enormous

---

[4] A seminal article in the field is by the American pediatrician, H.C. Kempe, "The Battered Child Syndrome" (1962) 181 J. Amer. Med. Assoc. 17.

increases in the rate of reporting of sexual abuse in the past decade, though it is questionable whether there has really been a significant increase in actual rates of abuse. There have also been changes in legislation to facilitate the prosecution of those who abuse children.[5]

While child protection agencies are dealing with more cases of physical and sexual abuse, their involvement in other areas has declined. Illegitimacy is no longer of great social significance; in many provinces it has ceased to be a legal concept. Single parents receive more social and financial support than in the past. Though their position is not an easy one, many more single mothers are keeping their children, resulting in a major decline in the adoption work of child welfare agencies. With the proclamation of the *Young Offenders Act*[6] in 1984, Canadian child protection agencies have also ceased to have direct responsibility for delinquent youth.

The last decades have witnessed a number of highly publicized cases of physical and sexual abuse, some of which resulted in tragic deaths. There has also been growing attention to the inadequacy of the state's child protection efforts. There have been cases where state agencies and protection workers have faced legal sanction for failing to protect children, and others where children have been abused or maltreated while in the care of state agencies. The media reports have focused on the most sensational cases, but they have produced an increased level of public and political awareness of the child protection field. There have been a number of public inquiries and government reports on issues in the child protection field in Canada during the past 15 years, some of which have resulted in significant legal and administrative reform.

THE LEGAL REVOLUTION

Related to some of the fundamental changes in the child protection field has been a veritable revolution in the role of law and the courts in Canadian society. Until the last quarter century, the law was primarily concerned with the regulation of economic, commercial and property affairs, and with the control of deviant personal behaviour by means of the criminal law.

In the last 25 years, however, the nature of law has changed dramatically. Law has become a social policy tool, affecting virtually every aspect of Canadian society. We are living in an increasingly "rights-based" society, in which individuals look to the courts to redress wrongs. For example, the courts have been called upon to deal with such political issues as abortion, language rights and native land claims.

---

[5] Bill C–15, *An Act to Amend the Criminal Code and the Canada Evidence Act*, 2d Sess., 33d Parl., 1986. (S.C. 1987, c. 24) came into effect in Canada on January 1, 1988.

[6] R.S.C. 1985, c. 4–1.

Reflecting and reinforcing the trend to rely on the law has been the introduction of the *Canadian Charter of Rights and Freedoms*[7] in 1982. This constitutional document has a number of important provisions, and is having a profound impact on many aspects of Canadian society, including child welfare. It has, for example, been cited by the courts to ensure that parents whose children are apprehended from their care are entitled to a judicial hearing within a reasonable time, and to restrict the authority of child protection workers to apprehend children without prior judicial authorization.[8] This recognizes the importance of due process in our society. The *Charter* has also been used by the courts to eliminate unjustified discrimination and has, for example, been invoked to give biological fathers greater rights in the adoption process.[9] As will become clear from the discussion of the *Charter* in this book, the rights it guarantees are not absolute, but rather are subject to "such reasonable limits ... as can be demonstrably justified in a free and democratic society."[10]

The increased emphasis on individual rights has had a strong impact on child protection proceedings in Canada. The protection process has been legalized. There is a greater recognition of the rights of parents and children; there are greater controls placed on the power of the state to intervene in the family. The child protection system is now premised on notions of due process. This reflects fundamental values in our society, as well as ensuring that decisions about state intervention are based on careful consideration of the issues by an impartial arbiter.

Due process is not without costs, however. With the legalization of the child protection system has come an expanded legal aid system, to ensure representation for indigent parents and, in many Canadian jurisdictions, legal representation for children. Perhaps more serious than the financial costs of due process have been the human costs. Due process takes time. Delays due to the court process can be very stressful for children and families, though sometimes parents can take advantage of delays to improve their parenting skills and relationships with their children.

While due process may ensure fairness and considered decision-making, it can make the work of various professionals seem more difficult. The child protection system now has a more sharply adversarial nature, and professionals in that system may have their opinions and decisions challenged in the sometimes hostile environment of the courtroom, by lawyers who may seem insensitive to constraints placed on those in the child protection system. It must be recognized

---

[7] Part I of the *Constitution Act, 1982*, being Schedule B of the *Canada Act 1982 (U.K.)*, 1982, c. 11.

[8] *Re C.P.L.* (1988), 70 Nfld & P.E.I.R. 287 (Nfld U.F.C.); and *H.M.* v. *Director of Child Welfare* (1989), 22 R.F.L. (3d) 398 (P.E.I.S.C.).

[9] *MacVicar* v. *British Columbia Superintendent of Family and Child Services* (1986), 34 D.L.R. (4th) 488 (B.C.S.C.).

[10] *Supra*, note 7, s. 1.

that parents and children who were separated from one another by the child welfare system have always felt a level of hostility. However, it is only with the rise of due process that they have had a forum to effectively challenge decisions that profoundly affect their lives.

LEGAL CONTEXTS AND THE PROTECTION OF CHILDREN

There are a number of different legal contexts in which issues related to the protection of children from abuse, neglect or ill treatment can arise.

Historically, the criminal law was the only legal tool employed to protect children. It still has an important role. It is a criminal offence to sexually abuse or physically assault a child. However, with regard to physical assault, caretakers can raise the defence of "using force by way of correction ... if the force used does not exceed what is reasonable under the circumstances."[11] It is also an offence for a parent or guardian to fail to provide a child with "necessaries of life" or to abandon a child under the age of 10.[12] While the *Criminal Code* can be used to prosecute those who harm children, it is a blunt tool which is often difficult to use.

Persons charged with criminal offences are guaranteed a broad set of rights under the *Charter*. There is an onus upon the prosecutor to prove guilt according to the highest legal standard, "proof beyond a reasonable doubt." Abuse cases are especially difficult to prove because it is often necessary to rely heavily on the evidence of the child who was the victim of abuse. The traditional rules of evidence and procedure governing criminal cases made it difficult for children to testify and discounted their evidence. Bill C–15, which came into effect in 1988, has made it easier for children to testify and there has recently been a significant increase in the number of prosecutions in Canada, especially for sexual abuse.

Criminal investigations are handled by the police, and the presentation of the case in court rests with the Crown attorney. There are sometimes disagreements between these authorities and child protection agencies about how cases should be handled. Child protection agencies may be concerned about the effect on a child of prosecuting a parent; alternatively, the agency may favour a prosecution, but the police may be unwilling to proceed. There has recently been an effort to improve liaison and coordination between child protection agencies and those responsible for criminal prosecutions. This has tended to result in more support for the prosecution of cases. Even now, criminal prosecutions for physical abuse are rare, except in cases involving serious physical injury or death.

It is generally easier to prove abuse or neglect in a civil proceeding than in a criminal case. The rules of evidence are somewhat more relaxed in a civil trial, and the standard of proof is lower, requiring only proof "on the balance of

---

[11] *Criminal Code*, R.S.C. 1985, c. C–46, s. 43.

[12] *Ibid.*, ss. 215, 218.

probabilities." The *Charter of Rights* has more limited applicability to civil proceedings.

Abuse and neglect are most commonly dealt with as a child protection case. This is a civil proceeding in which the state-mandated child protection agency seeks to intervene in the family, either by making the child the subject of court-ordered supervision, or by having the child removed from parental care, on either a temporary or permanent basis.

Sometimes abuse or neglect issues are raised in a civil case involving separated parents who are in a dispute over custody or access to their children. With growing awareness of the problem of child abuse, the number of cases involving this type of allegation has increased.

It is also possible for a child who has been the victim of abuse, or a guardian acting on behalf of the child, to bring a civil suit for monetary damages. However, abusers frequently lack the financial resources to satisfy a judgment and such suits have been rare. Further, children are often reluctant to sue their parents, even after they reach adulthood. However, victims may feel a sense of psychological vindication from recovering an award, and such civil suits are becoming more common.[13] It is also becoming more common for victims of abuse to seek monetary awards from their provincial Criminal Injuries Compensation Board. It is not necessary for there actually to be a criminal conviction for compensation to be granted, though there must be proof an offence occurred. In theory, the Board may seek reimbursement from an abuser for compensation paid, but in practice the Boards do not pursue abusers if they are without assets or reasonable income.

Complex issues may arise if there is more than one proceeding dealing with allegations of abuse or neglect; for example, it is possible for a criminal prosecution and a child protection application to occur simultaneously. Although the major focus of this book is on child protection proceedings, Chapter 10 considers parental custody or access disputes in which abuse allegations have been made and Chapter 11 deals with criminal prosecutions.

THE ROLE OF THE CHILD PROTECTION AGENCY

In every Canadian jurisdiction there is an agency which has legal responsibility for investigating reports that a child may be in need of protection and taking appropriate steps to protect children from ill-treatment. This may involve providing services to the child and parents in their home, or removing the child from the home on a temporary or permanent wardship basis. The child protection agency may provide services on either a voluntary basis, or an involuntary basis, making use of the legal system to require families to receive services. Child protection agencies are also responsible for arranging adoptions, though private agencies may be involved as well. In some localities child protection agencies

---

[13] See D. Brillinger, "Sex Assault Victim wins $125,000 award against father" (15 September 1989) Lawyers Weekly 8.

assume other responsibilities related to their principal mandates, such as organizing programs for the prevention of child abuse.

Child protection agencies are given very significant powers under legislation to search for children who may be in need of protection and, if necessary, to force parents to surrender custody. These agencies receive all or most of their funding from the state. From a conceptual perspective, child protection agencies are agents of the state, exercising the coercive power of the state. In most Canadian jurisdictions, child protection services are provided by provincial employees serving out of local offices, typically of the Ministry of Social Services.

In Manitoba, Nova Scotia and Ontario there are local child protection agencies, called Children's Aid Societies or Child and Family Service Agencies. These agencies typically serve a particular geographical area. In Ontario, a few Children's Aid Societies are denominational, serving only Catholic or Jewish families and children in a particular region. Recently, child protection agencies have been established in Ontario and Manitoba to serve native children exclusively. Even in provinces with these local semi-autonomous child protection agencies, ultimate statutory and financial responsibility for the agencies rests with the provincial government, and their employees should be viewed in many respects as agents of the state.

The structure of each child protection agency or local office is unique but they do share certain common features. Agencies have two basic functions: child protection (or family services) and child care. In some agencies workers have both child protection and child care responsibilities. Other agencies, however, have two types of workers.

Child protection workers are responsible for investigating suspected cases of abuse or neglect, and working with children and parents in their homes. Some agencies have intake departments, with a special mandate to deal with initial investigations and crisis situations; in such agencies if ongoing service is required, the cases are usually transferred to a family service worker after the initial investigation is completed by the intake worker.

Child care workers have responsibility for children who have been taken into care on either a temporary or permanent basis. Typically, children are actually cared for in foster or group homes, and child care workers have a liaison function with foster parents and group home staff. In some agencies, adoption work is done as part of child care while in others it is the responsibility of a separate department.

In some agencies there are specialized workers who are responsible for dealing with specific problems, such as adolescents living on the streets or child sexual abuse; in others, workers have a more generalized protection caseload. In some localities, particularly smaller agencies, staff members are responsible for both child protection and child care work.

In Québec, there are regionalized Social Service Centres with a mandate for providing a broad range of social services to children and adults. Workers in that province may have a mixed caseload including, for example, young offenders, child protection cases and marital counselling cases.

Child protection agencies are involved with the court system and must have access to adequate legal services. In some localities, especially larger centres, there are staff lawyers who are exclusively involved in representing agencies in child protection cases. In other places, child protection agencies hire lawyers in private practice to provide representation, typically establishing a relationship with a specific law firm. Use may also be made of court workers; these are employees of child protection agencies who are not lawyers but who are familiar with the court system. They are engaged to handle certain cases in court, typically those which are less contentious.

Child protection agencies provide services in conjunction with other agencies and professionals in private practice. For example, initial reports of suspected abuse or neglect may come from doctors in hospital emergency departments, public health nurses or teachers. When determining how a case should be handled, a protection agency may refer a case to a psychologist, psychiatrist or mental health clinic for an assessment, sometimes as part of the court process. If a child is taken into the care of an agency, it may be necessary for agency staff to work with therapists or educators. If there is a criminal prosecution, child protection workers will have to maintain contact with the police and Crown attorney's office. To be effective, child protection agencies must have good working relationships with others in the community.

Working for a child protection agency can be a difficult, stressful job. There are high turnover rates in these agencies. While most workers in this field are well-educated, having a college diploma or university degree, often in social work, they are typically relatively young and inexperienced. Young professionals often start their careers in these agencies and, after gaining some experience, move to less stressful work elsewhere in the helping professions.

Much of the stress in the child protection field relates to both the nature of the cases and the nature of the work. There is an inevitable degree of tension, as the role of child protection workers has both supportive and investigative functions. Child protection workers generally try to be supportive to parents and to provide services on an informal, voluntary basis. Indeed, most families that a worker comes into contact with do not end up in court, and in these cases the role of the protection worker can be regarded as similar to that of a therapist or counsellor, or an educator in parenting skills. However, the role of a child protection worker can also in some ways be viewed as similar to that of a police officer. Protection workers have legal responsibility for investigating allegations of abuse or neglect. Even if their involvement with a family is voluntary, in the event of later difficulties, anything a parent or child has told a worker may be relevant and admissible in a subsequent protection hearing.

Through education and disposition, most child protection workers want to have a therapeutic role, helping children and parents. But, understandably, workers may be viewed with hostility and distrust by parents. This often makes the job frustrating and contributes to the high turnover rate.

Some would argue that legal constraints make child protection work even more demanding. The law sometimes makes it difficult for child protection staff to take effective measures to protect a child. It is not enough for a worker to feel or believe that a child is at risk and should be removed from parental care. Involuntary removal can only occur if legal requirements are satisfied and the need for this is documented in court. However, if a child is inappropriately left in parental care and suffers further abuse, the worker will inevitably feel a sense of guilt and moral responsibility, and may even face civil or criminal liability for the failure to protect a child.[14]

THE LAW AND THE CHILD PROTECTION PROCESS

Child protection agencies are charged with the legal and moral obligation of promoting the welfare of children, by ensuring that they are not subject to abuse or neglect. Provincial and territorial legislation gives these agencies the authority to intervene in the lives of parents and children in order to provide protection. While the legislation varies from one jurisdiction to another, and different judges have conflicting views about how to interpret and apply the legislation, the law clearly presumes that parents are capable of raising their children without state interference. The law places a burden on child protection agencies to clearly establish the need for intervention.

The nature of this burden was discussed by Judge Stortini in *Re Brown*:

> In attempting to establish what is best for the children, I must accept the realities and accidents of life and refrain from judging the needs of the children and the parents' ability to satisfy them on an unfair or unrealistic basis ...

> In other words, the community ought not to interfere merely because our institutions may be able to offer a greater opportunity to the children to achieve their potential. Society's interference in the natural family is only justified when the level of care of the children falls below that which no child in this country should be subjected to.[15]

In another case, *Re Chrysler*, Judge Karswick frankly recognized the potential risk of placing the burden on the Children's Aid Society (C.A.S.) to prove its case.

---

[14] Fortunately, the courts have made it clear that child protection workers will only have liability for failure to protect a child in circumstances where there has clearly been inappropriate conduct. See *M.M.* v. *K.K.* (1989), 38 B.C.L.R. (2d) 273 (C.A.) which held that workers or an agency would only have civil liability for a monetary award if it could be proven that their negligence caused the subsequent injury to the child. In rejecting the claim in this particular case, the court was sympathetic to the fact that the workers had a "very onerous" caseload and had to set priorities. In *R.* v. *Leslie* (1982), 7 W.C.B. 431 (Ont. Co. Ct) the Court held that workers could only have criminal liability for the failure to protect a child who was injured by his mother if their conduct was proven to be "so negligent as to constitute a reckless or callous disregard for the safety" of the child.

[15] (1975), 9 O.R. (2d) 185 at 189 (Ont. Co. Ct).

It seems to me that ... the potential for real and immediate abuse must be clear before the state should be permitted to intervene by removing the child from her parents. If it were otherwise, it would allow a C.A.S. to be the final arbitrator in a so-called child abuse case and would leave the parents and the child with no real recourse to a really independent and impartial court. In adopting this principle, I realize that there is always the danger that some real and even irreparable harm may be inflicted upon the child if the parents are really potential child abusers, but the C.A.S. has not been able to prove that fact because of the unavailability of witnesses who can testify to the alleged abuse and therefore has not been able to meet the standard of proof required by the court.

I think that this risk must still give way to the greater risk of the irreparable harm that can be inflicted upon a child and the danger to society of the serious undermining of the parents and the family if a C.A.S. is permitted to act in an arbitrary way, even though its intentions are motivated by the highest ideals and concerns.[16]

At least part of the rationale for placing an onus on child protection agencies to justify their intervention is based on fundamental values of our society. Parents are viewed as having the moral right to raise their children in the manner they see fit; state restrictions on individual freedom, including the right to bear and raise children, require justification.

Legislation which restricts involuntary state interference may also serve to promote the welfare of children. It is difficult to make accurate predictions about a child's long-term psychological development simply by observing child-rearing practices in the home. Except for children who have been seriously harmed, there may not be sound empirical evidence to justify removing children from parental care. Research studies on children in the care of protection agencies offer a very mixed picture of the effects of removing children from their homes.[17]

Studies have revealed many problems with the treatment of children in the care of protection agencies.[18] Children often experience emotionally damaging moves from one placement to another. Placements that are intended to be temporary and short-term often turn out to be long-term, sometimes extending over several years. Parental contact during foster care placements frequently is limited or nonexistent. Insufficient efforts may be made to try to maintain children with their parents rather than removing them and placing them in foster care. It has also been found that the longer children remain in care and the less contact they have with their parents, the more likely that they will never return home.

---

[16] (1978), 5 R.F.L. (2d) 50 at 58. (Ont. Prov. Ct - Fam. Div.).

[17] M. Wald, J. Carlsmith and P. Leiderman, *Protecting Abused and Neglected Children* (Standford, CA: Standford University Press, 1988) at 14.

[18] See N. Trocmé, "Permanency Planning: Minimum Standard or Innovative Practice?", a report prepared for the Child, Youth and Family Policy Research Centre, (Toronto: 1989).

Concern over the damaging effects of removing children from their homes and over the problems of substitute care led to a move towards permanency planning in child protection legislation, policy and practice to varying degrees throughout North America. The permanency planning approach attempts to ensure that a child lives in a permanent family setting. Under permanency planning, the preferred approach is to keep children in their home, unless the danger to the child is clearly too great. This may involve family support services from child protection authorities or other social agencies while the child remains in the home.

If the child must be removed from the home, the goal is to return the child as soon as possible and to maintain parent-child contact during the separation. If the child cannot be returned within a reasonable time, the goal is to place the child in a long-term, stable family setting. The preferred long-term setting is an adoptive home because it provides the child with a new permanent family.

CHILD PROTECTION LEGISLATION

Every Canadian jurisdiction has legislation in place to regulate child protection. While all of the legislative regimes deal with the same fundamental issues, there are significant variations in philosophy and approach.

Each statute defines "child in need of protection," a key legal concept, as only children within this definition are subject to involuntary state intervention. Also, child protection legislation in every jurisdiction grants agencies the authority to apprehend children, that is, to take them into care prior to a court hearing, and provides for some form of interim custody hearing, at which a decision will be made about the care of the child pending a full hearing. If after a full protection hearing the court makes a finding that a child is in need of protection, there are essentially three types of orders that can be made: supervision, temporary wardship or permanent wardship.

Under a supervision order the child remains at home under parental care, but the home is subject to supervisory visits by the protection agency and any other conditions the court may impose. Temporary wards are placed in the care of the protection agency, usually in a foster or group home. Reunification with parents is generally contemplated when a child is made a temporary ward, and parents typically have the right to visit children who are temporary wards. Children made permanent or Crown wards are generally expected to be wards of the protection agency until they reach adulthood, though they may be placed for adoption without parental consent and occasionally are eventually returned to parental care.

Child protection legislation in each jurisdiction also provides for court review of prior orders to terminate, extend or change the nature of a prior order. Generally speaking, once a permanent ward is placed for adoption, the parents forfeit the opportunity to seek review.

In some jurisdictions adoption is governed by the same piece of legislation as child protection, as part of a comprehensive child welfare scheme. In other jurisdictions adoption is dealt with in a separate statute, though even in these jurisdictions child protection authorities are involved in some, though not all, adoptions.

There are significant differences in the philosophies reflected in different jurisdictions.[19] Most statutes can be characterized as having a social work oriented or interventionist approach. They tend to have relatively vague definitions of child in need of protection, a broad scope for pre-trial apprehension, limited concern for procedural issues, and a relatively unsupervised scope for agency decision-making once a child is in care. Running through these statutes is a policy in favour of flexible, individualized decision-making. Intervention by the agency is seemingly presumed to be beneficial, though courts remain responsible for supervising and sanctioning the process.

By contrast, other jurisdictions, most notably Ontario and Alberta, have enacted more legalistic schemes, which narrow the grounds for state intervention. These statutes place greater emphasis on due process for parents, and have been more heavily influenced by the permanency planning movement.

Just as legislation differs from one jurisdiction to another, judges within a single jurisdiction often have differing views and philosophies about the child protection process. Some judges view the process as adversarial in nature, with a high onus on the state agency, which is challenging the integrity of the family unit, to justify its position. Other judges tend to view the process as a less adversarial inquiry intended to promote the welfare of the child. The attitude of the presiding judge can have a significant impact on the manner in which child protection legislation is interpreted and applied.

The basic legislative features of Canadian child protection statutes and the differences in fundamental philosophy are more fully discussed in Chapter 2, and Chapter 14 offers the differing personal perspectives of four judges on the child protection process.

WHO SPEAKS FOR THE CHILD?

A fundamental question in the child protection area is: "Who speaks for the child?" It is a question which defies an easy answer. Some would argue that the protection agency, with its concern about the child's welfare, is speaking on behalf of the child. Others would point out that agencies often have institutional and professional constraints which prevent them from truly advocating what is best for the child. There may also be disagreement between the agency and foster parents or within the agency about how a particular case should be handled. While the agency will have an administrative mechanism for establishing how such disagreements will be resolved, there may still be controversy over what is truly best for the child.

---

[19] For a further discussion of the philosophical differences in legislation in various Canadian jurisdiction, see Chapter 2. See also, D.A.R. Thompson, "Taking Children and Facts Seriously: Evidence in Child Protection Proceedings: Part I" (1988) 7 Can. J.F.L. 11 at 16–18.

In Ontario and Alberta the government has established offices of child advocacy, separate from child protection agencies, with responsibility to act as advocates for children involved in the protection process or in the legal care of a protection agency. These offices are not intended to provide legal representation for children in court, but rather to act as advocates for them within the context of the child protection system. The establishment of these offices reflects a concern that the bureaucratic nature of child protection agencies may not always be in the best interests of children.

Parents involved in protection cases typically believe that they know and care for their children more than any of the professionals. Parents may thus claim that they speak for their children.

The children who are the subject of a protection case may also have their own views about what they want to have happen. Some children are too young to express their views and older children are sometimes reluctant or ambivalent about expressing their views. However, many children involved in the protection process have definite ideas about their futures. In a number of jurisdictions, legislation specifies that courts should consider the "child's views and wishes, if they can be reasonably ascertained."[20] In some jurisdictions children involved in child protection proceedings can have lawyers who represent them and claim to speak on their behalf. In some cases a psychologist or other mental health professional will interview or assess the child and report the child's views to the court, and in some situations the child may come to court and testify.

In some sense the judges who decide child protection cases may be considered to be speaking for the child. Although they have a responsibility for balancing the rights of the litigants and acting in accordance with the legislation, judges may be regarded as having ultimate responsibility for the protection of children and acting on their behalf.

The issue of legal representation for children in protection proceedings is discussed in detail in Chapter 9, but the broader questions of who speaks for the child, and who truly represents the interests of the child, are underlying themes of this book.

CHILD PROTECTION IN A SOCIAL CONTEXT

Child abuse and neglect are endemic to all parts of our society, and are not restricted to a particular region, economic or cultural group or race. One of the most infamous cases of physical abuse in the past decade in North America involved a prominent wealthy New York City lawyer, who was convicted of murdering his foster daughter. The Canadian public is gradually learning that even trusted and respected figures like doctors, teachers and priests can be guilty of sexual abuse.

Despite the widespread nature of child abuse and neglect, child protection agencies are more likely to be involved with families from certain economic,

---

[20] See, e.g., Ontario's *Child and Family Services Act*, S.O. 1984, c. 55, s. 37(3).

social and cultural groups. While child protection workers are typically white, well-educated and from middle-class backgrounds, their clients most often are poorly educated, living in or near poverty, and not infrequently members of a racial minority group and living in a family led by a single parent.

The National Council of Welfare observed that the clients of the child welfare system are "overwhelmingly drawn from the ranks of Canada's poor." In some cases, the personal or emotional problems that result in a life of poverty also may make it difficult to parent adequately. The Council also explained:

> There are two major reasons why poor families are more likely than those with higher incomes to use children's social services. First, low-income parents run a greater risk of encountering problems that reduce their capacity to provide adequate care for their children. Second, poor families are largely dependent upon a single, overburdened source of help—the child welfare system—in coping with their problems, whereas more affluent families enjoy access to a broader and superior range of supportive resources.

> Precisely because they cannot command the resources needed to deal with difficulties before they develop into more serious problems, low-income families' vulnerability is further increased as untreated problems accumulate and compound one another. By the time they come to the attention of a child welfare system, their problems often have become much more difficult to tackle in an effective manner ... [21]

The Council further wrote:

> Despite what most would consider a more enlightened and compassionate attitude than in the past, our society still stands in judgment on parents who are unable to care for their children. Whether a child is returned home under the supervision of a child welfare agency or sent to a foster home or treatment facility, the implication is the same: his or her parents have failed to perform adequately one of the most important roles of adult life.

> On the face of it, of course, parental inability is the reason underlying any decision to place a child in care. Whether the problem lies with the parent, the child, or both, and whether or not the initiative to remove the child is taken by the parents or by the child welfare authorities, the state can only intervene when it judges parents unable or unwilling to care properly for their children. What is often forgotten, however, is that the term 'unable or unwilling to provide care' is nothing more than a convenient administrative label lumping together a wide variety of family problems, many of which stem from inadequate income, unemployment and other factors that cannot fairly be blamed on their victims.[22]

Most judges seem aware of the need to be sensitive to the realities of poverty in Canada. In one child protection case, the judge wrote:

> In a hearing such as this there is danger in over-reliance upon any group of witnesses self-conscious respecting their professionalization. I resolved not to

---

[21] National Council of Welfare, *In the Best Interests of the Child* (Ottawa: 1979) at 2–3.

[22] *Ibid.* at 11.

fall victim to this specific bias of the profession, the group psychology of the social workers ...

It was manifest from the opening that this was a contest between the right of a subsocio-economic family to subsist together and the right of the public, represented by the Children's Aid Society, to insist upon higher standards of parental care than the couple in question were capable of offering. Many witnesses called for the Society were persons of superior education with post-graduate degrees in social work or some other related specialty. One could not listen to their testimony with all the somber implications of this application without resolving that this Court must not be persuaded to impose unrealistic or unfair middle-class standards of child care upon a poor family of extremely limited potential.[23]

Those who work in the child protection system must be sensitive to problems of poverty. They must also be sensitive to cultural and racial differences between themselves and their clients.

A number of racial minorities are overrepresented in Canada's child welfare system, but probably the most pervasive problems are with aboriginal children. Aboriginal children are apprehended and taken into care at more than three times the rate of other Canadian children. In some western provinces, more than half the children in care are aboriginal. Compounding conditions of poverty, chronic underemployment, inadequate housing and poor nutrition, are a history of racial discrimination and insensitivity to different child-rearing values. For those aboriginal people who come to live in cities, culture shock adds another source of stress and instability.

The special problems related to aboriginal children and the child protection system are addressed in Chapter 8, along with some of the recent innovations which are intended to increase the sensitivity of the system to needs of these children and their families. Like the role of the parent in society, the role of the child protection worker has become a complex and highly demanding one, requiring a unique blend of skill and dedication.

---

[23] *Re Warren* (1973), 13 R.F.L. 51 at 52 (Ont. Co. Ct), Matheson J.

2

CHILD PROTECTION LEGISLATION IN CANADA

*Dick Barnhorst** *and Bernd Walter*[†]

INTRODUCTION

This chapter discusses the major features of child protection legislation in Canada, including an analysis of the extent to which different jurisdictions emphasize due process or family autonomy. This approach supports notions of permanency planning, as opposed to a more interventionist approach, which tends to give social workers broader discretion to intervene in the family in situations they consider appropriate. Thus, the chapter provides an introduction to the child protection process, with individual topics more fully considered in subsequent chapters.

As discussed in Chapter 1, child protection statutes vary in philosophy[1] and approach, but deal with the same basic issues. Some begin with a statement of the principles to be used by agencies and judges in applying and interpreting the law. All include a definition of "child in need of protection," or an analogous concept like "endangered child." Such a definition is crucial to the legislative scheme, since it forms the basis for agency involvement. Most jurisdictions make statutory provision for a child to come into the care of an agency on a voluntary basis. Every jurisdiction provides for initiation of a protection proceeding by apprehending a child, and having an order made for the interim care of the child pending a full trial. For agency involvement to be justified, there must be a finding that a child is in need of protection. The court then has three basic dispositional alternatives: supervision of the child at home, temporary wardship or permanent wardship. Child protection statutes also provide a mechanism for reviewing prior orders, including the possibility of termination of a permanent wardship order if the child has not been placed for adoption.

In some Canadian jurisdictions, such as Ontario and Alberta, adoption is dealt with in the same legislation as child protection, as part of a total child welfare scheme. In other provinces, like British Columbia and Newfoundland, adoption

---

* Executive Director, The Child, Youth and Family Policy Research Centre (Ontario), Toronto, Ontario.

[†] Children's Advocate, Alberta Family and Social Services, Edmonton, Alberta.

[1] See Chapter 1, pp. 11-12, for a discussion of the concept of permanency planning and the broad differences in philosophy in various Canadian child protection schemes.

is governed by a separate statute. Adoption issues are clearly related to child protection, and child protection agencies have a role in some, but not all, adoptions. However, the philosophies and practical issues which arise in adoptions are somewhat distinct and are not addressed in this chapter.

STATEMENT OF PRINCIPLES

It is common for Canadian child protection statutes to include a statement of basic philosophy. Some statements are quite brief while others are long declarations of principles. These statements are intended to declare what the legislature considers to be the general policy underlying the specific sections and the provision of services to children and families. They are intended to serve as an interpretative guide to the courts and to protection agencies.

Some provinces (e.g., British Columbia and Prince Edward Island) provide short statements declaring that decisions are to be based on what is in the best interests of the child. For example, the *Family and Child Services Act* of Prince Edward Island simply states that "In the administration and interpretation of this Act the best interests of the child shall be the paramount consideration."[2]

The phrase "best interests of the child" is quite vague and such a statement is of little practical help to decision-makers. It is open to a wide range of interpretations and value judgments. It tends to support an interventionist approach, giving courts and agencies broad discretion to intervene in the family.

Other statutes contain statements of principles that recognize the importance of the best interests of the child, but also include other principles that recognize notions of permanency planning and the position of children in their families. Québec, Manitoba, Alberta, New Brunswick and Ontario have relatively long statements of principles that fall within this category. Some of the themes that appear in these more detailed declarations of philosophy are described below.

1. Family Autonomy. These declarations recognize the importance of respecting the family and the parents' primary responsibility in child rearing. For example, Ontario's *Child and Family Services Act* states that " ... while parents often need help in caring for their children, that help should give support to the autonomy and integrity of the family ... "[3] Manitoba's Act states that "The family is the basic source of care, nurture and acculturation of children and parents have the primary responsibility to ensure the well-being of their children."[4]

2. Least Disruptive Alternative. These statutes also state that if intervention in the family is necessary, the least disruptive alternative should be used. For example, the Alberta *Child Welfare Act* states:

[2]   R.S.P.E.I. 1974, c. F–2.01, s. 2.

[3]   S.O. 1984, c. 55, s. 1.

[4]   *The Child and Family Services Act*, R.S.M. 1987, c. C80, Declaration of Principles.

the family has the right to the least invasion of its privacy and interference with its freedom that is compatible with its own interest, the interest of the individual family members and society ... [5]

Similarly, Ontario's Act provides that "the least restrictive or disruptive course of action that is available and is appropriate in a particular case to help a child or family should be followed."[6] These kinds of provisions encourage providing help to a family without removing the child from the home. If removal of the child is necessary, it should be for a short period of time and contact with the parents should be maintained.

3. Continuity. Some statutes explicitly recognize the importance of continuity and stability for the child. For example, Manitoba's *Child and Family Services Act* states that "Children have a right to a continuous family environment in which they can flourish."[7] Québec's *Youth Protection Act* provides:

Every decision made under this Act must contemplate the child's remaining with his family. If in the interest of the child, his remaining with [his family] ... is impossible, the decision must contemplate his being provided with continuous care and stable conditions of life ... as nearly similar to those of a normal family environment as possible.[8]

These principles emphasize the importance of permanence for children, a preference for children remaining with their own family and, if removal is necessary, the need for a stable foster or adoptive family.

4. Prevention and Family Support. The declarations of principles in Québec, Manitoba, Alberta, New Brunswick and Ontario also acknowledge the importance of providing assistance to families in order to prevent more serious circumstances that could endanger children and lead to their removal from the family. For example, Manitoba's Act provides that "families are entitled to receive preventative and supportive services directed to preserving the family unit."[9]

5. Indian and Native Families. Some provincial statutes include statements of principle that explicitly recognize the special needs of Indian and native children, with particular emphasis on maintaining their cultural milieu. For example, Ontario's Declaration of Principles includes the statement that " ... all services to Indian and native children and families should be provided in a manner that recognizes their culture, heritage and traditions and the concept of the extended family."[10]

All of these principles directly or indirectly support continuity and stability for children and indicate a preference for maintaining children in their own

---

[5]   S.A. 1984, c. C–8.1, s. 2.

[6]   S.O. 1984, c. 55, s. 1.

[7]   R.S.M. 1987, c. C80, Declaration of Principles.

[8]   R.S.Q. 1977, c. P–34.1, s. 4.

[9]   R.S.M. 1987, c. C80, Declaration of Principles.

[10]   S.O. 1984, c. 55, s. 1.

homes. These principles may be of assistance to judges and social workers in making decisions under the legislation, especially when these decision-makers are applying the legislation to a particular case and the relevant, specific section does not provide sufficient guidance.

It is, however, difficult to determine whether statements of principles actually influence judges and child protection workers. Although they may be helpful, the legislature's policy is probably much more likely to be put into practice if the specific provisions of the legislation reflect the policy at critical decision-making points in the child protection process.

DEFINITION OF CHILD IN NEED OF PROTECTION

The definition of a "child in need of protection," or the analogous term "endangered child," is a crucial provision in protection legislation. The definition establishes the basis for whether or not involuntary intervention in the family is legally justified. Typically, a child may only be apprehended by a protection agency if there are reasonable grounds to believe that a child is within the definition. Similarly, a court can only order some form of intervention if it finds that the child is within the definition.

There are basically two approaches in Canada to the definition of a child in need of protection. One is the "interventionist" approach which leaves considerable discretion in the hands of social workers and judges. This type of definition contains relatively vague language that is open to a wide variety of interpretations. Using such a definition makes it relatively easy to determine that a child fits within its parameters and may be subject to involuntary intervention. However, such language offers little practical guidance to those making day-to-day decisions about protecting children.

Definitions taking a "family autonomy" approach contain language that is more precise and objective, and thus more likely to be interpreted in a consistent manner. This approach attempts to limit intervention to cases in which there is specific harm, or risk of harm, to the child. The family autonomy approach attempts to limit the range of discretion afforded to judges and social workers and restricts intervention in the family to relatively well-defined situations. The narrower, more specific approach is also consistent with notions of due process, since it gives parents a clearer idea of the problems they have to address.

In defining a "child in need of protection," the difficulty is to include provisions that allow intervention in order to protect children who truly need protection, yet are not so broad and vague that they allow intervention that may do more harm than good. Many commentators have argued that, from a permanency perspective, the narrower definition of the family autonomy approach is preferable.[11] They argue that a more precise and objective definition is more consistent

---

[11] R. Mnookin, "Child Custody Adjudication: Judicial Functions in the Face of Indeterminacy" (1975), 39 Law and Contemporary Problems 226; M. Wald, "State Intervention on Behalf of Neglected Children: A Search for Realistic Standards" (1975), 27 Stanford L. Rev. 983.

with the goal of keeping children with their own family whenever possible. It emphasizes the potential harm that may result from disrupting the child's continuity of care and relationships with parents and siblings.

Most Canadian statutes contain vague interventionist definitions of a child in need of protection. In fact, all but Ontario and Alberta are in this category.

New Brunswick's *Family Services Act* is fairly representative of the interventionist approach. In addition to such situations as physical or sexual abuse and failure to provide needed medical treatment, the definition includes the following situations:

(a) the child is without adequate care, supervision or control;

(b) the child is living in unfit or improper circumstances;

(c) the child is in the care of a person who is unable or unwilling to provide adequate care, supervision or control of the child; ...

(h) the child is beyond the control of the person caring for him;

(i) the child by his behaviour, condition, environment or association is likely to injure himself or others ... [12]

Some of the terms in this definition are broad and vague, leaving the definition open to a wide range of interpretations. Examples include "without adequate care," "living in unfit or improper circumstances" and "beyond control."

One problem with broad, vague definitions is that they increase the likelihood that the individual values of social workers and judges will have a major impact on how decisions are made. Such definitions also make it difficult for parents, children and their lawyers to determine whether or not child protection intervention is justified. Of course, vague language also makes social workers and judges more vulnerable to criticism because persons with different values may feel that these professionals have been too quick or too slow to intervene.

Another problem with this kind of definition is that it does not focus on harm to the child. In some situations, there may be agreement on the meaning of such provisions as "living in unfit or improper circumstances." For example, it might be agreed that it is not proper for children to be raised in a crowded, dirty home, or a home in which one of the parents is an alcoholic or in which there is physical fighting between the parents. However, it is possible that children raised in these situations do not suffer harm, or at least harm that is significant enough to justify involuntary intervention by a child protection agency.

These vague kinds of definitions tend to focus on home conditions and parental behaviour, rather than harm to the child. In many situations it is difficult to establish that home conditions or parental behaviour will necessarily harm the child's long-term development. There may be other positive factors in the child's home situation and the parent-child relationship, in particular, that outweigh the possible negative effects.

---

[12] S.N.B. 1980, c. F–2.2, s. 31(1).

In general, the Ontario and Alberta statutes contain definitions of a child in need of protection that are more precise than those found in other jurisdictions. Ontario includes the following provisions in its definition of a child in need of protection:

(a) the child has suffered physical harm, inflicted by the person having charge of the child or caused by that person's failure to care and provide for or supervise and protect the child adequately;

(b) there is a substantial risk that the child will suffer physical harm inflicted or caused as described in clause (a);

(c) the child has been sexually molested or sexually exploited, by the person having charge of the child or by another person where the person having charge of the child knows or should know of the possibility of sexual molestation or sexual exploitation and fails to protect the child;

(d) there is a substantial risk that the child will be sexually molested or sexually exploited as described in clause (c);

(e) the child requires medical treatment to cure, prevent or alleviate physical harm or suffering and the child's parent or the person having charge of the child does not provide, or refuses or is unavailable or unable to consent to, the treatment;

(f) the child has suffered emotional harm, demonstrated by severe

　(i) anxiety,

　(ii) depression,

　(iii) withdrawal, or

　(iv) self-destructive or aggressive behaviour

and the child's parent or the person having charge of the child does not provide, or refuses or is unavailable or unable to consent to, services or treatment to remedy or alleviate the harm;

(g) there is a substantial risk that the child will suffer emotional harm of the kind described in clause (f), and the child's parent or the person having charge of the child does not provide, or refuses or is unavailable or unable to consent to, services or treatment to prevent the harm;

(h) the child suffers from a mental, emotional or developmental condition that, if not remedied, could seriously impair the child's development and the child's parent or the person having charge of the child does not provide, or refuses or is unavailable or unable to consent to, treatment to remedy or alleviate the condition;

(i) the child has been abandoned, the child's parent has died or is unavailable to exercise his or her custodial rights over the child and has not made adequate provision for the child's care and custody ... [13]

These provisions, in general, focus on harm to the child, and in the case of emotional harm, require that the harm be severe.

Although Alberta's definition is similar to Ontario's in many respects, some provisions are even more specific. For example, the Alberta definition includes a

---

[13]　S.O. 1984, c. 55, s. 37(2).

child who has been, or is, at substantial risk for physical injury by the guardian of the child. It then goes on to specify what is meant by physical injury:

> a child is physically injured if there is substantial and observable injury to any part of the child's body as a result of the non-accidental application of force or an agent to the child's body that is evidenced by a laceration, a contusion, an abrasion, a scar, a fracture or other bony injury, a dislocation, a sprain, hemorrhaging, the rupture of viscus, a burn, a scald, frostbite, the loss or alteration of consciousness or physiological functioning or the loss of hair or teeth.[14]

This definition is by far the most specific, detailed provision of physical harm in Canadian legislation. It appears to reflect a legislative intention to be very clear about when intervention is warranted and to exclude minor and accidental injuries to children.

The Ontario and Alberta provisions also link harm to the child to the acts or omissions of the parents. In other words, it is not sufficient that a child has suffered harm. The harm must be the result of something the parent has done or failed to do. The definition includes risk of harm, but specifies that the risk must be substantial, thus indicating that minor or remote risks to the child are not sufficient to warrant involuntary intervention. In sum, the Ontario and Alberta definitions, compared to the definitions of a child in need of protection in other Canadian jurisdictions, are more specific and objective, and more focussed on harm or substantial risk of harm to the child. This reflects a legislative philosophy that appears to be more supportive of permanency planning by attempting to restrict intervention to more clearly-defined circumstances.

VOLUNTARY CARE AGREEMENTS

Nearly all Canadian child protection statutes provide for voluntary care agreements, by which the child is placed in the care of a child protection agency for a temporary period. These are agreements between the parents and the agency, and sometimes include the child as a party to the agreement.

The purpose of voluntary care agreements is to provide care for a child during a period in which the parents are unable to do so. A court proceeding is not required. The agreement is supposed to be voluntary and short term. Contact between parent and child is to be maintained. The goal is to return the child to the parents at the end of the period of the agreement. The parents' home is viewed as the child's permanent home and legal guardianship generally remains with the parents.

The concept of voluntary care agreements is consistent with the goal of continuity and stability for children. However, most Canadian statutes provide very little regulation or guidance regarding these agreements to ensure that they are used in ways that, in fact, promote a child's sense of continuity and permanence.

Ideally, legislation would contain provisions that ensure that the agreement is truly voluntary, that it is used only in circumstances in which it is not feasible to

---

[14] *Child Welfare Act*, S.A. 1984, c. C–8.1, s. 1.

help the family with the child remaining in the home, that the time period is short, that the agreement is clear as to what services will be provided and that the child and parent will maintain regular contact.

Most statutes provide that voluntary care agreements may be entered when a parent, due to temporary circumstances, is unable to care for the child. The Alberta Act is more restrictive in that it allows the agreements only if:

(a) the child is in need of protective services, and

(b) the survival, security or development of the child cannot be adequately protected if the child remains with the guardian.[15]

The requirement that the child be in need of protective services makes it unlikely that such agreements are truly voluntary and preventive in focus. If a child is in need of protective services, then the child protection agency must take the matter to court if the parents do not consent to the agreement.

Ontario's Act does not require that the child be in need of protection. In addition to the parents' temporary inability to care for the child, the Ontario criteria are that the agency:

(a) has determined that an appropriate residential placement that is likely to benefit the child is available; and

(b) is satisfied that no less restrictive course of action, such as care in the child's own home, is appropriate in the circumstances.[16]

Most Canadian statutes include time limits for voluntary care agreements. Time limits for initial agreements are 6 months (e.g., Ontario and Alberta) or 12 months (e.g., Québec, Newfoundland and Saskatchewan). These agreements may be extended for an additional 6 to 12 months, depending on the jurisdiction. In some provinces (e.g., Québec), these agreements may be extended indefinitely, whereas in other provinces (e.g., Manitoba, Nova Scotia, Ontario and Alberta), there is a cumulative maximum, typically of 1 to 2 years.

From a permanency perspective, it is important to have a specified total maximum period for such agreements. Maximum periods can force judges and social workers to make difficult decisions regarding a child's future so that the child does not drift through foster care indefinitely in a state of limbo.

INITIATION OF COURT PROCEEDINGS AND APPREHENSIONS

If a child protection agency believes that a child is in need of protection and that court action is necessary, Canadian statutes allow the agency to bring the matter to court in a number of different ways. The agency can make an application to the court, with the child remaining at home pending a trial at a future date. A child protection proceeding may also be commenced in a more dramatic and interventionist fashion, with the child being "apprehended"—that is, physically removed from parental care. An apprehension may occur after the agency

---

[15] S.A. 1984, c. C–8.1, s. 8(1)(b).

[16] S.O. 1984, c. 55, s. 29(4).

has obtained a warrant in the form of a court order allowing removal of the child from parental care. Agencies also have the legislative authority to apprehend children without a warrant or court order on the basis of the judgment of a child protection worker or police officer.

Apprehension of children represents a dramatic instance of state intervention in the family. Concern about due process would suggest that the power to apprehend children should be subject to careful regulation and judicial scrutiny. From a permanency perspective, the decision as to whether or not to apprehend the child is very significant. Removal of children from their homes clearly interferes with their sense of continuity and stability and should only occur in serious situations. It can lead to a long period of separation of children from their parents if the court proceedings are prolonged.

A statute that reflects permanency planning would attempt to ensure that apprehension is used only as a last resort. It would indicate a preference for commencing a protection application without apprehension. It would include restrictive criteria for apprehension in order to limit the range of discretion of child protection workers and would contain procedural safeguards, such as the requirement to obtain a court order, except in urgent circumstances.

The goal of permanency planning at this stage of the protection process is to maintain children in their homes, if possible. Removal of a child would not be viewed as the normal way of responding after a child protection investigation. On the other hand, the criteria and procedures for apprehension should not be so restrictive that children are endangered. Intervention decisions at this point in the process are extremely difficult and must be made on the basis of limited information. The purpose of the relevant legislative provisions should be to provide guidance to child protection workers by reflecting a balance between the need to maintain children in their homes and the need to protect them from serious harm.

Most Canadian statutes provide very little guidance regarding how to initiate protection proceedings. Some statutes are very general and leave broad discretion to child protection workers. For example, Newfoundland's Act does not indicate that apprehension requires any greater caution than an ordinary court application without removal of the child. As long as the child protection worker has reasonable and probable grounds to believe that a child is in need of protection, either method of initiating proceedings is permitted.[17]

---

[17] *Child Welfare Act*, S. Nfld 1972, No. 37, s. 11. Prince Edward Island had the least restrictions, allowing an apprehension without a warrant in any situation where the Director believed a child to be in need of protection. This was held to violate s.8 of the *Charter of Rights*; *H.M.* v. *Director of Child Welfare* (1989), 22 R.F.L. (3d) 399 (P.E.I.S.C.), and new, more restrictive legislation was enacted: Bill 39, 2d Sess., 58th Assembly P.E.I., (third reading 11 April 1990).

In some jurisdictions, the legislation includes criteria for apprehension without a warrant. The Yukon requires that there be "immediate danger to [the child's] life, health or safety."[18] Nova Scotia and Saskatchewan require that the child must be in "immediate jeopardy."[19] New Brunswick's Act allows apprehension without a warrant if there is reason to suspect that the child fits within the definition of a child whose security or development may be in danger and is in need of protective care.[20]

Ontario takes a much more detailed approach, one which expressly favours maintaining the child in the home and using the least disruptive means of bringing the matter to court. The Ontario Act permits apprehension with a warrant only if a judge determines that there are reasonable and probable grounds to believe that the child is in need of protection and that no less restrictive alternative, such as voluntary services or a court application without apprehension, would provide adequate protection for the child. Ontario allows apprehension without a warrant only if the child protection worker has reasonable grounds to believe that the child is in need of protection, and that "there would be a substantial risk to the child's health or safety during the time necessary ... to obtain a warrant or to bring an ordinary application."[21]

Alberta takes a similarly restrictive approach by allowing apprehension without a warrant only where the worker has a reasonable basis for believing that the child has been abandoned, has absconded and is without the necessities of life, or is in imminent danger of physical or sexual abuse.[22]

INTERIM CUSTODY

Once a child protection case is brought to court, it is very likely that a final decision will not be made at the first court appearance unless there is agreement between the parties as to the type of order that should be made. The case will be adjourned and the court will need to decide who should care for the child during the adjournment. The adjournment may be long and may be only the first of several during the course of the court proceedings.

The decision about the interim custody of the child during the adjournment is important from a permanency perspective. As discussed above with respect to apprehension decisions, placing the child in the care of the agency is clearly disruptive. Depending on the length of the court proceedings, interim custody

---

[18] *Children's Act*, R.S.Y. 1986, c. 22, s. 119(1).

[19] *Children's Services Act*, S.N.S. 1976, c. 8, s. 46; *The Family Services Act*, R.S.S. 1978, c. F–7, s. 19.

[20] S.N.B. 1980, c. F–2.2, s. 31(5).

[21] S.O. 1984, c. 55 s. 40(6).

[22] S.A. 1984, c. C–8.1, s. 17(9).

may continue for several months and, therefore, from a permanency perspective, should be done only with great caution. Decisions about interim custody also have the potential to dramatically affect parental rights, and due process concerns support judicial regulation under clear legislative standards.

In general, Canadian statutes give very little guidance to judges on the interim custody issue. Some statutes use the vague "best interests" test (e.g., New Brunswick). Manitoba's Act does not explicitly recognize the possibility that the child could be returned to the parents during the adjournment.[23] Saskatchewan takes an approach that is contrary to a permanency planning perspective by including a presumption that the child should be placed with the child protection agency.[24]

Ontario's provisions are most consistent with a permanency approach and protection of parental rights. They include a presumption that the child should not be placed in the care of the agency unless remaining with the parents would create a "substantial risk to the child's health or safety and the child cannot be protected" adequately while in the care of the parents.[25]

DISPOSITION ORDERS

If the court finds that the child is in need of protection, it must then consider what form of intervention should be ordered. Canadian statutes provide three basic options for the court. First, the child may be returned to the parents, subject to supervision by the child protection agency. This order may include terms requiring the agency to provide certain services to the child and parents. Second, the child may be made a temporary ward of the protection agency for a limited period of time. Under this order, the agency assumes temporary legal guardianship of the child and places the child in a foster home or other residential setting. Third, the child may be made a permanent or Crown ward. In general, this order terminates the parents' guardianship rights and responsibilities and transfers them to the state. The child may then be placed in an adoptive home or a long-term foster home.

From a permanency perspective, there are several significant areas that should be addressed in the legislative provisions governing this stage of the proceedings: (a) criteria for deciding which of the three orders is most appropriate in a particular case; (b) criteria for determining whether parent-child contact should be maintained if a wardship order is made; and (c) requirements for case plans to be presented to the court by the agency.

---

[23] R.S.M. 1987, c. C80, s. 29.

[24] R.S.S. 1978, c. F–7, s. 28.

[25] S.O. 1984, c. 55, s. 47(3).

Decision-Making Criteria

The most common approach to dispositional criteria in Canadian legislation is to simply state that the judge should make the order that promotes the child's welfare or is in the child's best interests. For example, Nova Scotia's Act provides that "In an action taken under this Act, the court shall apply the principle that the welfare of the child is the paramount consideration."[26]

Several Canadian statutes attempt to clarify the meaning of "best interests" by listing several factors for the court to consider. Newfoundland, New Brunswick, Prince Edward Island, Québec, Ontario, Manitoba, Alberta and the Yukon include the following kinds of factors that address issues related to permanence for the child:

- the stability of the child's relationships;
- the merits of helping the family while the child remains in the home;
- the importance of biological relationships;
- the child's need for permanence; and,
- the negative effects on the child of long delays in decision-making.[27]

As discussed earlier, the vagueness and indeterminacy of the concept of the "best interests of the child," render it a highly discretionary basis for decisions. However, the statutory addition of factors like the ones listed above at least helps to focus the judge's attention on matters that are relevant to ensuring permanence for children.

The Ontario and Alberta statutes specify that disposition orders are to be based on the "best interests of the child," listing the factors above as aspects of this concept. They also contain provisions that more clearly direct the judge to make orders that are consistent with permanency planning. In particular, they emphasize the importance of using the least restrictive alternative. For example, Ontario's *Child and Family Services Act* states:

The court shall not make an order removing the child from the [parents] ... unless the court is satisfied that less restrictive alternatives, including non-residential services and [previous efforts to assist the family]

(a) have been attempted and have failed;

(b) have been refused by the person having charge of the child; or

(c) would be inadequate to protect the child.[28]

The Ontario Act also requires the court to determine what previous efforts have been made by the child protection agency or another agency to assist the

---

[26] S.N.S. 1976, c. 8, s. 76.

[27] See B. Walter, "Legislative Dimensions of Permanency Planning," a report prepared for the Ontario Child, Youth and Family Policy Research Centre (Toronto, 1989) at 78.

[28] S.O. 1984, c. 55, s. 53(3).

child.[29] By knowing what efforts have been made in the past, the court is in a better position to consider the appropriateness of making a supervision order rather than a wardship order.

In cases in which removal from the parents is necessary, the legislation in Alberta and Ontario encourages the use of temporary wardship orders rather than permanent wardship orders. They also place a 2-year limit on the cumulative period during which a child may remain under temporary orders and agreements.[30] As noted earlier with respect to voluntary care agreements, the purpose of a time limit is to ensure that a definite decision about the child's future is made within a reasonable time so that the child does not drift in an uncertain state for a long and indefinite period.

The Ontario and Alberta statutes also include specific provisions that emphasize the seriousness of a permanent wardship order. Alberta's *Child Welfare Act* states that the court may not make a permanent order unless it is satisfied that the child cannot be adequately protected if the child remains with the parents, and the child cannot be returned to the custody of the parents within a reasonable time.[31] Ontario's Act contains similar criteria and specifies that the "reasonable time" within which a child cannot be returned home cannot exceed 24 months.

Access

If a child is ordered into the care of the child protection agency, another dispositional issue is whether the court should order that the parents be allowed to have access to the child. Some research suggests that a key factor in whether a child in care ever returns home is the extent of parent-child contact while the child is in care. If contact is not maintained, it is likely that the child will be placed in long-term foster care or an adoptive home.[32] Since reunification is a goal of permanency planning, it is important from a permanency perspective that legislation support parent-child contact after removal, especially in a temporary wardship situation.

There are various approaches to the issue of access in Canadian child protection statutes. Newfoundland and Nova Scotia do not explicitly refer to the possibility of access. The Prince Edward Island Act leaves the decision on access to

---

[29] S.O. 1984, c. 55, s. 53(2).

[30] S.O. 1984, c. 55, s. 66; S.A. 1984, c. C–8.1, s. 31. See however, s. 31(3) of Alberta's *Child Welfare Act*, which allows the court to make an extension for a further period of 1 year if "satisfied that there are good and sufficient reasons for doing so."

[31] S.A. 1984, c. C–8.1, s. 32(1); S.O. 1984, c. 55, s. 53(6).

[32] See Chapter 1.

the child protection agency rather than the court.[33] Some other statutes (Manitoba, Yukon, New Brunswick and Ontario) take a permanency approach by favouring parent-child contact while the child is in care. For example, Manitoba's *Child and Family Services Act* states that where the child is removed, "the parents or guardian shall have reasonable access to the child."[34] If the agency and the parents cannot agree as to what constitutes reasonable access, the court may decide.

In the case of permanent wardship orders, some statutes prohibit access or limit access to certain circumstances (Ontario, British Columbia and Yukon). For example, Ontario's Act permits access with a permanent order only if:

(a) permanent placement in a family setting has not been planned or is not possible, and the [parent's] access will not impair the child's future opportunities for such placement;

(b) the child is at least twelve years of age and wishes to maintain contact with the person;

(c) the child has been or will be placed with a person who does not wish to adopt the child; or

(d) some other special circumstance justifies making an order for access.[35]

This Ontario provision reflects concern for the child's need for permanence. The permanent wardship order terminates the parents' guardianship rights and responsibilities and the objective at this point is to find a new permanent family for the child. Finding a permanent family is given a higher priority than maintaining parent-child contact which, in some cases, may disrupt the child's adjustment to a new family.

Case Plans

Planning for a child's long-term future is fundamental to the permanency planning approach in child welfare. As noted earlier, the concern with ensuring permanence stemmed in part from research showing that some child welfare agencies failed to make plans for children, thus increasing the chances that they might drift in foster care for many years.

A legislative requirement that the child protection agency submit a case plan to the court can be valuable in many ways. First, it can help to ensure that the agency has actually developed a plan for the child. Second, it can lead to more informed and thoughtful decision-making by judges. In particular, the plan can allow the judge to compare what the agency has to provide with what the family can offer, perhaps with the addition of in-home services. Third, the plan can be an accountability mechanism because it provides a basis against which the

---

[33] R.S.P.E.I. 1974, c. F–2.01, s. 24.

[34] R.S.M. 1987, c. C80, s. 39(1).

[35] S.O. 1984, c. 55, s. 55(2).

agency's performance can later be evaluated; the failure to carry out a plan may be grounds for subsequent review of an order.

Only the Alberta and Ontario statutes include a requirement for case plans to be presented by the agency. Alberta's provision is limited, however, to temporary guardianship orders and it does not require that the plan be submitted to the court before the order is made; the agency is only obliged to file a plan with the court within 30 days of an order being made.[36] Ontario's legislation is clearly the most reflective of a permanency planning approach. The court is required to consider a written plan prepared by the child protection agency before making any dispositional order. The Act also requires that the plan contain the following:

(a) a description of the services to be provided to remedy the condition or situation on the basis of which the child was found to be in need of protection;

(b) a statement of the criteria by which the society will determine when its wardship or supervision is no longer required;

(c) an estimate of the time required to achieve the purpose of the society's intervention;

(d) where the society proposes to remove or has removed the child from a person's care,

(i) an explanation of why the child cannot be adequately protected while in the person's care, and a description of any past efforts to do so, and

(ii) a statement of what efforts, if any, are planned to maintain the child's contact with the person; and

(e) where the society proposes to remove or has removed the child from a person's care permanently, a description of the arrangements made or being made for the child's long-term stable placement.[37]

POST-DISPOSITION REVIEWS

Periodic court review of a case after the disposition order has been made is another accountability mechanism that supports permanency planning. From a permanency perspective, some of the purposes of post-dispositional review are:

• to ensure that the agency carries out a plan that has the goal of stable family placement for the child;

• to provide a means of settling disputes that may occur between the agency and the parents and/or child;

• to provide information needed to decide whether reunification or termination of parental rights is appropriate; and

• to evaluate the effectiveness of the plan and revise plan, if necessary.[38]

---

[36] S.A. 1984, c. C–8.1, s. 29(3).

[37] S.O. 1984, c. 55, s. 52.

[38] *Supra*, note 27 at 90.

All Canadian child protection statutes provide for court review of dispositional orders. In some jurisdictions, the rights of parents to initiate the reviews are restricted to situations of supervision and temporary wardship (e.g., Alberta and British Columbia). In Ontario, parents are entitled to initiate reviews of all three orders. If a child is placed for adoption, however, there cannot be a review of a permanent wardship order.

The decision-making standards at the review vary among the statutes. Some simply require the court to determine whether there has been "a change of circumstances" since the order was made (e.g., Yukon and British Columbia). As in many other areas, Alberta and Ontario take an approach that is more consistent with permanency planning. For example, the Alberta Act requires the court to consider several factors, including: the services that have been provided to the child or family, and whether the plan for the care of the child has been followed.[39] Ontario includes some other factors, such as whether the grounds on which the original order was made still exist; whether a future date for termination of the order can be estimated; whether the child or family requires further services; and, what is the least restrictive alternative that is in the child's best interests.[40]

CONCLUSION

Legislation can be viewed as a tool that can be used to promote greater permanence for children who come into contact with the child welfare system. As the discussion in this chapter suggests, there is considerable variation among Canadian child protection statutes in the extent to which they reflect a policy of guaranteeing due process and providing a formal structure for promoting permanence for children.

In general, many Canadian statutes tend to include broad statements of philosophy that are consistent with permanency planning. However, most statutes do not reflect a permanency approach with specific provisions at key decision-making points in the child protection process. They generally do not give much guidance at these points and leave broad discretion to judges and social workers.

The Ontario and Alberta Acts are the exceptions. More than any other Canadian statutes, they reflect the following commitments: (a) to keep children with their families, if possible; (b) if removal is necessary, to maintain parent-child contact; and (c) if reunification of parent and child is not possible, to establish a new and stable family for the child. These statutes provide more structure for the exercise of discretion in child protection proceedings and tend to afford children and parents a greater degree of due process. Legislation in other jurisdictions appears to afford a broader scope for state intervention in the family.

---

[39] S.A. 1984, c. C–8.1, s. 30(2).

[40] S.O. 1984, c. 55, s. 61(3).

3

INITIAL INVOLVEMENT

*Robin Vogl**

REPORTING ABUSE AND NEGLECT

Child protection agencies rely on members of the public to report situations appearing to involve abuse or neglect of children. In all Canadian jurisdictions except the Yukon, the law places a duty on the public to inform child protection authorities of situations in which there are reasonable grounds to suspect the abuse or neglect of children. Types of situations that require a report to be made vary among provinces. However, all require that suspected physical or sexual abuse of a child by a parent, guardian or caregiver be reported. The legislation in most provinces also offers the reporting person immunity from civil liability, unless the report is made maliciously or without reasonable grounds.

Some provinces, including Ontario, may only prosecute professionals such as doctors and teachers for failing to report suspected abuse. In any jurisdiction, the failure to report child abuse may theoretically give rise to civil liability for damages suffered by a child if reporting the abuse would have prevented harm to the child.[1]

Reports received from professionals are rarely malicious. Even so, a report from a professional regarding a child protection concern still calls for judgment and common sense on the part of the child protection agency. Despite the best of intentions, a concerned professional may not fully understand the constraints of the law and the limited resources of a child protection authority. Ontario's *Child and Family Services Act* provides an avenue for individuals who are dissatisfied with the response of a Children's Aid Society to bring an application before the court to review an agency's decision not to intervene.[2]

When a report of suspected abuse comes from a neighbour, family member or estranged spouse, motivation becomes a factor in the assessment. Good faith

---

* Former Senior Counsel, Metro Toronto Children's Aid Society; now a lawyer in private practice, Toronto, Ontario.

[1] See *O'Keefe* v. *Osorio* (1984), 27 American Trial Lawyers Assoc. L.R. 392, in which an Illinois jury awarded $186,851 against a doctor who negligently failed to report the physical abuse of a 1-year-old child, who subsequently suffered further abuse by the parent. The failure to report was because the doctor believed the parent was receiving adequate psychiatric care.

[2] S.O. 1984, c. 55, s. 40(3).

should be assumed until there is reason to believe that the report is malicious or unfounded. In most provinces child protection agencies are technically required to investigate any allegations of abuse or suspicion of the need for protection. However, in Alberta and the Yukon, child protection authorities are expressly afforded discretion to decide whether or not an allegation will be investigated. For example, in Alberta the Director of Child Welfare may decline to investigate allegations which are made maliciously, without reasonable grounds or where a referral to community services would protect the child. It is necessary to conduct investigations with a degree of care and common sense since child protection authorities in the United States have faced law suits when investigations were either overzealous or not intensive enough.[3] There is a possibility for similar liability in Canada. Lawsuits have been brought against child protection agencies in Canada for overzealous or incomplete investigations, but none have succeeded.[4]

Reporting a situation to child protection authorities can require courage. A family member may suffer guilt for exposing the caregiver, and other family members may be very hostile as a result of the report, even if it is justified. Likewise, a neighbour who expresses concern about a child can face open hostility from an angry parent or caregiver. Even if a complainant provides information out of anger or vindictive motivation, the information may still be accurate. It is often during a relationship breakdown that previously-held confidences are disclosed because there is no relationship left to protect. On the other hand, it is during conflict that the temptation to make false or exaggerated complaints is greatest.

Not all cases are referred by outside professionals or family members. Parents or children may approach child protection agencies either for assistance or when

---

[3] D. Besharov, *Criminal and Civil Liability in Child Welfare Work: The Growing Trend* (Washington, D.C.: National Legal Resource Center for Child Advocacy and Protection, American Bar Association, 1983) refers to American cases in which caseworkers were sued for violating parental rights by "harassing" a child and family in the investigation of anonymous concerns which were subsequently unfounded. Likewise, American agencies have been successfully sued for failing to conduct a sufficiently full or careful investigation. In one case cited by Besharov, a noncustodial father reported bruising of his 34-month-old daughter, alleging the mother's new partner as the likely perpetrator. The investigation bore out the bruising, but the partner was not interviewed. No follow-up visit was ever made. Eight days later the child was hospitalized in a comatose state and subsequently died.

[4] See *A.G.* v. *Superintendent of Family Services* (1989), 21 R.F.L. (3d) 425, a civil suit by parents and children for wrongful removal of the children from parental care. While the court concluded that the inexperienced worker who handled the case made "errors in judgment," she and the other workers did not act "so unreasonably" as to indicate that they were not "acting in good faith." The British Columbia Court of Appeal dismissed the civil actions against the workers and the Superintendent.

In another Canadian case, the court rejected a claim that workers should be liable for injury suffered by an abused child. In *M.M.* v. *K.K.* (1989), 38 B.C.L.R. (2d) 273 (C.A.) it was held that workers or an agency would only have civil liability if it could be proven that their "negligence" caused the subsequent injury to the child. In rejecting the claim in this particular case, the court was sympathetic to the fact that the workers had a "very onerous" caseload and had to set priorities.

placement outside the family is necessary. In these cases, help is usually provided on a voluntary basis.

THE INTAKE PROCESS

Initial Assessment of Case

The initial assessment of a case reported to a child protection agency is one of the most significant and sensitive stages of investigation. Often faced with time pressures and the disadvantage of limited information, an intake worker must have the necessary skills and experience to assess its urgency or appropriateness. A caller may initially characterize a situation as one of neglect, and then may respond to further questioning with more information which indicates abuse. Conversely, a caller may label a situation as abuse, and then describe a situation which clearly does not constitute abuse, even if further investigation would verify the reported facts. The intake worker, with the support of a supervisor and occasional legal advice, must determine whether or not a case requires protective intervention, the urgency of any such intervention, and whether or not that intervention will be carried out with the consent of the caregiver.

Most agencies encourage a close working relationship between child protection staff and police, particularly in the investigation of physical or sexual abuse, as the possibility of criminal charges exists. In many areas formal protocols have been developed to assist in a coordinated response by child protection workers and the police.

When talking to a person reporting suspected abuse, it is important to obtain as much information as possible relating to the expressed concerns. A worker must often ask probing questions of a reluctant caller to determine the origin and extent of the concerns. The exact words of a complaint should be accurately noted, and the worker can facilitate the assessment process by asking the caller to provide objective information such as observations and statements, rather than general impressions.

Confidentiality of Callers

It is possible for individuals to register anonymously concerns of child abuse or neglect, analogous to the anonymous tips received by police departments. The fact that callers refuse to identify themselves should not obviate the need to conduct an appropriate investigation, provided they supply sufficient information to identify the child involved and to justify a child protection concern. If the information provided is substantiated upon investigation, the identity of the caller is not needed. However, if the investigation does not yield any evidence of the caller's concerns, it is obviously impossible to obtain further details which might assist in the ongoing investigation.

Some callers will identify themselves, but request that their name not be revealed to the child's parent due to fear of retaliation. This is a realistic fear, and should be respected when possible. However, the nature of the complaint may identify the source, and attempts to protect the caller may be of no practical effect. Though the informant's identity may ultimately be revealed to the parents, there is some basis in case law for arguing in favour of non-disclosure,[5] and legislation in Prince Edward Island, New Brunswick, Québec and Manitoba provides that names of informants be kept confidential. Despite this protection, it may be necessary for the reluctant informant to come forward and testify if investigation yields neither objective evidence nor an admission by the parties, or if the informant observed direct evidence of abuse or neglect.

The Child's Age and Protection of the Unborn

A child's age is critical in determining whether or not the agency has the legal mandate to investigate and protect the child. The provinces have varying age thresholds which allow the involvement of child protective services. On the low end of the age continuum emerges the issue of protecting the unborn. Over the past few years, there have been some Canadian cases involving attempts to protect an unborn child. With the passions of the abortion debate running high, it is not surprising to see the issue of rights of the unborn raised in the context of child protection. Cases before the courts have generally involved drug abuse or lack of physical self-care by the mother, especially immediately prior to expected delivery. Agencies have generally been concerned about risk to the child and mother during the birth process, as well as about risks to the unborn child prior to birth.

Only New Brunswick specifically refers to the "unborn child" in its definition of "child" for protection purposes.[6] Child protection authorities have been un-clear about their responsibility and authority with respect to the unborn, but are concerned in view of the growing scientific knowledge establishing the impact of the pregnant woman's health upon fetal development. While the Yukon does not specifically include the unborn in its definition of child, its *Children's Act* includes a provision allowing the Director of Child Welfare to apply for an order of supervision if a pregnant woman subjects herself to addictive or intoxicating substances which might endanger her fetus.[7]

The issue of protecting the unborn child has found its way to the courtroom in provinces where the definition of child does not clearly indicate whether the legislation applies to the unborn. Though some judges have been prepared to rule that the unborn child falls under the definition of "child" for protection purposes, the British Columbia Supreme Court in *Re Baby R.*, refused to find that a fetus is

---

[5] *D. v. National Society for the Prevention of Cruelty to Children,* [1977] 1 All E.R. 589 (H.L.).

[6] *Family Services Act,* S.N.B. 1980, c. F–2.2, s. 1(a).

[7] R.S.Y. 1986, c. 22, s. 133.

a child. The court found there was no jurisdiction to order a pre-birth apprehension of a child when the mother refused to undergo a Caesarian section despite fetal distress.[8]

However, a judge in an Ontario case took a different approach. An expectant mother was leading a nomadic life and sleeping in an underground parking lot. The protection agency believed that she was mentally unstable and about to deliver, and that her living conditions would place the unborn child at risk during the birthing process. The court held that there was jurisdiction to make an order to protect an unborn child and ordered that the child be made a temporary ward prior to its birth.[9] The judge simultaneously ordered that the mother be detained for assessment under the provincial mental health legislation.

Even if the courts do not permit intervention prior to birth in the absence of specific legislative authority, the risks to which a child is subjected prior to birth may well justify apprehension at the time of birth. For example, in a British Columbia decision, the court concluded that a drug-addicted baby is born abused.[10]

The upper age limit of child protective services varies significantly across Canada. In Ontario, Nova Scotia, Newfoundland, Saskatchewan and the Northwest Territories, the upper age limit is 16, with the qualification that in Ontario and Nova Scotia, if proceedings are commenced before a child attains the age of 16, an order can be made or extended after the child turns 16 years of age. In Alberta, Québec, Manitoba, Prince Edward Island and the Yukon, the upper age limit is 18, whereas British Columbia and New Brunswick have upper age limits of 19 for child protective services.

When a report is received regarding an individual beyond the legal age mandate of a child protection agency, it is often important to direct the involved individual or family to an appropriate agency for follow-up. A family or individual in crisis can be dissuaded from seeking needed support by a response that echoes the "not my department" indifference which is all too common in a stressed government agency.

Native Children

It is important to identify a child as native promptly if a native agency exists or if child protection legislation requires special treatment for native children. For example, legislation may require that notice of a court application be given to bands or that specialized arrangements be made for care of the child. Identify-

---

[8] (1988), 15 R.F.L. (3d) 225.

[9] *Children's Aid Society of Belleville* v. *Linda T. and Gary K.* (1987), 7 R.F.L. (3d) 191 (Ont. Prov. Ct—Fam. Div.). This decision has to be reconsidered in light of the decision of the Supreme Court of Canada in *Tremblay* v. *Daigle* (1989), 62 D.L.R. (4th) 634 (S.C.C.), where it was held until birth, a fetus is not a "person" for the purposes of civil law or the Québec *Charter of Human Rights and Freedoms*.

[10] *Superintendent of Family and Child Service* v. *M.(B) and O.(D)* (1982), [1982] B.C.D. Civ. 1568–06 (B.C.S.C.) Proudfoot J.

ing the child as native may affect how the case is handled in these and similar situations.

THE INVESTIGATION PROCESS

Skills required to investigate an allegation of abuse or neglect are similar to those required in police work. They include keen listening and observation skills, the ability to record observations in an objective manner, maintaining an objective stance throughout the investigation and professional discretion to plan an appropriate intervention. In addition, the investigator must minimize the emotional discomfort of the individuals being questioned. The overall investigation must strike a balance to protect the interests of a highly vulnerable population of children while respecting the rights of the parent and the family.

Experienced child protection workers are very good sources of knowledge about the overall investigation process. It is also worthwhile for child protection workers to become familiar with the specific legal aspects of the process as this will enhance the credibility of an investigation regardless of the outcome.

Some would argue that the power to remove children from their parents or caregivers is more profound than the power to send an individual to jail. It is a power not to be taken lightly, and one for which a worker can anticipate public and judicial scrutiny. The decision to remove a child should be made only after consultation with a supervisor, provided time permits.

In one Ontario case, *D.B.* v. *Children's Aid Society of Durham Region*, the court dismissed the protection application and ordered the agency to pay most of the father's legal fees. Judge Dunn spelled out his expectations of the agency during the investigation of abuse or neglect. The case involved allegations by a mother that the children's father had sexually abused them on an access visit. This is usually a difficult situation to assess. Judge Dunn highlighted the following six points: [11]

1. The Society has an obligation to conduct a thorough investigation before acting. In particular, the agency was chastised for failing to contact two doctors who were in a position to provide information prior to bringing an application before the court. Obviously, in a situation involving the life or physical safety of children, it is not always reasonable to delay their removal from home until all avenues of information have been explored. However, it is advisable to afford the family the maximum possible recognition of their civil liberties without compromising the life or safety of the child.

2. The Society has an obligation to work with the police in conducting a sexual abuse investigation. When the investigation involves an allegation of physical or sexual abuse, the spectre of criminal charges hangs over the parties. If the police interview the parents first, subsequent interviews with protection workers may not occur or may be delayed. It is essential to understand the

---

[11] *D.B.* v. *Children's Aid Society of Durham Region* (1987), 20 C.P.C. (2d) 61 at 66–73 (Ont. Prov. Ct—Fam. Div.).

alleged perpetrator's situation. For example, if a separated father is alleged to have abused his children and only the mother and child have been questioned prior to protection proceedings, the father may well feel ignored and victimized. As soon as the police interrogation of an alleged abuser concludes, the individual and their lawyer should always be directly involved in the child protection investigation process, unless they object. Until proven in a court of law, a suspected abuser is only that. The impartiality of the investigation should be evident in the language used and in the process itself.

3. The Society has an obligation to consider alternative measures for protection of the children before proceeding to court. In the 1970s, the concept of "permanency planning" emerged as an approach to child protection.[12] The researchers who coined the phrase argued that a lengthy period of intervention by child protection or juvenile justice authorities obtained questionable results. They argued that less intervention in the lives of families and children was often more reasonable than the inconsistent and sometimes highly intrusive approach of the previous decades.

The concept of the "least restrictive alternative" has emerged as an aspect of permanency planning and is reflected in the approaches of many Canadian judges. In some jurisdictions, such as Ontario and Alberta, the least restrictive alternative is enshrined in the child protection legislation. The principle is translated into practice when one works in a cooperative, voluntary manner with families, whenever possible. When involuntary intervention is required, one should use the least intrusive involvement that will ensure the child's safety. For example, voluntary contractual involvement is preferable to court ordered, supervision at home is preferable to a child in care, placement within the community or extended family is preferable to placement in foster or institutional care, and temporary care and custody is preferable to permanent care.

It is important to interpret the principle of the least restrictive alternative with common sense. The principle needs to be qualified by the realities of the situation. Available facts and appropriate responses differ from case to case. In a situation of life-threatening abuse, the child's removal may be warranted until an alternative plan can be properly investigated and implemented. Even in the context of a permanency planning perspective, it occasionally may be important to err on the side of caution in protecting children.

4. The Society has an obligation to treat all clients fairly and equally and with as much dignity as possible. When parents are separated and one parent is alleging abuse by the other, it is natural to view the parent with whom you have your first contact as your "client" in an investigation. In reality, you have several potential clients, including any parent or caregiver with whom you have contact and, most importantly, the child or children who are the subject of the investigation. Maintaining a neutral stance is also important. Remember that one party's

---

[12] B. Walter, *Legislative Dimensions of Permanency Planning* (Toronto: Child, Youth & Family Policy Research Centre, 1989) at 1–2. See also discussion in Chapters 1 and 2 of this book.

information may seem reasonable and sincere when it is received, and then may be seen from a new perspective after interviewing other parents, family members or caregivers. The rights of all parties must be respected. It is best to avoid appearing allied with one side or the other, even if the position adopted by the agency following investigation supports one party.

5. *The Society has an obligation to continue an investigation up until the time of a final court determination in a vigorous, professional manner.* It is often tempting to think of a case as being static, especially after an assessment has been made and a position has been taken. However, it is sometimes frustrating and occasionally rewarding that child protection cases are capable of dramatic changes. With the delays inherent in the court system and the constant exchange of information which accompanies the legal process, it is not unusual for family circumstances or assessments to change over time. For some workers, it may be embarrassing to alter a professional opinion about the nature of an incident, the risks to a child, or the ability of a caregiver to protect a child. And yet, such modifications are inevitable in the ongoing professional monitoring of a family situation. The change of position may be seen as a highly professional response, provided it is based upon new case information.

6. *The Society has an obligation to reassess their position as more information becomes available.* Information received from police or agencies may cast a new light on the situation. The child may provide new information which substantiates, refutes, or alters the nature of the protection concerns.

A responsible investigation includes not only collecting and evaluating information offered by various parties; it can also involve actively seeking information from relevant sources. For example, it would be important to know the extent of a parent's psychiatric illness, its chronicity and the degree to which it would impair their parenting ability.

Parents may refuse to sign necessary releases for disclosure of medical record information. In this case, Ontario's legislation provides for obtaining a court order compelling the records' custodian to release relevant records to the protection agency.[13] The agency must establish: (a) that the record contains information which may be relevant to a consideration of whether a child is suffering abuse or is likely to suffer abuse; and, (b) that the custodian of the record has refused to release it. The Yukon's *Children's Act* contains similar provisions.[14]

If a social worker thinks immediate action is required to protect a child before the investigation is complete, the worker should be candid about the limited information upon which the decision to apprehend is being made, and should clarify that the investigation will be continuing.

---

[13] *Child and Family Services Act*, S.O. 1984, c. 55, s. 70.

[14] R.S.Y. 1986, c. 22, s. 117(5)(6).

CHILD ABUSE REGISTERS

A number of Canadian provinces have formal child abuse registers. In these jurisdictions, child protection agencies are required to report cases of abuse to the centralized register. The purpose of these registers is to track and identify abuse, and to provide information for research purposes. Proponents also argue that placing an abuser's name on a register may act as a deterrent to further abuse, which may be especially important if no criminal prosecution is commenced.

Ontario's controversial register is currently under review. At present, an individual on the register may be identified as an abuser if there is "credible evidence" that the acts occurred. In practical terms, this means a protection worker's strong belief that abuse occurred is sufficient evidence to justify placing a name on the register, even without legal proof of the abuse. However, access to the register in Ontario is limited and in most cases it is used only by child protection staff and researchers.

In contrast, Manitoba's legislation provides that placing a name on the abuse register requires proof on the ordinary civil standard, the balance of probabilities. This legislation allows a review process for named individuals, including an appeal to the courts. However, access to the Manitoba register is significantly wider than in Ontario and permits screening of individuals seeking employment in positions of responsibility for children. Naming an individual on the register should entail due process if a fundamental right such as the right to earn a living is directly affected. Other provinces are studying the Manitoba model.[15]

Most other provinces do not maintain formal registers, but do keep centralized indexes of all child protection cases. Typically, there is no formal review process available to an identified individual. While the identification of individuals by these indexes may raise some valid civil liberties concerns, use of the information is generally strictly limited.

VOLUNTARY VS. INVOLUNTARY INVOLVEMENT

Some provincial legislation encourages families to become involved with child protection agencies on a cooperative, voluntary basis. This may, in part, be a reaction to public perception that protection agencies are unduly authoritarian. In fact, most protection workers have caseloads with a significant number of cases where the family has either voluntarily approached the agency for service, or was referred by an individual or outside agency and agrees to the involvement of the protection agency. However, it is possible for a case to move from voluntary to involuntary at any point.

---

[15] Nova Scotia and Ontario seem particularly interested in establishing a register allowing screening and due process. See N. Bala, *Ontario Child Abuse Register Review* (Toronto: Ontario Ministry of Community and Social Services, 1987).

The distinction between voluntary and involuntary involvement is often quite subtle, and there are often situations where a family will reluctantly agree to work voluntarily with the agency. Given the authority of the child protection agency to remove children if necessary, it is not surprising that families often do not realize their right to decline services of the child protection agency. It is only with legal advice that a family can accurately determine the legal authority of the intervening agency. It is important for a protection worker to respect and even encourage use of a family's right to seek legal advice at any stage of involvement.

VOLUNTARY ARRANGEMENTS

Contracting with Parents

When protection concerns have been identified, it is good practice to discuss agency objectives and the steps required to meet them with the parents. For example, an effective parenting course or a period of involvement with a child management worker may need to be arranged to combat a discipline problem. If these terms are written in a simple contract, the parties can be clear about the intervention goals. If the objectives are not met, the contract may be an important piece of evidence in justifying the need for court-ordered intervention. This offers an example of the dual helper/enforcer role. The preparation of such a contract not only represents cooperative planning with a family, it also anticipates the possibility of later court involvement.

Homemakers

Many provinces will provide homemakers for the family if a parent is absent from the home or prevented from assuming normal parental duties by a temporary illness or disability. This option is contained in the legislation of Alberta, Manitoba, New Brunswick, Ontario and Prince Edward Island. In Alberta, Manitoba and Ontario, the child protection authority is obliged to obtain a judge's order if the placement exceeds a few days. Use of a homemaker minimizes disruption to the children, but is clearly only a solution to a short-term family problem.

Voluntary Placement With a Relative or Friend

When a temporary or permanent alternative to parental care is required, it is best to discuss the options with the parent and the child. Individuals such as neighbours, grandparents, aunts, uncles or family friends can often provide the short- or long-term care needed by children under these circumstances. A custodial parent may discourage a worker from investigating a plan of care with a noncustodial parent or other family member because of lingering feelings of anger or resentment. A caregiver experiencing parenting difficulties may also feel guilty or embarrassed about revealing the situation to the other parent or a relative. However, from the child's standpoint, if voluntary arrangements with a known and trusted person are feasible, they are usually a far better option than care by strangers.

If the child has had minimal ongoing contact with the potential temporary caregiver, it is often better to explore that plan, especially if the alternate care required is expected to be of short duration. However, if the custodial parent has objections to placement with a particular individual, these concerns must be carefully addressed. As a general rule, whenever there is an apparent conflict between a parent and the child protection agency, it is advisable to bring the matter before a court to protect the rights of all parties.

Care By Agreement

Sometimes parents cannot care for their children and voluntary placement with a friend or relative is inappropriate or impossible. If it then becomes necessary to use foster care or a group home, placement may be authorized by a signed agreement between the parent and the child protection agency. A child who is old enough to participate in the decision may also be a party to the agreement. It is important to review the contents of the agreement with the family in some detail. A parent being asked to enter an agreement for care should be given an opportunity to consult a lawyer before signing.

The maximum period for any voluntary care agreement varies from province to province. Most agreements provide for an early termination if one of the parties wishes to end the placement, as long as the required notice is provided to the other contracting parties. In some cases parents retain certain rights and responsibilities concerning their children, even though the children are in the agency's care. In other cases, parents may specifically authorize the agency to make decisions related to the child's care, such as routine medical or dental care. The agreements may include a regular amount to be paid by the parent for the support of the child in care if parents are able.

In most cases, an agreement can be extended for further periods. Some provinces have limited the period of time a child can be kept in care under agreement because children were seen as drifting in the system without direction. For example, in Ontario, a temporary care agreement can be renewed for no longer than a total of 12 months.

INVOLUNTARY INTERVENTION

Without parental consent, a child protection agency must be granted authority from the court to: (a) supervise the care of a child at home, or (b) remove a child either temporarily or permanently.

To bring a matter before the court, one of these four routes is normally followed:

1. Application to court;
2. Notice to the parent to produce the child in court;

3. Apprehension with a warrant or court order; or

4. Apprehension without a warrant or court order.

These options are discussed below. Not all options are available in every jurisdiction.

Application

In some jurisdictions, an agency may bring a case before the court by way of an application or written request to have the matter heard without taking the child into care prior to the court hearing. This option is particularly useful when a supervision order is being requested, or when the family circumstances are not urgent but chronic in nature and would not justify an apprehension. For example, with an isolated incident of physical abuse which occurred while the parents were disciplining a child, the agency may want to see the parents involved in a child management course as a condition of a supervision order. A court application may provide the appropriate vehicle to accomplish this. The court application is available in Alberta, Saskatchewan, Ontario, Québec, New Brunswick, Prince Edward Island and the Yukon.

Notice To Produce the Child

As an alternative to apprehension, legislation in Nova Scotia and the Yukon allows a "notice to produce" which literally requires that a parent or guardian produce the child before the court at the time and place specified in the notice. The notice to produce is used when a child protection agency is having difficulty completing an investigation or when access to a family is otherwise impeded.

Apprehension With or Without a Warrant or Order

One of a protection worker's most difficult professional decisions is whether or not to remove a child against the wishes of a parent or caregiver. This represents the strongest flexing of state powers in the lives of families. If a child is old enough to verbalize the wish to be cared for outside the home, the decision to remove may be easier for everyone involved. Other situations are also quite clear, such as that of an abandoned child, or a teenager who is out of the parents' control and agrees to be removed from the home. However, if the child is too young to communicate, or wishes to stay home despite the dangers to health and safety posed by the home situation, removal becomes more difficult for everyone.

Above all, apprehension should not be used to punish uncooperative families. It is an extreme step which should be taken only to ensure the health and safety of a child. Removal from home is often traumatic to a child and should be reserved for those cases where a situation cannot be addressed safely with the child remaining in the home.

It is impossible to define exhaustively all situations that might warrant apprehension. In a case where there has been a series of "accidental" injuries to a child, removal may be appropriate. One of the accidents seen in isolation may not warrant such a radical step, but in the context of repeated injuries would raise questions about the possibility of physical abuse or serious chronic neglect.

On the other hand, a single incident with convincing evidence of abusive behaviour may warrant removal of a child. For example, cigarette burns, severe burns resulting from direct contact of a child's buttock with a burner on a stove or medical evidence of sexual abuse may justify immediate removal, especially when there is no admission of responsibility from the parent and no accurate determination of risk can be made.

In some cases, a child's removal is made necessary by a lack of information about the risk of further injury to the child. With suspected child abuse, there is often a frustrating absence of information from the parents or caregivers who face the possibility of criminal charges and invoke their constitutional right to silence. From the child protection point of view, it then becomes impossible to ascertain what has happened in the family, what steps, if any, might reduce the risk to the child, and whether or not it is feasible to return the child to the family.

Most provincial laws do not require that a child be abused before being removed, only that there be a substantial risk of harm. Removal may be the only practical alternative if parents have a history of violence toward children or are suffering from a condition that places their children at significant risk, (e.g., addiction to drugs or alcohol) and support is unavailable to reduce the risks to a tolerable level. While courts are demonstrating reluctance to remove children on a preventive basis, the law provides for this option, and it is one which a child protection worker ought to consider when the risks to a child seem high. The age of the child is a crucial factor in this decision, since it is assumed that an older child may be more capable of avoiding harm or reaching out for help than an infant.

All provinces have given child protection authorities the right to apprehend without a warrant, and if necessary, to enter premises with force to remove a child at risk.[16] The use of forced entry is generally restricted to situations where the life or safety of the child is in immediate danger. In some provinces, protection workers appear to have a choice of apprehending with or without a warrant, but other provinces (including Ontario) require that a warrant be obtained for the

---

[16] In most provinces, legislation stipulates that apprehension without a warrant requires a worker to have "reasonable and probable grounds" to believe that a child is in need of protection. The Prince Edward Island Supreme Court recently held that provincial legislation which did not contain such a requirement was unconstitutional as it violated a citizen's right under s.8 of the *Charter* to be free from "unreasonable search and seizure." *H.M.* v. *Director of Child Welfare* (1989), 22 R.F.L. (3d) 399 (P.E.I.S.C.). Legislation in that province has been amended to restrict the use of warrantless apprehensions; Bill 39, 2d Sess., 58th Assembly P.E.I., (third reading 11 April 1990). This decision raises questions as to the constitutionality of laws in provinces like B.C., Manitoba, Newfoundland and Nova Scotia where statutes permit warrantless searches in non-emergency circumstances.

removal of a child unless the time necessary to obtain a warrant or order might endanger the child.[17]

The process of obtaining a warrant begins with the swearing of an "information," which is a written statement signed by a worker and sworn to be true, stating the facts giving rise to the belief that a child is endangered, and asking that a warrant be issued authorizing the child's apprehension. A judge or justice of the peace must then agree to issue the warrant. In most provinces there must be a court appearance to have a warrant issued, but in Alberta it may be obtained by telephone.

In situations where a child protection worker who is planning to apprehend a child anticipates some resistance, a request will be made for police assistance. Many police departments prefer to wait until a warrant has been obtained before they will intervene so that there is an authoritative document to show a resistant and often bewildered family. If the police are involved, it is important to work in a cooperative manner, strategizing roles during and after the apprehension. Where time permits, careful planning of an apprehension can alleviate a great deal of stress and confusion for all concerned.

Occasionally a voluntary agreement is not a practical option. In this case, an apprehension will be planned with the family's consent. Most judges are willing to accept an apprehension "on consent," as long as no legal rights are adversely affected.

The technical legal requirements of apprehension are that a child be physically removed from the care and custody of a parent, usually without the parent's consent. It is wise to state clearly that the child is being apprehended, for example, by saying: "I am apprehending Johnny." The moment of apprehension is then crystallized for everyone, rather than leaving parents with the feeling they were coerced into agreeing to have their child taken from them.

Normally, an apprehended child will be taken to a place of safety which includes hospitals, foster homes and group homes. If a child in hospital is apprehended, it is customary to provide a letter indicating that the child has been apprehended, which can then be placed on the child's chart for easy reference. The parents, as well as the hospital, must be informed of the fact that the child has been apprehended. Whenever possible, this should occur in a face-to-face meeting between the social worker and the parents.

Some child protection statutes allow a child protection worker to apprehend a child for the specific purpose of having the child medically examined, with the possibility of return if there is no need for a continued apprehension. Occasionally, the circumstances warranting apprehension are resolved within days following the apprehension, or the agency enters into a voluntary agreement with the parent as an alternative to a court application.

---

[17] *Child and Family Services Act*, S.O. 1984, c. 55, s. 40(6)(b).

COURT APPEARANCE FOLLOWING APPREHENSION

All provinces require that the child protection agency appear before court to justify an apprehension and to permit the family to present its position to the court. The time limit for this to take place varies from 24 hours (with discretion to extend the time frame under certain circumstances in the case of Québec's *Youth Protection Act*[18]) to 45 days, in the case of the Northwest Territories' *Child Welfare Ordinance*[19]. Many provinces provide some discretion, setting out a maximum period within which a child protection application must be brought before the court. For example, in Nova Scotia, the application must be brought not earlier than 4 clear days and not later than 21 days after the date the child is taken into care.[20] By contrast, the Ontario statute affords little discretion in its requirement that an application be brought before the court within 5 days of bringing a child to a place of safety.

The first appearance in court may be little more than a formality at which the court documents are placed before the judge and an adjournment is requested. This would likely occur where an apprehension is on consent, or in a situation where parents either cannot be located at the outset, or need time to obtain legal counsel. In other cases, especially where the apprehension has been strongly opposed by the parent, the court may be asked to hold an interim care hearing to determine the validity of the apprehension and the care and custody of the children pending a full hearing.

INTERIM CARE

The court process is often slow and cumbersome. In a contested child protection case, a court will inevitably be asked to adjourn the matter on more than one occasion. Depending upon the case and the availability of trial time, the proceedings may be adjourned for many months awaiting a final determination. Because delays are inevitable in the court process, most child protection laws specifically provide for a summary (or brief) hearing at the outset of the proceedings. This is to determine where a child will reside while a final determination of the application is made.

The evidence in such a hearing may be by oral testimony or by affidavit (a written statement, sworn to be true). For example, in a child abuse case the

---

[18] R.S.Q. 1977. c. P–34.1, s. 47.

[19] R.O.N.W.T. 1974, c. C–3, s. 16(3). Alberta, Nova Scotia and P.E.I require that parents be notified "forthwith" of the apprehension.

[20] *Children's Services Act*, S.N.S. 1976, c. 8, s. 47(3).

evidence at an interim care hearing[21] may consist of a physician's report which explains the type of injuries observed and gives an opinion that the injuries were likely not accidental. The protection worker may also be required to testify about the information obtained from the parents, police or other sources, and the reasons for a care and custody request. The court will usually be asked to consider the risks to a child if the child remains in the home pending a full trial.

There is substantial variation among provinces and courts in the test to be applied at this early stage. Some legislation and some judges favour caution by authorizing protective care pending a hearing if there is possibility of further harm to a child while in parental care. In some provinces, such as Ontario, the child protection agency must prove substantial risk of harm to justify an order that the child remain in care at this early stage, and protective care is ordered only as a last option.

In many cases, the parties agree about the nature of the interim order. For example, a child protection agency may be willing to return a child to the parent's care, providing that an order is made permitting supervision of the home situation. In this case, the court would be asked to make the interim order which is agreed upon by the parties, without necessarily hearing or receiving evidence.

Assuming the parties have had an opportunity to retain counsel, the negotiations at this early stage can be pivotal to the future of the case. It is not uncommon for the entire application to be settled on consent, once the concerns are openly discussed. In this situation, an interim order may not be necessary, and the parties may proceed to a final order on the first occasion in court.

REQUIREMENT OF NOTICE

Those affected by the court proceeding must be properly notified of the time, place, and nature of the proceedings. All provinces require notification of parents, although the term used in the Alberta legislation is "all the guardians of the child."[22] It is important to review the definition of "parent" when determining who should actually receive notice. For example, Ontario's *Child and Family Services Act* defines "parent" quite broadly, by including individuals who are not necessarily biological parents, at the same time excluding biological fathers who are not married to the mother and have had little or no involvement with the child or mother.[23]

In addition to parents, many provinces provide for service of notice on any person who had custody of the child at the time of the apprehension, on older

---

[21] In some jurisdictions the interim care hearing is colloquially referred to as a "show cause" hearing, as the onus is on the child protection agency to show cause why the child should remain in care pending a full hearing.

[22] *Child Welfare Act*, S.A. 1984, c. C–8.1, s. 21(1)(a).

[23] S.O. 1984, c. 55, s. 3.

children and on foster parents who have been caring continuously for the child for an extended period. If the child is native, a number of provinces require that the band be notified of the proceedings.

In Ontario and other provinces, a child under the age of 12 may also receive notice at the discretion of the judge if the court is satisfied that the child is capable of understanding the hearing and will not suffer emotional harm by being present. Some provincial legislation permits a child protection agency to omit service of notice of the hearing on a child over the age of 12 if it can be established that the child may be emotionally harmed by being present at the hearing.

The form of written notice varies among provinces, but usually contains the information necessary to allow a party to respond to the application of the child protection agency including the date, time and place of the hearing, the order requested and a summary of the facts alleged by the child protection agency.

The child protection agency is expected to make a diligent effort to identify, locate and serve the notice by following every reasonable lead which may assist in locating every individual entitled to notice. Despite the efforts of the worker, the missing party occasionally cannot be located or formally served by the first court appearance. In this case, it is usually necessary to seek an adjournment in order to effect service of the notice. If, after repeated efforts to locate a party, the protection agency is still unable to effect service, an order from the court may be requested dispensing with service on the missing party. Occasionally the court will order a form of substitutional service, that is, a form of service other than delivery of the documents in person to the individual. This includes mailing the documents to an address where the individual is believed to live, leaving them with someone believed to be in contact with the individual, or publishing a newspaper advertisement.

DISCLOSURE AND PRE-TRIAL DISCUSSIONS: THE SOCIAL WORKER'S ROLE

This section offers direct advice to social workers about disclosing information to other parties and about the social worker's role in pre-trial discussions.

Contested litigation is slow, crude and costly in monetary and emotional terms. One can simply watch a child whose future is tied up in the litigation process to be convinced of its high toll. The child whose future is before the courts is forced to deal with constant uncertainty. Children ask questions like: "Will I be going to the cottage next summer? What school will I be going to? Can I join Boy Scouts? Where will I be living next year? When will the adults tell me what's going to happen?" The court process often forces children to spend their most important developmental years in the care of temporary caregivers.

The courtroom translates into headaches for protection workers: filling out forms; arranging for service of documents; dealing with seemingly aggressive lawyers; waiting; and then after possibly countless adjournments, participating in a hearing of which the outcome may be a great disappointment. However, the courtroom is a fact of professional life for the protection worker. Imagine the terror a court proceeding invokes for the parent or caregiver whose child is before the court.

The best approach to court avoidance is clear communication with families from the beginning. In many cases, your concerns will not be a surprise to them. The courtroom should never be the first place a family hears your protection concerns clearly stated.

Disclosure

Most provinces have acknowledged a positive duty for child protection agencies to disclose to the parties the information forming the basis of their protection application. The duty to disclose in this particular situation modifies the normal duty to protect confidentiality of client information.

If you invite one lawyer to a disclosure meeting, other counsel should also be invited. Because notions of fairness play an important role in the court process, it may embarrass the agency in subsequent court proceedings to appear to have treated one counsel in a manner perceived as special. A request for disclosure by the child's lawyer should receive the same response as a request by the parents' lawyer.

When you embark on a process of information-sharing, it is important not to assume the child's lawyer will agree with the agency's position. Although a lawyer may agree to use the information you provide with discretion, the bottom line is that information of the counsel is information of the client. Likewise, you should not assume that you can have an "off-the-record" conversation with a lawyer for the parents or child. The lawyer is duty-bound to use every opportunity to advance the client's case.

The nature of disclosure on each case varies depending upon issues or the interests of individuals to be protected (e.g., the identity of foster parents or informants). The disclosure practices of child protection agencies vary a great deal: some virtually open the file to counsel seeking disclosure, whereas others take a highly restrictive approach. Protection workers need to become familiar with the disclosure policies of their particular agency. Most child protection agencies encourage workers to consult with their lawyers before offering access to documentary evidence.

In some agencies, virtually all disclosure takes place through the agency's lawyer. In others, the workers respond to requests for disclosure, with occasional guidance from counsel. With a highly contentious case, it is advisable to defer requests for disclosure entirely to the agency's lawyer.

Often a lawyer for a parent or child will ask a worker for copies of file documents. This is usually a reasonable request, especially if the file contains a great deal of information. It is time-consuming and frustrating for a lawyer to take notes of the file's contents. Copies are often made and provided to the lawyer at cost provided agency policy permits this.[24]

Failure to provide opposing lawyers with information required to do their jobs may result in acrimony and unnecessary adversarial attitudes. The case may be delayed while they seek disclosure by way of court order. In several provinces, the rules of court specifically require disclosure. Failure to comply with the requirement of disclosure could attract an order of costs against the agency or a possible argument under the *Charter of Rights and Freedoms*.[25] There is also a risk that the failure to disclose information may raise doubts about the agency's overall management of the case.

In some jurisdictions, the child protection agency may be required to share only material upon which it plans to rely in making its case. In Ontario and some other jurisdictions, child protection agencies may be ordered by the court to disclose "facts relating to any matter in issue in the proceeding ... "[26]

An agency may legitimately wish to withhold some file information from the litigating parties. Reports in the file may have been prepared on a confidential basis for the child protection agency, and the agency may feel compelled to respect the confidence. Some information may fall within the realm of that which is protected by solicitor-client privilege. The agency may also wish to hold back information which, if released, could prejudice or endanger a third party, such as an informant or a foster family. Before providing disclosure, it is advisable to review the entire file, and seek legal advice about any questionable material it contains. If the protection agency wishes to withhold information from an opposing party, counsel representing the agency will often advise the parties of the document being withheld. They are then free to request the document from the author, or through formal procedures at court.

---

[24] In an Ontario decision, *Catholic Children's Aid Society of Metro Toronto* v. *Mr. and Mrs. P.* (2 May 1985), York (Ont. Prov. Ct—Fam. Div.) [unreported], Thomson P.C.J., the judge ordered that photocopies of the agency's records be provided to parents' counsel on certain conditions. The agency was authorized to delete any personal information about workers, or information which would identify the whereabouts of the child and the foster parents. The agency was to be compensated for any costs assumed in that process. The parents' counsel specifically undertook that he would not reveal any identifying information to his clients. However, see *C.A.S. of Stormont, Dundas, & Glengarry* v. *K.G.* (1989), 23 R.F.L. (3d) 382 (Ont. Dist. C.A.) where the court allowed counsel for the parents to inspect a child protection worker's case notes before the worker testified, but would not permit photocopying of the notes by the counsel.

[25] *Canadian Charter of Rights and Freedoms*, Part I of the *Constitution Act, 1982*, being Schedule B of the *Canada Act 1982 (U.K.)*, 1982, c. 11.

[26] *Rules of the Provincial Court*, (Fam. Div.), Reg. 810 under the *Courts of Justice Act*, S.O. 1984, s. 20(1).

Disclosure of audio- or video-taped interviews with the child may warrant exceptional handling, especially if they may be used as evidence in a concurrent criminal prosecution. Some judges have held that child protection agencies are not required to share the contents with parents' counsel, unless the tapes themselves will be tendered in evidence in the protection proceeding. This is particularly true when the child complainant has requested the tapes be kept confidential. However, if the agency intends to present the tapes in evidence, the court may well compel their disclosure as a prerequisite.[27]

If there is a difference of opinion regarding access to information, it may be possible to bring the matter before a judge for a determination at an early stage. Except for some compelling reason, a policy of full disclosure to the litigating parties makes good sense. Frequently the process of meaningful disclosure is instrumental in bringing about a consent resolution of the case without the necessity of contested litigation.

Pre-Trial Discussions

Conversations with lawyers representing other parties to a proceeding can be of benefit to everyone. Despite the conversational informality, the objectives of such discussions will be one or more of the following:

1. Exchange of Information. The concept of "trial by surprise" may be part of television dramas, but it is not part of our legal system, especially in cases involving children. The protection worker usually provides the information to the other parties, but it does not need to be a one-way street. Use the opportunity of pre-trial discussions to ask questions that are relevant to an ongoing assessment of the case. What is the exact nature of the parent's plan for the child? Is the parent working? What is the address of the new apartment? Will she be living with anyone at that address? What role will the grandmother be playing? What is the name of the drug program she will be attending? Ask all questions you need answered. If a meeting is convened prior to court, copies of all reports to be tendered in court should be provided to all parties. Ask other parties for copies of such documentation.

2. Settlement. Once the facts are disclosed, there may be room to negotiate a settlement. Remember that up to that point, the parents' lawyer may only have heard the story from their perspective. Disclosure of the agency's case can often be an educational experience for opposing counsel. It is unrealistic to expect a lawyer to commit the client to a resolution at an initial meeting. Likewise, you should not feel obliged to respond immediately to a settlement offer if time is needed to consider it or to consult with a supervisor or lawyer privately. While not unheard of, agreements are rarely concluded at a meeting between counsel. The parent's lawyer will frequently need an opportunity to review the evidence

---

[27] If a videotape is to be used in a concurrent criminal proceeding under s. 715.1 of the *Criminal Code*, R.S.C. 1985, c. C–46, the Crown attorney will invariably feel obliged to provide defence counsel with access to the tape prior to the criminal trial.

privately with the client. A gruelling session between the counsel and parent is often needed to bring about the possibility of settlement. However, the lawyer is duty-bound to take instructions from the client and may be instructed to fight the case, despite attempts to convince the client otherwise.

3. Narrowing Issues. Even if the ultimate issue cannot be settled by way of agreement, it is often possible to narrow the areas of conflict. Can the special needs of the child be agreed upon? Is wardship understood to be necessary, but its duration the real issue? Do the parties agree on the period of wardship but disagree about the nature of the access? All efforts should be made to establish those areas of the case not in dispute so the hearing can focus on the actual issues to be litigated.

4. Resolving Evidentiary Issues and Streamlining Trial. If a case must go to trial, cooperative planning will help ensure the hearing is not unduly protracted. Resolving legal issues can only be done by the lawyer acting on behalf of the child protection agency. If the lawyers are present at a pre-trial meeting or conference, legal issues can be raised in the context of the general discussion about the case.

Sometimes the parties can agree to have certain evidence admitted without the necessity of the authors attending. For example, in a permanent wardship application with adoption as the agency plan, all may agree that an affidavit regarding adoptability can be filed instead of calling an agency adoption worker to testify. To resolve a question about evidence admissibility, it is sometimes possible, prior to the trial, to bring a preliminary motion before the judge who will be presiding. This practice minimizes the inconvenience to witnesses who are waiting to testify at the trial. As well, knowing whether or not the controversial evidence will be admitted assists counsel in making decisions about what witnesses will be required before the commencement of trial. Lawyers can often agree to accommodate the testimony of an expert witness at a specific time, thus minimizing the inconvenience for that person.

FORMAL PRE-TRIAL MEETING

In a number of provinces, the Rules of Court provide for a formal pre-trial meeting before a judge. The meeting can be in the form of an informal chat in the judge's chambers (office) with only lawyers present, or a meeting in the courtroom with all lawyers and their clients. The style of the judge and the wishes of the parties usually determine the form of the meeting.

Lawyers representing the parties usually outline the positions being taken, and briefly summarize the nature of the evidence they will provide. If there are any documents to be filed, they are provided to the judge, who returns them after the pre-trial is completed. In some localities, the child protection agency is required to file a pre-trial brief, containing copies of all court documents, reports, and other written information which the judge may require.

After hearing from all parties, the judge will usually indicate what he or she would decide if acting as presiding judge. The parties are then given an opportunity to consider the judge's pre-trial indication, and to accept or reject it. If the parties accept the views of the judge, the judge will call the court reporter, and permit the parties to resolve the case by way of consent order. If the parties do not accept these views, they may request a trial date with the assurance that the matter will be heard by a different judge. However, if all parties wish to have the pre-trial judge preside at trial, this can usually be arranged.

In some courts, a formal pre-trial is required before a matter will be set for trial. In other courts, the pre-trial is available upon request, but is not required in every case. As a general rule, a formal pre-trial is of limited value when the parties are deeply entrenched in their positions, or when the case hinges on conflicting evidence. The pre-trial can be particularly useful in two types of situations:

1. Where a child protection agency takes a position it believes to be correct, but will accept a court's ruling that the position is not justified by the evidence. If, at pre-trial, the court does not support the agency position, the agency may agree to a consent order but may ask that the judge put on record that a pre-trial was held and its outcome. This allows a formal explanation of why the original agency position was ultimately changed.

2. Even though the outcome of a case appears obvious, a parent or a child may resist the advice of their counsel. In this case, a judge may convince the resisting client that the order being asked for is inevitable. The lawyer for the resisting party may be the best person to assist in assessing the usefulness of a pre-trial for this purpose.

It is always important to consider any reasonable settlement proposal and to keep an open mind as the case changes during the months prior to court, as well as during the trial itself. However, child protection litigation is different from other types of litigation in some significant respects. First, it is litigation that arises out of a statutory duty. Second, the probability of success, is not the only factor in deciding whether to proceed to court. Sometimes it is important to bring a matter before the court even when the probability of success is low. The decision to proceed under those circumstances is a difficult one, and deserves legal guidance.

THE PROTECTION HEARING

Anne Genereux[*]

INTRODUCTION

The protection hearing is the court hearing at which the child protection agency presents evidence to a judge to establish the need for protection of the child. Unless the evidence can justify a court finding that the child is in need of protection, the court has no legal authority to order any form of intervention, no matter how urgent it may seem from a social work perspective.

Because of its nature and the significant effect it has on the lives of children and their families, child protection legislation is constantly under review, and sometimes under attack. It is important to know which people within your agency are reliable resources in keeping up to date on legislation.

It seems to be increasingly difficult for child protection workers to fulfill the requirements of the legislation and provide the quality of service they expect of themselves. Agencies are under financial constraints. It often seems that workers are constantly being required to spend more time performing administrative tasks and less time in direct contact with their clients. Review mechanisms, recording requirements and other accountability issues now face front line workers. Social workers occasionally find that legislative amendments assist them in their work. One such example in Ontario is *An Act to Amend the Child and Family Services Act, 1984*,[1] which provides new mechanisms for social workers and police to apprehend adolescents who run away from their placements or parents.

THE CHILD IN NEED OF PROTECTION

Every provincial protection statute defines a "child in need of protection," though the specific criteria vary. Understanding the definition, and being able to apply it to the cases that confront social workers on a daily basis is essential. The specific grounds for intervention are interpreted against a philosophical backdrop that recognizes the need for protection of the best interests and well-being of children. Some provincial statutes expressly outline the philosophical bases or

---

[*] Manager of Accreditation and Legal Support, Ontario Association of Children's Aid Societies, Toronto, Ontario.

[1] S.O. 1988, c. 36, s. 40a-d.

principles within which the statutes are to be interpreted. Definitions in all jurisdictions generally include the following:

- physical, sexual or emotional abuse;
- abandonment;
- orphanhood;
- parental failure to meet health needs of the child;
- inadequate parental care, supervision or control; and,
- absence of the parent in circumstances that endanger the child's safety or well-being.

All child protection workers should know how the concept of the "child in need of protection" is defined in their jurisdiction, and what the specific words of the statute mean. Statutory interpretations by judges who hear these cases arise on a case-by-case basis, often in subtle statements rather than major pronouncements. Each case is decided on the facts presented, and leading judicial precedents rarely play a significant role in the outcome of a case. It is essential that all the criteria indicating a child's need for protection are established with clear evidence in court. Although definitions of a "child in need of protection" vary from province to province, there is substantial commonality in the types of cases which are brought before the court.

Cases of physical abuse are often noticed when a parent has used excessive force in disciplining. A doctor or hospital emergency professional may observe injuries which do not appear to be the result of a childhood accident or appear inconsistent with the explanation provided by the parent. For example, a very young infant suffering multiple broken bones would, in the absence of a reasonable explanation, raise questions about the possibility of abuse by a caregiver. It is often difficult to distinguish an abusive incident from a childhood accident. Even when a parent offers a credible explanation, issues may be raised about the quality of supervision, particularly if accidents happen on more than one occasion. It is important for child abuse investigators to remember that as a young child becomes mobile, it is normal for falls and other accidents to occur. One should enter an investigation with an open mind and not draw firm conclusions of abuse, or confront parents with child abuse allegations before a thorough investigation has been made.

A parent's use of corporal punishment alone does not usually justify agency involvement. Rather, the use of force resulting in demonstrable harm to the child, perhaps in the form of bruises, welts, cuts, burns, broken bones or internal injuries should be cause for agency concern. These situations can range from a single incident of excessive punishment to life-threatening injuries. It is often possible to obtain medical evidence of physical abuse, but even when harm is clearly documented, these cases are difficult. With a very young child, there is no way of ascertaining what happened directly from the child, and older children sometimes do not tell the full story of their injuries in order to "protect" their parents. In these cases, the protection worker must rely heavily on the medical findings and interviews with the parents or caregivers to assess the likelihood of abuse. A doctor can often advise whether the injuries are consistent with the explanation offered.

There has been a great increase in the number of reported cases of child sexual abuse in Canada. Heightened professional and public awareness has increased sensitivity, and created an atmosphere in which allegations are more likely to be believed. Protection agencies are most likely to be involved when the allegation concerns a parent or guardian, or if the parent is failing to protect the child from the abuse of a relative or friend. Even without physical evidence of sexual abuse, the child's statement may form sufficient evidentiary basis for a court proceeding. The presence of confirming physical evidence strengthens such an application, but it is not essential. Sexual abuse includes a wide range of sexual activities, and is not restricted to the act of intercourse.

Cases of emotional abuse are less frequently dealt with by protection agencies, perhaps because it has always been difficult in these cases to meet the requirements of an objective court inquiry. Although emotional abuse is extremely difficult to prove in court, the scars are frequently permanent and deep, especially when no remedial intervention is effected. Some have suggested that emotional abuse is too esoteric to form the basis of state intervention. However, when a child is exhibiting signs of deep emotional pain, and the action or inaction of a parent or caregiver is documented and believed to be a major causative factor, an agency may be able to establish a protection case. These cases generally succeed only if there is detailed testimony by a social worker or other professional (such as a teacher) combined with an expert psychological or psychiatric opinion which interprets those observations.

Applications because of abandonment are not common, but are generally straightforward when they occur. Referral sources are usually babysitters with whom the children have been abandoned or relatives who are no longer willing to care for a child left by a parent. In these cases it is sometimes difficult to notify parents of the apprehension and court proceedings. However, as discussed in Chapter 3, if a parent cannot be located, a court order can be obtained to dispense with notice, or the parent may be notified by leaving court documents with another person or by some other means. Although orders authorizing agency care of a child under these circumstances are not usually difficult to obtain, workers are expected to make diligent efforts on an ongoing basis to locate parents or other relatives who may provide for the child's care.

Many agency court applications involve children at risk because a parent's judgment and caregiving are impaired by intellectual limitations, physical or mental health problems, or an addiction to drugs or alcohol. Sometimes the family can be supported in caring for the children, but during a crisis or if the problem is chronic a court application for removal may be necessary, especially if extended family are not available or capable of providing care.

In many situations of abuse, there is also some form of neglect. Further, there are many situations which have no direct physical, sexual or emotional abuse, but the child's physical or emotional needs are clearly not being met. Unfortunately, the subject of neglect seems to have been overshadowed in recent years by the more dramatic cases of abuse. However, it must be remembered that neglect, particularly in the case of young totally dependent children, can cause serious harm or death.

Most agencies are sensitive to the relationship between poverty and child neglect, and often attempt to provide practical assistance to families who are struggling to raise children without sufficient financial resources. However, chronic misuse of resources to the children's detriment may necessitate court involvement.

Physical evidence of neglect may include a physical description of the child's hygiene, dress and living environment. If issues relate to the adequacy of nutrition, medical evidence may be useful.

In cases where parental drug or alcohol addiction is suspected but denied, the agency is usually forced to rely on information from reported incidents, each of which alone might be viewed as relatively innocuous, but which together reveal a pattern of parenting posing a serious risk to a child's physical or emotional well-being. Parents may be affected by mental illness (e.g., depression or addiction), and may be unaware of the impact of their behaviours on the children in their care. Documented observations of the parent while he or she is under the influence of an intoxicant may be important to the agency case.

Parents who are rendered unstable by addiction, mental illness, or immaturity, may demonstrate the instability in various aspects of their lives such as housing, employment and relationships. A long history of criminal activity raises issues of a parent's ability to transmit social values to a child, as well as the practical issues raised by frequent incarcerations.

Chronic domestic violence and its influence on children is a frequent cause for agency concern. In New Brunswick, Newfoundland, Prince Edward Island and Alberta, spousal violence is specifically included in the statute as a situation where a child is in need of protection. While most child protection professionals have little difficulty recognizing that a child living in a "war zone" is at risk, some courts require expert testimony to establish a causal relationship between spousal violence and harm to the child, especially if there is no history of direct abuse of the child.

Lack of supervision or control is a frequent protection issue. Agencies are often forced to bring applications before the court when a young child is repeatedly left at home alone, or when an older child is seen regularly engaging in potentially dangerous activities with no adult supervision. Sometimes the older child will be referred to child protection agencies by police. By far the most frequent situation involving lack of supervision or control is that of the adolescent/parent conflict, sometimes escalating to the point where the adolescent is totally estranged and living on the streets.

Violations of the law by a child or young person may be the basis of a protection application, especially when the act involved is seen by investigating police as an attempt to get help. Under the *Young Offenders Act*[2], criminal charges cannot be laid against a child under age 12, thus the only alternatives available to police are to suggest that parents take appropriate measures, or to involve child protection authorities. Ontario and Nova Scotia have a specific provision in their protection legislation which refers to a child under age 12 who has committed an offence. In other provinces, more general parts of the definition of a "child in need of protection" are used for the child who persistently or seriously breaks the law under circumstances which suggest that protection issues exist.

Not infrequently, cases involve a combination of abuse and neglect issues. A case may surface on one basis and subsequently reveal a constellation of protection issues. A worker concerned about a child's safety, or emotional or physical health, can discuss with the agency lawyer the existing legal definition of "child in need of protection" most relevant to a given situation.

All jurisdictions have legislation identifying a need for protection if the guardian, parent or person having charge of the child is unwilling or unable to obtain essential medical treatment that is recommended by a physician. The issue of provision of medical treatment is very complex, partially because it often involves strong advocacy of religious beliefs, such as a Jehovah's Witness parent refusing a blood transfusion. There may also be a need for quick hearings, and dispensing with some of the basic provisions for notifying parents prior to a hearing. These cases may involve careful balancing of competing interests.

Canadian courts have generally upheld the constitutional validity of child welfare statutes requiring that a child receive needed medical attention, even though this may violate the religious views of parents or children.[3] However, in a Newfoundland case, it was held that the legislation in that province was unconstitutional for failing to require notice to parents and a court hearing within a reasonable period of time after an emergency apprehension and blood transfusion.[4] The legislation in Newfoundland was amended to ensure that parents and children are afforded these procedural safeguards, though still allowing emergency treatment to be provided with authorization from the child protection authorities, prior to a court hearing.

In an Ontario case, a 12-year-old Jehovah's Witness girl with acute leukemia was refused chemotherapy as this would necessitate blood transfusions, which were contrary to the religious beliefs of the girl and her parents. The agency applied to have her made a ward in order to allow the treatment to occur, even

---

[2]   S.C. 1980–81–82–83, c. 110, s. 2.

[3]   See, e.g., *Re S.E.M.*, [1987] 1 W.W.R. 327 (Alta Q.B.).

[4]   *Re C.P.L* (1988), 70 Nfld & P.E.I.R. and 215 A.P.R. 287 (Nfld U.F.C.). The decision offers a good discussion and comparison of the provisions for medical treatment of apprehended children in other Canadian provinces.

though her prognosis with treatment was poor. The court considered the applicability of ss. 7 and 15(1) of the *Canadian Charter of Rights and Freedoms* which provide:

> 7. Everyone has the right to life, liberty and security of the person and the right not to be deprived thereof except in accordance with the principles of fundamental justice ...

> 15.(1) Every individual is equal before and under the law and has the right to the equal protection and equal benefit of the law without discrimination and, in particular, without discrimination based on race, national or ethnic origin, colour, religion, sex, age or mental or physical disability.[5]

Judge Main cited the *Charter* and refused to make the order sought:

> I must find that she has been discriminated against on the basis of her religion and her age pursuant to s. 15(1). In these circumstances, upon being given a blood transfusion, her right to the security of her person pursuant to s. 7 was infringed. As a result, even if she could be said to be a child in need of protection, the application must be dismissed pursuant to ... the *Charter*. Dismissal is a remedy which I consider appropriate and just in the circumstances. There is no question that this court has that jurisdiction. In granting such relief, I take into consideration the interests of the community, the interests of justice and, most importantly, the interests of L.D.K ...

> I am satisfied that this family is a warm and close-knit unit. L.'s parents are both loving and concerned individuals. L. is a beautiful, extremely intelligent, articulate, courteous, sensitive and, most importantly, a courageous person. She has wisdom and maturity well beyond her years and I think it would be safe to say that she has all of the positive attributes that any parent would want in a child. She has a well thought out, firm and clear religious belief. In my view, no amount of counselling from whatever source or pressure from her parents or anyone else, including an order of this court, would shake or alter her religious beliefs.

> I believe that L.K. should be given the opportunity to fight this disease with dignity and peace of mind. That can only be achieved by acceptance of the plan put forward by her and her parents.[6]

The girl soon thereafter died. It should be appreciated that in this case it was far from clear that the girl would have survived even if she had accepted the proposed treatment. The case illustrates that the courts respect a zone of privacy and will be reluctant to intervene in the family, though they will not allow parents or children to refuse treatment that has a high probability of saving a child's life.

Not all medical issues are emergency situations. In another Ontario case, Judge Karswick found a child to be in need of protection because she required medical treatment which the parent was unable to provide. Both the mother and grandmother requested custody of the child, but neither was able to provide the

---

[5] *Canadian Charter of Rights and Freedoms*, Part I of the *Constitution Act, 1982*, being Schedule B of the *Canada Act 1982 (U.K.)*, 1982, c. 11.

[6] *Re L.D.K.* (1985), 48 R.F.L. (2d) 164 at 171 (Ont. Prov. Ct - Fam. Div.).

extensive care required by the child on a consistent basis. Born with cystic fibrosis, the child required extensive daily home care procedures of a basic nature. The mother and the grandmother were not supportive of each other, and each requested sole custody of the child. Neither was able to maintain the strict diet and regimen required by the child. As a result, and after evidence from many medical personnel who spoke to the needs of this child, the judge ordered a period of temporary wardship for 6 months. This period of wardship, among other things, permitted the agency to consent to a medical procedure which the mother was unwilling to authorize. Given a change in any one of the major factual components of this case, the decision of the judge could well have been different. Judge Karswick stated:

> In my mind, there is no question about the love, care and commitment that the mother has for her daughter. I am also convinced that the grandmother is committed to providing as best as she can for her grandchild.

> However, there is overwhelming, uncontradicted, highly reputable medical evidence and opinion which argues emphatically against the return of the child to the mother or to the grandmother at this time.[7]

THE LEGAL FRAMEWORK OF PROTECTION PROCEEDINGS

It is important to remember that, in addition to child protection legislation, other statutes and legal rules have an effect on the conduct of a hearing. Provincial evidence law, rules of court procedure and relevant case law must also be considered in presenting these cases to court.

Ontario's *Child and Family Services Act*[8] has the most comprehensive procedural provisions. From the point of view of the agency this is both a help and a hindrance, in that it tells everyone involved exactly what is to be done but leaves relatively little discretion to the judge.

Parties to the protection hearing are identified in s. 39(1) of the Act, and include the child protection agency, the child's parent or parents, and a band representative if the child is native. Foster parents who have cared for a child continuously for 6 months immediately prior to the hearing will also have the right to address the court, though they are not awarded full legal status as parties. Individuals providing the actual physical care of a child, like foster parents, often have more information to offer a court than the workers of the child protection agency. These individuals may also have a very specific interest in the decision of the court, and their role and importance is more than that of a witness.

---

[7] *Children's Aid Society of Peel* v. *B.B. and C.*, [1988] W.D.F.L. 794 (Ont. Prov. Ct - Fam. Div.) Karswick P.C.J.

[8] S.O. 1984, c. 55.

A Child's Involvement

The child may also be involved in the protection proceeding. Generally speaking, under Ontario's Act a child 12 years of age or older is presumed to be entitled to be present at the hearing. However, there are provisions for excluding a child age 12 or older, and for including a child under age 12.[9] Some considerations weighed by the judge in determining whether or not a child will be permitted to remain in the courtroom during the hearing include the child's age, level of understanding, emotional state and prior knowledge of the facts being presented. Other circumstances must also be considered. For example, if the protection hearing concerns three siblings, two being 12 years of age or older while one is just under age 12, the judge may determine that the youngest child can attend. On the other hand, a 12-year-old child may be excluded if the younger siblings will not be attending, the child is immature or the allegations about the parents are unknown to the child.

Not all jurisdictions are this clear regarding who is entitled to be present at a hearing. Québec legislation requires the court to hear "all persons concerned," which could include a wide range of people, depending upon the allegations; the legislation also permits any person to intervene if they demonstrate to the court that they are acting in the interests of the child. However, the judge may exclude the child from the courtroom if the evidence being produced could cause prejudice to the child. The child's advocate must remain.[10]

Most jurisdictions provide an opportunity for the child's wishes, where ascertainable, to be put before the court. However, this is not always done directly. In some jurisdictions, the child may be excluded from court at the outset or may be excluded from court at the judge's discretion. In an Ontario case, Judge Lissaman had to rule as to whether he would interview the two children who were the subjects of the protection hearing. This case involved two children, aged 5 and 6, for whom the agency was requesting permanent wardship with no access to the parents. The parents opposed the termination of access. The judge refused to interview them, but indicated in his ruling that he would have less concern about interviewing children 10 or 13 years of age. Judge Lissaman stated:

> ... it would be extremely easy for me to say I must find out in any event what these children think. What would I ask them? Would I ask them whether they wish to be adopted with no access or whether they wish to be adopted with access? Would I have a conversation with them about issues, about the problems that might arise in the future? These are the things that concern me as a judge asked to interview children ... I, therefore, have come to the conclusion that I would be wrong to interview the children, and I decline to do so.[11]

---

[9] *Child and Family Services Act*, S.O. 1984, c. 55, s. 39.

[10] *Youth Protection Act*, R.S.Q. 1977, c. P–34.1, ss. 81, 84.

[11] *Catholic Children's Aid Society of Metro Toronto* v. *S.and S. (No. 2)* (15 September 1987), (Ont. Prov. Ct - Fam. Div.) [unreported], Lissaman J.

However, in an Alberta case, Judge Fitch agreed to see a 9-year-old child in his office in the presence of the lawyers, after all the other evidence had been presented. In this case, the mother was seeking custody of her son who had been raised by his great-grandmother until her death. His father was requesting that custody go to the boy's aunt and uncle, who had also resided with the great-grandmother. Custody was granted to the mother, with generous access provisions to the other parties. The child wished to reside with his mother and had clearly stated that to the judge and lawyers. The judge based his decision on other factors as well as the boy's wishes. Judge Fitch stated:

> Measures which are frequently taken by courts to reduce stress on young persons involved in custody cases proved unnecessary in this case. The court has seldom seen in a courtroom a young person of such tender years who appeared as alert, pleasant, informed, self-confident and aware.[12]

As will be discussed more fully in Chapter 9, a number of Canadian jurisdictions allow the child's views and wishes to be conveyed to the court by a lawyer who represents the child. It is also quite common for witnesses to relate what children have told them about where they would like to live and how they would like to be treated. Although there may be concerns that such evidence is technically "hearsay," the courts in child protection cases are generally quite flexible about receiving this type of evidence, especially if it is given by an "expert." Issues related to hearsay and expert evidence, as well as communicating a child's wishes to the court are discussed in Chapter 13.

Privacy and Exclusion of the Media

In Ontario, legislation provides that the protection hearing must be held separately from the hearings in criminal proceedings. The Ontario statute also specifies that protection hearings are to be conducted in private unless the judge expressly permits them to be open.[13] This may occur by having completely separate facilities or by having hearings on separate days or at separate times; other jurisdictions have similar provisions to ensure that hearings are private.[14]

With the recent public interest in child abuse matters, questions have been raised about the public's right to information in the context of a private hearing. Media presence in the courtroom during a hearing is dealt with specifically in s. 41 of the *Child and Family Services Act* of Ontario. "Media" is defined as press,

---

[12] *In the matter of the custody of and access to the child Re A.J.G.*, [1988] W.D.F.L. 1730 (Alta Prov. Ct) Fitch P.C.J.

[13] *Child and Family Services Act*, S.O. 1984, c. 55, s. 41(3). The constitutionality of this provision is being challenged by a newspaper which argues that it is an unjustified restriction on freedom of the press; see Kingston *Whig Standard* (27 November 1989) 1.

[14] These jurisdictions are British Columbia, the Northwest Territories, Québec, New Brunswick and Nova Scotia.

radio and television media; and not more than two media representatives either by their choice or, if they cannot agree, by the court's choice, are permitted unless the court orders otherwise. The court is also given discretion to ban any particular media representative or all media representatives from part or all of the hearing. There is also a prohibition on publication of any information that would identify a child participating in, or subject of, the hearing, and the court may further order a ban on publication of information that would identify an adult charged with abuse under the protection legislation. Most other jurisdictions have a variety of provisions that are similar to the Ontario legislation, but no other legislation is as comprehensive.[15]

Adjournments

Adjournments occur for a wide range of reasons. They happen most frequently when a case is first before the court and one or more of the parties (e.g., the parents or the child) want time to obtain a lawyer. At other times during the trial, adjournments may occur to permit an assessment to be done, to permit preparation of submissions by the lawyers at the completion of a lengthy trial, or to allow continuation of the trial when sufficient days were not booked ahead of time.

While the provisions exist to grant adjournments, the courts are becoming more reluctant to permit either lengthy or multiple adjournments. The responsibility for justifying the adjournment rests with the person who requests it. Even if all the parties involved in a case agree to an adjournment, the judge is not obliged to comply. As discussed in Chapter 3, a critical issue whenever an adjournment is granted, is whether the child will remain at home or be placed in the care of the protection agency during the adjournment.

Conduct of the Hearing

Not all statutes specifically address the issues of the order of evidence being given, who may present evidence, whether witnesses may be called by the court, in what manner a child's evidence may be given, or whether a transcript of evidence given at a prior hearing can be used at a new hearing.

Ontario legislation,[16] in s. 46(2), in theory appears to require a two-step hearing, with an initial finding that a child is in need of protection. Only if there is such a finding can the court receive "evidence relating only to disposition" (i.e., the type of order the judge should make: supervisory, temporary wardship or permanent wardship). From a practical standpoint, this division of proceedings into two distinct stages typically occurs in certain larger urban centers; more often in smaller communities there is a single hearing dealing with both issues.

---

[15] See, e.g., *Child Welfare Act*, S.A. 1984, c. C–8.1, s. 23 which prohibits publication by any means of the name of the child or guardian of the child or identifying information about either, without the consent of the court.

[16] *Child and Family Services Act*, S.O. 1984, c. 55.

The availability of court time and the complexity and length of the trial are factors in determining whether the proceedings will be divided. The division of the hearing into two stages affects the type of evidence that must be assembled for each stage, and the amount of time involved social workers must spend in court. The workers need to know ahead of time what information will be asked and what can be offered, and whether the trial will occur in two stages or one.

No other provincial legislation requires a two-stage process in respect to the court's reception of evidence, but the statutes in Newfoundland and Prince Edward Island do specifically require a finding of the need for protection prior to an order being made.[17]

In most provinces, the court may, on its own initiative, summon a person to give evidence and to produce any documents relevant to the case. This gives the judge the opportunity to hear all the evidence available with respect to a child's need for protection. In practice, most judges rely on the parties and their lawyers to bring forward evidence, and rarely use their statutory powers to call their own witnesses.

Typically, if a judge is concerned that a person with relevant evidence has not been called, the judge will indicate this in court and leave it up to the lawyers involved to call the evidence and witnesses they believe necessary. The trend in most jurisdictions is away from the informal and towards formality, with adherence to rules of procedure and protection of the rights of the parties without judicial interference. This suggests that a judge will refrain from calling a witness, though it is not uncommon for judges to ask clarifying questions of a witness.

FINDING A CHILD IS IN NEED OF PROTECTION

A crucial aspect of any hearing is the judge's determination of whether or not the child is in need of protection. Without such a finding, the court cannot require that the parent or guardian have any involvement with the protection agency. Once such a finding has been made, subsequent orders can be for supervision, temporary wardship or permanent wardship.

The purpose of the hearing and the responsibility for proving the case are generally the same in all provinces: the agency must prove its case on the civil standard of proof, the balance of probabilities. This means the judge must be convinced that it is more probable than not that the facts alleged by the agency are true.

In the case of *Re T.M.M. and the Catholic Children's Aid Society of Metropolitan Toronto*, Judge Karswick stated:

---

[17] The *Child Welfare Act*, S. Nfld 1972, No. 37, s. 19(4); *Family and Child Services Act*, R.S.P.E.I. 1974, c. F–2.01, s. 29(1).

It is my view that when all of the evidence is in and all the submissions completed and the court must make its final decision, at that point, the ultimate burden must remain with the Children's Aid Society, who must satisfy the judge that it is in the best interests of the child to deprive the child and the parents of their relationship.[18]

As discussed in Chapter 2, the concept of "best interests of the child" has a specific meaning in the context of protection proceedings. It does not simply mean what is best for the child in an absolute sense, but rather, that the onus is on the agency to prove that it is best for the child that the state intervene in the family and overcome the normal presumption of family autonomy. The court must be satisfied that the agency has proven the child is within one or more of the legal definitions of a child in need of protection. If the child is found to be in need of protection, the court will look at all the circumstances of the case in order to make the appropriate disposition.

Child protection hearings are decided on the basis of the evidence presented to the court. It is the responsibility of the workers involved in the case, together with their counsel, to present all the information in an understandable, professional manner.

The onus is on the agency to satisfy the court that the child is within the statutory definition of "child in need of protection" or the analogous concept of "endangered child," which is used in some provinces. The workers and agency need to be aware of the relevant judicial precedents interpreting the related provincial statute. There is also a need to be aware of what constitutes sufficient, relevant information and what is the beginning of excessive, irrelevant or repetitive evidence. The fact that the onus is on the child protection agency means that it must rely on the information and evidence it can put forward itself.

It is sometimes said that the agency is only justified in interfering if parental conduct falls below a minimum social standard. The *Brown* case involved a mother who was developmentally delayed and who suffered from uncontrolled epilepsy. The father was unstable and had a low level of intelligence. The court expressed the view that the level of care available to the children from the parents was below the standard required and that the children were in need of protection. As stated by Judge Stortini in *Re Brown*:

> ... the community ought not to interfere merely because our institutions may be able to offer a greater opportunity to achieve their potential. Society's interference in the natural family is only justified when the level of care of the children falls below that which no child in this country should be subjected to.[19]

In *Children's Aid Society of Ottawa-Carleton* v. *Steven W. and Monica W.*, Judge Sheffield considered the standard of care the community should expect:

---

[18] *Re T.M.M. and the Catholic Children's Aid Society of Metropolitan Toronto* (1981), 4 F.L.R.R. 3 (Ont. Prov. Ct - Fam. Div.).

[19] *Re Brown* (1975), 9 O.R. (2d) 185 at 189 (Ont. Prov. Ct - Fam. Div.).

The relevant community is definable by reference to the principles determining a jury panel, whether or not trial is by jury. Provincial child welfare laws focus, however, not upon the guilt and punishment of the parents but upon the protection of children.

The need for protection exists independently of parental culpability, and may be objectively assessed by concepts of causation rooted in appropriate professional disciplines rather than by reference to the level of harm a given community has been accustomed to tolerate.[20]

The children in this case were aged 8 months and 2½ years. Their father, a minister of a congregation in a small community outside of Ottawa, was alleged to have used corporal punishment on the children, and indicated he would continue to do so. There was also evidence at the hearing that the father advocated the use of corporal punishment in lectures and sermons. The children were found in need of protection due to physical abuse and the substantial risk of further physical abuse, and were made the subjects of a supervision order.

When trying to determine if a child is in need of protection and state intervention appropriate, it is important for the agency and court to be realistic and to appreciate the cultural diversity of Canada. As one judge observed, one must not "impose unrealistic or unfair middle class standards of child care upon a poor family of extremely limited potential."[21]

The need for sensitivity is particularly apparent in regard to native families and children, as noted by Judge Moxley in *Re E.C.D.M.*:

In my view, in order for a child to be found in need of protection there must be a significant departure from a standard of child care that one would generally expect for a child of the age of the child in question. Furthermore, while there is a minimum parental standard for all society, a secondary standard must be established for parents of the age of the parent in question and for the type of community in which the parent resides. A teen-aged parent cannot live up to the standard expected for a middle-aged parent. Similarly, different standards of parenting apply to parents of Cree ancestry who reside in a small rural community in Northern Saskatchewan than would apply to white middle-class parents living, for example, in Regina. What is an acceptable standard for the former might be unacceptable to the latter.[22]

Judge Moxley considered the evidence in the case and made the child a permanent ward, concluding:

Relating these facts to the community standards, a single parent in Pelican Narrows might be expected to live in crowded conditions in a house owned by a relative. It is not a significant departure from the community standard for her to be unemployed and to lack skills and employment opportunities. To have had problems with alcohol is commonplace in this community.

---

[20] *Children's Aid Society of Ottawa-Carleton* v. *Steven W. and Monica W.* (4 December 1987), (Ont. Prov. Ct - Fam. Div.) [unreported] at 24, digested in [1988] W.D.F.L. 458, Sheffield P.C.J.

[21] *Re Warren* (1973) 13 R.F.L. 51 (Ont. Prov. Ct - Fam. Div.), Matheson P.C.J.

[22] *Re E.C.D.M.* (1980), 17 R.F.L. (2d) 274 at 275 (Sask. Prov. Ct).

Where this mother does depart from the standard is in three areas: first, her lack of interest in her children, exhibited by her giving up of her son, her leaving her daughter in the care of others and her infrequent and short visits with her daughter when the daughter was in care of the Department; second, her inability to look after her own most basic needs, as shown by her failure to acquire glasses and to apply for social assistance payments; and, third, real problems with the living arrangement proposed by the mother ... The mother is obviously concerned about her inability to get along with her uncle and his children. It was a dispute with the uncle that brought on her last drinking bout. I do not expect this living arrangement to work out for very long, and the mother has no plan to deal with this problem.[23]

If the child is not found to be in need of protection, there is no authority in any provincial statute that requires parents to be subject to involuntary intervention. The statutory definition prescribes the basis for state intervention for dealing with social problems. However, the definitions do not provide a total redress of the social problems and are framed in the context of individual rights and responsibilities. Child protection statutes must also be interpreted in a social context to be meaningful. For example, even a decade ago, an 11-year-old child left at home without an adult might have raised potential protection issues. With the decline of stay-at-home parents, however, the "latch-key" kid is no longer seen as a priority for child protection agency involvement unless other questionable circumstances are involved.

Determination of Religion

In Ontario, a judicial finding concerning the child's religion is a preliminary step in the protection process, as it may determine which agency is responsible for the child. In some locations in the province there are Jewish and Catholic agencies, in addition to the public agency. In Prince Edward Island, Nova Scotia and the Northwest Territories, the court must establish a child's religion if there has been a finding that a child is in need of protection.

In all four jurisdictions, legislation requires that the agency make efforts to find placements that permit children to maintain their religion. In other jurisdictions, agencies also attempt to do this as a matter of practice.

DISPOSITION

If a child is found to be in need of protection, the court has the responsibility to determine what kind of disposition, or intervention, is appropriate. As stated in *Children's Aid Society of Ottawa-Carleton* v. *Steven W. and Monica W.*:

The court has a positive obligation imposed on it, where a finding of protection has been made, to consider the degree of intervention in the family unit that is least likely to be disruptive to the continued harmony of that family, and at the same time address the best interests of the child or children.

---

[23] *Re E.C.D.M.*, *ibid.* at 279.

The court has very broad jurisdiction under the Act once a finding has been made. It has quite obviously the authority to take these children away from their parents and to place them in a home where they will at least be ensured physical protection. The court also has the ultimate authority of making the children wards of the Crown, where very severe circumstances exist, and authority, of course, to make the order of supervision that is suggested.[24]

This quotation outlines the two areas that must be considered regarding disposition: (a) the orders available under governing legislation; and, (b) the basis upon which to determine the order to be made.

Types of Dispositional Orders

The three basic orders that are available to judges in all Canadian jurisdictions are:

1. Supervision orders;
2. Temporary wardship orders; and,
3. Permanent wardship orders.

Supervision Order

The least intrusive intervention, because it does not require the child to be removed from the custody of the parents, is the supervision order. All jurisdictions provide for an order of supervision, and also for conditions of the supervision order. The conditions included in a supervision order, while permitting the child to remain in the parent's custody, may be intrusive in the lives of the family. Examples of terms which might be imposed are: visits to the home by a public health nurse, a homemaker service or a teaching homemaker; participation in infant stimulation classes, day care programs or parenting courses; or, the child's attendance at medical appointments, school or extra-curricular activities.

It should be noted that in Ontario the court may make a supervision order under s. 53(1) of the *Child and Family Services Act*[25] resulting in a child being placed with a person other than the parent who had custody prior to the apprehension, subject to supervision and possible conditions. For example, subject to the agency monitoring the placement, the child may be placed with a grandparent or other relative, or with a parent who lost custody after divorce.

---

[24] *Supra*, note 20.

[25] S.O. 1984, c. 55.

Temporary Wardship Order

The second type of order the court may make is for temporary wardship.[26] This order removes the child from the control and custody of the parents and places the child, on a temporary basis, with the protection agency. The agency arranges to place a child in its care with foster parents, in a group home, or in an institution, depending upon the needs of the child.

With the greater understanding of the child's need for stability and permanency planning, statutory limitations have been placed on the length of time for temporary wardship. As long as wardship is temporary and under constant review by the courts, little, if any, planning of a long-term nature is done for the child. Time limitations also impose an onus on the parents to do whatever is required to regain custody of their child within a reasonable period of time. The length of a temporary order, a combination of temporary orders, or voluntary placement followed by temporary orders varies from 12 to 36 months depending on the jurisdiction; in Manitoba temporary orders are limited to shorter periods for infants and younger children.

Permanent Wardship Order

The most intrusive order available under the protection legislation is the order for permanent wardship,[27] which removes the child or children from the care, custody and control of the parents on a long-term basis, and often permanently. Although a permanent wardship order always transfers parental rights and responsibilities to the state, an order can allow for ongoing contact with the natural family in certain circumstances. In Ontario, even permanent wardship orders can be reviewed at the request of parents or older children if the child has not been placed for adoption.

Selection of a Dispositional Order

Most of the child protection statutes provide a test or a series of criteria to be considered by the judge in deciding what type of order to issue. Once a finding that a child is in need of protection has been made, the judge then considers these statutory criteria.

Provincial legislation provides that the dispositional order must be in the interests, welfare or best interests of the child. This type of test has been criticized because it does not provide clear, reliable, consistent standards. In some jurisdictions, such as Nova Scotia, there is a simple statement that decisions must be made with the "paramount consideration" being the welfare of the child.[28] In most jurisdictions, including Newfoundland, New Brunswick, Prince Edward

---

[26] In Ontario, this is called Society wardship. In some jurisdictions, the terms "guardianship" or "custody" are used instead of wardship.

[27] In Ontario, generally referred to as Crown wardship.

[28] *Children's Services Act*, S.N.S. 1976, c. 8, s. 76.

Island, Québec, Ontario, Manitoba, Alberta and the Yukon, the statute offers a series of criteria to be used in determining the child's best interests and making a disposition. Even in these jurisdictions, the term "best interests" is vague. There is no statutory weighing of various factors, as the criteria applied by a judge are based on the facts of each case, in the context of parental rights and the judge's value base. The test does not give consideration to what is best for the child in absolute terms, but is a balancing of rights, opportunities, values and the child's needs.

The primary considerations for those jurisdictions that do delineate what should be weighed in assessing the child's best interests include:

- the child's preferences, if obtainable, though they are not determinative;
- the child's cultural background and relationships;
- the importance of continuity in the child's care and the possible effect of disruption of that continuity;
- the relative merit of the plans being proposed by the agency and parents for the child's care;
- the least restrictive alternative; and,
- the physical, mental and emotional needs, and the care required to meet them.

Even in those jurisdictions without a statutory specification of the elements of a "best interests" test, the courts are influenced by these types of factors.

Alberta and Ontario statutorily require that the agency develop a plan of care for the child, and present it to the court.[29] The Ontario legislation requires the plan of care to be prepared in writing before the court makes a decision about disposition. The relevant section also identifies the concerns that must be addressed and explanations that must be provided. If permanent wardship is requested, the arrangements being made for the child's long-term, stable placement must also be included. The importance of the plan of care is illustrated by the fact that an application to review the child's status can be brought earlier than the ordinary statutory minimum 6-month period if the court is satisfied that a major element of the plan is not being carried out.[30]

The determination of what constitutes the best interest of the child has been considered in a wide range of cases. In *Children's Aid Society of the Districts of Sudbury and Manitoulin v. J.H. and C.H.*, Judge Runciman stated:

> ... what is the least restrictive alternative that is in the child's best interests. This is really the keystone or pivotal criteria ... Crown wardship is the most

---

[29] *Child and Family Services Act*, S.O. 1984, c. 55, s. 52; for Alberta see *Re S.D.* (1988), 17 R.F.L. (3d) 183 (Alta Prov. Ct).

[30] *Child and Family Services Act, ibid.*, s. 60(8).

intrusive alternative in that the child will be taken out of the family constellation and placed for adoption ...

and later in the same decision:

Child welfare proceedings are not a win and lose type of situation. The ultimate goal is to reintegrate a family and that, always, the best interests of the child are paramount.[31]

In the case of *Children's Aid Society of the City of Kingston* v. *Mr. and Mrs. H.*, Judge Thomson discussed the disposition orders available to the court:

I have rejected either a supervisory order or a temporary wardship for these children. Both contemplate an atmosphere of constructive planning for the children with (in the case of a temporary wardship) and within (in the case of a supervisory order) the existing family unit. The goal of both classes of remedial action is the rehabilitation of the family so that the children can be reintegrated into it.[32]

It must be recognized, however, that the resources of an agency to help a child are limited. This is illustrated in *Heather Ann T.* v. *The Family and Children's Services of the Regional Municipality of Waterloo*, where the child was a 14-year-old girl who alleged to have been sexually assaulted but who ran from placements made by the agency once she was in care. None of the plans or assistance proposed by the agency could be implemented because of her conduct. Judge Robson concluded:

... there is substantial risk to this child if she returned home. However, there is only so much that human beings can do for other human beings. There is only so much that this court or the law can impose on a group of social workers. Knowing that she needs protection, knowing that she is at risk in returning home isn't quite the same as being able to do anything about it ...

and further, the judge stated:

I don't believe in imposing on Societies obligations that they can't deliver. It creates expectations that are unreasonable.[33]

This case illustrates the fact that, despite their best efforts, agencies cannot always provide for children, particularly adolescents, who cannot be cared for by their own families. Regardless of the order made, the agency must be in a position to work with the family, or at least with the child, at the completion of the hearing. In some situations, a change of worker may resolve the hostility between the family and the agency. Unfortunately, protection hearings tend to polarize the family and the worker, and promote animosity between them. The

---

[31] [1988] W.D.F.L. 733 (Ont. Prov. Ct - Fam. Div.). In this case, the mother had a severe drug addiction problem, and both parents were incarcerated for criminal activity; the father for substantially longer than the mother. The decision was to have the child remain as a temporary ward for a further period of time.

[32] (June 1977), Frontenac (Ont. Prov. Ct - Fam. Div.) [unreported].

[33] *Heather Ann T.* v. *The Family and Children's Services of the Regional Municipality of Waterloo* (November 1986), (Ont. Prov. Ct - Fam. Div.) at 12 [unreported].

worker must be able to work through the issues with the family. However, as in the case described above, supervision is sometimes not a viable option.

The most difficult dispositional decision a court can face is that of permanent wardship since it may permanently sever the child's tie to the biological family. It is never an easy decision for a judge to make, but the focus must always be on the child's future. In a Manitoba Court of Appeal decision, Justice Monnin stated:

> The test is: What is in the best interests of these children, and not whether the mother has merely seen the light and is now prepared to be a good mother, while in the past, on her own admission she was not such. The test is whether the mother has in fact turned a new leaf and whether she is now able to give to the children the care which is in their best interests. Good intentions are not sufficient ... to give this mother another chance is to give these children one less chance in life.[34]

In a decision of the District Court of Ontario, Judge Corbett considered the relative positions of the child and the parent:

> The law no longer treats children as the property of those who gave them birth but focuses on what is in their best interests. A child's tie with a natural parent is very relevant in a determination as to what is in the child's best interests. But it is the parental tie as a meaningful and positive force in the life of the child and not in the life of the parent that the court has to be concerned about. As has been emphasized many times in custody cases, a child is not a chattel in which its parents have a proprietary interest; it is a human being to whom they owe serious obligations.[35]

Access Orders

If the disposition is temporary or permanent wardship of the child, the judge may make an order for access by the parents or other persons. If the order is for temporary wardship, then access between child and parents, or brothers and sisters, is meant to maintain family unity and assist the child to reintegrate into the family. Where permanent wardship is granted, access is usually for the purpose of maintaining some family ties, for the sake of an older child, or because it is best for the child's well-being.

When a temporary wardship order is made, Ontario's *Child and Family Services Act* creates a presumption in favour of access by the parents or other person

---

[34] *Children's Aid Society of Winnipeg* v. *Redwood* (1980), 19 R.F.L. (2d) 232 at 234 (Man. C.A.).

[35] *Catholic Children's Aid Society of Metro-Toronto* v. *H.C.K.* (1988), 21 R.F.L (3d) 115 at 129 (Ont. Prov. Ct - Fam. Div.).

who had charge of the child immediately before intervention.[36] This presumption can be rebutted if the court is satisfied that continued contact would not be in the child's best interests. On the other hand, there is a presumption against access by the parents where an order of Crown (or permanent) wardship has been made. Again, the presumption can be rebutted if the court is satisfied that provisions are met.[37]

The court has the authority to make an order regarding access rights to a child.[38] In the Ontario legislation, an application for access may be made by the child, the parent or any other person, including a representative of the child's native community if the child is native, in conjunction with a protection hearing or separately.[39]

Access is often provided to parents where permanent wardship is granted, provided the child is not expected to be placed for adoption after completion of the child protection hearing. Generally speaking, an order for parental access must be terminated if the child is to be adopted. The issue of post-adoption access is controversial and is further discussed in Chapter 7.

Child Support Orders

In most provinces, the court has the authority to order payment by a parent to a protection agency to help care for a child. Ontario legislation sets out criteria for such a court order, and provides for the order ceasing when the child is 18. It also permits variation of the court order upon proof of change of circumstances on the part of the child or parent.[40]

Although child protection agencies in many jurisdictions may request an order for payment towards the care of a child, such requests are not frequently sought by the agency, and applications for maintenance orders are sometimes rejected by the courts.

Often, families who have children in the care of a child protection agency have low incomes and are not able to pay child support without incurring severe difficulties. In addition, the agencies are reluctant to make such requests, as they tend to create difficulties with families. Some agencies view the bookkeeping requirements of what are usually small payments as time-consuming to administer and not cost-effective. Some judges view protection agencies as government bodies which should not place further demands on low income and stressed families. However, in these times of increasing government restraint, it seems likely that some agencies will be taking more aggressive steps towards seeking support, at least where parents have sufficient financial resources.

---

[36] S.O. 1984, c. 55, s. 55(10).

[37] *Ibid.*, s. 55(2).

[38] *Ibid.*, s. 54.

[39] *Ibid.*, s. 54(2).

[40] S.O. 1984, c. 55, s. 56.

Restraining Orders

A restraining order prohibits a person's access to, or contact with, a specified child. Such orders are typically made in the context of abuse, where there is the potential for physical, emotional or sexual harm to the child. The orders may restrict living arrangements by not allowing a person to reside in the same place as the child, limiting contact with the child, or preventing any contact with the child; for example, such an order may be made if a child is placed with the mother under a supervision order, with a restraining order to keep an abusive father away from the child.

Alberta, British Columbia, Manitoba and Ontario specifically provide the court with the authority to make a restraining order in a protection case. If such an order is made, the police may be called to assist in its enforcement, and the person who violates the order commits an offence and may be arrested.

FINDING THAT A CHILD IS NOT IN NEED OF PROTECTION

An application by a child protection agency may be dismissed by the court after a full or partial hearing if there is no finding of a need for protection. In provinces without specific legislation, the child must be returned to the person with custody prior to the hearing unless a court order to the contrary is made under other legislation. Sometimes a court will hear a protection application and a custody application between parents at the same time. In this situation, if appropriate, the court may dismiss the protection application and make a custody order.

Only three jurisdictions specifically address this issue in the legislation. Nova Scotia's *Children's Services Act* provides that the judge may dismiss the case and determine custody as between parents or guardians with conditions the judge deems proper.[41] In Prince Edward Island and the Yukon, legislation requires that the child be returned to the person who had custody at the time of apprehension or application.[42]

APPEALS

An appeal is theoretically distinct from a status review since an appeal is based on a claim that the trial judge made an error of law, while a review is based on a claim that there has been a change in circumstances. In practice there may be some overlap, since an appeal court in a protection case has the discretion to receive evidence about matters that occurred between the time of trial and the appeal.

---

[41] S.N.S. 1976, c. 8, s. 49(1)(b).

[42] *Family and Child Services Act*, R.S.P.E.I. 1974, c. F–2.01, s. 34(1); *Children's Act*, R.S.Y. 1986, c. 22, s. 126(2).

Appeals are governed by provincial child protection legislation; other statutes and the rules of court may also affect the process. In child protection cases, appellate courts are reluctant to reverse the original ruling because trial judges hear extensive testimony enabling them to evaluate the demeanour of the witnesses and the personality of the parents.

A major difficulty when appeals are launched is the length of time required for them to be heard. During that time, the plans for the child are in many respects left in limbo. No adoption placement can be made and no steps can be taken towards permanency for the child.

In addition, the parent who requests the appeal may bring forth a motion for interim access or custody pending the appeal. In order to vary the trial judge's decision regarding custody or access pending the appeal, the parent must show either that there is a substantial material change in the circumstances affecting the best interests of the child, or that the judgment of the trial judge was substantially in error clearly contrary to the best interests of the child.[43]

The primary consideration in permitting access pending appeal is the best interests of the child.

---

[43] *C.A.S. for County of Kent* v. *Drouillard* (1980), 2 A.C.W.S. (2d) 258 (Ont. Prov. Ct - Fam. Div.); this was an interim application for custody pending appeal.

5

THE CHILD IN CARE

*David A. Cruickshank**

INTRODUCTION

After the child protection hearing, a sigh of relief can often be heard from the child protection worker. The difficult decision has been made by someone else. In reality, the spotlight now shifts to the worker and the supervisor, because they now bear responsibility for a host of new and difficult choices. The worker faces a complex legislative scheme requiring the balancing of parental rights, governmental interests, substitute parents' rights and the child's needs and rights. The worker and supervisor also make placement and access decisions for which they will be accountable to the court.

How should the worker reconcile the desire to provide the best available child welfare services with the limitations of resources, waiting lists, court-ordered deadlines, and the legal rights of all the actors? This chapter does not provide all the answers, but it does attempt to focus attention on accountability to the courts, internal systems, parents and children in a way that helps the social worker dealing with children in care to understand and work within the legal constraints.

The child welfare worker's mandate to protect the child is set in an emerging philosophical context of family unity and reunification. A number of provinces now recognize that their legislative philosophy is to promote the best interests of the child, but also:

> ... to recognize that while parents often need help in caring for their children, that help should give support to the autonomy and integrity of the family unit and, wherever possible, be provided on the basis of mutual consent.[1]

---

* Visiting Professor, Faculty of Law, University of British Columbia and Director, Professional Legal Training Course, Continuing Legal Education Society of B.C.

[1] *Child and Family Services Act*, S.O. 1984, c. 55, s. 1(b); see also *Child Welfare Act*, S.A. 1984, C–8.1, s. 2(a)(c); and *Family Services Act*, S.N.B. 1980, c. F–2.2, preamble and s. 2.

Even the best interests ideology is becoming balanced by phrases which echo Goldstein, Freud and Solnit's "least detrimental alternative."[2] Ontario's law, for example, calls on judges and workers:

> ... to recognize that the least restrictive or disruptive course of action that is available and is appropriate in a particular case to help a child or family should be followed.[3]

The combination of "least restrictive alternative" and a family reunification policy means that the child welfare worker should not view placements "as best" for a child. Rather, the worker should recognize that what is being done is often the least harmful until family support services can bring the parent to the point of resuming custody. Because we know that being in care is harmful for children, the worker is always balancing the risks of keeping the child in care against the risks of returning the child to the parent. This chapter demonstrates how various legislative checks and balances attempt to spread the risks and distribute legal rights so that the entire burden of responsibility does not rest with the worker.

THE CHILD CARE SYSTEM—AN OVERVIEW[4]

The child care system in Canada consists of literally thousands of components. Some accommodate only one or two children, others over a hundred. A detailed examination of this system is clearly beyond the scope of this book, but a few of the salient features of the system can be described.

Though there are many different types of facilities, they can be classified as fitting into three broad categories: foster homes, group homes, and large institutions. Before considering each type of facility, a few general characteristics should be mentioned.

The child care system as a whole tends to suffer from a chronic lack of funds, and this is reflected in the quality of care provided. In many localities there is a real shortage of facilities. The people who are caring for the children, children who are often suffering from various emotional and behavioural problems, frequently have little or no training.

At the time of initial entry into the system, a child is generally assigned to a child care or social worker, who has primary responsibility for that child. Some kind of assessment of the child's needs is made, and the child is sent to the most suitable facility which has a vacancy. The nature of the assessment will depend upon the nature of the child's problems and his age, the duration of the wardship order, the facilities available, and the budget of the protection authority. The

---

[2] J. Goldstein, A. Freud & A.J. Solnit, *Beyond the Best Interests of the Child* (New York: Free Press, 1973). The authors argued that "best interests" disguises the reality of removing the child from the family to a placement that was "best." Their proposed language to justify state intervention and placement was "the least detrimental alternative," a term that has been more frequently taken up in American legislation.

[3] *Child and Family Services Act*, *supra*, note 1, s. 1(c).

[4] This section is a revised version of N. Bala and K. Clarke, *The Child and the Law* (Toronto: McGraw-Hill Ryerson, 1981) at 120–23. Reprinted with permission.

assessment may range from a conversation between a worker and a supervisor, lasting a few minutes, to a stay of several weeks in an assessment facility which can conduct a range of physical and psychological tests.

The experience of the child, once in care, tends to be characterized by considerable instability, something which is undesirable for any child, especially one who has an unhappy background and has been characterized by an unstable relationship with parents. In one study, it was discovered that more than one third of permanent wards lived in three or more placements since becoming permanent wards, and that almost one half had three or more social workers.[5]

Placements may break down because the child cannot adjust, or because the people offering the placement find that a child is unmanageable, or the facility is closing. The failings of the child care system should not necessarily be blamed upon the people who operate the system. They are largely people who are dedicated and hard working. Given the virtually intractable nature of the problems of some of the children in the system and the lack of resources, there will inevitably be serious shortcomings. Judges, however, when considering removing a child from the home, are always aware of the fact that committal to care is not a magic solution to the problems of a child, and this influences the decisions they make.

The backbone of the child care system is the foster home. There are more children in this type of facility than all of the others combined. A foster home is simply an ordinary home in which people have agreed to take children who have been committed to the care of protection authorities. Foster parents are recruited by the protection authorities and go through a screening process which may consist of one or more interviews, but very rarely includes any form of psychological testing. Foster parents are not required to have any specialized education or training, and efforts have only recently been made to offer even rudimentary training courses. Foster parents receive a minimal sum for each foster child they have, generally from $10 to $30 a day, an amount which barely covers the cost of feeding the child. Clearly, this is the least expensive form of care which can be provided, as foster parents are virtually in a volunteer status, taking in children out of a sense of love. Many foster parents have children of their own, as well as taking in one or more foster children, and they generally are people who care about children. In recent years it has become increasingly difficult to recruit people to serve as foster parents.

Many foster home placements work out very successfully, especially when younger children are involved. A child may stay many years in the same home, eventually being adopted by the foster parents. Unfortunately, with older children, particularly if they have problems, foster placements are frequently less successful. Foster parents tend to be members of the white Canadian middle class, and this can create adjustment problems for children with a different social

---

[5] See B. Raychaba, *To Be On Our Own With No Direction From Home: A Report On Special Needs Of Youth Leaving The Care Of The Child Welfare System* (Ottawa: National Youth in Care Network, 1988); and Ontario Association of Children's Aid Societies, *The Future of Foster Care* (Toronto: 1988).

and cultural background, and unfortunately most children in care do have a different background. Children from low-income and aboriginal families tend to be disproportionately represented among children in care, and there have recently been efforts to increase the number of aboriginal foster families. Breakdowns in foster home placements are quite common, and incidents of physical, and even sexual, abuse occur with disturbing frequency.

Group homes are facilities operated by a paid staff for the express purpose of caring for children. There are generally 5 to 10 children in each group home, though there may be fewer or more. They tend to have more structured programs than foster homes. The amount of training and education of the staff varies, but given the generally low salaries, the staff tend to have limited educational qualifications, and turnover frequently. There are many different types of group homes. Some have a particular philosophical or psychological approach. Some are operated by a husband and wife and are known as group foster homes, while others have staff on rotating shifts. The staff are more professionally oriented than ordinary foster parents, which is hardly surprising in view of the pay differentials. It costs the protection authorities much more to keep a child in a group home than in a foster home, but it is possible to place older and more difficult children in these homes. Group homes may be operated directly by the child welfare authorities, though most are privately owned and take children on a contractual basis; many are operated by non-profit corporations, though for some this can be quite a lucrative operation.

Some child welfare agencies operate receiving homes, which are group homes intended for short-term stays immediately following the apprehension of a child or after actual placement breaks down. Both foster homes and group homes are located in the community, and an effort is made to integrate children into the community, for example, by having them attend local schools.

There are a number of large institutions which are sometimes used by child welfare authorities. In some provinces a child in need of protection may be sent to a training school or other institution for young offenders. Various institutional settings are also used for children who have very serious problems that may require considerable supervision and care, and perhaps medical or psychiatric care. These facilities include mental health centres and facilities for disabled children.

In recent years there has been an increased emphasis on placing children in care in community settings wherever possible, and large institutions, like Newfoundland's infamous Mt. Cashel orphanage, have been closing.

THE PLACEMENT DECISION

The decision on placement has three main elements: (a) where; (b) with whom; and, (c) for how long. In many cases, the first two are merged (e.g., a foster home placement). In most provinces, "where" and "with whom" are decisions ultimately controlled by the administrative side of the child welfare system (i.e., the Minister, Director, Superintendent or Society).[6] At least in part, the length of placement is controlled by the legislation (e.g., maximum duration for temporary wardship) and the courts (e.g., a specified length of wardship order).

In some provinces there is some tension between the judiciary and child welfare administrators about who should control placement. The judges, who often have more continuity on the job than the workers, may believe they know the best move for the child. But workers are closer to the inside of group homes, foster homes and treatment programs. They know about the waiting lists, the changes in group home staff and the needs of the child. In the end, the knowledgeable worker and supervisor must place the child. Yet with that control comes accountability to the court, to be considered later in this chapter.

Some provinces have balanced the judicial desire to get involved in placement with the administrative need to control those decisions. Ontario and Alberta require a child care plan to be presented to court at the time of a wardship application. The previous chapter describes the elements of a plan.[7] At the outset, the requirement for a plan gives the judge a certain amount of leverage. If the placement recommended in the plan is not followed and no adequate reason is offered when the case comes up for review, the judge can take that departure into account.[8] In Ontario, a judge may be requested to review the child's status if a major element of the plan is not being carried out.[9] In addition to its function as an accountability device, the child service plan requires the worker to focus on the very specific needs of the child and to make a prediction about what is best for the child. In jurisdictions where the plan is not required by law, the worker may sometimes get by with demonstrating parental unfitness now and worrying about placement needs later. The lesson for all jurisdictions is that where there is an absence of good placement planning in advance of a protection hearing, there

---

[6] See Chapter 4, pp. 69–70, for a review of the various orders available. None of legislation permits a judge to name a specific placement. In practice, the judge hears a plan for placement then makes a general committal to care. The judge cannot, for example, designate foster care, let alone a specific foster home.

[7] See Chapter 4, p. 71. See also *Child and Family Services Act*, S.O. 1984, c. 55, s.52.

[8] *Child and Family Services Act*, S.O. 1984, c.55, ss. 49, 61(3); see also *Child Welfare Act*, S.A. 1984, c. C–8.1, s. 29(3).

[9] *Child and Family Services Act, ibid.*, s. 60(8)(b).

will be an inevitable pressure to legislate planning and to provide more judicial say in placement.

What are the placement choices? These depend on the order sought in court. A supervision order can return the child to the parent.[10] A broader use of the supervision order is called the "community placement" and it encompasses placement "with a relative, neighbour, or other member of the child's community."[11] The supervision order should be a vehicle for providing support services to the family, from homemaker services, to counselling and adequate medical care. The risk factor for the protection worker is the likelihood of further abuse or neglect. Therefore, some supervision orders will require regular visits, medical check-ups, or attention to who visits the family. In cases of suspected sexual abuse, for example, the visits of the nonresident father may be have to be restrained by court order.[12] The typical initial supervision order has a maximum duration of 6 months.[13]

The broadest range of placements is available after a temporary guardianship (or wardship) order. In some jurisdictions legislation lists a variety of placement choices, such as a foster home, group home, receiving home or a treatment centre.[14]

The legislation in other jurisdictions uses generic terms for the placement options, oriented to the broader concept of service, rather than a place. Ontario's definitions, for example, encompass a "child development service," a "child treatment service," a "child welfare service" and a "residential service."[15] It is the author's view that these terms permit more flexibility and creativity in the use of placement options. The negative side is that, unless accompanied by a specific plan put before the court, these generic terms could disguise to a judge what is really going to happen to a child.[16]

In most provinces, the guidance on what placement to use will not come from legislation or the courts. It will come from a child welfare manual, an assessment report, or the direction of a supervisor. However, there is a move toward some general legislative criteria that all placements must be measured against. The

---

[10] See Chapter 4, pp. 69–70.

[11] *Child and Family Services Act*, S.O. 1984, c. 55, s. 53(4).

[12] See, e.g., *Family Services Act*, S.N.B. 1980, c. F–2.2, s. 58.

[13] *Ibid.*, s. 39(4); see also *Family and Child Service Act*, S.B.C. 1980, c. 11, s. 13(2). Some jurisdictions permit 12-month orders: e.g., *Children's Services Act*, S.N.S. 1976, c. 8, s. 49(1)(c); *The Family Services Act*, R.S.S. 1978, s. F–7, s. 29(a).

[14] These examples come from: *Family Services Act*, S.N.B. 1980, c. F–2.2, s. 23; *Children's Act*, R.S.Y. 1986, c. 22, s. 104; and *Child and Family Services Act*, R.S.M. 1987, c. C80, s. 1.

[15] *Child and Family Services Act*, S.O. 1984, c. 55, s. 3.

[16] Ontario requires placement plans at the time of the protection hearing; see note 6.

Ontario statute directs the child protection agency to choose residential care for temporary wardship that, to the greatest extent possible:

- represents the least restrictive alternative for the child;
- respects the child's religious faith;
- respects the child's linguistic and cultural heritage;
- places the native child with a member of that child's family, band or community;
- takes account of the child's wishes and the wishes of a parent who is entitled to access;
- ensures that the child receives an education that corresponds to his or her aptitudes and abilities; and,
- keeps the child in Ontario, unless there are extraordinary circumstances.[17]

These criteria would be useful in any jurisdiction. They are probably part of the policy manuals in most other provinces. By putting them into legislation, the Ontario government is asking its workers to be accountable for the failure to adhere to these criteria. Therefore, the worker's justification for a sound placement decision is important.

This chapter will not attempt to describe all the administrative systems for decision-making. But with increased scrutiny of what went wrong there is no doubt that child welfare workers must document their placement choices carefully. This means they must review the choice with the supervisor or an administrative committee,[18] provide a detailed written description for the file, and implement a bring-forward system to force regular review of the placement.

Before discussing permanent wardship orders, there is a unique "combination order" in Ontario that should be explained. There, the court may make a single order for temporary wardship followed by a supervision order in the home, to last a total of up to 12 months.[19] This type of order will be quite rare since a judge normally would be reluctant to return the child to the parent without first reviewing the matter in court. Nevertheless, it could save the disruption of a court hearing when it is anticipated that the parents' difficulties are short-term and that they will soon be able to care for the child.

As discussed in Chapter 4, temporary wardship orders can initially be made for up to 12 months, and can be followed by further order for between 12 and 36 months, depending on the province. If the placements and services provided during temporary wardship are not leading to the goal of family reunification, the

---

[17] *Child and Family Services Act*, S.O. 1984 c. 55, s. 57(2)(3)(4).

[18] In Québec, a "Comité de la protection de la jeunesse" helps administer the *Youth Protection Act*, R.S.Q. 1977, c. P–34.1, ss. 12–30, and is involved in placement decisions. Other jurisdictions (e.g., Alberta) have local or regional placement committees which set priorities and allocate placements.

[19] *Child and Family Services Act*, S.O. 1984, c. 55, s. 53(1).

child welfare worker will have to consider a permanent wardship order. The criteria for getting these orders normally involve clearing a further hurdle in court. Alberta, for example, requires the court to be satisfied that:

> ... it cannot be anticipated that the child could or should be returned to the custody of his guardian within a reasonable time ... [20]

While it is technically possible to obtain a permanent wardship order at an initial child protection hearing, that is quite rare. Unless the parents are dead or have abandoned the child, the temporary wardship order will usually be the vehicle for the child's first period in care.

There is an unfortunate tendency in some child welfare agencies to seek a series of temporary wardship orders, knowing that they will fail, in order to build a case for permanent wardship. This tendency is sometimes supported by the judicial attitude toward a case. The court will often want to make several attempts at temporary wardship before moving toward more permanent planning for the child. In some agencies, this has led to an unwritten set of rules about moving through levels of care on the way to permanent wardship. The notion has been imported from the correctional system which speaks of levels of custody. Although it is hard to identify who should be blamed for such an approach to placement decision-making, it seems clear that placement decisions should be based on the child's needs and the resources available, not some checklist of care stages. In a truly needs-driven system, it should be possible to obtain a permanent wardship order very early if one can quickly determine parental incapacity and the need for stability and continuity in the child's care.

Placement following a permanent wardship order usually involves a choice between long-term foster care and adoption. Younger children will have a good chance of being adopted, while older children or disabled children may have to be placed in government-supported foster homes or group homes. Some jurisdictions have recognized that long-term foster care should be encouraged and that a relationship like adoption can be legally guaranteed without cutting off financial support to the adoptive parents. Alberta has achieved this end result by creating joint guardianship between the Director of Child Welfare and the foster parents who are rearing the child.[21]

Alberta also has "private guardianship," which can be obtained by an adult who has cared for the child for at least 6 months.[22] The court can order private guardianship with the consent of the parent or existing legal guardian, or it can terminate existing rights in order to permit private guardianship. The status for the child is similar to adoption, but it leaves open the possibility of a parent applying to resume guardianship. Other provinces have a policy of subsidized adoption to encourage the adoption of hard-to-place children.

---

[20] *Child Welfare Act*, S.A. 1984, c. C–8.1, s. 32(1)(c), as am. S.A. 1988, c. 15, s. 45(2).

[21] *Ibid.*, s. 34.

[22] *Ibid.*, ss. 49–54.

ACCOUNTABILITY TO THE COURT AND CHILD WELFARE ADMINISTRATION

Accountability in child welfare legislation is built in by four devices:

1. required planning;
2. time limits on temporary wardship orders;
3. status reviews of wardship orders by courts or administrative bodies; and,
4. right of children and parents.

Required planning for the child in care in Alberta and Ontario has been explained earlier. It is worth adding that Alberta's statute calls for a plan to be filed 30 days after the protection hearing. Ontario law not only requires a plan of care for the child to be filed with the court, it sets out a detailed list of the issues to be addressed in the plan.[23] The concern for workers will be whether the paperwork in Ontario overwhelms their ability to work with families and children. The author is not in a position to assess the bureaucratic impact, but the Ontario legislation does force early thinking about the child's needs by protection workers and parents. It appears to reduce the tendency to warehouse children under temporary wardship orders while a plan of care is developed.

Time limits on temporary wardship orders also act as a brake on the child welfare system. There has been an increased recognition that the child's sense of time is different than adults, particularly for young children.[24] This idea has produced shorter statutory maximum duration for initial orders in child welfare legislation—as brief as 6 months in Prince Edward Island.[25] Some jurisdictions differentiate for the younger child by placing shorter upper ceilings on total time in care.[26]

Of course, a judge is free to establish a shorter time for temporary wardship within the prescribed maximum time. This may be done because the judge wants to monitor progress or because the court wants to consider an early return to the parents. The worker should listen carefully to the judge's reasons for a shorter order. If early return is contemplated, there should be extensive parental involvement and visitation, particularly toward the end of the period. On occasion, the judge's short duration order is used to test the worker or the child welfare system. Will there be activity on this case or will the judge have to recall the case quickly to force attention to the file?

---

[23] *Child and Family Services Act*, S.O. 1984, c. 55 s. 52. Elements of the plan include "a description of the services to be provided" and "a statement of the criteria by which the society will determine when its wardship or supervision is no longer required."

[24] "Fifth Report of the Royal Commission on Family and Children's Law, Part V," *The Protection of Children (Child Care)* (Vancouver: 1975) at 8.

[25] *Family and Child Services Act*, R.S.P.E.I. 1974, c. F–2.01, as am., s. 34(2)(b).

[26] In *Children's Act*, R.S.Y. 1986, c. 22, s. 129, maximum periods are: under 2 years—12 months; under 4 years—15 months; over 4 years—24 months. See also *The Child and Family Services Act*, R.S.M. 1987, c. C80, s. 38(1).

No matter what duration is set for the temporary order, the worker must give the placement attention as soon as an order is made. At any subsequent hearing, one of the first cross-examination questions by counsel for the parents to the child welfare worker will be: "Can you explain to the court why nothing was done for this child until the 5th month (in a 6-month order)?" The judge will ask the same question if activity toward a stable placement is not evident in the first few weeks. Most child welfare workers regularly review and update their files; this is a good time to remember that a time-limited temporary wardship order gives the court, the parents and the lawyers an opportunity to ask whether the in-care option continues to be better (or less detrimental) than returning the child home. The worker's efforts, whatever shortcoming there may be in the system, are necessarily going to be scrutinized.

STATUS REVIEWS

Status reviews involve a court hearing to review the child's time in care, and to consider the potential for return to the parents and the plan for the future. They are a standard feature of modern child welfare legislation. Reviews are obviously necessary if a child's temporary wardship order is about to expire and the agency wishes to continue wardship. Reviews also have three other important functions:

1. they permit the court to take into account new circumstances that require a change in the original order; [27]

2. they encourage child welfare agencies to find permanent placements or adoption for children who are the subject of permanent guardianship orders; and,

3. they put power in the hands of the parents and some children to initiate accountability for a placement that they find unacceptable.

Most status reviews are initiated by the child welfare authorities. Indeed, Prince Edward Island permits only the Director of Child Welfare to initiate a review, thus eliminating the accountability function.[28] The underlying concern, that the child or parents could immediately ask for a review of an order if they were given the right to apply, is dealt with in other provinces by requiring 6 months to elapse before someone other than the child welfare authorities can apply for a status review.[29]

Status reviews should be flexible instruments which permit a wide number of circumstances to be considered before the court makes a further order. Ontario's *Child and Family Services Act* provides the broadest list of criteria:

---

[27] *Family and Child Service Act*, S.B.C. 1980, c. 11. s 13(6) provides for an application to vary or rescind based on changed circumstances. This form of review is like a child custody variation proceeding, in which the applicant must show a "significant" change in circumstances. Ontario, by contrast, has more flexible access to a status review and much broader criteria, as discussed below.

[28] *Family and Child Services Act*, R.S.P.E.I. 1974, c. F–2.01, s. 36.

[29] *Child and Family Services Act*, S.O. 1984, c. 55, s. 60(7).

60.(3) Before making an order under subsection (1), the court shall consider,

    (a) whether the grounds on which the original order was made still exist;

    (b) whether the plan for the child's care that the court applied in its decision is being carried out;

    (c) what services have been provided or offered under this Act to the person who had charge of the child immediately before intervention ... ;

    (d) whether the person is satisfied with those services;

    (e) whether the society is satisfied with those services;

    (f) whether the person or the child requires further services;

    (g) whether, where immediate termination of an order has been applied for but is not appropriate, a future date for termination of the order can be estimated; and

    (h) what is the least restrictive alternative that is in the child's best interests.[30]

These criteria are considered but judges do not have to make specific findings before they make a further order.

While the term "permanent" (or Crown) ward appears to suggest an end of court activity, and often in practice it does, the term really connotes an end of mandatory court reviews. There is still a possibility of a later court hearing to terminate a permanent order, provided that the child has not been placed for adoption. The child welfare authorities may bring such an application. Some provinces have more extensive provisions allowing for a status review of a permanent wardship. In Ontario, a child who is 12 years of age or older, or a parent, may seek such a review, though if a child has resided with the same foster parents for 2 years, special permission of the court is required for such a review.[31]

OTHER REVIEW MECHANISMS

Review of permanent wardship orders is critical in a system that is fully accountable. There is a concern that children in permanent care will not have an external watchdog because their parents may no longer be involved. Most jurisdictions require the child welfare authorities to administratively review permanent wardship cases at regular intervals, usually every 12 months.[32] The agency should consider progress toward adoption, long-term foster care, or other permanency plans for the child. In addition to existing rights to review before a court, a more recent trend in legislation is to create a nonjudicial structure for review of permanent wardship and other child welfare functions.

[30] *Ibid.*, s. 60(3).

[31] *Child and Family Services Act*, S.O. 1984, c. 55, s. 60(4)&(5).

[32] *Children's Act*, R.S.Y. 1986, c. 22, s. 138; *Child and Family Services Act*, S.O. 1984, c. 55, s. 62; *The Child and Family Services Act*, R.S.M. 1987, c. C80, s. 54.

In addition to regular judicial scrutiny of children who are temporary or permanent wards, increasingly, Canadian jurisdictions are employing nonjudicial and administrative accountability. There have always been internal administrative checks in the worker-supervisor relationship and in child welfare agencies. The administrative accountability discussed here goes beyond that. First, some legislation recognizes administrative bodies which work independently within the child welfare system to review orders or actions by an agency or worker. In addition, many administrative decisions are open to review by a court under a whole different legal regime known as administrative law. Using administrative law principles, a court can exercise judicial review of administrative decisions that are biased, unfair or without jurisdiction.[33]

Québec, Ontario and Alberta have each introduced different administrative accountability devices into their child welfare systems. Each initiative has a slightly different purpose, but there is a unifying theme of accountability. The other provinces have confined accountability to court remedies like status reviews and judicial appeals.

Québec has a community-based "Comité de la protection de la jeunesse."[34] The Comité has broad powers to protect specified rights of children, to conduct its own investigations, and recommend improvements in the system. Although the Comité has review functions in cases of compulsory foster care,[35] it acts more as the community standard body for the Director of Youth Protection (child welfare director). It can make a Director accountable by independent investigations or direct action on a case. The Comité does not appear to function as an appeal body.

Ontario has created, for children in care, two types of internal review by independent bodies. For residential placement, there is a Residential Placement Advisory Committee.[36] The Committee must review every placement in an institution (10 or more children) of 90 days or more. The Committee can also accept complaints about any placement from children aged 12 or older. The Committee

---

[33] This chapter will not analyze the administrative law remedies. In brief, where an administrator makes a decision that affects rights or privileges, that person must act fairly (i.e., provide fair procedures and act within the legislation) and without bias (i.e., no prior involvement in the earlier decisions, no appearance that the matter is decided already). If the administrator fails in these responsibilities, the individual can ask for judicial review of the decision by a court. The court will not substitute its own decision, but it may require the administrator to reconsider the case and act fairly. In a case of bias, the administrator will have to step aside and let someone else make the decision. In child welfare law, administrative law principles have rarely been used because the courts have all the significant decision-making power that affects rights. Nevertheless, some placement or review decisions by workers or the director could be challenged on administrative law principles if all statutory remedies were first exhausted.

[34] *Youth Protection Act*, R.S.Q. 1977, c. P–34.1, ss. 12–30.

[35] *Ibid.*, s. 63.

[36] *Child and Family Services Act*, S.O. 1984, c. 55, ss. 34–35.

only has the power to recommend placement changes or improvements to the service providers and to inform the agency and Minister of its recommendations. However, a child (12 years of age or older) may seek further redress from the Children's Services Review Board.[37] After the Residential Placement Advisory Committee process, the Board can hold a hearing and can order a change in placement or a discharge of the child from residential care. The idea behind these bodies is to have an accessible, swift determination by decision-makers with child welfare expertise. These features are not always available in a court-centred review system.

Ontario also has a formalized complaints process for children in care, including an Office of Child and Family Service Advocacy, which is responsible for dealing with complaints of children in care and their parents, as well as advocating on their behalf for appropriate services.

In Alberta, there is a system of Appeal Panels, established in 1984 and amended in 1989 to respond to a court decision ruling that the former Child Welfare Commission appeal process amounted to no appeal at all.[38] The new Appeal Panels were also called into question by the courts, but the Panels' final authority over decisions of the Alberta Children's Guardian was confirmed.[39] Most recently, Alberta provided a further avenue of appeal to the Court of Queen's Bench if parties are dissatisfied with the Appeal Panel decision.[40] The new Panels can receive an application from the child (no minimum age limit), the parent or guardian, or from foster parents who have had the child for 6 of the last 12 months.[41]

The Appeal Panel process can review most key decisions of the Director: placement changes during temporary or permanent guardianship, refusal of visitation privileges, refusal to disclose information and similar decisions. Because the Appeal Panels are independent of the administrative system and because their decisions can be appealed to the Court of Queen's Bench, the Panels are likely to be deemed fair and unbiased in the administrative law sense.[42] The Panels also represent forward thinking about an accessible, swift and inexpensive means of

---

[37] *Ibid.*, s. 36.

[38] *B.M. and M.M.* v. *R. in Right of Alberta et al.*, (1985), 45 R.F.L. (2d) 113 (Alta Q.B.); the case followed the reasoning in *Beson* v. *Director of Child Welfare (Nfld)*, [1982] 2 S.C.R. 716, 30 R.F.L. (2d) 438 (S.C.C.).

[39] *Tschritter* v. *Children's Guardian for Alberta et al.* (1989), 19 R.F.L. (3d) 1 (Alta C.A.) and B. Mahoney, "Annotation". The commentary explains the political furore surrounding the office of the Children's Guardian.

[40] *Child Welfare Amendment Act of 1988*, S.A. 1988, c. 15, ss. 38, 39 (proclaimed in force 1 September, 1989).

[41] *Child Welfare Act*, S.A. 1984, c. C–8.1, s. 86, as am.

[42] In *B.M.*, and *Beson*, *supra*, note 38, the courts expressed a willingness to make child welfare decisions on placement subject to the "fairness doctrine" in administrative law. See discussion, *supra*, note 33.

holding the child welfare administrative system and workers in it accountable for their decisions.

The Alberta approach is more impressive when one looks at the role of the Children's Advocate. This is an office, created by legislation, that operates within the Ministry, but separate from the Director of Child Welfare.[43] The Advocate has rights-protecting functions and investigative powers similar to those of the Comité in Québec or the Office of Child Advocacy in Ontario. Like a provincial ombudsman, the Children's Advocate has access to the Legislature because the Advocate reports annually to the Minister, who must table the Report in the Legislative Assembly. The Advocate can also assist a child in an appeal and can be called upon to advise an Appeal Panel or court in their deliberations. These important functions fit nicely between the Director's decisions (i.e., the worker's decisions) and the more formal appeal system. Nevertheless, the rights to appeal or to call upon a Children's Advocate will be of little use unless child welfare workers diligently advise their clients that these rights exist.

Just because a province has not provided for appeals from administrative decisions in its legislation, does not make such decisions immune from court review. The fairness doctrine in administrative law might be invoked by lawyers to challenge administrative decisions (e.g., placement, denial of visitation, etc.) that have been made without fair procedures.[44] A court reviewing the decision would look at the interests requiring protection; if they are interests or rights with serious consequences when breached, the court will ask whether the decision-maker acted fairly or in accordance with the rules of natural justice. The parents or child must know the case against them, have an opportunity to be "heard" (orally or in writing) and face an unbiased decision-maker. There should be reasons given for the decision.

The desired result of the administrative law approach is to have an unfair decision ruled void and have the matter reconsidered by the original decision-maker. In unique cases, however, a superior court may invoke its inherent jurisdiction and substitute its own decision in the best interests of the child.

In one noted case, *Beson* v. *Director of Child Welfare for Newfoundland*,[45] a

---

[43] *Supra*, note 40, s. 4.

[44] *Nicholson* v. *Haldimand Norfolk Regional Board of Commissioners of Police*, [1979] 1 S.C.R. 311. This landmark decision in the Supreme Court of Canada has been followed in many administrative settings, from immigration to child welfare, since 1979. See also note 32.

[45] *Beson* v. *Director of Child Welfare (Nfld)*, *supra*, note 38.

child was removed by the Director of Child Welfare from prospective adoptive parents after 5 months on probationary placement with them. This was done because of allegations of abuse. They were given no notice of hearing, and the allegations eventually proved unfounded, but by then the child had been placed with another couple. The Supreme Court of Canada ruled the child should be returned to the first couple and adopted by them. In doing so, the court specifically invoked its inherent power (the so-called *parens patriae* power[46]) to act in the best interests of a child in a situation where legislation offered no remedy, but it also indicated that the Director of Child Welfare had acted unfairly and violated principles of administrative law.

The significant drawbacks of the administrative law approach are that it is slow, expensive and carries little assurance of a different final decision. The *Beson* case was before the courts for almost two years. For these reasons, legislated internal appeal mechanisms should be advocated for all jurisdictions.

The most recent development in accountability of decision-makers arises under the *Canadian Charter of Rights and Freedoms*. Section 7 of the *Charter* provides:

> 7. Everyone has the right to life, liberty and security of the person and the right not to be deprived thereof except in accordance with the principles of fundamental justice.

Arguably, many child welfare decisions affect the liberty interests of parents and children or the security of the child. This *Charter* right does not prevent the state from depriving persons of those rights, but it requires the state to act "in accordance with the principles of fundamental justice." This means granting at least procedural fairness, and it could mean striking down an unfair law.[47]

---

[46] The term *parens patriae* is latin for "parent of the country," and refers to an ancient jurisdiction of superior courts in England (and Canada) to act to promote the best interests of children, mental incompetents and others who lack the capacity to protect themselves. It only exists to the extent not supplanted by a legislative scheme.

[47] *Singh* v. *Minister of Employment and Immigration*, [1985] 1 S.C.R. 177 (S.C.C.) (procedural fairness); *Ref. re s. 94(2) of Motor Vehicle Act (B.C.)*, [1985] 2 S.C.R. 486 (substantively unfair law struck down); *Morgentaler* v. *The Queen*, [1988] 1 S.C.R. 30 (abortion law struck down).

Professor Bala and the present author have examined *Charter* arguments in detail elsewhere.[48] Applied to the status of the child in care, many of the arguments meet a barrier. Because the child is under the custody and protection of the state, the courts will reason that the child is receiving treatment or care, not a loss of liberty or security.[49] Therefore, placement or visitation decisions will most often be left alone by the courts, even where a child is placed in a secure treatment facility.[50]

The *Charter* developments in prison law may eventually have some impact on administrative decisions in child welfare. In cases of solitary confinement or the loss of parole, the courts have called for procedural fairness.[51] The analogous loss of liberty or security in a child welfare case would have to be somewhat drastic. Moving a child from foster care to a confined setting without using legislated secure treatment hearings[52] or placing a child in the home of a known sexual abuser are examples where a *Charter* challenge might succeed.

PLACEMENT CHANGES

When a worker decides to change a child's placement during a court-authorized period of care, the long-range goal for the child must be in view. Will the child go back to the family eventually? Is adoption possible? Is another form of stable, permanent placement available? The worker's documentation of the placement change should relate to one of these goals.

---

[48] N. Bala and D. Cruickshank, "Children and the Charter of Rights and Freedoms" in B. Landau, ed., *Children's Rights In the Practice of Family Law*, (Toronto: Carswell, 1986); see also D.A.R. Thompson, "A Family Law Hitchhiker's Guide to the Charter Galaxy" (1988) 3 Can. Fam. L. Q. 313.

[49] *Nova Scotia (Min. of Social Services)* v. *E. (P.D.)* (1987), 6 R.F.L. (3d) 377 (N.S.C.A.).

[50] Secure treatment provisions permit the province to confine the child who is a "danger to himself or others" (or similar grounds). Normally, the period of confinement is short (e.g., 90 days) and it must be authorized and reviewed by a Provincial Court Judge (e.g., Alberta's *Child Welfare Act*, S.A. 1984, c. C–8.1, ss. 41–48.1).

[51] *R.* v. *Caddedu* (1982), 32 C.R. (3d) 355 (Ont. H.C.) (*Charter* remedy); *Cardinal and Oswald* v. *Director of Kent Institution*, [1985] 2 S.C.R. 643 (S.C.C.) (solitary confinement non-*Charter* remedy).

[52] *D. (D.L.)* v. *Family and Children's Services of London and Middlesex* (1986), 1 R.F.L. (3d) 326 (Ont. Fam. Ct) (held that s. 7 infringed but no declaration remedy was available to the court).

There will be legislative[53] or administrative criteria[54] that governed the original placement; these should continue to govern in a changed placement. Factors such as native heritage, the child's views, and the least detrimental alternative should be considered and articulated in written file reports. Proposed continuity or progress in education, health treatment, or counselling should also be documented.

One of the hardest decisions for a worker is to return the child to a family where there has been abuse or neglect in the past. Normally, the matter goes back to court and the ultimate responsibility for a change lies with a judge.[55] Nevertheless, there are circumstances where the child could be returned to the parents without a court review.[56] By simply allowing a temporary wardship order to expire, the child will go back to parental care without judicial review. In some jurisdictions, child protection agencies have the authority in a situation of temporary wardship to place the child with the natural parents; [57] with a temporary order in place, the Director can remove the child any time, without a court review or a finding that the child is in need of protection.

The decision to return the child home carries risks; those risk factors should be documented and countered by a description of the increased capacity of the parents. Regrettably, the worker must always imagine the worst and write up the file as though he or she might face a public inquiry later. Although the decision is an agonizing one, it should be remembered that leaving a child in care also carries risks that can be recorded. The worker may also have the backing of a supervisor or a placement committee. These internal second looks at the worker's judgment will be helpful if a case is later opened to scrutiny.

Ontario also has Review Teams to assist in dealing with child abuse cases.[58] These teams of experts are available to a child protection agency for referrals. If the agency sends a case for a review and recommendations, they get an important second opinion. The agency is also made accountable to the team, for it cannot return a child to parents suspected of abuse unless it has received and considered the team's recommendations. In the alternative, the agency must go to court to have its temporary or permanent wardship order rescinded. This type of accountability should be welcomed by the child protection agency because it

---

[53] *Supra*, note 14. Ontario adds criteria for changed placements; *Child and Family Services Act, supra*, note 36, s. 61(3).

[54] Child welfare manuals may set the criteria; in some provinces, a placement committee establishes criteria.

[55] The child welfare authority is not bound by a waiting period before seeking a review and change of status and placement, see, e.g., *Children's Services Act*, S.N.S. 1976, c. 8, s. 52 (1)(b).

[56] See, e.g., *The Child and Family Services Act*, R.S.M. 1987, c. C80, s. 14 (voluntary placement agreements for up to 12 months).

[57] *Ibid.*, s. 51 (the agency has all "rights and powers of a parent").

[58] *Child and Family Services Act*, S.O. 1984, c. 55, s. 69.

protects the agency from total exposure if its decision to return the child to the parents goes wrong.

Although judges seem central to most child welfare decision-making, they rarely learn about the ultimate success or failure of many placement changes. Since most jurisdictions have only administrative control of the placement, the judge gets little feedback. Too often, the child protection authorities only go by the letter of court orders, not the spirit. If no judicial review or report back is required by law, judges will not be informed of placement changes. The judge would benefit from hearing about the success stories or the new placement resources that are being attempted for a child. Therefore, administrative systems should develop ways to advise the judge of placement changes without having to resort to a formal hearing, for example, by sending a progress report. The judge has no power to approve or disapprove, unless there is an application before the court, but feedback will help the judge to understand what works and does not work, and it may make life less lonely at the top.

There are three exceptions to the general rule that placement decisions during care belong to the sole discretion of the child protection agency. Some jurisdictions will not permit a placement to be changed to a resource outside of the province without some special procedure.[59] Where the child is in foster care and removal from that foster home is contemplated, the foster parents may have a right to notice and a right to have the removal decision reviewed. This right is typically granted where the foster parents have had the child continuously for at least 6 months.[60]

Placement for adoption may also be subject to special criteria or judicial review; in all jurisdictions, the child in care must be subject to a permanent wardship order or there must be parental consent to adoption.[61]

It is also typical for legislation to provide, as it does in New Brunswick, that only the child welfare authorities may place children who are wards for adoption or that private placements must be approved in advance.[62] Some jurisdictions, like Ontario, facilitate adoption planning and finalization by prohibiting further judicial review once the child has been placed for adoption.[63] This means that natural parents will not be able to disrupt the status reviews or applications for visitation once the child is placed for adoption. This makes sense because, once the decision is made to terminate the parental rights, the adoptive parents should

---

[59] See, e.g., *Child and Family Services Act*, S.O. 1984, c. 55, s. 57(4) (Director from outside the local agency must be satisfied that "extraordinary circumstances" justify removal).

[60] *Ibid.*, s. 60(6)(d); Alberta's *Child Welfare Act, supra*, note 50 and Manitoba's *The Child and Family Services Act, supra*, note 56, s. 55 (no 6-month care limitation; any foster parent can appeal removal to director).

[61] See, e.g., *Family Services Act*, S.N.B. 1980, c. F–2.2, ss. 69–70.

[62] *Ibid.*

[63] See, e.g., *supra*, note 59, s. 134(2).

have a chance to both legally and psychologically establish permanent relationships with the child.

Adoption placements for a native child require special attention. Provincial governments are becoming more sensitive to the problems of placing native children in non-native homes. Typical legislative controls require that the child welfare authorities consult with the chief or band council of a native community before placing the child for adoption outside that community.[64]

SCREENING OF PLACEMENT RESOURCES

Because of increased professional awareness and media attention to cases of child abuse in foster homes or group homes, child welfare authorities have improved the screening of placement resources. Foster homes are subject to few legislative guidelines. The usual provision is that it must be a home approved by the appropriate child welfare authority.[65] Under provincial regulations or policy, there will be screening inquiries about such matters as marital status, criminal records, mental health, and child care experience. These inquiries require skill and sensitivity, since most foster parents are legitimate candidates. A screening procedure that deters too many applicants may inappropriately reduce foster parent resources.

The control of foster homes and the removal of approved status is a matter of complete discretion for the child welfare authority, though as discussed below in some situations foster parents may have some rights with respect to removal of a child in their care. But their status as foster parents can be granted or withdrawn without much explanation, unless they are under a statutory licensing regime.[66]

In several jurisdictions, however, group homes have more extensive rights than foster homes if child welfare authorities wish to close them. In most jurisdictions, group homes are screened through a licensing mechanism.[67] The licens-

---

[64] *Ibid.*, s. 134(3); see also Alberta's *Child Welfare Act, supra*, note 50, s. 62.1.

[65] See, e.g., *Family and Child Service Act, S.B.C. 1980, c. 11, s. 1; Children's Act*, R.S.Y. 1986, c. 22, ss. 147, 148, 150(1).

[66] Most provinces exempt foster homes from licensing and the rights of a licensee that go with it. However, some have a licensing regime available: e.g., Saskatchewan has regulations for licensing foster homes and group homes: *The Family Services Act*, R.S.S. 1978, c. F–7, s. 87(1)(e).

[67] See, e.g., *Child and Family Services Act*, S.O. 1984, c. 55, ss. 175–190. An alternative to licensing is to exert controls through "contracts for service" with child care resources. The legal contract between government and provider is the means for control, rather than the threat of lifting the licence: e.g., *Family Services Act*, S.N.B. 1980, c. F–2.2, ss. 23–29.

ing brings greater accountability and scrutiny at the outset, but the licensee also receives rights that cannot be removed without some form of hearing.[68]

The screening and regular monitoring of individual group homes is an important goal achieved by licensing. Perhaps even more important is the imposition of general standards for group homes. The establishment of high standards for the physical facility and the child care being provided can be achieved through regulations.[69] These standards are welcomed by the responsible group home service providers because they force out fringe or short-term operators. The improvement of standards and programs within group homes should be a priority issue for provincial governments because group home care is so prevalent, so exposed to negative publicity, and so critical to the development of the child in care. Frequently, group homes are licensed to provide service not only to children in care but also to children channelled through the young offender system. This can create problems for both the group home and for the child protection agency if a child in care is required to follow a highly restricted program, or if the child is exposed to children exhibiting much greater antisocial tendencies.

The screening of placement resources has become increasingly important because of the spectre of negligence suits against child welfare authorities. Negligence or malpractice suits for poor placements or child care failures are common in the United States, and Canadian courts appear prepared to accept the application of negligence law to child welfare malpractice.[70] A cornerstone of negligence law is the standard of care owed by the alleged wrongdoer to the person who was a victim. The courts will look at accepted standards in the profession and ask whether the agency, individual, or care provider met that standard. Even accepted standards will not be good enough if the court finds that an objective outsider, (or a reasonable person) would expect more. To use a stark example, if parents found that their child in care was malnourished or receiving no education whatsoever, they might use a negligence claim to seek redress on behalf of the child. The fact that a foster home or group home followed accepted standards for meals, or had no standard to follow, would not be an adequate defence. However, if the agency uses reasonable efforts to screen and monitor the placement, it is not liable for wrongful acts committed by foster parents or group home operators.

As a purely defensive stance, therefore, child welfare authorities should be very interested in the development of standards and procedures for screening and

---

[68] See, e.g., Ontario's *Child and Family Services Act, ibid.*: The licensee is entitled to a hearing before a "Child and Family Services Review Board" if the government proposes to revoke or not review a licence. An appeal to the Divisional Court lies beyond the Board's decision.

[69] See, e.g., Ontario's *Child and Family Services Act, ibid.*, s. 205; Saskatchewan's *The Family Services Act, supra,* note 66; New Brunswick's *Family Services Act, supra,* note 67, s. 24.

[70] W. Holder & K. Hayes, eds, *Malpractice and Liability in Child Protective Services* (Longmont, Colo.: Bookmakers Guild, 1984). In *Gareau* v. *B.C. (Supt. Family and Child Services)* (1986), 5 B.C.L.R. (2d) 352 (B.C.S.C.) the court considered a negligence claim seriously, but held that the Superintendent had an "honest (but mistaken) belief" that the facts leading to an apprehension were true.

monitoring placement resources. In addition to the agency, the front line workers who make the placement decisions could be sued for malpractice. These workers deserve the protection of careful screening and well-enforced standards for placement resources.

THE MEANING AND SCOPE OF WARDSHIP

Child welfare authorities are often concerned about the degree to which the court's temporary or permanent wardship orders give them decision-making powers on behalf of children. Does the wardship simply mean the right of legal custody, does it mean complete control over the child's life, or is it something in between? A combination of common law cases and specific statutes provides a different answer to these questions in each province. Some of the most typical provincial schemes for defining wardship will be described here.

First of all, provincial statutes often will distinguish "guardianship of the person" from "guardianship of the estate" of the child.[71] Guardianship of the person involves physical care and control, decisions concerning education, health care, consent to the marriage of a minor and where the child will reside.[72]

The powers of "guardianship of the person" in regard to a child are normally granted to a child welfare authority by temporary or permanent wardship (or guardianship) orders, unless there are statutory exceptions. In brief, the powers are a bundle of rights and duties that the state can assume while acting as parent to the child.

---

[71] See, e.g., *Family and Child Service Act*, S.B.C. 1980, c. 11, ss. 10(2), 13(5), 14(4)(5) (British Columbia Superintendent of Child Welfare is guardian of the person; Public Trustee is guardian of the estate). See also: *Child Welfare Act*, S.A. 1984, c. C–8.1, s. 32(3); *The Child and Family Services Act*, R.S.M. 1987, c. C80, s. 1 (definition); The *Child Welfare Act*, S. Nfld 1972, No. 37, s. 15(1) (child committed only to "care and custody" of Director, but by *Adoption of Children Act*, S. Nfld 1972, No. 36, s. 9(4) the Director has sole authority to consent to adoption of permanent wards; therefore, "care and custody" here amounts to guardianship of the person, at least for permanent orders). The *Children's Services Act*, S.N.S. 1976, c. 8, ss. 49, 53 and 16(5) in Nova Scotia operates to the same effect as the Newfoundland statute.

[72] No Canadian jurisdiction has attempted to fully define guardianship by statute. Yukon's *Children's Act*, R.S.Y. 1986, c. 22, s. 28(1), has defined "custody" in a broad manner: "'custody,' in relation to a child, includes the right to care and nurturance of the child, the right to consent to medical treatment for the child, the right to consent to the adoption or the marriage of the child, and the responsibilities concomitant with those rights, including the duty of supporting the child and of ensuring that the child is appropriately clothed, fed, educated and disciplined, and supplied with the other necessaries of life and a good upbringing."

Since case law in divorce matters is expanding the meaning of custody to be as broad as guardianship (e.g., *Anson* v. *Anson* (1987), 10 B.C.L.R. (2d) 357), it is submitted that Yukon's definition is the modern equivalent of guardianship of the person.

Guardianship of the estate refers to the authority over the administration of a child's property, inheritance, contracts, and decision-making about property, income and expenditure of income. Some provinces separate guardianship of the estate of a child in the care of the welfare authorities and assign those powers to a separate official like a Public Trustee.[73] Others, like the Northwest Territories and Prince Edward Island, do not distinguish the two, so it seems that the child welfare authority obtains full guardianship.[74] New Brunswick and Saskatchewan distinguish the two, but assign guardianship over both person and estate to the responsible Minister.[75]

Québec uses the *Civil Code* concept of tutorship for guardianship. The Director of Child Protection must apply to the Superior Court to terminate parental rights and assume tutorship or have it assigned to another parent. Tutorship is the equivalent of a permanent guardianship order assigning guardianship of the person to the Director.[76] The termination of parental rights by the Court clears the way for adoption of the child.[77]

The next distinction one must look for in provincial legislation is between the scope of a temporary wardship order and a permanent wardship order. For this discussion, it is assumed that a child welfare authority only has guardianship of the person. The scope of permanent wardship is reasonably uniform in Canada. Provincial legislation normally assigns full guardianship of the person to the child welfare authority, including the right to consent to medical treatment or to consent to adopt. Indeed, the main purposes of permanent wardship are to termi-

---

[73] *Family and Child Services Act*, S.B.C., *supra*, note 71.

[74] *Family and Child Services Act*, R.S.P.E.I 1974, c. F–2.01, s. 37(1); *Child Welfare Ordinance*, R.O.N.W.T. 1974, c. C–3, ss. 24(2), 25(2).

[75] *Family Services Act*, S.N.B. 1980, c. F–2.2, ss. 4(1)(2); *The Family Services Act*, R.S.S. 1978, c. F–7, s. 43(1).

[76] *Youth Protection Act*, R.S.Q. 1977, c. P–34.1, s. 71.

[77] *Ibid.*, s. 72. See, generally, B.M. Knoppers "From Parental Authority to Judicial Interventionism: The New Family Law of Québec," K. Connell-Thouez & B. Knoppers, eds, *Contemporary Trends in Family Law: A National Perspective* (Toronto: Carswell, 1984).

nate parental rights and prepare for adoption,[78] and to ensure that a child receives appropriate medical treatment.

Jurisdictions like Ontario give the child welfare authority "care, custody, and control," not "guardianship of the person" at the time of a permanent order. This is an attempt to leave open some narrow avenues for parental rights, such as access, but the central assumption by child welfare authorities of full parental rights remains intact.[79]

The bundle of rights and duties that go with temporary wardship has more variation from one jurisdiction to another. In most provinces, the legislation is not explicit about this issue.[80] By implication, in these jurisdictions temporary guardianship rights will include at least physical care and control and medical consent, but will not extend to the right to give adoption consents.[81] Temporary wardship powers regarding such matters as religious upbringing or education decisions sometimes preserve parental rights or input, depending on the provincial statute.

Some Canadian jurisdictions enacted legislation to deal more explicitly with the temporary wardship rights of a child welfare authority. The philosophy is the same—to keep the parents involved while working toward family reunification, although they have taken two separate paths toward giving parents more rights and input during temporary guardianship. In Ontario, the legislation presumes that access will be granted to parents during temporary wardship (society wardship), unless it is not in the child's best interests.[82] Similarly, the parents retain the absolute right to consent to marriage of a child under 16.[83] If the withholding of medical treatment was not the reason for the protection order, a court can grant the parents the right to give or refuse medical consent during temporary

---

[78] *Supra*, note 76, s. 72; see also Newfoundland and Nova Scotia statutes.

[79] *Child and Family Services Act*, S.O. 1984, c. 55, s. 59. Ontario does not use the language of "guardianship of the person," but it is submitted that the language encompasses all "guardianship of the person" rights, except for access and religious upbringing, which can be subject to further court direction. Yukon is also a "care and custody" jurisdiction: *Children's Act*, R.S.Y., 1986, c. 22, s. 126; but the director's powers over a child in his "care and custody" are later defined as the "custody of and the guardianship for the child" (s. 137).

[80] See, e.g., discussion of Newfoundland and Nova Scotia, *supra*, note 71; the "care and custody" of the child welfare authority during temporary and permanent guardianship is not separately defined.

[81] See, e.g., *Child Welfare Act*, S.A. 1984, c. C–8.1, s. 29(2).

[82] *Child and Family Services Act*, S.O. 1984, c. 55, s. 55.

[83] *Ibid.*, s. 58(4).

wardship.[84] The child's education, however, is the sole responsibility of the child welfare authority.[85] The Ontario approach is to give parents specific rights, as exceptions to the general care, control and custody given to the child protection authorities over their wards. Yukon has followed a similar pattern in its recent reform.[86]

Alberta has achieved the parental involvement goal by a more general device. During a temporary guardianship order, the Director of Child Welfare becomes a "joint guardian" with the parents, and may exercise all parental rights except in connection with adoption.[87] The Alberta legislation gives the court discretion to grant parental access, require financial contributions from the parents, and generally set "conditions under which the Director shall consult with the guardian on matters affecting the child."[88] This gives the court flexible scope for granting parental input, without wholly allocating specific rights (e.g., consent to medical treatment) to the parents. The exceptions to the general custodial authority of the Director are more general and more flexible.

Wardship, while the child is in care, has a public interest purpose. It gives the child welfare agency security in its placement planning. Subject to regular court or administrative reviews, the agency knows that the natural parents cannot interfere with the child's stability and upbringing. There is more than administrative convenience behind such a policy. The agency's security is necessary for permanency planning, especially when it applies for permanent wardship.

The developing concept of private guardianship, contrasted to the public wardship (or guardianship) of an agency, is helping some jurisdictions find more options for permanent placements. Manitoba and Alberta have private guardianship provisions in their child welfare legislation.[89] These statutes make it possible for a foster parent or other proposed guardian to apply to court for sole

---

[84] *Ibid.*, s. 58(1) - (3).

[85] *Ibid.*, s. 57(3).

[86] *Children's Act*, R.S.Y. 1986, c. 22, c. 137(2).

[87] *Child Welfare Act*, S.A. 1984, c. C–8.1, s. 29(2).

[88] *Ibid.*, s. 29(4).

[89] *Child and Family Services Act*, R.S.M. 1987, c. C80, s. 77; *Child Welfare Act*, S.A. 1984, c. C–8.1, s. 49.

guardianship of a child who is in the permanent care of the child welfare authorities. If an order of private guardianship is made, the public wardship of the child welfare agency ceases and the foster parents (or other applicants) become the sole legal guardians of the person.[90] This arrangement falls just short of adoption. The child may retain his or her name and may preserve some inheritance rights. In addition, private guardianship is reversible upon application to court.[91]

The private guardianship option may be helpful for disabled children, who are hard to place for adoption. It may also help older children or those who have positive contact with natural parents who are permanently unable to care for them. If government policy permits continued payment to the foster parents during private guardianship, this option may be preferable to adoption by some other person, as this might disrupt a stable foster care situation.

At least in theory, in other provinces there is custody or guardianship legislation that could be used for similar purposes to private guardianship. This legislation is designed for a relative or friend to take over care of the child in the plea of a deceased parent or one who has abandoned the child.[92] If a provincial child welfare authority was prepared to consent to an application by a foster parent, this general legislation could be used to accomplish the same ends as the Manitoba and Alberta statutes.

THE RIGHTS OF CHILDREN IN CARE

In 1977 Québec led the way in Canada in statutory recognition of the rights of children in its *Youth Protection Act*. This Act expressly recognizes the rights of children in care to: [93]

- be informed of rights and appeals under the Act;
- consult an advocate;

---

[90] The Alberta statute is ambiguous about whether "guardianship of the estate" also passes to the foster parents. Because the "guardianship of the estate" goes to the Public Trustee at the time of a permanent guardianship order (s. 34(3)), and the private guardianship sections make no express change to this status (s.54(1)), it can be argued that guardianship of the estate remains in public hands, while all other incidents of guardianship go to private persons. This was probably an oversight of the legislative drafters.

[91] In Alberta, the *Child Welfare Act*, S.A. 1984, c. C–8.1, s. 54(3), permits a guardian (parent) whose rights have not been terminated to apply to end the private guardianship.

[92] This legislation is normally in a separate statute dealing with child custody and maintenance, or is standing alone: e.g., *Guardianship of Children Act*, R.S.N.B. 1973, c. G–8; *Infants Act*, R.S.B.C. 1979, c. 121, ss. 21–33; *Children's Law Reform Act*, R.S.O. 1980, c. 68, ss. 48–79.

[93] *Youth Protection Act*, R.S.Q. 1977, c. P–34.1, ss. 2.2 - 11.3. The central principle is declared in s. 3: "Decisions made under this Act must be in the interest of the child and respect his rights."

- learn of a child care plan;
- be heard in court or other decision-making settings;
- be consulted before a placement change;
- health, social, and educational services while in care;
- communicate in confidence with certain persons;
- be disciplined only in accordance with established rules;
- freedom from adult detention;
- a placement in accordance with his or her needs; and,
- privacy (non-disclosure of identity).

To the extent that these rights are procedural, they are enforced by the courts (e.g., right to notice of a proceeding). In the social services domain, they are enforceable through the Comité de la protection de la jeunesse (e.g., right to an appropriate education). There is not much information on the effectiveness of the Québec Comité in enforcement matters.

Ontario has also legislated a Code of rights for children in care, but has set up an internal complaints procedure.[94] A service provider or child welfare agency must have an internal procedure for hearing alleged violations of the rights of children. Following an internal review, a further complaint can be made to the Minister of Community and Social Services, who can appoint an independent person to review the complaint and take action.

The 1984 Ontario legislation goes beyond the Québec law to detail very concrete rights of children while in care. They include rights to: [95]

- not be subjected to punishment;
- receive religious instruction;
- participate in the development of the child care plan;
- quality meals, clothing, medical and dental care;
- education and recreational activities; and,
- be informed of all procedural rights under the Act.

In addition to the specific list, Ontario has given the most extensive set of procedural rights in Canada to children in child protection cases. The child aged 12 or older will usually receive notice and attend a hearing, can see assessment reports, can consent to an order, and can initiate a review of a placement or of an

---

[94] *Child and Family Services Act*, S.O. 1984, c. 55, ss. 105–107.

[95] *Ibid.*, ss. 95–104.

order.[96] Even the children under 12 may be granted some of these rights, if the court is satisfied that the child "is capable of understanding the hearing and will not suffer emotional harm by being present at the hearing."[97] All children may have legal representation and the court may direct that a lawyer be appointed for the child.[98]

Other jurisdictions which have recently reformed their child protection laws, such as Yukon and Alberta, have been more cautious. They have granted procedural rights, such as a right to be informed about hearings or placement[99] and a right to seek review of wardship or access orders,[100] but "quality of care" rights for children in care have not been explicitly granted. Alberta carefully legislated decision-making factors that never put "rights" and "children" in the same sentence. Instead, the "interests of a child should be recognized and protected."[101] Yukon subordinated the notion of a child's right to the paramount principle of best interests of the child, which may be somewhat more paternalistic than the rights-based approach of Québec and Ontario.[102] The cautious approach to the rights of children in care highlights a difference in attitude toward the status of children.[103] The idea of an independent status for the child has been accepted in Québec and Ontario, but acknowledged only in a few procedural ways in other jurisdictions.

---

[96] *Ibid.*, s. 39 (hearings), s. 51 (consent orders), s. 60(4) (review applications), s. 50(4) (assessments).

[97] *Ibid.*, s. 39(5).

[98] *Ibid.*, s. 38.

[99] *Children's Act*, R.S.Y. 1986, c. 22, s. 121(2); *Child Welfare Act*, S.A. 1984, c. C–8.1, s. 21(1.1).

[100] *Children's Act, ibid.*, s. 143(2) (Child 14 or over can apply to vary); *Child Welfare Act, ibid.*, ss. 30, 32(8).

[101] *Child Welfare Act*, S.A. 1984, c. C–8.1: s. 2(b). In hearings leading up to legislative reform, many submissions promoted legislated rights for children, so the avoidance of them was a conscious legislative choice.

[102] *Children's Act, supra*, note 99, ss. 1, 131.

[103] For a review of the status of children in the Canadian context see *Admittance Restricted: The Child as Citizen in Canada* (Ottawa: Canadian Council on Children and Youth, 1978).

PARENTAL RIGHTS

The rights of the natural parents while the child is in care are dependent upon how many incidents of guardianship are assumed by the child welfare authority. The starting point, therefore, is to examine the scope of the rights and duties granted to the child welfare authority. What is left over belongs to the natural parents. As discussed above, some provincial laws have carefully described what rights parents retain during a temporary wardship order or after permanent wardship.[104] Generally speaking, parental rights diminish as permanency planning moves toward adoption.

While the child is in care on a temporary order, the parents will normally have rights to:

- access; [105]
- be consulted on placement, education, religious upbringing, and health care;[106] and
- seek a review of the order at least once during the order. [107]

The child welfare authority will have final authority over placement, care, custody, and control of the child.

The most serious loss of parental rights occurs if the child welfare agency obtains permanent wardship. Parents should have legal representation at a hearing concerning permanent wardship and they should be aware that, if they lose, the child welfare agency may have no further duty to involve them, consult them

---

[104] See section from this chapter: "The Meaning and Scope of Wardship", pp. 97–101.

[105] See, e.g., *Child and Family Services Act*, S.O. 1984, c. 55, ss. 53(2), 55. Courts generally grant access (or visitation) between children who are temporary wards and their parents, though sometimes it is supervised or even suspended, for example, if there is a risk of abuse or the child expresses a wish that there be no contact. Where access is ordered, it is necessary to establish a schedule which is sensitive to the needs of the child, the natural parents and the foster family. Problems in regard to visitation will be exacerbated if an agency worker must supervise the visits, or transport the child to and from the visits; this may be necessary if there is concern about relations between the natural parents and the foster parents. Sometimes a child is placed by the agency far from his or her home; in appropriate cases, the agency should consider financial assistance to allow a parent to maintain contact with the child. For a further discussion of access, see Chapter 4, pp. 73–74.

[106] *Ibid.*, s. 57(5) (input on major decisions); s. 58 (consent to medical treatment). Contrast the complete control of the child care authority once care and custody is awarded in Nova Scotia: *Children's Services Act*, S.N.S. 1976, c. 8, s. 51.

[107] See, e.g., *Child Welfare Act*, S.A. 1984, c. C–8.1, s. 30(1). *Family and Child Service Act*, S.B.C. 1980, c. 11, s. 13(6) (based on changed circumstances, not limited to once during order).

or seek their consent on any matter, including adoption. Though, if a child is not placed for adoption, there is the possibility of continued contact and visitation with the natural parents.[108]

THE RIGHTS OF FOSTER PARENTS

Legislators have begun to recognize how important foster parents are in the child welfare system, and have responded by giving them a voice in child welfare decisions. Ontario, Manitoba and Alberta have been the pioneers in establishing these rights. There is usually a qualification period of 6 months' continuous care of a child before the foster parents have statutory rights.[109] Some provinces grant them the right to notice of any court hearings, including renewal or review hearings, which affect the child they have cared for.[110] Foster parents may also receive the right to initiate an administrative complaint procedure about an agency decision on the child's status.[111]

It is important to distinguish the rights foster parents have as intervenors (or participants) in a hearing from the rights of a party to a proceeding.[112] A party, such as a natural parent, is in court to assert custody or guardianship rights. The foster parents are there to have their opinion heard on the future of the child. They have the right to address the court, but generally may not call their own witnesses or cross-examine the witnesses called by others. Generally, their rights to care for the child can only be asserted through the child welfare authority. To assert rights as a party the foster parents would have to apply to court indepen-

[108] *Child and Family Services Act*, S.O. 1984, c. 55, s. 55(2). See also section in this chapter: "Placement Changes," and *The Child and Family Services Act*, R.S.M. 1987, c. C80, s. 45(3).

[109] *Child Welfare Act*, S.A. 1984, c. C–8.1, s. 21; *Child and Family Services Act*, S.O. 1984, s. 39(3).

[110] *Child Welfare Act, ibid.*, s. 32(8). See also *The Child and Family Services Act*, R.S.M. 1987, c. C80, ss. 30(1)(d), 40(4).

[111] *Child and Family Services Act, supra*, note 108, ss. 57(7), 64.

[112] *Child and Family Services Act, supra*, note 108, ss. 39(1)(3).

dently, at their own expense, for custody or private guardianship.[113] In provinces without explicit recognition of their rights to participate in a protection or status review hearing, the foster parents may still have input by asking the court to recognize them as interested persons who wish to intervene and be heard.[114] In addition to any statutory rights to participate in court hearings, foster parents may be called as witnesses, most commonly by the child welfare authority.

Probably the most important right for foster parents is the ability to challenge removal of the child from their home. Ontario requires that foster parents receive notice 10 days before a proposed removal, if they have had continuous care of the child for two years.[115] The foster parents can then request an administration review by an official outside the agency, and the child will remain in their care pending the review unless there is some substantial risk to the child.[116] Other provinces do not yet have such significant pre-removal rights, although Manitoba grants post-removal rights.[117] A rationale for not granting foster parents rights is that the child welfare authority and foster parents will clash in court. It should be appreciated that these conflicts already arise within the current system. Is there not something to be gained by an open procedure with a neutral decision-maker instead of discouraging foster parents through unilateral administrative decisions?

CONCLUSION

Though not present in all jurisdictions, in recent years in Canada there have been two major legislative trends in the child welfare field. There is a move away from total child welfare authority control and toward greater accountability. Consistent with this trend is a movement toward concrete, defined rights for children in care and foster parents. These new directions have a unifying theme of reducing unquestioned state power over the lives of children.

The directions may be perceived as threatening by some child welfare workers and agencies. Nevertheless, they will find it difficult to argue that state control over decision-making in the past has produced better child welfare judgments, or to argue that parental input and shared decision-making will produce

---

[113] *Supra*, notes 89, 92. It may also be that foster parents can argue that they, or the child in their care, have a right under s. 7 of the *Charter of Rights*, to a fair hearing before their "liberty and security of the person" are infringed by the action of child welfare authorities. See, *N.P.P.* v. *Regional Children's Guardian* (1988), 14 R.F.L. (3d) 55 (Alta Q.B.) and *Smith* v. *Organization of Foster Families*, 97A Sup. Ct R. 2094 (1977, U.S.S.C.).

[114] *Family Services Act*, S.N.B. 1980, c. F–2.2, s. 52(3); *The Child and Family Services Act*, R.S.M. 1987, c. C80, s. 31.

[115] *Child and Family Services Act*, S.O. 1984, c. 55, s. 57(7).

[116] *Ibid.*, s. 57(9).

[117] *The Child and Family Services Act, supra*, note 114, s. 51(2).

worse decisions. Child welfare workers now have a tougher job. They cannot leave it to the judge because they face greater internal administrative accountability and a duty to give children a high quality of care rights. It seems likely that the legislators will increasingly accede to the reasonable demands of children and parents for more rights. Acceptance of the new legislative trends, although they maintain some of the traditional authority of the state, finally gives voices to the people most affected by child welfare decisions.

6

STREET KIDS AND ADOLESCENT PROSTITUTION: A CHALLENGE FOR LEGAL AND SOCIAL SERVICES

Christopher Bagley*, Barbara A. Burrows†
and Carol Yaworski‡

INTRODUCTION

Prostitution is an ancient and troubling institution. In North America prostitution is a major industry which prevents a significant number of women and adolescents from living at or below formal poverty lines or from making demands on formal systems of social and financial assistance.[1] Yet, for western society, prostitution is offensive to the Judeo-Christian ethic, as it institutionalizes both fornication (licentious sex) and adultery (sex outside the institution of marriage). Tensions between the functional aspects of prostitution (sexual outlets for men and economic supports, primarily for adolescents and women) and the moralistic motives of society are reflected in the ambiguities of attempts to control prostitution.

These ambiguities are well illustrated in Canada today, where the practice of prostitution is not itself illegal, but where many of the transactions that lead to such relationships are deemed unlawful. Apparently rational solutions, such as licensing adult prostitutes and allowing them to advertize in newspapers and magazines, are shunned by policy makers.

Until recently, juvenile prostitution (commercial sex involving both males and females under the age of 18) was generally considered as part of the general problem of prostitution. However, current social concern about the widespread problem of child sexual abuse has been paralleled by an increased concern about juvenile prostitution. Various legal solutions have been incorporated into recent legislation to address the problems of juvenile prostitutes.[2]

*   Professor, Faculty of Social Work, The University of Calgary, Calgary, Alberta.

†   Research Associate, Canadian Research Institute for Law and the Family, Calgary, Alberta.

‡   Director, Henwood Homes, Oshawa, Ontario.

[1]   H. Reynolds, *The Economics of Prostitution* (Springfield, Il: Charles C. Thomas, 1986).

[2]   For a discussion of these initiatives, see R. Dawson, "Child Sexual Abuse, Juvenile Prostitution and Child Pornography: The Federal Response" (1987) 3 J. Child Care 19.

This chapter begins by describing contemporary knowledge of juvenile prostitution. Recent social policy and legal initiatives that have been undertaken to address the problems of juvenile prostitutes are then discussed and assessed. The central contention is that there is little evidence of any rationality or success in these approaches. Finally, some practical suggestions are made about how social service agencies and practitioners might deal more effectively with the problem of juvenile prostitution.

CURRENT KNOWLEDGE ABOUT ADOLESCENT PROSTITUTION

It is appropriate to review findings from recent Canadian, American and European studies on juvenile prostitution before considering the legal and social policy problems involved in controlling this trade, and the more acute dilemmas and difficulties in helping young people who are likely to be lured into the world of prostitution, drugs, pornography, petty crime and street violence. These empirical studies help us to understand the failure of child protection services in preventing or adequately treating child abuse (a major factor in the drift into adolescent prostitution). The studies reveal the complex and heterogeneous nature of young prostitutes and the areas in which they work—a complexity which has, so far, defied successful legal and social service intervention.

Although the sexual exploitation of adolescents by older individuals (almost universally male) through the misuse of authority, through sexual assault, rape, or by commercial transaction has existed since the earliest times[3], it was only in the 1970s that North American society began to understand both the dimensions of this problem and the destructive force of such exploitation in the lives of young people.[4] This increased consciousness reflected the development of a feminist critique of society and its institutions.[5] This new consciousness also led to a better understanding of adolescent male prostitutes, who serve the needs of adult males, who otherwise typically lead ordinary heterosexual lives.[6] Ironically, adolescent prostitution is still seen by many as an institution involving

---

[3] F. Henriques, *Prostitution and Society*, Vols. 1,2 & 3 (London: McGibbon and Key, 1966); F. Rush, *Child Sexual Abuse: The Best Kept Secret* (New York: McGraw-Hill, 1980); L. Otis, *Prostitution in Medieval Society* (Chicago: University of Chicago Press, 1985).

[4] C. Bagley & K. King, *Child Sexual Abuse: The Search for Healing* (London: Tavistock, Routledge & Kegan Paul, 1990).

[5] Rush, *supra*, note 3; D. Russell, *The Secret Trauma: Incest in the Lives of Girls and Women* (New York: Basic Books, 1984).

[6] D. Campagna & D. Poffenberger, *The Sexual Trafficking in Children* (Dover, MA: Auburn House Publishing, 1988).

voluntary transactions which should be subject to regulation by statutes relating to public order rather than those designed to protect children.[7]

Factors Influencing Entry to Prostitution: Child Abuse, Home Environment and Runaway Behaviour

Juvenile prostitution was described in 1975[8] as a problem of young people who have suffered abuse and rejection within their families and who then move onto the streets. These young people are psychologically and physically vulnerable. Benward and Densen-Gerber found that 44% of adolescents in a residential treatment and community centre in New York had suffered incestuous abuse prior to leaving home. They also found that leaving home following sexual abuse put the young person at considerable risk for rape by strangers and acquaintances. This secondary abuse appeared to be a major antecedent of entry into prostitution. A Canadian study supports these findings.[9]

One of the most comprehensive studies[10] of adolescent female prostitutes found that 60% of the women sampled were victims of sexual abuse in their childhood or early adolescence before entering prostitution.[11] Two-thirds of these victims were sexually assaulted by a father or a father figure. Most women entered prostitution after running away from home because of sexual, physical or emotional abuse. The teenager who runs from home in order to escape abuse often has a repertoire of sexual experience to draw upon in trying to survive on

---

[7] A. Brannigan, L. Knafla & D. Levy, *Evaluation of Bill C–49 in Calgary, Regina and Winnipeg* (Ottawa: Ministry of Justice and Attorney General of Canada, 1988).

[8] J. Benward & J. Densen-Gerber, "Incest as a Causative Factor in Anti-Social Behaviour: An Explanatory Study" (1975) 4 Contemporary Drug Problems 323.

[9] C. Bagley & L. Young, "Juvenile Prostitution and Child Sexual Abuse: A Controlled Study" (1987) 6 Can. J. Comm. Mental Hlth 5.

[10] M. Silbert & A. Pines, "Sexual Child Abuse as an Antecedent to Prostitution" (1981) 5 Child Abuse and Neglect 407. Bagley and Young, *ibid.*, replicated the work of Silbert and Pines with an opportunity sample of 45 young women who had left prostitution in the previous 2 years. All had begun prostitution as juveniles. In this respect, they appear to be representative of prostitutes in Canada as a whole, where the average age of entry to the profession is 15.5 years. See Government of Canada, *Sexual Offences Against Children: Report of the Committee on Sexual Offences against Children and Youths*, Vols 1 & 2 (Ottawa: Ministry of Justice, Attorney General of Canada and Ministry of National Health and Welfare, 1984) [referred to in the text as the Badgley Report, after the Committee's chairman]. See also Government of Canada, *Pornography and Prostitution in Canada: Report of the Special Committee on Pornography and Prostitution*, Vols. 1 and 2 (Ottawa: Ministry of Justice and Attorney General of Canada, 1985) [referred to in the text as the Fraser Report, after the Committee's chairman].

[11] Numerous other studies have found that early sexual abuse influences the process of entering prostitution. See, e.g., R. Deisher, G. Robinson & D. Boyer, "The Adolescent Female and Male Prostitute" (1982) 11 Ped. Ann. 819; C. Fletcher, "Early Sexual Experience and Female Prostitution" (1982) 43 Dissertation Abs. International 3027-B.

the street. Seventy-eight percent of the women in this study became prostitutes while they were still juveniles.

A Canadian study argued that an additional factor in the drift into prostitution was the stigmatized sexual identity that girls developed as a result of sexual abuse. Often these adolescents became highly promiscuous and were victims of multiple abuse, both inside their families and in school and the community, before entering prostitution.[12]

Thus, a picture emerges of adolescent prostitutes as young women whose psychosexual development has been disrupted by pathological factors within the home; street life and prostitution further undermine their already fragile mental health.[13] The finding of much poorer mental health in adolescent prostitutes has also been replicated in work from New York and California.[14]

Janus and his colleagues conducted a detailed study of the antecedents and current problems of adolescent male prostitutes in Boston, a sizeable but often unrecognized sub-population within the youth prostitution group.[15] These researchers argue that while the vulnerability-drift model can explain the entry of female "street kids" into prostitution, different models of motivation must be explored for males. It is quite rare for a male hustler to work for a pimp; the opposite is true of teenaged female prostitutes. Nevertheless, the self-employment and mutual support of the male hustlers seems to do little to alleviate the wretchedness of their condition. Janus et al. divide the male prostitute population into five rather distinct groups:

1. Permanent street hustlers who live on the streets, lack a home, and are very mobile. These youth seem to have little sense of the future and are unable to organize their survival skills to redirect their lives. They describe themselves as gay but display confused sexuality.

2. Heterosexuals who maintain contact with the community and may even live at home. They work hard to look conventional, and will abuse women whenever the opportunity presents. They are also often involved in various delinquent activities.

3. Young adolescent males who flirt with the hustling scene. They have marginal involvement with home and school; they experiment with drugs and sexuality and are more immature than youth from other groups.

---

[12] This promiscuity could simply be learned behaviour or it could have psychodynamic significance. See Bagley & Young, *supra*, note 9.

[13] C. Bagley & W. Thurston, *Preventing Child Sexual Abuse: Reviews and Research* (Calgary, AB: University of Calgary, 1989). Rehabilitation and Health Monograph Series, No. 18.

[14] I. Gibson-Ainyette et al., "Adolescent Female Prostitutes" (1988) 17 Archives Sexual Behav. 431.

[15] M. Janus, B. Scanlon & V. Price, "Youth Prostitution" in A. Burgess & M. Lindquist, eds, *Child Pornography and Sex Rings* (Toronto: Lexington Books, 1984) 127.

4. Youths who disassociate themselves from any peer group of hustlers. They hustle less frequently and have a broader range of social contacts and interests. Their motivation is likely to be mainly financial.

5. Youths who are isolated from a peer group as a result of their complete lack of social skills. They are often graduates of child welfare or mental health systems that have been unable to help them. They lurch from crisis to crisis and often deter potential "tricks" by their appearance and aggressiveness. Almost all of the youth in this last group had been physically and sexually abused in their childhood, sometimes in foster homes.

Three-quarters of the male prostitutes surveyed by Janus et al., had been involved in the production of pornography; this finding is supported by other studies as well.[16] Half of the Boston subjects had participated in sado-masochistic sex. Searching for factors motivating entry into prostitution, Janus points to a common feature in about half of his subjects: coercive and traumatic sexual assault earlier in life, with the boy either identifying with the perpetrator or adopting the role of permanent victim. In Boston (as in other American and Canadian cities), helping services for these young males are conspicuous by their absence. The primary needs of these youngsters are for food, shelter, safety and formal education without the seemingly coercive ties of conventional social service intervention. One particular problem for adolescent male hustlers is that their attractiveness to customers lies in their youth; in their teenage years they often become addicted to lifestyles associated with a high income, permitting the purchase of drugs and other items associated with rich, young lifestyles. By the age of 20 years, however, the male prostitute loses his attractiveness and his income.[17] No long-term studies exist, but it is likely that the future for many of these young men is one of crime, dealing in drugs, and prison.

Weisberg's findings with respect to male adolescent prostitutes in San Francisco are compatible with these findings.[18] Weisberg describes in detail the lifestyles of three contrasting groups of young male hookers who work in different parts of the city. The first group work in a lower-class sex-trade zone, marked by cheap rooming houses and many kinds of sexual activity. The youth here tend to be habitual prostitutes who are more aggressive, less attractive and more likely to be on drugs than male hookers in other areas. They present themselves as heterosexual, even macho in appearance. Their aggressiveness may relate to doubts about their sexual identity. These youth tend to be peer-delinquent, have lower-class origins and to come from generally disrupted and abusing families. Prosti-

[16] S. O'Brien, *Child Pornography* (Dubuque, IA: Kendall-Hunt, 1983); A. Burgess & M. V. Clark, *Child Pornography and Sex Rings* (Toronto: Lexington, 1984).

[17] V. Price, B. Scanlon & M. Janus, "Social Characteristics of Adolescent Male Prostitution" (1984) 9 Victimology: Int'l J. 211.

[18] D. Weisberg, *Children of the Night: A Study of Adolescent Prostitution* (Lexington, MA: Lexington Books, 1985).

tution is a way of surviving economically (as is theft or drug trading). Selling themselves for sex is not seen as anything but an unpleasant, temporary activity.

Weisberg identifies the second area of male prostitution in San Francisco as a primarily gay area of bars and restaurants. These adolescents see themselves as gay, and usually cater to men who themselves are explicitly gay. Boys from the suburbs who are exploring their new-found sexuality also trade sex for money in intermittent visits to the area.

The third area of male prostitution identified by Weisberg is a more affluent region of hotels. Males working this area tend to be older (over 17 years), well dressed and middle class in origin. Some engage in prostitution to support their careers in the arts. These young men were largely ignored by merchants and police until younger male hookers from other areas moved in and conflict developed. Weisberg's research raises the possibility that the ecology and cultural climate of particular cities may produce different patterns of prostitution, even though the background and motivation of many of the youth entering the sex trade may be quite similar. The possibilities for ecological variation are also raised in the various Canadian studies undertaken for the Fraser Report (discussed below).

The Canadian government recently commissioned a major study of juvenile prostitution in Canada.[19] Of the 229 juvenile prostitutes interviewed for the Badgley Report, 145 were females and 84 were males. The average age of both groups was 18 years. About 75% of the males said they were homosexual or bisexual in orientation, but it is not clear whether this sex-role orientation emerged because of prostitution or homosexual seduction, or whether young, gay males lacking acceptance in other social settings drifted into prostitution. Whatever the pattern of cause and effect, both male and female subjects reported similar types of home background, with desertion or long-term absence of father in 44% and of mother in 21% of the homes. For a third of females and 17% of males, a parent had been chronically dependent on public assistance. Nevertheless, the majority came from economically stable backgrounds, often a two-parent, middle-class family. However, according to the young people's reports, these apparently stable families were often beset by marital strife and alcoholism in one or both parents.

Comparison of data from the national survey of sexual assault in childhood commissioned for the Badgley Report with data from the young prostitutes indicates that they were at least twice as likely as "ordinary" children to have been sexually abused before leaving home in their early teens.[20] A third of females who later became prostitutes had experienced intercourse before their 12th birthday, compared with 0.8% of those in the national survey; [21] overall, 42% of the

---

[19] Government of Canada, *Sexual Offences Against Children, supra,* note 10.

[20] C. Bagley, "Child Sexual Abuse and Juvenile Prostitution" (1985) 76 Can. J. Public Hlth 65.

[21] C. Bagley, "Prevalence and Correlates of Unwanted Sexual Acts in Childhood in a National Canadian Sample" (1989) 80 Can. J. Public Hlth 295.

145 female prostitutes had their first sexual experience in a non-consensual situation, usually involving a blood relative. However, as the authors of the Badgley Report acknowledge, the research setting was certainly not ideal (subjects were contacted on the street and interviewed that same day or evening, and interviews generally took place in rented rooms or coffee bars), and the subjects may have concealed information or misled the researchers in a number of areas, including those of sensitive issues in childhood. The researchers were not particularly skilled, consisting in some cases of students with minimal training.[22]

Data on the educational history of the young prostitutes can, however, be regarded as fairly reliable. Their formal educational achievements stood in marked contrast to those of their parents. Over two in five (42%) had not progressed beyond junior high school, and two in three (66.8%) had not completed more than one year of high school. The reason for this poor school achievement lay in both voluntary drop-out and drop-out forced when the young person ran away from home. It is simply not possible to enroll in another school when the only address a young person can give is "the street." Many of the young people had been in foster care, group homes or shelters, but none of these institutions seemed able to address the angry rebellion against conventional norms which these young people brought with them from their disturbed home life.

There is some evidence that although the kinds of adolescents who could be drawn into prostitution are similar in many cultures, the legal and political climate of a country may influence both entry into prostitution, and the conduct of this trade. Kiedrowski and Van Dijk studied prostitution in Denmark, France, the Netherlands and Sweden.[23] In cultures (particularly the Netherlands) where prostitution is officially tolerated and even encouraged in defined geographical zones, adult prostitutes (who rarely work for pimps) provide their own self-policing. There are strong social controls from the adult prostitutes themselves (based on both self-interest and social concern) that prevent juveniles from entering the trade.

Street Life—Drugs, Abuse, Disease and Criminal Activity

A prominent aspect of street life is that of power, status and hierarchy. Schaffer and DeBlassie,[24] reviewing American evidence, argue that the young adolescent female on the streets is at the bottom of an exploitation hierarchy. She is used, sexually and otherwise, by a motley street crew, consisting of pimps and drug dealers. Also, police view the problems of the street from a model of social

---

[22] Bagley, *supra*, note 20.

[23] J. Kiedrowski & J. Van Dijk, *Pornography and Prostitution in Denmark, France, the Netherlands and Sweden* (Ottawa: Gov't of Canada—Policy, Programs & Research Branch, 1984).

[24] B. Schaffer & R. DeBlassie, "Adolescent Prostitution" (1984) 7 Adolescence 689.

order, not one of absolute morality. Their role is not to help or protect the young runaways, but to maintain a balance of power in which, ultimately, police control the streets and curb and arrest the major players. McMullen, in a study of young prostitutes in London, England, elaborated this model of power in terms of the subcultural norms which govern the workings of Soho, the "pleasure centre" of the capital city.[25] Within these hierarchies of power, male prostitutes have somewhat higher status, often doubling as pimps or drug pushers. Young girls are often used as "packers," carrying drugs concealed on their body. She takes the rap for drug possession; if she loses the drugs or disposes of them herself, her physical safety is in peril.[26]

Another study found that once the juvenile prostitutes were in the streets they were victimized by pimps; they were beaten, raped, robbed and abused. In addition to being victimized through prostitution, they were also victimized in situations that had nothing to do with their street work.[27] Three-quarters of the subjects were raped, in most cases by total strangers; these rapes often involved brutal force. Despite the fact that virtually all victims described physical injuries and extremely negative emotional impact, very few reported their victimization to authorities or sought help.

The Badgley Report portrays the life of a young prostitute in Canada as one of horror and continued abuse. A little over 25% of the females began prostitution by age 13 and 59% had begun working as prostitutes by the time they were 16. Just over half of the young male prostitutes and 30% of the females regularly used street drugs. Often prostitution was a means of earning money to buy drugs, even though the original motivation was simply to obtain money for a bed and a meal. Most hoped that having to sell themselves for sex would be temporary, but it rarely worked out this way. Over half of both females and males had contracted a sexually transmitted disease; and 70% of females and 51% of males had been beaten or injured while working as prostitutes. The assailants varied from tricks, pimps and other prostitutes to police and strangers. All females and males had been charged with soliciting, loitering, property offences, sexual offences, assaults and alcohol, drug or other offences. However, the involvement of the criminal justice system resulted in no new social service intervention to address the needs of these young people. The life of a young prostitute is a passport to a more general criminal career. According to evidence from these young people, pimps both imposed the most extreme violence on them and inducted them into broader ranges of deviance, including theft, assault and drug dealing.

A second major study initiated by the Canadian government was the Fraser Report.[28] Research conducted through the Fraser Committee produced regional

---

[25] R. McMullen, "Youth Prostitution: A Balance of Power" (1987) 10 J. Adolescence 35.

[26] K. Kufeldt & M. Nimmo, "Kids on the Street—They Have Something to Say: Survey of Runaway and Homeless Youth" (1987) 3 J. Child Care 53.

[27] M. Silbert, *Sexual Assault of Prostitutes* (San Francisco: Delancey Street Foundation, 1981).

[28] Government of Canada, *Pornography and Prostitution in Canada, supra,* note 10.

studies of prostitution in Canada. This research is both interesting and important. It shows that in each city studied there are different zones in which prostitution is practised. Each zone has a particular character, associated with the types of prostitutes available and prostitution practised. Older women, juveniles, males, native women, transvestites and others tend to solicit in different parts of cities, and their support (or exploitation) groups differ too. Prostitution in Canada is a complex sociological problem.

CANADIAN LEGAL AND SOCIAL RESPONSES

As noted above, two major Canadian reports recently considered the issue of juvenile prostitution. The *Report of the Committee on Sexual Offences Against Children and Youths*[29] considered juvenile prostitution within the context of the problem of child sexual abuse, while the *Report of the Committee on Pornography and Prostitution*[30] considered juvenile prostitution within the context of the institution of prostitution in Canada. Both Committees commissioned considerable background research; many of these research findings were discussed above. Both reported, with one key exception, similar conclusions and strongly overlapping recommendations. To date, at least with regard to prostitution, the recommendations have been largely ignored (with a few notable exceptions) by the government to which the reports were presented and by subsequent administrations.[31]

The Badgley Committee

The Committee on Sexual Offences Against Children and Youths (subsequently referred to as the Badgley Committee, after its chairman, sociologist Robin Badgley) opened the set of six chapters on juvenile prostitution with the following observation:

> The issue of prostitution in Canada, in particular, juvenile prostitution, is clothed with ambiguity, myths and hypocrisy. Publicly, there is widespread indignation and condemnation concerning the plight of these youths. Their visible presence on the downtown street corners of many large Canadian cities is seen in some quarters as a failure of existing public services—social, enforcement and legal—to deal adequately with the problem. A sharp disparity exists between what is publicly said and what should be done to reduce the occurrence of juvenile prostitution. While in the rhetoric of public debate, the

---

[29] Government of Canada, *Sexual Offences Against Children, supra,* note 10.

[30] Government of Canada, *Pornography and Prostitution in Canada, supra,* note 10.

[31] R. Dawson, "Child Sexual Abuse, Juvenile Prostitution and Child Pornography: The Federal Response" (1987) 3 J. Child Care 19.

needs of these youths are allegedly recognized, the services available to them are limited in scope, or in some instances, have been curtailed.[32]

These remarks were made in the early 1980s, yet remained entirely true in 1990. The Badgley Committee based its recommendations and conclusions on a review of existing law, reports from hospitals and social service agencies, and a special survey of 229 juvenile prostitutes who were working the streets in eight major cities across Canada.

It should be noted that obtaining samples of juvenile prostitutes is fraught with difficulty. A true random sample is impossible to obtain, because the population from which to sample is undefined. Purveyors of a clandestine trade may be difficult to locate[33], and their participation in a research interview poses problems of danger (from pimps and others) for both the prostitute and the interviewer. Also because juvenile prostitutes are victims of sexual abuse in the terms of provincial child welfare statutes, the interviewer might have a legal or ethical obligation to report such abuse to child welfare authorities; however, such an obligation could make research interviews with young prostitutes impossible.[34]

In reviewing the history of these young people, the Badgley Report concluded that, " ... existing social services had been ineffective and had provided inadequate protection and assistance. In this respect, there can be no doubt in the Committee's judgment that special programs must be funded to meet their needs."[35] As of 1990, there was little evidence of the provision of increased service or innovative programs for young prostitutes and street kids through federal initiatives.

In reference to juvenile prostitution, the Badgley Report concluded:

In the Committee's judgment, the relationship between young prostitutes and pimps encompasses one of the most severe forms of the abuse of children and youths, sexual or otherwise, that currently occurs in Canadian society. The relationship is based on two forms of ruthless exploitation: psychological and economic. The pimp exploits and cultivates the prostitute's vulnerabilities— her low self-esteem, her feelings of helplessness, her loneliness on the street and her need for love and protection. These weaknesses are the fetters with which the pimp binds the girl to him and keeps her on the street. Economically, pimps exploit prostitutes by drawing them into a form of virtual slave labour, or at least into a relationship in which ... the pimp, provides a service whose value is vastly outweighed by the amount which ... the prostitute, is required to pay for it. The cost to the prostitute of working for a pimp goes far beyond the earnings that she gives him; it amounts to the girl's forfeiture of her future.

---

[32] Government of Canada, *Sexual Offences Against Children, supra*, note 10 at 947.

[33] *Supra*, note 20.

[34] *Supra*, note 9.

[35] Government of Canada, *Sexual Offences Against Children, supra*, note 10 at 1075.

Opportunities to obtain a better education, to become free of drug and alcohol addiction, to sort out emotional problems, to return to a normal lifestyle and to enter into healthy, caring relationships, are seriously jeopardized or permanently destroyed. The relationship between juvenile prostitutes and pimps is parasitic and life-destroying. In the Committee's judgment, it must be viewed as a problem of the utmost gravity. It must be stopped.[36]

How can this problem be stopped, and the needs of the homeless adolescent runaways be met? Eight of the Badgley Committee recommendations might, if implemented, provide some useful and viable approaches to the problem. As of the end of 1989, the following progress had been made in acting on the Report's recommendations.

Recommendation 41: *As part of a national program of public education, special educational programs should be developed, based on the findings of the Committee on juvenile prostitution. These special programs should be made available to parent-teachers associations, schools, and educational television.* By 1989, a special fund of $20 million (to be spent at the rate of $5 million a year) was allocated for research, education and demonstration projects concerning all aspects of child sexual abuse. A total of 10 projects were funded which related to juvenile prostitution, including two conferences and four projects to facilitate the development of special education programs related to this problem. None of these projects involved very substantial expenditures of funds.[37]

Recommendation 42: *Provincial Child Protection Services should develop special programs geared to serve the needs of young prostitutes and to identify the early warning signs of troubled home conditions warranting the provision of special services.* As of 1990, it was difficult to obtain information on special initiatives, but in British Columbia and Alberta most initiatives have relied on private funding. These initiatives, while excellent in concept, have been privately funded or only partially funded by government sources. Furthermore, they have been able to cope with only a few dozen cases, whereas the need is for comprehensive programs reaching hundreds of street kids in each city.[38] Ontario allocated $1.3 million in 1985 for drop-in shelters and counselling services for street children practicing, or at risk of, prostitution.[39] Research in Ontario found that

[36] *Ibid.* at 1061.

[37] An overview of the federal government's response to the Badgley Report 1984–1989 is found in Appendix B to R. Rogers, *Reaching for Solutions: The Report of the Special Advisor to the Minister of National Health and Welfare on Child Sexual Abuse in Canada* (Ottawa: Health and Welfare Canada, 1990) at 126–143.

[38] See M. Benjamin, *Juvenile Prostitution: A Portrait of "The Life"* (Toronto: Ministry of Community and Social Services, 1985); Kufeldt & Nimmo, *supra*, note 26; L. Zingaro, *Working With Street Kids* (1987) 3 J. Child Care 63; M. Dorais & D. Menard, *Les enfants de la prostitution* (Montreal, VLB Editions, 1987).

[39] "Ontario Plans All-Out Attack on Prostitution" *The* [Ottawa] *Citizen* (5 February 1985) A5.

nearly half of all female prostitutes in Toronto were juveniles, and a growing number were under 16 years old.[40] Thus, given the dimension of the problem in Toronto, the special allocation of $1.3 million by the Minister of Social Services seems more of a symbolic gesture, rather than an attempt to address the problem comprehensively.

Recommendation 43: *The Office of the Special Commissioner on Child Abuse (established through the Committee's key, first recommendation) should, in conjunction with various branches of government, establish a series of five-year demonstration projects aimed at protection, counselling, education and job training for young prostitutes and others on the street.* The Office of Special Commissioner for children was never established, although a Special Advisor on Child Sexual Abuse was appointed to report to the Minister of Health and Welfare, and he did so in June 1990. While the federal Department of Health and Welfare's demonstration funding is theoretically available for such projects, no special initiative, funding or competition was aimed at juvenile prostitution. By the end of 1989 only one project was established in this area. The Coastal Community Services of Victoria received funding for a downtown emergency services co-ordinator to oversee a multi-agency service for youth at risk. Strategies include intervention, education and advocacy to improve the health and quality of life of street youth, including juvenile prostitutes.

Recommendation 44: *The Office of the Special Commissioner, with the Federal Department of Justice and the Solicitor General, should provide support to municipalities for the provision of special police force units, with prime responsibility for investigating and charging pimps and clients of young prostitutes.* As of early 1990, no action had been taken on this recommendation by the federal government, though some urban police forces, such as the Metro Toronto Police, have formed special units to address the problem of street youth and juvenile prostitutes.

Recommendation 45: *The practice of juvenile prostitution (i.e., by someone under 18) should become a "status offence" (just like under-age liquor consumption), so that police and social service workers would have the power to intervene directly with young prostitutes, and offer direct and immediate help.* No action had been undertaken on this recommendation by 1989. The Fraser Committee (see below) actually argued against this criminalization of juvenile prostitution.

Recommendation 46: *The Criminal Code should be amended so that anyone offering or exchanging money with a young person (under 18) for purposes of sex should be guilty of a criminal offence.* Bill C–15 became effective in 1988 and provides that: "Every person who, in any place, obtains or attempts to obtain, for consideration, the sexual services of a person who is under the age of

---

[40] Benjamin, *supra*, note 38.

eighteen years is guilty of an indictable offence and is liable to imprisonment for a term not exceeding five years."[41]

Recommendation 47: *The Office of the Special Commissioner should promote the publication of names of men convicted of soliciting juveniles for the purpose of prostitution.* By 1989, the Office of the Commissioner had not been established and despite the continued, extensive practice of juvenile prostitution in Canadian cities, very few charges have been brought against men who engage the services of a juvenile prostitute.

Recommendation 48: *Various changes should be made in the law relating to sexual offences to make it easier to convict pimps involved with juvenile prostitutes, with a minimum, mandatory sentence of two years and a maximum of 14 years for "liv[ing] ... on the avails of prostitution of another person who is under the age of eighteen years."* As part of Bill C–15, changes to the *Criminal Code* had largely adopted these recommendations.[42] It seems, however, that relatively few convictions have been obtained under these provisions.

In summary, the Badgley Report was well-researched and persuasively written. It contained a comprehensive set of proposals which could have addressed the profound problems of young teenagers who run from home because of abuse, then fall prey to the perils of street life, and drift into various destructive lifestyles, including prostitution. The government has acted on a few of these proposals, particularly in the areas of legal change. However, virtually nothing has been done with regard to those proposals requiring financial expenditure and coordination of work between federal and provincial government departments.

The Fraser Committee

This special Committee of enquiry was commissioned by the federal Minister of Justice to examine what appeared to be a growing problem of the visibility of prostitutes and pornography in Canadian cities. The work of this committee overlapped with that of the Badgley Committee. However, the Fraser Committee (chaired by lawyer Paul Fraser and reporting in 1985) considered the problem from a public order standpoint, rather than from the child-centred focus employed in the Badgley Report.

The various research reports on prostitution prepared for the Fraser Committee are in many respects similar to accounts of youth prostitution elsewhere in North America and in Europe. There are many similarities: prior sexual and physical abuse; average age of entry into prostitution in mid-teens; few available alternatives for survival; and continued exploitation, abuse and degradation by pimps, tricks and others. However, there are also important differences: propor-

---

[41] Bill C–15, *An Act to Amend the Criminal Code and the Canada Evidence Act*, 2d Sess., 33d Parl., 1986, s. 9(4). See *Criminal Code*, R.S.C. 1985, c. C–46, s. 212(2)-(4).

[42] *An Act to Amend the Criminal Code, ibid.*, s. 9(2); *Criminal Code*, R.S.C. 1985, c. C–46, s. 212(2).

tion of males trading for sex; types of clients; degrees of degradation and exploitation; and different types of police harassment and control. Most of the Fraser Committee research reports focus on the issue of social control, rather than on helping exploited young people escape from prostitution. There is some scattered evidence that police responses vary according to officers' perceptions of the adolescent. For example, a middle-class girl "gone astray" may be helped but native and Métis girls are likely to be treated with contempt or even abuse by police.

Of all the reports for the Fraser Committee, the research on Vancouver prostitutes by John Lowman is the most sympathetic to the adolescents involved.[43] Lowman and his team interviewed 272 prostitutes. Lowman argues convincingly that most previous approaches have failed to give enough weight to the problems of juvenile prostitutes as vulnerable young people, rather than as a class of prostitutes providing trouble for society, their families, and the moral order in general. Lowman, like Raychaba,[44] argues that approaches to these young people must focus on how they define their own social and personal situations. Paternalistic and authoritarian approaches to the problems of young women on the street are bound to fail.

Research conducted for the Fraser Report indicated that prevention approaches must employ community-based strategies, using peer networks to alleviate the conditions of young prostitutes and to help them leave the street. Young people cannot be "saved" by any type of moralistic approach, or by child protection strategy operating under provincial law, or by any evangelical organization. Not only must the structural problems causing young people to flee from home be addressed, the structure of street life itself has to be understood.[45]

The Fraser Report did address the special problems of juvenile prostitutes. It referred to evidence provided by a Winnipeg agency which reported that 80% of

---

[43] J. Lowman, *Vancouver Field Study of Prostitution* (Ottawa: Gov't of Canada—Policy, Programs and Research Branch, 1984); *Taking Young Prostitutes Seriously* (Burnaby, BC: Simon Fraser University, School of Criminology, 1985); "Prostitution in Vancouver: Some Notes in the Genesis of a Social Problem" (1986) 28 Can. J. Crim. 1.

[44] B. Raychaba, *To Be on Our Own* (Ottawa: National Youth in Care Network, 1988).

[45] See L. Zingaro, *supra*, note 38, which outlines helping strategies for Vancouver street kids. These young people have rebelled against all forms of authority, legitimate and illegitimate. They are cynical of the approaches of adults, whether to exploit or to help. Yet self-help strategies, with financial support from existing organizations, could provide significant exits from the street. Many of the young people who are dragged into prostitution have previously been "in care" with child welfare systems. Young people from the care system demanding that they be allowed to determine their own futures is a valuable indicator of possible strategies for "reaching the unreachable;" see also *ibid.*

the youth in their programs had been victims of sexual abuse at home. This agency reported that:

> As we delved into the literature in the area, we discovered ... that our observations were consistent with experts in the field who have acknowledged that teenage prostitution is a point on a continuum of an early destructive sexual experience. One recent case in which we were involved was that of a young woman who used to obtain her allowance for performing fellatio on her father; for her it was a natural progression to move on to other forms of selling sex.[46]

It was extraordinary that the man in this case could not be prosecuted for this act because sexual relations with a minor were not illegal if that minor was "not of previously chaste character" or engaged in sex in return for money. The statute on incest did not apply, so long as the father did not actually engage in vaginal intercourse with his daughter—the very limited statute on incest in Canada refers only to completed, vaginal intercourse between members of the opposite sex, closely related by blood.[47] Intercourse by a father with his adoptive or step-daughter is not, in legal terms, incest. The father could now be prosecuted, as Bill C–15[48] criminalized clients of adolescent prostitutes. It also criminalized "touching for a sexual purpose" and "sexual exploitation" of a child by a person in a position of "trust or authority", whether or not money is involved.

The Fraser Committee recommendations advocated the decriminalization of prostitution, allowing women aged 18 and over, to work from their homes or small, licensed establishments. However, they advocated the criminalization of pimps and customers using juvenile prostitutes, and would not have permitted the licensing of juveniles to work as prostitutes. Educational programs and economic and social service supports were proposed in order to help young people on the street, prevent the entry of juveniles into prostitution, and encourage their exit from street life.

Licensing adult prostitutes and "allowing small numbers of prostitutes to organize their activities out of a place of residence ... "[49] appears to be a sensible and well-reasoned suggestion. Moreover, it would allow the delivery of direct assistance to juvenile prostitutes through prosecution of customers who use unlicensed juveniles. Fraser and his colleagues argued (unlike the Badgley Committee) that juvenile prostitution should not be a status offence, concluding from the research studies that such criminalization would be unlikely to assist in helping strategies.

---

[46] Government of Canada, *Pornography and Prostitution in Canada, supra*, note 10 at 352.

[47] C. Bagley "Mental Health and the Sexual Abuse of Children and Adolescents" (1984) 2 (June) Canada's Mental Health 17.

[48] Bill C–15, *supra*, note 41.

[49] Government of Canada, *Pornography and Prostitution in Canada, supra*, note 10 at 538.

Federal Legislative Responses

Federal government response to the Badgley and Fraser recommendations has been mixed. Bill C–15 did criminalize the customers of juvenile prostitutes, but Bill C–49 (aimed at controlling public soliciting) was passed in direct contradiction to Fraser's recommendations. Very few of the recommendations for educational and social service assistance for young prostitutes have been taken up by the federal government. Government response to the Reports seems to have been based on ideology, rather than on reason or a careful study of the two reports which brought together the presentations of thousands of concerned groups and individuals across Canada.

One of the federal government's principal responses to the Fraser Committee recommendations was to introduce Bill C–49 to cope with the public nuisance associated with street soliciting, as identified by many witnesses in their submissions to the Fraser Committee. Fraser and his colleagues advocated that only "active or bawdy soliciting" should be subject to summary conviction.[50] The Committee clearly hoped that legalizing houses of prostitution would end or diminish the public nuisance aspect of prostitution.

It appears that the government used this recommendation to bring in a bill that went far beyond the Fraser recommendations. While ignoring proposals for establishment of services that might have tended to exclude juveniles from prostitution, the government brought in legislation that was punitive to prostitutes in a manner that went beyond the intention of the Fraser Committee. This law prohibits any kind of communication in a public place, however orderly, for the purposes of prostitution: both customer and prostitute may be prosecuted.[51] The law also allows the use of "sting" operations by male and female police officers pretending to be prostitutes or customers.

The federal Department of Justice commissioned research on the effects of the controversial aspects of Bill C–49 on street prostitution in Calgary, Regina and Winnipeg. These studies provide important data on how the institution of prostitution is evolving in Canada. One thing is clear—the number of juveniles, and their exploitation, has not diminished as a result of any government legislation.

In the Calgary study, interviews were conducted with 70 prostitutes, 51 females and 19 males.[52] The majority of women interviewed had been victims of sexual or physical abuse before leaving home, or had been raped or beaten up

---

[50] Government of Canada, *Pornography and Prostitution in Canada, supra,* note 10 at 538–39.

[51] Bill C–49, *An Act to amend the Criminal Code,* 1st Sess., 33d Parl., 1984–85. See *Criminal Code,* R.S.C. 1985, c. C–46, s. 213(1). Outlawing a form of communication opens this law to challenges under the *Canadian Charter of Rights and Freedoms,* as a violation of freedom of expression.

[52] A. Brannigan, L. Knafla & C. Levy, *Evaluation of Bill C–49 in Calgary, Regina and Winnipeg* (Ottawa: Ministry of Justice & Attorney General of Canada, 1990).

while working on the street. Rates of abuse were higher for the female prostitutes.

> We were astounded by the recurrent accounts of hookers and hustlers being confronted by armed assailants, stabbed, threatened with death, beaten up and robbed. During 1986, two female hookers from Calgary were found murdered in rural Alberta, their bodies disposed of in the country. The interviews suggest that the gravest source of aggression comes from their customers.[53]

The new police posers under Bill C–49 appeared to be an additional factor by which the lives of prostitutes (including juveniles) are harassed. The new law and the police interpretation of it appear to have done nothing to assist adolescent prostitutes. Indeed, the exact opposite may be the case. In Calgary, for example, a halfway house for young prostitutes closed, ostensibly because it was underused. However, police action against soliciting appears to have "pushed the problem of young prostitutes out of sight."[54] While the number of adolescent prostitutes on the street has been reduced, their actual number has not diminished. They are now much more likely to work for pimps or through intermediaries, and are simply not accessible at street level.[55] Traditional agencies working at the street level now have few visible or easily available clients. Bill C–49 may have driven adolescent prostitutes off the streets, but now they are both invisible and under the tighter control of pimps. Their opportunities for escaping from prostitution may have been reduced.

Evaluations of the workings of Bill C–49 for the Department of Justice were also carried out in Vancouver, Halifax, Toronto and Montreal. These studies, together with the report on the Prairie provinces by Brannigan et al. show marked ecological variations in the type and manner of prostitution between cities, public reactions to prostitution, and the type of control strategies used by police.[56] Nowhere, however, is there evidence of any particular concern by police and public for the problems of adolescent prostitutes; the one thing that unites Canadian cities is the perception of prostitution as a problem of public order and public morals, not as a problem of adolescent victims.

THE JUVENILE JUSTICE RESPONSE TO YOUNG OFFENDERS

Until quite recently, in both Canada and the United States, adolescents whose promiscuous sexual behaviour (sometimes including prostitution) displeased

---

[53] *Ibid.* at 47.

[54] S. Braungart, "Closure Leaves Teens Desperate" *The Calgary Herald* (19 October 1989) B3.

[55] G. Brannigan, Personal Communication (1989).

[56] L. Knafla, Personal Communication (1989).

adults were processed and sometimes incarcerated with little attention to basic rights, or the luxury of a criminal trial with the production of formal evidence and defence by counsel. Young people, especially adolescent females assumed to be sexually active and at odds with their families, could be held in custody by child welfare jurisdictions for long periods.[57] Under the old *Juvenile Delinquents Act*[58], adolescents could be indefinitely detained if they engaged in "sexual immorality or any similar form of vice," which included engaging in prostitution. Ismael, for example, in an examination of the juvenile courts in Calgary, found that one judge was particularly likely to order the incarceration of adolescent females who had allegedly been sexually precocious, on the grounds that they were at risk for juvenile prostitution.[59]

In the 1980s there was an increased recognition of the legal rights of adolescents and a move to afford them the same rights as adults. This was reflected in the *Young Offenders Act*, which came into force in 1984 and put an end to the arbitrary detention of young females who were suspected of engaging in, or likely to engage in, prostitution.[60] The *Young Offenders Act* now allows young persons the same legal rights as adults, with the onus on the Crown to prove a violation of the criminal law beyond reasonable doubt. The power of judges to invoke delinquency legislation to order protective custody for adolescents whom they perceive to be at risk has been eliminated. The youth court now more closely resembles the adult court.

Many observers argue that the court's function as a helping agency has been diminished by the enactment of the *Young Offenders Act*.[61] Although we have no good comparative evidence, it seems likely that Canada's young people are now more poorly served by social welfare agencies than they were before the advent of the *Young Offenders Act*. In Alberta, for example, many services previously administered by the Department of Social Services came under the jurisdiction of the Department of the Solicitor General following passage of the *Young Offenders Act*. In the process, services for care and counselling of young people were lost. Social service records from child protection proceedings are not trans-

---

[57] J. Ismael, *Juvenile Detention: A Study in Decision-Making* (Calgary, AB: University of Calgary, Faculty of Social Work, 1982) Faculty of Social Welfare Monograph Series.

[58] R.S.C. 1970. c. J–3. s. 2; first enacted in 1908.

[59] Ismael, *supra*, note 57.

[60] Government of Canada, *Pornography and Prostitution in Canada, supra* note 10; *Young Offenders Act*, R.S.C. 1985, c. 4–1.

[61] Judge Herbert Allard, senior judge of the Family and Youth Court in Calgary, has commented publicly on many occasions that the *Young Offenders Act* had the disastrous effect of curbing ways in which the judicial system could help young people. Judge Allard was one of the Badgley Commissioners, and had a major hand in the writing of the chapters on juvenile prostitution, including the recommendation that juvenile prostitution should become a status offence.

ferred to the Department of the Solicitor General, and the young offender is less likely to receive any continuity of care between child protection and juvenile correctional systems.

While in theory counselling or residency requirements may be imposed as conditions of probation, in practice the most common sentence for an adolescent prostitute prosecuted for soliciting under Bill C–49 is a fine in youth court. The young person will probably pay off the fine by turning extra tricks. It is open to judges in Family Court to order secure treatment under a section of the Alberta *Child Welfare Act*, but only if the adolescent is a "danger to himself or others."[62] This section is rarely used, and is applied only to psychotic, extremely aggressive or actively suicidal youth. While we do not have systematic data for other provinces, there do not appear to be grounds for supposing that any other jurisdiction had been successful in using young offender or child welfare legislation to assist young people practising, or in danger of entering, prostitution.[63]

Bracey observes that in North America the criminal justice system treats the adolescent prostitute as an offender, rather than as a victim—despite the social science evidence to the contrary.[64] The fundamental dilemmas of using various kinds of legalistic approaches to the problems of youth prostitution are well illustrated in the work of Hawkins and Zimring:

> Traditional powers to lock up status offenders, allegedly for their own good, allowed the police and juvenile courts considerable control over truants, runaways, vagrants, and the insubordinate, at least in theory. Removing the power to arbitrarily lock up the young also removed leverage on the part of the police to protect juveniles from real dangers. In effect, the decriminalization of status offences has led to the deregulation of youth.

> The police, deprived of the power to lock the children up, have often staged a strategic withdrawal; many no longer regard themselves as responsible for the welfare of 15- and 16-year-olds. Other public agencies lack the incentives and resources to fill the gap.

> The withdrawal from the coercive regulation of adolescents can be justified because the costs of regulation—in dollars, in liberty, and most importantly, in youth welfare—exceeded their benefits. But withdrawal of the use of coercive state power has not been costless. The dangers of exercising immature judgment on the streets of major urban areas, living in squalor, and risking disease and death are quite real ...[65]

Thus the crux of the matter is that previous delinquency legislation and social service interventions have failed to help adolescents who are on the streets, and

---

[62] S.A. 1984, c. C–8.1, s. 41.

[63] Dorais & Menard, *supra*, note 38.

[64] D. Bracy, "Concurrent and Consecutive Abuse: The Juvenile Prostitute" in B. R. Prize and N.J. Sokoloff, eds., *The Criminal Justice System and Women* (New York: Clark Broadman, 1982) c. 16 at 317.

[65] Hawkins & Zimring, *Pornography in a Free Society* (New York: Cambridge University Press, 1988) at 192.

in danger; the new legislation has also failed. Canadian governments have largely ignored key recommendations in recent reports which might assist in dealing with the problem. Thousands of Canadian adolescents are being sexually exploited each day. Police, judges and social workers at present lack the resources and commitment to address the problem of juvenile prostitution, except in quite a limited fashion.

SOME SUGGESTIONS FOR PRACTITIONERS:
WORKING WITH RUNAWAYS

Evidence suggests that simply returning runaway youths to their homes is futile. In working with runaways it is critical to elicit their reasons for running away. While sometimes these reasons may not seem very serious in the eyes of a social worker, they are obviously sufficient for the youth and therefore warrant serious consideration. Obtaining such information is vital to establishing the youth's perception of their situation and must form the basis of corrective action or counselling. It must also be appreciated that what a youth reveals to a worker, especially early in a relationship, may not be a complete picture. Even seemingly "street tough" adolescents may be slow to fully reveal their feelings, and may not understand their own feelings, motivations and past.

Many of the principles that apply to helping runaways also apply generally to juvenile prostitutes, a subgroup of runaways. In working with runaways, the long-term treatment emphasis must change from simple protection to behaviour change. Specifically, external controls must eventually be loosened; these youths must be given the opportunity to make their own decisions and mistakes. While workers must emphasize to youths the dangers of street life and the counter-productiveness of chronic running away, it must be recognized it is for youths themselves to truly learn the nature of these concerns. If running away is part of a pattern, it must be unlearned and not simply stopped. The environment from which the youth has run must also be critically examined, because returning the youth without effecting change in that environment will only lead to more of the same.

Many runaways yearn for independence and the opportunity to manage their own lives. They feel, with some justification, that they can do no worse for themselves than the adults in their lives have done for them. They thus seek the right to control their own destiny within the system; if that option does not exist within our systems, they look outside the system. The following are some helping strategies which may prove effective in treating runaways.

1. *Supported, Independent Living.* Such programs exist across the country in relatively small numbers and are virtually unavailable to youth under the age of 16 years. While 16 is the age at which most provinces provide less restricted programming for street youth, that age guideline may be artificially high. The lack of the opportunity to use such programs when youths feel ready for them leads them to seek unsupported alternatives (i.e., street life).

As well, there has been a disturbing trend in the past few years toward teen admission policies which restrict access to child welfare programs for youth who are under 16 years and whose situation is not viewed as critical. Left to their own devices, bad situations have a way of becoming critical, but by the time they do the child may be too old to qualify for the needed help.

2. *Alternative Education.* Chronic running away and regular school attendance are generally not compatible activities and in some instances school pressures and failures may have been the critical problem for the young person in the first place. At the same time a lack of education and training relegate youth to dependence on state financial assistance or crime. Alternative school programs which address learning problems and allow students to work at their own pace are more likely to provide the success necessary to sustain effort. Additionally, co-op programs which combine basic literacy with job placements are an alternative, especially for those youth who require tangible success.

3. *Counselling and Group Support.* Individual and group counselling can provide youth with some individualized support and the reassurance that they are not alone. The street's attraction for many youth is the opportunity to be with others who are supportive, understanding and most importantly, non-judgmental. Many street youth describe their supports on the street as their "family." In order to engage a youth in a productive counselling relationship, a worker must understand how the youth perceives the world and replicate, in a professionally appropriate manner, the support and acceptance that exists for the youth "on-the-run." Most teen prostitutes represent a subgroup of runaways and because of their involvement in prostitution, are usually at the bottom of the street hierarchy. Professional counselling of this type can provide an environment in which they can feel comfortable enough to explore the circumstances that led to their current situation.

For most runaways, the effective approach is the utilization of the fundamental principles of social work: listening, accepting and providing guidance. Runaways, like most people, learn experientially; they must therefore be offered the opportunity to make decisions in a climate which supports them when they make mistakes, and then gives them the chance to try again until they get it right.

CONCLUSIONS—SOCIAL POLICY DIRECTIONS

Canadian society is ambivalent about prostitution. We are undecided whether to tolerate prostitution as an institution, to suppress it, to control the practice in a punitive way to prevent young people from entering prostitution, or to help prostitutes leave the exploitation of street life. Despite the recommendations of two major reports and other Canadian research (showing that the majority of adolescents who enter prostitution were runaways who had been victims of physical, sexual and emotional abuse in their homes) the official approach has been based on a public order approach, rather than on principles of helping. Despite some initiatives, services that can help young prostitutes leave the street and obtain counselling, career guidance and education are woefully inadequate in all Canadian cities.

Research shows that there is much variety within the prostitution population. There is also geographical variation within urban areas and policy towards prostitution varies greatly throughout North America. Male and female adolescent prostitutes usually have different motivations for becoming involved in prostitution and therefore need different approaches from helping agencies. Agencies working with adolescent females must address the pain inflicted by earlier sexual abuse; otherwise the helpless, depressed, disorganized and self-harming behaviours manifested by many adolescent prostitutes are likely to continue.[66]

Part of the problem is the lack of affordable accommodation. Without a place to stay, a young person cannot have access to income assistance and cannot return to school. Moreover, many of these youths have rebelled against the often perverse and dictatorial authority imposed in their homes, and are likely to rebel against traditional social service and judicial interventions. New and imaginative approaches are needed and these should be funded by provincial and federal governments as demonstration projects, as the Badgley Report has advocated.

The one approach which our society has adopted for controlling the practice of juvenile prostitution is to criminalize the customers of young prostitutes and their pimps. Further criminalization of customers does not help those adolescents who have already fallen into prostitution. One possible solution would be to licence prostitutes over 18, requiring the customer to check this licence. However, licensing prostitutes and allowing them to work in small collectives of adults (as the Fraser Committee recommended) remain controversial issues and do not seem to be politically realistic for Canada at this time.[67] In addition, licensing also implies that a person under 18 might be prosecuted for prostitution in the same way that a person under 18 (or 21 according to province) can be prosecuted for obtaining liquor. This brings us back to the Badgley Committee recommendation, which was not endorsed by the Fraser Committee, nor acted on by government, that juvenile prostitution itself be made a status offence. To some observers, it remains puzzling and paradoxical that a young person may be prosecuted for buying liquor, but not for engaging in commercialized sex.

The situation of juvenile prostitutes in different Canadian cities should continue to be monitored. Social scientists must try to elucidate exactly how abusive home situations lead, directly or indirectly, to many young people entering prostitution. The development of prevention strategies is of the utmost significance. In this respect, the findings of Kufeldt and Nimmo[68] may prove very helpful.

---

[66] *Supra*, note 4.

[67] M. Bennett, "Prostitute Scheme Still a Hot Issue" *The Toronto Sun* (24 October 1985) 28.

[68] *Supra*, note 26.

Their survey of 408 adolescents living on the street in the downtown core of Calgary found that they were of two basic types. The "runners" had lost all contact with their family, and often came from other parts of Canada; nearly half of them had previously been in child care facilities, and most had criminal records, including soliciting offences. The "ins-and-outers" had run from difficult home situations, often more than once, but returned home for temporary periods, they were less likely to have tried prostitution as a means of surviving. The needs of these temporary runners are different, and social service strategies and specialized housing could meet the needs of this population in ways which could prevent the drift into permanent prostitution. An innovative strategy would involve use of affordable housing, linked to some non-authoritarian wardship or care, which is quite different from conventional child welfare approaches.[69]

Juvenile prostitution is deeply harmful to its participants. It is a deep-rooted problem, based in the manner in which conventional society approaches problems of child care and child abuse. The elimination or reduction of the incidence of juvenile prostitution will require fundamental changes in approach, and profound changes of attitude by both the Canadian public and the Canadian government.

---

[69] Zingaro, *supra*, note 38.

ADOPTION

Heather L. Katarynych[*]

THE ADOPTION CONCEPT

Adoption is a legal creation of a parent-child relationship between individuals who are not biologically related. It has been described as both a birth and a death. As it creates a new family, it extinguishes another. As a general rule, the effect of adoption is to place adopted children in the same position they would have had as the biological children of their adoptive parents, and terminate all of the legal ties arising from their relationship with the natural parents.

Adoption is an ancient concept. In Roman civil law, for example, it was intended to create kinship for men who did not have a male heir. At that time, continuity of the male line was a key political, economic and religious consideration, which meant that the adoptee was invariably an adult male. Adoption was unknown to the common law, where it was considered an attempt to assign the rights and duties of parentage, and therefore contrary to public policy.

In Canada, at the time of Confederation, adoption as a process for legally assigning parenting responsibility was generally unknown. However, North American Indians had evolved their own form of adoption as a means of providing care for children whose parents were unwilling or unable to do so. The earliest adoption law in Canada was enacted in New Brunswick in 1873, followed by Nova Scotia, Prince Edward Island and Alberta, all of which enacted adoption statutes prior to World War I. Five other provinces (Ontario, Québec, Manitoba, British Columbia and Saskatchewan) enacted adoption statutes in the 1920s, followed by three remaining jurisdictions (Newfoundland, Northwest Territories and the Yukon) in the 1940s. The statutory scheme in each jurisdiction creates a complete framework for adoption within that jurisdiction. These schemes deal with the same basic issues:

1. *Relinquishment of the child.* Legislative provisions concerning this issue are directed to obtaining the consent of the biological parents to the adoption, determining the suitability of the child for adoption placement, and regulating any intermediaries, such as an adoption agency.

2. *Placement of the child.* The focus here is on placing the child with the prospective adoptive parents and monitoring the attachment and bonding between the child and family during a time-limited probation period.

---

[*] Senior Counsel, Metropolitan Toronto Children's Aid Society, Toronto, Ontario.

3. *Finalization of adoption.* This stage represents the culmination of all that has gone before. Legislation regulates the process by which the newly constituted family proceeds to court, usually with the assistance of the person or agency that has placed the child with the family for the purpose of adoption. An adoption order will give the child the legal status of a child of the adoptive parents, as if the child were born to them, and sever the legal links to the biological parents.

4. *The possibility of reunification.* Legislative provisions dealing with this issue are concerned with the renewal of contact between the adult adoptee and the biological parent.

An adoption effects a change in legal status, and is said to be "binding upon the world", and not just on the parties to the proceeding itself. Because of the radical change it makes to the child's legal status, it is an order which is not made lightly, and only in circumstances where there is strict conformity with both the letter and the spirit of the applicable statutory law.

TYPES OF ADOPTION

Children are made available for adoption through a variety of legal routes: (a) court order for permanent wardship of a child, giving the provincial child welfare agency the right to seek an adoptive family for the child and place the child without any further involvement of the child's birth parents, including any necessity to obtain their consent to the adoption; (b) voluntary parental surrender of the child to a child welfare agency for adoption placement; (c) voluntary parental surrender to a private adoption agency or individual, who then arranges the child's placement for adoption; (d) parental placement of the child with a relative; (e) stepparent adoption, following remarriage of the custodial parent.

Each of these routes has its own particular set of legal rules and practices, designed to deal with its unique features. For example, the child welfare staff enjoy a broad discretion in the choice and monitoring of an adoption placement for a child who has been made a permanent ward through child protection proceedings. Proportionate to the wide discretion is a corresponding high degree of accountability for the decisions that are made. Statutory provisions governing consent adoptions, (or voluntary surrenders), arranged by the provincial child welfare authority, a private agency, or through private individuals, are designed to ensure that relinquishment of the child is not undertaken precipitously or in an ill-informed fashion. At the same time, private agencies and individuals who wish to undertake adoption work are subjected to strict rules to govern their operations—rules designed to guard against the marketing of children.

Relative and stepparent adoptions are usually subjected to a lesser degree of control than agency-arranged adoptions at the placement stage, because generally the child is already a part of the adoptive applicant's family. These adoptions often proceed with consent of all concerned. However, there will be a high degree of court scrutiny if an adoption order will cause a non-custodial parent to lose the right of access to the child and that person objects to the adoption.

These varying degrees of control and the impact they have on the participants to the adoption process are discussed throughout this chapter.

Adoption of Permanent Wards

The statutes of most provinces give the child protection agency the exclusive right and duty to determine the best interests of wards committed permanently to its care, including the decision and choice of adoptive parents. For example, Ontario's *Child and Family Services Act*[1] requires the Children's Aid Society to seek an adoptive family for permanent wards in the Society's care unless the child's best interests dictate otherwise, and to communicate with agencies both within and outside the province to assist in adoption planning for their permanent wards.

A central issue of the last decade has been the extent to which a court has the right to intervene and substitute its decision for decisions made by a child welfare official (usually a provincial Director of Child Welfare, relying on information provided by field staff), when both the Director and the court have responsibility to ensure that the best interests of the child are served.[2] The Director of Child Welfare is given this responsibility by specific provisions of the adoption statute. The superior courts, however, have an inherent historic jurisdiction to promote the best interests of children, which may continue to exist despite the enactment of legislation governing adoption. The struggle to resolve competing claims to the child when the court is asked to intervene and overturn a decision made by the provincial Director of Child Welfare, can result in protracted litigation for a child who may already have encountered a significant degree of insecurity while the machinery of the "protection" system determined that the birth family could not provide adequate care.

Madam Justice Bertha Wilson of the Supreme Court of Canada characterized this dilemma as "a rather sad saga which discloses how one small boy can be caught in a legislative and administrative net and have to come to the highest court in the land to extricate himself."[3] At issue for the Supreme Court was a decision of Newfoundland's Director of Child Welfare to remove a child from his adoption placement on unconfirmed information that the child was being ill-treated by the prospective adoptive parents. The child had been made a ward

---

[1] S.O. 1984, c. 55, s. 134(1). Although s. 134 does not specifically require the Society to be guided by the "best interests" test of s. 132(2), practice is to incorporate its factors into the Society's decision to seek and choose an adoptive family.

[2] See *Beson* v. *Director of Child Welfare (Nfld)*, [1982] 2. S.C.R. 716, 30 R.F.L. (2d) 438 [*sub. nom. D.B. and P.B.* v. *Director of Child Welfare (Nfld)]*, 142 D.L.R. (3d) 20, 39 Nfld & P.E.I.R. 246, 111 A.P.R. 246, 44 N.R. 602; See also *E.P. and E.P.* v. *Superintendent of Family and Child Service of British Columbia* (1987), 9 R.F.L. (3d) 158 (B.D.S.C.), Huddert J.

[3] *D.B. and P.B.* v. *Director of Child Welfare for Newfoundland* (1982), 30 R.F.L (2d) 438 at 439 (S.C.C.).

of Newfoundland's child welfare Director as a newborn infant. Shortly after his second birthday he was placed for adoption with a Mr. and Mrs. B. Six months later allegations of child abuse by Mr. B. were brought to the Director's attention. Despite the couple's denial of any maltreatment of the toddler, the Director refused to disclose the source of the allegations and demanded the child's return. No opportunity to respond to the allegations was given to the couple. The child was removed just 7 days short of the conclusion of the adoption probation period, during which the child had apparently thrived.

The couple immediately sought an appeal of the Director's decision to the province's Adoption Appeal Board. The Board refused to hear the appeal, ruling that the couple had no statutory right of appeal because the child had been removed from their home *during* the adoption probation period and not after the *expiry* of that period. The couple then attempted to gain the child's return through *habeas corpus*[4] proceedings. Newfoundland's Supreme Court, after a full hearing of the matter, ruled that the allegations of abuse against Mr. B. were unfounded, and that the couple had provided a "fine home" for the boy.[5] However, the court refused to order a return of the child. In its view, Newfoundland's adoption statute had given the Director the discretion to remove a child from adoption placement and the court should not substitute its views for the views of the Director. This decision was upheld by the Newfoundland Court of Appeal. The couple then sought intervention of the Supreme Court of Canada. At the hearing of their application for leave for the appeal, the couple discovered that the boy had been placed for adoption with another couple 10 months after his removal from the B. home. This other couple had no knowledge of the claim of the B.'s to the child "until the bombshell was dropped on them by the registrar [of the Supreme Court of Canada]."[6]

The Supreme Court of Canada agreed that the statute did not give the Adoption Appeal Board jurisdiction to hear an appeal of the Director's decision if the adoption placement was terminated during the adoption probation period. However, Madam Justice Wilson disagreed with the position of the lower courts that nothing could be done. She held that the court could and should have ordered the child's return to Mr. and Mrs. B.'s custody, using either its *parens patriae*[7] jurisdiction to protect the child's best interests where the statute was deficient, or

---

[4] *Habeas corpus* is Latin for "have the body." It is an expeditious type of proceeding available in the superior courts which allows a citizen to challenge the authority of a government agency to have custody of a child or adult.

[5] *Supra*, note 3 at 440.

[6] *Ibid.* at 446.

[7] The term *parens patriae* is Latin for "protector" or "father of the country." It refers to an inherent jurisdiction exercised by superior courts to protect the interests of children, mental incompetents and others who could not protect themselves. The superior courts are the Courts of Queen's Bench or the Supreme Court in each province, as distinguished from the statutory provincial courts, which in most provinces have statutory jurisdiction over child protection and adoption matters.

its power of judicial review of the Director's decision, based on the court's finding that the Director had failed to treat the couple fairly and had improperly exercised his discretion.

At the time of the Supreme Court's decision in the case, the child, who was by then 5 years old, had been residing with his second set of prospective adoptive parents for almost a year. Notwithstanding that time span and the court's cautious consideration of the effect on the child of disturbing the status quo by yet another move in his short life, the court ordered the child returned to Mr. and Mrs. B, and granted the adoption order.

The reasoning of the Supreme Court of Canada was applied by the Alberta Court of Queen's Bench to hear an appeal by foster parents of the provincial Director of Child Welfare's decision to reject them as adoptive applicants for a permanent ward they had fostered for almost 10 years. The boy had been moved to the home of a prospective adoptive father. The basis here for the court's willingness to intervene was that the remedy of review provided by Alberta's legislation was so inadequate that it constituted no fair appeal from the Director's decision at all.[8] What must be proved to the court in these circumstances, as in the situation where the contest is between competing adoptive applicants, is that the provincial Director of Child Welfare, in refusing his consent to the adoption of the child by the foster parents, acted capriciously or in bad faith.

It should be noted that if the superior courts believe that there is an adequate statutory route of appeal for prospective adoptive parents, the superior courts are unlikely to intervene. Thus, in Ontario, where s. 138 of the *Child and Family Services Act*[9] gives a statutory right of appeal to a person who is refused having a child placed for adoption, or who may have a child who has been placed removed before the adoption is completed, the courts have demonstrated great reluctance to override decisions made the appropriate authorities after a full and fair hearing.[10]

Assessment of the Child's Capacity for Adoption

Common wisdom in child welfare practice suggests that the key to healthy childhood growth and development is to give every child a secure place as a member of a family and a positive relationship with a parent. However, it is naive to believe that adoption will always be the best long-range planning for those children whose parents are unable to care for them. Ontario's legislation contains the fullest statutory itemization of the factors that are to be considered

---

[8] *B.M. and M.M. v. R. in Right of Alberta et al.* (1985), 45 R.F.L. (2d) 113 (Alta Q.B.), Veit J.

[9] *Supra*, note 1, s. 138.

[10] *Re Baby K.* (1988), 13 R.F.L. (3d) 209 (Ont. H.C.).

in deciding whether adoption is in a particular child's best interests.[11] Factors listed in the statute consist of the following:

- the child's physical, mental and emotional needs and whether a potential adopting parent is likely to be able to provide the care that is essential to meet those needs;
- the child's physical, mental and emotional level of development, and the extent to which a potential adopting parent is likely to be able to meet the child's needs;
- the child's existing relationships with members of the biological family or prior caregivers;
- the child's views and wishes about adoption;
- the child's cultural background, and the extent to which a potential adopting parent is likely to be able to accept it as an integral part of the child;
- the religious faith in which the child has been raised prior to adoption placement, and the extent to which a potential adopting parent is likely to be able to respect it, if it is important to the child;
- the availability and appropriateness of alternative long-term parenting options for the child; and,
- the effects on the child of further delay in planning.

The effect on the child of further delay in planning for the future has become an increasingly critical consideration for child welfare agencies and the courts, which sometimes struggle to settle the custody of children who may have been caught in a seemingly never-ending legal limbo through protracted protection litigation.

Regulation of Private Intermediaries

In a market where the "supply" of healthy newborns available for adoption is increasingly outstripped by the "demand," an entrepreneurial spirit has prevailed to spawn an increasing number of privately-based (rather than publicly-based) individuals and agencies who obtain children for persons willing and able to afford the costs. This development has led to increasing moves towards legislative regulation of the practice. The purpose of such legislation is to ensure that the best possible placement is made for the child and the adoptive parents. Also, prohibitions have been enacted to prevent the buying and selling of children by unscrupulous marketeers, and to ensure that children are not seen as a marketable commodity.

Most provinces prohibit the offer or acceptance of money or consideration of any kind to induce a person to make a child available for adoption, and strictly

---

[11] *Child and Family Services Act*, S.O. 1984, c. 55, s. 130(2).

regulate the costs that may be charged to persons receiving a child through the private adoption route. The British Columbia Supreme Court, using the discretionary power of the province's *Adoption Act*,[12] has permitted prospective adoptive parents to reimburse a birth mother for travel, legal aid and medical expenses that she had actually incurred in the relinquishment of her child, but articulated the following principles: [13]

1. No person should profit from the existence of a greater demand for than supply of children for adopting.

2. A birth mother's decision to give a child up for adoption should be unencumbered by any pre-birth agreements or arrangements.

3. A birth parent should not be allowed to coerce potential adoptive parents who have received the child into making payments as a condition for the birth parent's consent.

These principles underlie Ontario's statutory requirement that both agencies and private individuals (e.g., physicians, lawyers, clergy) involved in adoption be non-profit and licensed by the province to arrange adoption placements.

Ontario permits placement of a child who is under age 16 and unmarried only by a licensed adoption agency or a licensed individual, unless the prospective adoptive parent is the child's grandparent, great-uncle or great-aunt, uncle or aunt, a spouse[14] of the child's mother or one of the child's parents. Regulations under the statute strictly control any financial or other form of compensation for any aspect of the adoption.

Such prohibitions can create particular difficulties for individuals and agencies acting as intermediaries to obtain a child for persons who have been unsuccessful in obtaining a child through the province's child welfare authority (the so-called public route) or who choose not to use the provincial adoption placement resources. A 1987 decision of the Alberta Queen's Bench[15] illustrates the difficulty. The Baby J. Adoption Agency brought together natural mothers and the proposed adopting parents, so that the mother had an opportunity to select parents for her child. In accordance with their philosophy that prospective adopting parents must be properly qualified, the agency sought to educate adopting parents through a $500 course. Prospective adoptive parents were required to take the course to be on the private adoption list of the agency and were responsible for paying the course fee. The court ruled that such arrangements breached the statute, and that a private adoption service could not escape the consequences

---

[12] R.S.B.C. 1979, c. 4, s. 15.1 as amended.

[13] *Re Adoption Act*, (1982), 27 R.F.L. (2d) 72 at 74 (B.C.S.C.) per Huddart L.J.S.C.

[14] "Spouse" is defined by the legislation to mean a person to whom a person of the opposite sex is married or with whom the person is living in a conjugal relationship outside marriage. *Child and Family Services Act, supra,* note 1, s. 130(1)(b).

[15] *Re J.; R.G.J.S. and G.M.S.* v. *B.L.P.* (1987), 7 R.F.L. (3d) 58 (Alta Q.B.), Berger J.

of the prohibition by disguising the payment as tuition for a course of instruction when the course is a prerequisite to being placed on an adoption list.

Such prohibition against compensation does not prevent a government scheme from making subsidy payments to adoptive parents, where the particular child's special needs require subsidy. Without subsidy, these children are unlikely to find an adoptive home because of the special expenses that are likely to be incurred in parenting them. A number of provinces, including Ontario, allow for subsidized adoptions.

RELINQUISHMENT

Relinquishment may be accomplished through a court order of permanent wardship or by parental surrender.

Permanent Wardship Order

Children who are presented for adoption through a permanent wardship order may have been the subject of litigation in a court that has decided that their parents are not presently able to parent them, have not been able to do so in the past, and are unlikely to be able to do so in the foreseeable future. The permanent wardship order may have been made on a consent basis. Parental consent is not required for this type of adoption, and the parents do not receive notice of the adoption hearing, unless the court has preserved a right of access to the child.

Parental Surrender

Parents may voluntarily surrender their rights to their children for adoption. In cases of voluntary parental surrender, legislation in most provinces requires the identification of all persons whose consent is required for the child's adoption, and the consent of each of those persons or alternatively a court order dispensing with the consent. The legislation also requires specific assurances that parents giving such consent are aware of both the short- and long-term consequences of their decision.

The Significance of Consent

In recognition of the awesome consequences of consenting to the adoption of one's child, the law attends the giving of consent with a variety of safeguards in an effort to guard against precipitous or ill-informed decision-making. Statutory provisions governing consent typically include the following:

1. a time period following a child's birth during which the parent is not permitted to sign a consent—if one has been signed during this time period, it has no legal effect;

2. a period immediately following the signing of the consent, within which birth parents can change their mind—during this time period the consent

is considered to be only partially crystallized and has no binding legal effect;

3. the requirement that counselling be offered to birth parents to assist in decision-making—such counselling may only be provided by professionals specifically authorized by the provincial child welfare authority for that purpose;

4. the requirement that the consent be witnessed by a social worker authorized by the provincial regulating authority to undertake this task;

5. special protection for a minor parent (e.g., in Ontario, the requirement that the Official Guardian be satisfied that the consent reflects the true and informed wishes of any parent less than 18 years of age); and,

6. the requirement that the judge, before whom the adoption application is presented, be satisfied that every person who has given consent understands the nature and effect of an adoption order.

In order to be legally valid, parental consent must be informed. Basic facts that parents need in order to make their decision include the following:

1. the child will no longer be known by the birth name, but will instead acquire the name given by the adoptive parents;

2. the child will cease to be the legal child of the birth parents, and will become the child of the adoptive parents as if born to them;

3. the birth parent will be barred from contact with the child, unless the provincial law permits post-adoption access to the child; and,

4. reunification with the child, if desired by a birth parent, may not occur until the child reaches adulthood, and even then, is possible only if the child also seeks to reestablish contact.

Like any consent in law, a consent to adoption obtained by fraud or through duress or trickery is not a valid consent. Adoption based on an invalid consent may be set aside at a later date. In one British Columbia case, the court set aside the birth mother's consent, and effectively blocked the adoption because the mother's consent had been obtained fraudulently. In this case, the paternal grandparents of a child were seeking to adopt him.[16] The mother was 16 years old, and the father 18. The child was born less than 3 months after the marriage. When the child was 4 months old, the parents separated, placing him with the paternal grandparents, who then made the adoption application. The grandfather and father pressured the reluctant mother into signing the consent for the adoption. They led her to believe that doing so would assist in the reconciliation of the couple, that she and her husband would regain the child upon reconciliation, and that in any event she could see the child at any time. In fact, the husband found married life distasteful and restrictive, and had no intention of resuming cohabi-

---

[16] *Re Adoption No. 71–09–013131* (1973), 9 R.F.L. 196 (B.C.S.C.), Harvey L.J.S.C.

tation. The consent was signed in the presence of a lawyer, about whom the judge remarked:

> While I am not prepared to find that the solicitor wholly failed in his duty I do find that he was mistaken in the opinions expressed in … his affidavit appended to the form of consent, that it "appeared to be signed freely and voluntarily," and that the mother "appeared to understand fully the effect of her consent and of adoption."[17]

The judge stated:

> A consent, induced as this one was by fraud and undue influence, is neither free nor voluntary and is not binding. It is no consent at all. Equally it is plain that the mother, in the induced belief that the adoption of the child would not hinder her right to see the child at will or to regain the child upon reconciliation with her husband, had little or no understanding of the effect of adoption and of her consent thereto.

> It is true that the misrepresentation of the husband was as to his intention but it was nevertheless a representation that the alleged intention did indeed exist and, as it was untrue, there was a clear misrepresentation … The misrepresentation was clearly intended to and did in fact cause the mother to sign the form of consent. It brought about in her mind a misunderstanding which induced her to act as she did. The misrepresentation was clearly fraudulent as there was, admittedly, a complete absence of honest belief in the husband's mind that there was any possibility of reconciliation or of regaining the child in a united home.[18]

A significant factor in this case was that the proposed adoptive parents were actively involved in deceiving the mother. In other cases where this element was absent, the courts have shown considerable reluctance to allow a parent to argue that a consent that appeared to have been freely given was invalid.

A common problem is deciding when to determine who must give consent under a relinquishment statute. Good social work practice would have the determination made before the child is placed, so that the child is fully freed from claims of the birth parents. This gives an optimum measure of security to the adoptive family during the adoption probation period, so that they can concentrate on the integration of the child to the family, secure in the knowledge that the child is legally ready for adoption. However, judges in Ontario have held that the determination of who is legally a parent, and thus entitled to give or withhold consent to the child's adoption, must be made at the time of the application for adoption. A determination made at the time of the child's placement, without further inquiry during the probationary period to ascertain whether a person has acquired parental status during that time, is not adequate.[19]

---

[17] *Ibid.* at 199.

[18] *Ibid.* at 200.

[19] *Koziar* v. *Morra* (1986), 3 R.F.L. (3d) 225 (Ont. S.C.), Galligan J.

Good practice requires making a determination prior to the placement of the child, to maximize the stability of the placement, but then inquiring again at the time of adoption. For example, in Ontario, a man might file a declaration of paternity with the Registrar General during the adoption probationary period, in which case he would be entitled to notice of the adoption proceeding, and would either have to consent to the adoption or his consent would have to be dispensed with by court order.

Whose Consent is Required?

Critically important is the task of identifying those who are entitled to participate in the legal relinquishment of the child, and ensuring that the necessary consents are obtained, or alternatively that a court order is obtained waiving the necessity of any particular consent. Persons having the status to give or withhold consent vary from one province to another.

Ontario's legislation provides a broad definition of "parent" for the purposes of adoption. Only the "casual fornicator" who shows no interest in the child is excluded from consideration. In some other provinces, the definition of "parent" for the purpose of consenting to an adoption is more limited.

In 1978, Ontario enacted a statutory definition that encompassed all biological fathers, as well as biological mothers. After 6 months the definition was amended because delays were often encountered in identifying and locating the father and getting or dispensing with his consent to the adoption. Such delays were felt to frustrate the legislative objective of expeditious adoptions and compromise the best interests of children and adoptive families. The new definition, enacted in November 1979, does not recognize as a statutory parent for adoption consent purposes a biological father who has neither taken any active steps to identify himself nor had a relationship of some permanence with the mother or the child. Rather, the legislation places an onus on such a man to come forward and identify himself. It is legally irrelevant that a man may not know that he fathered a child.[20]

In a 1988 decision, the Ontario Divisional Court held that such discrimination against unwed fathers does not offend the *Canadian Charter of Rights and Freedoms*.[21] In overturning the decision of the lower court that the Ontario definition of "parent" offended s. 15 of the *Charter*, the appellate court stated:

> Adoption is a very important matter. It is clear that in establishing the legal framework for it the legislature has given careful study to the complex issues involved in it. It has obviously considered that the best interests of the child

---

[20] Until recently, legislation in several provinces required the consent of only the mother of a child born out of wedlock to the child's adoption. Such legislation has been held unconstitutional as unjustified discrimination against fathers; *MacVicar* v. *B.C. Superintendent of Family and Child Services* (1986), 34 D.L.R. (4th) 488 (B.C.S.C.). It is significant that Ontario legislation excludes only fathers who have not had a relationship of some permanence with the mother of the child and have not formally identified themselves.

[21] Part I of the *Constitution Act, 1982*, being Schedule B of the *Canada Act 1982 (U.K.)*, 1982, c. 11.

are the paramount concern and that all so-called rights of the biological parents are subsidiary to what is best for the child. Debate could go on forever as to whether or not the legislative scheme that is embodied in the law of Ontario is the best one that can be devised by human beings. But the legislature considered all of the competing positions and decided the issue as it saw it in the best interests of the child. The legislation before the court has been carefully thought out after experiments with other legislative schemes had been tried and found by the legislature not to be in the child's best interests.

... it is an erroneous oversimplification to say that the mother and a father who does not fall within the statutory definition of "parent" are similarly situated. The mother because of physical necessity has shown responsibility to the child. She carried and gave birth to it. The casual fornicator who has not demonstrated any interest in whether he did cause a pregnancy or demonstrate even the minimum responsibility to the child ... cannot be said to be similarly situated to the mother. The statute recognizes as a parent a father who demonstrates the minimum interest in the consequences of his sexual activity. Most fathers are defined as parents. Only those who do not demonstrate some responsibility to the child are not. It is thus apparent to us that the different statutory treatment of the two persons is based upon their respective demonstrated responsibility to the child, not upon their different sexes.

We do not think that a statutory difference in treatment between a natural parent who is responsible to her child and one who has not shown even minimal interest in whether a child exists because of his sexual activity can be said to be irrational, insidious or unfair ...

It is we suppose possible, in the sense that anything is possible provided one has a fertile enough imagination, to conjure up a scenario where a casual fornicator is not told about the pregnancy and, despite his best efforts to do so, is unable to find out the good news that he is to be a father, has any prospect of being a real father to the child frustrated because of the Act. It is worth noting that counsel have been unable to find anywhere in the voluminous evidence any trace of the existence of the hypothetical man who has casual sexual intercourse, seeks to find out if it resulted in a birth and then assumes responsibility for the child he fathered ...

It is our opinion that the obvious objective of this legislation is to ensure that children whose parents are unwilling or unable to care for them receive early placement in a permanent home where they will have the opportunity to be reared as members of a family. There was ample evidence before the legislature, and there is ample evidence before this court, that such placement should be made as early in the child's life as possible, and that there should be a maximum feeling of certainty on the part of the adoptive parents and the child that the placement is permanent ...

The evidence in this case is overwhelming that delay in placement or in finalizing the adoption incurs serious risks of long-term behavioural, emotional or psychological harm for the child. Delay in finalization of an adoption can cause intolerable strains on the prospective adoptive parents. The legislature has on reasonable grounds concluded that it is in the best interests of the child and the families by whom he or she is to be adopted that the process be as quick and certain as is reasonably possible.[22]

A father who is a parent within the meaning of the legislation and comes forward wanting to care for his child when the mother has relinquished her right to do so will be given very serious consideration by the courts in any competition between him and the persons with whom the child has been placed for adoption. Typical of the recent judicial attitudes is a decision of the British Columbia Court of Appeal, giving interim custody of a 5-month-old infant to his 19-year-old father who, with the support of his parents, was seeking permanent custody of the child.[23]

The lower court had ruled that the status quo should be preserved pending full hearing of the father's application for permanent custody. The Court of Appeal, in reversing the ruling, reasoned as follows: (a) an arrangement whereby a child is parented by his father and paternal grandparents is not unusual in this day and age; (b) a biological parent's claim to his child's custody must be given very serious consideration; and, (c) where the legislation requires the child's best interests to be the determining factor, and the scales are relatively evenly balanced between what the biological father can offer the child and what the prospective adopting parents can offer, the blood tie should be the deciding factor. This emphasis could be seen as the reemergence of the so-called "parental right" that treated the child much like property. However, the focus of the modern law is on the right and well-being of the child, and it is from this particular perspective that the courts consider the parent's claim.

In Ontario, a judge can find that the natural father is not a "parent" on the uncontested affidavit of a mother stating that the biological father does not qualify as a "parent" within the meaning of the statutory definition. A judge

> ... errs in law in refusing the uncontroverted evidence before him. He had no right to simply disregard the evidence before him and shed some doubt or cast ... aspersions on the truth of the materials submitted to him since no other materials contradicted the information presented to him.[24]

Conditional Consent

A consent given by a parent to adoption by a specific person or couple is termed "conditional consent." The basic effect of a conditional consent is that if the conditions upon which the consent is premised are not met, the consent has no legal effect. In an Alberta case, the court held that a 16-year-old birth mother

---

[22] *Ontario (Attorney General)* v, *Nevins, Prov. J.* (1988), 13 R.F.L. (3d) 113 at 115–120 (Ont. Div. Ct).

[23] *M. (C.G.)* v. *W. (C.)* (1989), 23 R.F.L. (3d) 1 (B.C.C.A.).

[24] *Re R.* (1985), 53 O.R. (2d) 54 at 59 (Ont. Dist. Ct), Fleury D.C.J.

had given her consent to her child's adoption by a specific couple. When the couple divorced, the husband and his new wife applied for guardianship and the birth mother applied for custody herself.[25] The court ruled that the mother's consent to the adoption had no legal effect. However, that was not the end of the matter. The child's best interests dictated that he remain with the man he regarded as his father and with whom he had a strong bond. Although the court was not asked to make an adoption order, it indicated, in preserving guardianship, that it would have been prepared to dispense with the mother's consent to the adoption in the circumstances of the case.

Revocation of Consent

The statutes of most provinces recognize that a parent may have a change of heart about relinquishing the child; thus they provide specific time frames within which a parent may revoke consent to adoption. This appears to be the law's acknowledgement that a child's first birthright should be the opportunity to be raised by his own biological family. In Ontario, for example, a parent has the right to revoke the consent for a period of 21 days from the date the consent is signed, without having to justify the decision.

A parent seeking to revoke a consent after the expiry period provided by the provincial statute permitting cancellation of the consent must be able to prove to the court that it is in the child's best interests to permit such a revocation. The benefits to the child of maintaining ties to a biological parent and being in the care of that person must be balanced against the benefits to the child of maintaining stability and parental bonds to those with whom the child has been placed for adoption. How that balance tips depends on the circumstances of the particular case.

In a 1985 decision, the Supreme Court of Canada refused to overturn a decision refusing to allow a mother to revoke her consent to the adoption of the son whom she had placed with a couple for adoption shortly after the birth.[26] The Court's rationale was that the welfare of the child was the predominating consideration, and that the court's task was to:

> ... choose the course which will best provide for the healthy growth, development and education of the child so that he will be equipped to face the problems of life as a mature adult. Parental claims must be seriously considered but must be set aside ... where it is clear that the welfare of the child requires it.[27]

---

[25] See *S.L.B.* v. *J.M.C. and P.S.C.* (1987), 10 R.F.L. (3d) 96 (Alta Q.B.), Legg J.

[26] *King* v. *Low.* [1985], 1 S.C.R. 87, 44 R.F.L. (2d) 113 (S.C.C.), McIntyre J.

[27] *Ibid.* at 126.

It was significant in this case that the mother acknowledged that she had given a free and fully-informed consent to the adoption and that she herself had chosen the adoptive parents. Perhaps most important was the evidence that the process of bonding—what the court termed " ... the formation of a relationship of love and obligation which is essential to the normal development of a child"[28]—had progressed to the point where removal of the child would be traumatic enough to adversely affect his health and development. By the time the Supreme Court of Canada heard the appeal, the child was 3 years of age and the biological mother was a virtual stranger to the child.

The Court cited with approval the following statement of the trial judge:

> The law gives rights to the natural parents of a child in order that such very important and natural bonding may be protected and fostered, in the best interests of the child. The court recognizes those rights on that basis and for that purpose. But where, as in the present case, such bonding does not exist between the natural parent and child, having instead developed between the child and other parent figures, the court must perforce give recognition to the facts of the case accordingly. To do otherwise would be to substitute an empty formula for the substance which the law must embody and express.[29]

The legislation of some jurisdictions does not provide a specific time frame for revocation of consent; in such cases the parent may exercise that right until the adoption order is made. New Brunswick's adoption law permits a parent to revoke consent at any time prior to the granting of an adoption order, unless the child has been placed for adoption by the Minister.

Recently the New Brunswick Court of Appeal considered a case in which an unwed mother placed her child with a couple for the purposes of adoption, and some 4½ months later revoked her consent. By statute, no adoption order is permitted in New Brunswick until a 6-month probationary period has expired. The prospective adoptive parents' had initiated an application to dispense with the mother's consent, based on the child's best interests; that litigation and competing application by the birth mother resulted in the 14-month delay, but the court was not prepared to allow the prospective adopters to benefit from their refusal to return the child pending the trial. In ordering the child's prospective adoptive parents to return the infant to her birth mother, Angere J.A. ruled that the evidence did not show that such return would harm the child, even though the little girl had resided some 14 months with the prospective adoptive parents. They had changed her name and she was doing well in the prospective adoptive home. The New Brunswick Court of Appeal has recently determined that the law of the province does not require a natural parent who has revoked consent to her child's adoption to give a reason for her revocation.[30]

---

[28] *Ibid.* at 118.

[29] *Ibid.* at 129.

[30] *R.S. and M.E.S.* v. *C.H.* (1989), 20 R.F.L. (3d) 456 (N.B.C.A.).

Where, however, the statute does provide a specific time period, parents who wish to revoke their consent after its expiry must seek a court order permitting it. For example, in Ontario, if the child has not yet been placed for adoption, the court may hear the parent's application to withdraw consent to the adoption, but may grant it only if satisfied that withdrawal is in the child's best interests. Where the child has been placed for adoption, such application cannot be made at all.

Dispensing with Parental Consent

The adoption laws of each province provide a mechanism whereby a court may waive or dispense with the rights of a person who has been given legal status to give consent to a child's adoption, if the inability to obtain the consent is barring an adoption that would otherwise be in the child's best interests. The issue sometimes arises in cases where the child is being placed for adoption with strangers, particularly where a birth parent has arranged the adoption privately and without the intervention and assistance of the local child welfare authority. It more frequently arises when it is a stepparent who seeks to adopt the child, and consent to the adoption is being withheld by the child's noncustodial birth parent, usually, but not always, the father.

The person who desires an order dispensing with the missing consent must prove to the court that the child's best interests require it. Regardless of the reasons put forth, the order is only granted if, in the court's opinion, the likely benefits of adoption outweigh those that would accrue to the child if the court preserved the legal right of the person whose consent is missing.

It is an order not easily granted. Courts have considered the following factors essential to a determination of whether an order should be made dispensing with a birth parent's consent:

- the extent to which the child has an ongoing and meaningful relationship with the parent who is withholding consent to the child's adoption;[31]
- the extent to which the child has a meaningful relationship with extended family of the parent withholding consent (e.g., grandparents, aunts, uncles, cousins, etc.);[32]
- what positive contributions may be made to the child's welfare by dispensing with the consent;[33]

---

[31] *Stoodley v. Blunden* (1981), 17 R.F.L. (2d) 280 (N.S.S.C. - C.A.).

[32] *Ibid.*

[33] *Ibid.*

- the fact that an adoption order will terminate rights of access granted by a court at the time of divorce;[34]
- the fact that the law does not require a non-custodial parent to show "exceptional circumstances" to argue that his rights to access should supersede the adoption;[35] and,
- the fact that a parent had virtually no contact with her child for over 4 years, but had contacted child welfare authorities on numerous occasions asking them to assist her to regain custody of the child from foster parents, and had been emotionally upset when she placed the child and refused to dispense with her consent.[36]

The rationale for being reluctant to dispense with parental consent is rooted in the court's recognition of the far-reaching and final effects that adoption has on the rights of a parent and child. An order dispensing with the consent of a noncustodial parent to the adoption will only be made in special or unusual circumstances, and on the clearest evidence of benefit to the child.[37]

Notice of the Application to Dispense With Consent

As a general rule, provincial adoption laws require anyone seeking a court order to waive a person's right to give consent to the child's adoption to make a reasonable attempt to locate the person whose consent is at issue and formally notify that person of the application. Such notification is intended to alert the affected persons of when and where the court will consider and decide the application. It is also intended to notify them that if they do not consent, they have a right to attend a court hearing where the judge will decide on the application to dispense with their consent. Failure to respond to this notice of a hearing allows the court to make its decision in the person's absence, and will usually result in the court dispensing with the required consent.

Most provincial adoption statutes stipulate a time frame within which the court's decision can be appealed. Until this time period has expired, the order has been appealed, or the appellate courts have made a final decision, the child cannot be adopted.

---

[34] *W. v. H. and Attorney General of Alberta* (1982), 25 R.F.L (2d) 337 (Alta C.A.).

[35] *Williams v. Hillier and Hillier* (1982), 26 R.F.L. (2d) 164 (Man. C.A.).

[36] *Re W.; W. v. R. and R.; R. and R. v. W.* (1983), 32 R.F.L (2d) 153 (Man. C.A.).

[37] See, for example, *M. v. B.* (1984), 41 R.F.L. 187 (Ont. Dist. Ct), Keenan J., and *Re British Columbia Birth Registration No 82–09–032673* (1988), 12 R.F.L. (3d) 167 (B.C.S.C.), Paris J.

ELIGIBILITY TO ADOPT

Age and Marital Status

Statutory requirements regarding the age and marital status of prospective adoptive parents govern the capacity to adopt in all provinces. These standards exist to establish the basic age differences and life circumstances that these children would have had if they had been born to the prospective adoptive parents and thus to ensure the probability of a successful adoption. For example, in Ontario special circumstances must be shown to justify adoption if the prospective adoptive parent is less than 18 years of age.

While in Ontario couples who reside in a stable common law relationship can jointly apply to adopt a child, in some provinces only those who are legally married can do so. In a recent British Columbia case, the Court refused to permit an adoption by an unmarried couple, reasoning that because adoption is a statutory creation, a court had no inherent jurisdiction and British Columbia's *Adoption Act* had exhaustively specified the parties who are authorized to adopt a child in British Columbia. British Columbia legislation permitted adoption only by an adult person or by a husband and wife; there was no provision for adoption by an unmarried couple.[38]

Residency of Adoptive Parents and Child

Most provinces require the adoptive parents to be resident in that province at the time the application is made. For example, Ontario's legislation refuses to permit the court to make an adoption order unless both the child and the prospective adoptive parent are residents of Ontario. Questions of residency most frequently arise when the child to be adopted is brought to Canada for that purpose.

Under existing immigration regulations, a Canadian citizen intending to adopt a child under 13 is allowed to sponsor that child as a landed immigrant, provided that the child genuinely is in need of adoption. For example, a child who has been orphaned or abandoned would be eligible, but adoptions cannot be arranged solely to permit immigration of the child to Canada. In this way, children from outside the country can be sponsored into Canada, become landed immigrants, and be adopted.

When the child does not have landed immigrant status, the issue of residence is not as easily resolved. Problems can arise in determining whether a child in Canada under the authority of a visitor's visa or Minister's permit is a resident for the purpose of the province's adoption legislation.

---

[38] *Re British Columbia Birth Registration No. 77–09–004–368* (1988), 18 R.F.L. (3d) 222.

Assessment of the Potential Adopter

Home assessments are essentially investigations into an individual's fitness to adopt and may be undertaken only by those persons approved by the provincial child protection agency for that purpose. As a general rule, responsibility is given to those trained in social work assessment and theory. Assessing the suitability of a person wishing to adopt a child is the central task of the home assessment process.

In Manitoba, for example, individuals apply to an adoption agency, which in turn ascertains the person's suitability as a potential adopting parent. If suitability is established, the agency forwards relevant details to the Provincial Director, who enters the names and particulars on a central adoption registry. The agency may then recommend that applicants entered in the central registry be permitted to adopt a particular child. If the Director approves, the agency may then place a child with the applicant.

Other provinces, such as Ontario, do not maintain a central register of applicants, but allow approved adoption agencies to establish their own lists of approved adoptees. The agencies then consult one another to suitably match a child with an adopting family.

The central question for professional staff selecting a potential adoptive parent is whether the person can create and sustain a parent-child relationship. The following tangible parental characteristics are typically identified in the legislation:

- ability to financially maintain and educate the child;
- adulthood, or in its absence, demonstration of special circumstances to justify the adoption;
- a sufficient age gap between the prospective adopter and the child to effectively simulate the parent-child relationship. In Newfoundland, for example, this age gap must be at least 25 years, unless the consent of the Director is obtained; and
- special circumstances in some provinces, if the adoption will result in the single parenthood of the child.

More difficult qualities to assess are the intangibles, the most significant of which include the individual's understanding of and commitment to the uniqueness of the adoptive parenting role. It requires an assessment of the prospective adopting parent's ability and commitment to accept the child's reality, and to explain the adoption with an understanding of the child's ability and need to understand it at various stages of maturity.

Selection of Adoptive Parents

The process that ultimately leads to the selection of an appropriate adoptive family for a child is complex. It involves matching the parents' fitness to assume parenting responsibilities for a child not born to them with the child's suitability for such parenting. It is, in a sense, simulating a role, usually reserved for nature. It is an awesome responsibility.

It is essential to dispel any myths that the prospective adoptive parents bring to the process and to ensure that they understand and appreciate both the short- and, more importantly, the long-term consequences of adopting a child. In particular, prospective adopters need to know that:

- Children who cease to be the legal offspring of their biological families at the date of the adoption order may nonetheless keep them very much alive, even if only in the far reaches of their minds.
- Provincial adoption legislation may preserve cultural rights children have, particularly aboriginal rights.
- Children gain a right to inherit from and through the adoptive parents and their kindred, unless specifically excluded by the terms of their last will.
- The secrecy of the child's pre-adoptive identity may dissolve when the child reaches adulthood.
- The prospect of reunification through provincial disclosure mechanisms that have emerged in the last decade may also attract other members wishing to seek out the adoptee.
- Adoption does not have the sophistication to rework life, despite the law's presumptuous pronouncement of rebirth, which for example includes listing the adoptive mother on the child's birth certificate as if she physically bore the child.

A decade ago, the two sets of parents never met prior to an adoption if the intermediary was a child protection agency, (e.g., a Children's Aid Society in Ontario), and only seldom met in the case of an adoption arranged through some other intermediary. Now the practice in some provinces is to permit such meetings if the adoptive parents are willing and no identifying information is disclosed.[39]

The Children's Aid Society of Metropolitan Toronto, for example, will arrange for a meeting between the birth parents who are relinquishing and the adoptive parents who are receiving the child, to allow them to convey to one another what is important to them in the adoption process. The birth parent may, for example, have prepared a letter to be given to the child and discussed later if the child raises questions about the birth parent's inability to care for the child. The prospective adoptive parents may agree to provide the birth parent with periodic photographs or updates on the child. Such meetings can be pivotal for adoptive parents in ensuring that the reality of the child and his history are kept firmly in mind, and can give a measure of peace to a birth parent who wishes to

---

[39] Some private adoption agencies, at least in the United States, are experimenting with an even more "open adoption" process that, for example, involves the exchange of identifying information and permits for occasional visits between the birth parents and the adoptive family. See L. Caplan, "A Reporter at Large: An Open Adoption, Part I" (21 May 1990) The New Yorker 40, and "Part II" (28 May 1990) The New Yorker 73.

be assured that the child goes into an adoption in which the parental wishes for the child will be conveyed directly to those who will raise the child.

THE PLACEMENT PROCESS

Placement and Probation

Placement of a child for adoption can involve an "actual" or "deemed" placement. With an "actual" placement the agency with responsibility for the child reviews the applicants and selects the parents who are considered most likely to provide stability and support; to some extent, the length of time that the applicants have been in the queue will be a factor, but a placement decision is never based solely on "waiting in line". Some agencies in Canada have recently begun to give birth parents a role in selecting among suitable applicants, without providing identifying information. After the agency selects the applicants, and confirms their interest, the child is placed in their home and the adoption probationary period begins. A "deemed placement" refers to the crystallization of a decision that a child will be adopted after having been initially placed in a home on a different understanding.[40] This occurs when foster parents receive approval to adopt a child already in their home on foster placement. The placement process is usually acknowledged by the signing of a written document by adoptive applicants and witnessed by the placing agency or licensee.

Adoption probation is the process following the child's placement with the selected family. The central goal of adoption probation is the attachment of the child to the adoptive parents and other family members and the bonding of the adoptive parent to the child. Thus, adoption probation prohibits making an adoption order when the child is initially placed for adoption. In the case of a child placed with strangers, it is the law's most outwardly visible acknowledgement that the security for the child intended by the placement has a fragility that can gain strength only with careful and committed nurturing.

The usual time for the adoption probation is 6 months, but the period may be lengthened or shortened to meet the particular circumstances of the child and family. If, for example, the child is being adopted by the foster parents, adoption probation may be waived altogether, since there is already a basis upon which to measure the extent to which the child and prospective adopters have bonded. On the other hand, it is not unusual for adoption probation to extend to a full year in the case of an older child who is being adopted by strangers, if the child needs the additional time to throw off the emotional baggage that has been carried from pre-adoptive life.

If the child is being adopted by a relative or a stepparent, legislation in most provinces does not require a probationary period, on the reasoning that the child is already a part of the adoptive family. However, if at the time that the relative

---

[40] See *Catholic Children's Aid Society of Metropolitan Toronto* v. *T. S. et al.*, (1989), 20 R.F.L. (3d) 337 (Ont. C.A.).

or stepparent seeks the adoption order the court has concerns about the child's adjustment to the adoptive family, the court may adjourn the application and order an investigation and assessment of the child's situation by the provincial child welfare authority. The report prepared for the court as a result of this investigation assists the presiding judge in determining whether the adoption is in the child's best interests.

Adoption probation is generally supervised by a social worker designated by the provincial child welfare authority to monitor and support the new family unit. That social worker will ultimately prepare a report for the court outlining the child's adjustment to the adoptive family and the family's adjustment to the child. Ontario's legislation, for example, requires a formal written report recommending whether the court should finalize the adoption in any case where the child is less than 16 years of age and is not being adopted by a relative or stepparent.

What should be subjected to precise assessment during the probationary period depends on the particular circumstances of each case. Typically, the social worker considers the characteristics of both the child and the adoptive parents, and addresses those factors that will provide the court with information to satisfy it that finalization of the adoption is in the child's best interests. The factors that are usually considered in an assessment of probation are:

- the extent to which the prospective adoptive parents are meeting the child's physical, mental and emotional needs;
- the extent to which the parents recognize and accept the child's physical, mental and emotional levels of development;
- the extent to which the child is developing a positive relationship with the adopting parents, siblings and extended family, and establishing a secure place as a member of the adoptive family;
- the extent to which the child has been able to let go of prior relationships;
- the extent to which the adoptive family is providing the child with continuity of care;
- the extent to which the child's cultural background and religious faith is respected and nurtured within the adoptive family;
- the child's views and wishes about the adoption, in whatever verbal or nonverbal manner that they are communicated;
- the extent to which the child is ready to have the adoption finalized; and,
- the extent to which the adoptive parents show themselves able to accept the child as an individual in his or her own right, not made in their image or there to satisfy their needs.

A Manitoba court recently had to consider the appropriateness of permitting a protection agency to intervene in a private adoption proceeding in which the court was being asked by the applicants to ignore the agency's homestudy report disapproving of the biological mother's choice of adoptive parents for her child.[41] The agency's request for intervenor status was opposed by both the prospective adoptive parents and the mother. The court permitted the agency to intervene in the court proceeding on the basis that the agency might be able to assist the court in a way that the parties might not. The court felt that it was unreasonable to expect the applicants to call evidence which, by its nature, might be detrimental to their case. The court also determined that the intervenor would not delay the litigation.

Protection of the Placement

The laws of most provinces attempt to shelter the newly formed family from interference from the child's birth family. This is considered to be the best means of ensuring a safe and secure environment for the child and new family as they integrate.[42] In Ontario, any interference with a child placed for adoption is an offence under the statute. As indicated earlier, once the child is placed for adoption, most provinces prohibit any applications by a birth parent for return of the child.

Guardianship of the Child During Placement: Interim Guardianship

Legislative provisions specifying who has the legal right and responsibility for decisions related to the child during the adoption probation period vary between the provinces. In British Columbia, for example, once the child is surrendered by the birth parents to the Superintendent of Child Welfare, guardianship of the child transfers to the Superintendent. Guardianship of the child's estate transfers by operation of law to the Public Trustee.

In Ontario, rights and responsibilities rest in the placing agency or licensee, once all parental consents to the child's adoption are signed and the 21-day period for cancellation has passed without incident. The adoptive parents do not have the legal right and responsibility for decisions related to the child during the adoption probation period, except insofar as the agency or licensee with guardianship responsibility delegates authority to them. (e.g., permission to take the child out of the country on vacation, authority to make medical care decisions, etc.).

Interim guardianship orders are sometimes granted to prospective adoptive parents if the prospective adoptive parents wish to secure the child's custody from others during the adoption probation period, and the court considering an adoption application is not satisfied that the adoption should be finalized at a particular point in time.

---

[41] *D.D.W. and D.D.W.* v. *V.M.* (1988), 17 R.F.L. (3d) 292 (Man. Q.B. - Fam. Div.).

[42] See, for example *C.G.W.* v. *M.J. and A.C.* (1981), 24 R.F.L. (2d) 342 (Ont. C.A.).

FINALIZATION: THE ADOPTION ORDER

The process of relinquishment and acquisition come together in the application that is made to the court at the conclusion of the adoption probation period to finalize the adoption. Each provincial adoption statute specifies which level of court has authority to finalize adoptions. In most provinces, the court with jurisdiction over child protection matters also has responsibility for adoption; in Ontario this is the Provincial Court (Family Division).

The course of the proceeding depends on the type of adoption, especially on whether the child is being adopted by applicants who are, and are intended to remain, unknown to his/her birth family. In such cases, the legal process ensures that the identity of the adoptive family is protected. The hearing, which will result in the presentation of a new status binding on the world, is a private one.

Most provinces require the child's birth identity to be supplanted by his birth registration number on the adoption application and on the order itself. The documents relating to the adoption application which reveal the child's biological parentage are kept confidential, for example in a sealed envelope in court files, and cannot be disclosed without a court order. In cases where the birth identity is known to the adoptive applicants and the birth family is actively involved in the adoption (e.g., adoption by a relative or stepparent), such secrecy is meaningless. The judge may finalize the adoption in Chambers (i.e., the judge's office) on simple scrutiny of the evidentiary documents filed in support of the adoption order.

In Ontario a formal hearing is not a strict necessity if the application is not opposed and the supporting documents are in order, unless issues are raised regarding notice of the application or consents to the adoption, or the court is of the opinion that the child should be heard on the issue of the capacity to appreciate the nature of the application.[43]

Notice of the Adoption Hearing

In some provinces, such as Ontario, legislation specifies that a person who has consented to adoption is not entitled to notice of the adoption hearing. In some provinces, the courts have ruled that the absence of a specific provision in the statute directing that notice is not to be given, means that it must be given to persons who gave consent to the adoption or whose consent is to be dispensed with by court order. The rationale is that these persons have a right to ask the court to permit withdrawal of their consents up to and including the date of the hearing.

---

[43] *Re M.L.A. and three other applications* (1979), 25 O.R. (2d) 779 (Ont. Prov. Ct - Fam. Div.), Beaulieu P.C.J.

Notwithstanding a provision in Alberta's *Domestic Relations Act*,[44] stipulating that the mother of a child born outside marriage is the child's sole guardian, and the silence of Alberta's *Child Welfare Act*, on whether notice of adoption proceedings is to be given to the biological father of a child born out of wedlock, the court ruled that the province's adoption scheme did not exclude this father's entitlement to notice of the proceeding:

> ... an adoption order should be predicated on the welfare and interests of the child. The continuing presence of the biological father and his interest in and willingness to support the child, as here, must surely be weighed in that process.

> I do not wish to be taken as deciding that notice to biological fathers must be given in all proposed adoptions. The worth of such a requirement would have to be resolved in the legislative arena, having regard to the need for finality in these matters, the interests of mother, child, and biological father and, not the least, those of the adopting parents.

> But where Social Services has information that the biological father remains a real presence in the life of the proposed adoptee, that information must be accurately conveyed to the chambers judge in order that an informed decision concerning the giving, or dispensation, of notice can be taken. The judge may require further information such as additional affidavit evidence, additional investigation by Social Services or perhaps an appearance of the mother. The problem would not arise where the father or his whereabouts are unknown, or where he has never evinced interest in the welfare of the child. But that is not the case here.[45]

British Columbia's adoption law requires notice of the adoption application to be given to any parent who has consented to the child's adoption or to any parent whose consent has been dispensed with, only if the parent has a court order preserving a right of access. However, jurisprudence in that province has required applicants for an adoption order to disclose the identity of other persons who might be interested in the adoption application. This enables the judge to direct notice if none has been given.[46] This requires identification and notice to a person with a right of access by order or by agreement, a parent in whose home the child has lived and any other person who has shown an ongoing interest in the child, and provides the court with a way of ensuring that the child will not be deprived of contact with a prior significant care giver, if that person comes forward with a plan that promotes the child's best interests more than the proposed adoption.[47]

---

[44] R.S.A. 1980, c. D–37, s. 47.

[45] *H.J.L.* v. *L.A. and R.D.A.* (1986), 1 R.F.L. (3d) 395 at 399 (Alta C.A.).

[46] *Re British Columbia Birth Registration 84–09–044294* (1986), 5 R.F.L. (3d) 302 (B.C.S.C.), Spencer J.

[47] See *E.S.* v. *Minister of Social Services* (1983), 35 R.F.L. (2d) 213 (Sask. C.A.); *S.* v. *Minister of Social Services* (1983), 33 R.F.L. (2d) 1 (Sask. C.A.).

Where a parent is entitled by law to formal notice of the adoption hearing and cannot be located, the court may waive the statute's notice requirement, thus paving the way for the adoption application to be heard on its merits. The court must be satisfied, before dispensing with the requirement of notice, that a reasonable attempt has been made to locate and provide notice to the missing parent and may order "substituted" service of the notice, for example, by a newspaper advertisement or sending notice to a relative of the parent.

The Child's Participation in the Hearing

Most provincial statutes permit the child who is the subject of the application to be present at the adoption hearing. Some provinces require the court to satisfy itself that the child understands and appreciates the nature and consequences of the adoption. For example, the statutes of New Brunswick and Manitoba require the court to consider the wishes of a child where the court considers it "appropriate and feasible."

The Manitoba Court of Appeal condemned a trial judge's practice of allowing the opinions or feelings of a 7-year-old child who was the subject of the adoption application to be made known to the court through the mouth of one or other of the parents.[48]

The Child's Consent to Adoption

Except in Ontario, where the statutory age is 7 years, all children 12 years of age and over who are the subject of adoption proceedings have a right to give consent to their adoption, unless the court dispenses with their consent. In order to maximize the child's opportunity to make a choice about something that is already understood by the child, it is usual to wait until some time late in the adoption probationary period before formally discussing the issue with the child. Good social work practice requires that prior to any placement for adoption the prospective adoption should be discussed with the child, in accordance with the child's capacity to appreciate the circumstances and communicate. In Ontario, the child's consent must be witnessed by a social worker authorized by a Children's Aid Society to witness adoption consents. The role of that social worker is to ensure that the child: (a) is able to understand and appreciate the consequences of the adoption; (b) gives the consent freely, without fear of punishment or promise of reward; and (c) has sufficient information, explained in appropriate language, to weigh the alternatives that are available.

---

[48] *McCullagh and McCullagh* v. *Flannery* (1986), 49 R.F.L. (2d) 155 (Man. C.A.), Huband J.A.

Dispensing With the Child's Consent

All provinces provide a statutory mechanism to dispense with the child's consent to the adoption. The test varies from province to province, but typically focuses on the appropriateness of such exclusion of the child from participation in the adoption process when the statute gives him that specific right.

An Ontario court ruled that the right of a 12-year-old boy to know his true origins should give rise to a substantial onus on the applicants to show why that right should be withheld from him. In that case, the reason advanced for dispensing with the child's consent was that the child already believed that the adoptive applicant (mother's spouse) was his father. The mother had withheld from him the true facts of his paternity, and he would discover this fact if his consent was sought.

The court considered the importance of evidence attesting to a child's particular sensitivity and vulnerabilities and was not prepared to rely solely on the parent's opinion that the child was not ready for the information about his true origins. Judge Nasmith did, however, dispense with the child's consent, for essentially the following reasons:

1. the parents [had] convinced [the court] through affidavit evidence and subsequently through *viva voce* evidence that they sincerely believed that the child [was] particularly sensitive and vulnerable at [that] time and would be devastated if he learned the truth about his natural father; and,

2. the correct information if given would be that the psychological father is not the natural father and it would not be possible to identify the natural father or to make constructive use of the information.[49]

The Test for Finalization: Making the Adoption Order

The first duty of the presiding judge is to be satisfied that the statutory requirements (e.g., those pertaining to residence and age of the prospective adopters) have been met. The next duty is to be satisfied that the adoption order is in the child's best interests. The latter is essentially a judge's scrutiny of the processes that have now come together before the court in support of an order securing the newly formed family unit against the world. The burden of satisfying the court rests with those who seek the adoption order.

In Ontario, the court charged with hearing the adoption application must also examine the relinquishing documents to satisfy itself that the interests of the child's birth parents were properly protected and that those persons who signed consent to the child's adoption understood the nature and effect of it. The report on the child's adjustment to the adoptive family that is prepared by the social worker designated to monitor the probationary period is a critical (although not necessarily determining) piece of evidence considered by the court.

---

[49] *Re the Adoption of "A"*, (1980), 3 F.L.R.R. 47 (Ont. Prov. Ct - Fam. Div.), Nasmith P.C.J.

Appeal and Annulments

The rights of appeal in the case of an adoption are strictly circumscribed by the provincial statute. For example, s. 150 of Ontario's *Child and Family Services Act*[50] specifically provides the right to appeal a decision granting or refusing an adoption order, but requires it to be launched within 30 days of the original decision. No extension of that time period may be permitted. The appeal is to the District Court, with the possibility of a further appeal to the Ontario Court of Appeal. As with most other types of appeals, there is not an actual rehearing of the case, but instead a review of the record that was before the judge who made the decision. The essential task of the appeal court is to determine whether the lower court judge made an error in law. New evidence may be introduced at the appeal level only if the provincial statute permits it, and even then, the introduction of new material is usually left to the discretion of the appeal court. The appeal court will be most reluctant to overturn the decision of a trial judge who had the opportunity to see all of the participants in person, and will only overturn the decision if there clearly was an error in the lower court's application of the relevant law.

In addition to the possibility of appealing a decision in regard to adoption, some provinces permit application for an annulment, or revocation, of the original order. An annulment is a declaration from a court that the original order is invalid because there was a fatal defect in making the original order. Arguably, in some situations an application for annulment can be made at any time, though some statutes specifically limit the time for making such an application. Some provinces, such as Alberta and Nova Scotia, have legislation specifically dealing with annulment of an adoption order. In other provinces, it appears that courts might have an inherent power to grant an annulment, for example, if parental consent to an adoption was obtained through fraud or duress.

In a recent Alberta case, the Court of Appeal set aside an adoption order of a 5-year-old child on application by the child's putative birth father, because the child's mother and her new husband had not given complete information to the social worker who had prepared a report for the court in support of the adoption.[51] They had not disclosed the real history and extent of the relationship between the child's mother and father, had not told the worker that a court order had given him access and that he had abided by its terms when allowed to do so, and had misled the court by not informing it that the biological father had stopped his support payments because he had been advised in writing by provincial Social Services that the mother's marriage meant that he was no longer responsible for maintenance of the child.

---

[50] S.O. 1984, c. 55, s. 150.

[51] *H.J.L.* v. *L.A. and R.D.A.*, *supra*, note 46.

It should be noted that, unless there are grounds for an appeal or annulment, an adoption order, once made, cannot be rescinded. In *Re Chappell and the Superintendent of Child Welfare*,[52] a 22-year-old man sought to have an adoption order made when he was 4 years old rescinded. The adoption placement was not successful, and at the age of 10 years he moved out of his adoptive home and began a series of placements in the care of the child welfare authorities and in training schools. At the age of 20 he located his natural mother, resumed a relationship with her, and adopted her surname. The young man, the natural mother, the adoptive parents and the child welfare authorities all agreed that it would be in the young man's best interests to have the initial order rescinded, but the court simply found that it lacked the jurisdiction to do so.

RELATIVE AND STEPPARENT ADOPTIONS

Different social and legal considerations arise when a child is to be adopted by a relative or stepparent than when the adoption is by a stranger and arranged through an intermediary or by a child protection agency. Although no national statistics are available, it is clear that a significant portion of all adoptions involve stepparents and relatives, perhaps as many as half of all adoptions.

In a number of jurisdictions there are special statutory provisions governing this type of adoption. The provincial statute typically specifies the classes of persons who qualify as relatives or stepparents for the purpose of such adoptions. For example, in Ontario if there is a proposed adoption by a relative of the child, or a spouse of the child's parent, the application can be made without the necessity of a homestudy. In such intrafamilial adoptions, there is no need for a probationary period before the application is made (although a court may order one at the hearing).

Applicants in stepparent adoptions typically assert that a number of benefits will accrue to the child through adoption. First, it is argued that a legal change in the child's surname will simplify life in terms of records and all the other documentary and statistical requirements facing all citizens as they progress through life. It is also argued that adoption will stabilize and finalize the circumstances of the child's environment. Thus, for example, if something were to happen to the natural mother, the stepfather would be the guardian of the child and the new family would not be split up; there would be no uncertainty as to the custody of the child. The adoptive parent will also be able to give parental consent for such things as hospitalization of the child. The child can inherit the adoptive parent's estate without the need for a will, and the child's wishes for the stepparent to become his or her legal parent would be formalized. Finally, any contact by the children with the noncustodial natural parent will be subject to the control of the custodial parent and stepparent.

In deciding whether to grant an adoption order in favour of a stepparent, the courts typically consider:

---

[52] (1977), 81 D.L.R. (3d) 643 (B.C.S.C.).

- the extent to which the child has experienced any difficulty using a surname different from the mother's;
- whether the child has expressed any desire to keep his or her surname;
- whether the child has expressed any desire to maintain ongoing contact with the noncustodial birth parent;
- whether there has been, or is likely to be, any practical difficulty (as opposed to awkwardness) with, for example, consent to hospitalization remaining with the custodial parent and not the new spouse;
- the fact that the matter of inheritance can be resolved by writing a will to provide for the child;
- the extent to which the bond between the new spouse and the children would be practically affected by granting or refusing an adoption order;
- the concern that an adoption order could completely sever the relationship between the noncustodial natural parent and the child;
- the extent to which the noncustodial parent has shown genuine interest in maintaining contact with the child (even if contact has been lost for a while and the natural parent is now trying to rekindle the relationship);
- whether the noncustodial parent would be denied access if it was applied for. (Abdication of access rights is not enough. The test is whether past shortcomings would preclude rekindling of the relationship with the child.); and,
- the child's present relationship with the noncustodial parent.

The court is particularly wary of recent marriages that have not, at the time of application, existed for a reasonable period of time. The courts are also cognizant of provisions in general custody legislation that permit a stepparent to apply for custody of the child if circumstances warrant, for example, in the case of the custodial parent's death or incapacitating illness.

It is interesting to note that in cases where a woman with children has remarried and the stepfather does not want to adopt the children, or cannot adopt them, the children will sometimes use their stepfather's last name. Such a change of name may be the result of a formal, legal name change, or may simply result from the informal use of the stepfather's surname, for example, when registering for school. The effect of such a name change is to present the community with the impression that the stepfather is the legal father of the child, either as a result of adoption or from birth. The attitude of the courts to such a change of name, affecting the appearance of a change in status, is somewhat mixed. Though in some jurisdictions an injunction might be granted to prevent a change of name, particularly if the natural father continues to see the children and contribute to their support, the courts have often been prepared to allow such a change of name. Further, in some jurisdictions, such as Ontario, a custodial parent may be able to change a child's surname without the other parent's consent, in the absence of a court order or agreement requiring such consent.

EFFECTS OF ADOPTION

Changing the Child's Name

The general rule in all provinces is that the child assumes the surname of the adopting parents unless the court orders otherwise. Some provinces give the child no statutory say in changing either his of her given name or surname at the time of the adoption order. In New Brunswick, Ontario and Alberta, at the time of adoption the court may change the given name of a child 12 years of age or over only with that child's consent. In New Brunswick, the court must be satisfied that the change is being made with the child's knowledge and agreement, insofar as the child's wishes can be ascertained.

Changing the Child's Status

For almost all purposes adoption creates a new status for the adoptee and adoptive parents. The effect of an adoption order is to terminate both the natural parents' rights to custody of their child and their duty to support their child, while at the same time giving the adoptive parents the right of custody and the responsibility of support.

In any will or other document, a reference to a person or group of persons shall be deemed to include a person who has acquired status by adoption, unless such an inference is expressly excluded. Thus, if a man in his will leaves his estate "to my nephews," this includes the adopted son of the man's brother. Also, adopted children acquire all of the rights to inherit property upon intestacy (if a person dies without a will), which they would have if they were biologically related children, unless the legislation specifically removes this right of inheritance. For example, New Brunswick's *Adoption Act* provides that for inheritance purposes only some of the closest kindred relationships will be legally created by adoption, such as brother and sister, but others, such as nephew and grandchild, will not be created.

Post-Adoption Contact

The door shut at placement is locked on the date of the adoption order. Behind it is sealed and sheltered all identifying information pertaining to the adoption, whether filed with the court or housed within provincial government offices or agencies involved in the adoption process. The keys to access are held by the authority responsible for maintaining the province's adoption records.

In addition, the wall that is put around the adoption placement to separate and shield the child and the adopting parents from the birth family becomes virtually impenetrable after the court orders the adoption. In Newfoundland, for example, the court has the discretion to order that the adopted child's place of birth be changed on any substituted birth registration so that the adoptive parents can appear to have physically given birth to the child. This confidentiality barrier becomes firmly established once an adoption is finalized, yet it generates considerable controversy with respect to the concerned parties' rights of access both to each other and to adoption records.

One of the thorniest issues facing adoption in the past decade is the extent to which a pre-existing right of access can survive an adoption order, or whether the court can attach an access order to the adoption itself. In most jurisdictions the legislation does not distinguish between adoption by strangers, where there will usually be no ties with the past, and adoption by a stepparent or relative where there might well be ties with a former parent and others (e.g., grandparents). This makes the issue particularly difficult. When a child has been adopted by persons unknown to the natural parents, for example, in an adoption arranged by an agency, it is easy to appreciate that allowing the natural parents access could be most disruptive. On the other hand, in the case of adoption by a stepparent or relative, allowing a natural parent access might sometimes be appropriate.

Although the law has evolved in the last decade, this issue has not been fully settled. Some judges have held that there is nothing inconsistent between the child's adoption and the continuing right of access for a parent whose rights have been terminated by the adoption order itself. Typical of the ongoing attempt to provide the child with both adoption and continuing access is a 1986 decision of the British Columbia Court of Appeal which held that a pre-existing access order in favour of one person does not bar the granting of an adoption order in favour of another person, but an adoption order has the effect of terminating a pre-existing right of access, unless the judge granting the adoption exercises his discretion to make an access order or order that an outstanding order continue in force.[53] The court's rationale hinged on its consideration of access as a benefit for the child, rather than a right given to the parent; the court was prepared to exercise inherent jurisdiction to fill a gap in British Columbia's legislation, which was silent on the point.

Other courts continue to rule that ongoing contact between child and birth parent is an unjustified interference with the adoptive parent's role, and that the courts have no jurisdiction to diminish the rights granted by an adoption order by granting a right of access to another person over the objections of the adopting parents.

In Ontario, an access order attached to an adoption is not permitted. Any access order granted in preceding child protection proceedings must be terminated before the child is placed for adoption, and a judge has no authority to make a permanent wardship order on the understanding or anticipation that the

[53] *Re Alberta Birth Registration 78–08–022716* (1986), 1 R.F.L. (3d) 1 (B.C.C.A.), Seaton J.A.

prospective adoptive parents will allow birth family members access to the child after the adoption.

Ontario's case law indicates that an adoption order should not be made if continuing access to birth parents would be of significant benefit to the child. If, on the other hand, adoption is more important to the overall welfare of the child, then the child should be free of the complications that may be caused by continued involvement of the birth family in the child's life.[54]

Although probably not legally enforceable, post-adoption access in Ontario is possible if an agreement is worked out between the adoptive parents and birth family members. Such an arrangement probably makes the birth family dependent upon the adoptive parents not changing their minds although it also may expose the adoptive parents to future access or custody litigation if the birth family member attempts to pursue such a claim through the courts. For these reasons, such arrangements should be entered into with caution.

Ontario's legislative prohibition of a post-adoption access order has survived an attack under sections 2, 7 and 15 of the *Canadian Charter of Rights and Freedoms*.[55] Ontario's Court of Appeal has ruled that the *Charter's* protections of freedom of association under section 2(d) does not extend to the protection of family relationships, but is restricted to associations outside the family circle. Thus the adoptive parents have the exclusive right to associate with the adopted child, as is the case in any natural family.

Ontario's Court of Appeal has also ruled that termination of access to a permanent ward in order to free the child for adoption does not deprive the birth parent of life, liberty or security of the person as contemplated by s. 7 of the *Charter*. The Court further held that denying birth parents the possibility to seek access to their children in the situation of adoption, even though they can seek access in other circumstances, did not constitute unjustified discrimination and hence did not violate s. 15 of the *Charter*.

An access order can be sought after an adoption order has been made, if the province's statute governing general custody and access matters is wide enough to give the person standing to apply. The position taken by the British Columbia Court of Appeal is that an adoption order gives the adoptive parents no greater or lesser right than the natural parents to resist an application on the basis of status.[56]

---

[54] See *Catholic Children's Aid Society of Metropolitan Toronto* v. *T.S. et al., supra*, note 40. Upholding Lissaman D.C.J., in *Re J.S. and C.S.; Catholic Children's Aid Society of Metropolitan Toronto* (1987), 10 R.F.L. (3d) 343 and overturning Nasmith P.C.J. in *Re J. and C.; Catholic Children's Aid Society of Metropolitan Toronto* v. *S. and S.* (1985), 48 R.F.L. (2d) 371 (Ont. Prov. Ct).

[55] *Supra*, note 21; *Catholic Children's Aid Society* v. *T. S. et al., supra*, note 40.

[56] *Bosworth* v. *Cochrane*, [1984] 2 W.W.R. 86 (B.C.S.C.).

Disclosure of Information

One of the most controversial issues in the adoption field is whether adopted children should have the right to know the identity of their natural parents, and to meet them. Both sides of this question were addressed in *Lyttle* v. *C.A.S. of Metropolitan Toronto*.

> There can surely be no doubt but that any child, knowing he has been adopted, will be curious about his origins ... there is more than mere curiosity but a basic, if sometimes unexpressed, need for a child, who knows he has been adopted, to get in touch with his natural parents. This need becomes most apparent during early adolescence. To know who his real parents are gives a child a sense of identity, an assurance of belonging, and an awareness that he has not come from nowhere, but has his own place in history as the child of known parents ...
>
> On the other hand, the sense of security of the child in his new home ought not to be disturbed readily. He must continue to know that this is indeed his home; that he is entitled to demand the loyalty of his new parents and that he is obliged to give them his loyalty in return. That sense of security and loyalty would be diminished if the adopting parents felt that a natural parent could interfere with the affection of the child, or their authority over him. They might feel that they were mere custodians of the child, with less than ordinary parental rights and responsibilities. Another factor, of general public policy, which I think is almost conclusive with children's aid societies, is that prospective adopting parents would be more difficult to find if they were generally aware that natural parents might be permitted to regain contact with adopted children.[57]

There are two kinds of information that participants in the adoption process may be interested in: identifying and non-identifying. Identifying information includes names, addresses or other information that could permit the identification of a person involved in the process. Non-identifying information that an adoptee might want would include the reasons that the adoption occurred, a medical history of the birth parents, and some general information about the background of the biological family. Birth parents may be interested in such non-identifying information as learning about the child's progress in school, sports or a career; birth parents may want periodic updates of this type of information. In general, the laws governing disclosure of identifying information are much stricter than those governing disclosure of non-identifying information.

In some jurisdictions the disclosure of non-identifying information is governed by policies of agencies involved, while in others, it is a matter of statutory guidance.[58] Some non-identifying information is provided to the adults involved at the time of the placement, in particular, related to the medical history of the birth parents. If the adoptee seeks out further non-identifying information, for

---

[57] (1976), 24 R.F.L. 134 at 136 (Ont. H.C.), Weatherston J.

[58] See, e.g., *Child and Family Services Act*, S.O. 1984, c. 55, s. 158b, as amended by S.O. 1987, c. 4.

example relating to the reasons for the adoption, it can be provided with the consent of the adoptive parents until the adoptee reaches adulthood when this consent is no longer required.

The release of identifying information is accomplished only pursuant to a strict set of statutory controls designed to ensure that the rights of privacy are respected for those participants to the adoption who wish to remain unidentified. Thus, as a general rule, identifying information is released from adoption records only if all persons to be identified agree in writing that it ought to happen.

The movement towards increased disclosure of information between adoptee and birth parents has led to some political controversy. Most provinces were slow to introduce legislation to deal with the problem. In 1976, a scheme to provide adopted children with information about their natural parents was introduced in Britain. In a close vote, a similar scheme was adopted by the Ontario Legislature in 1978.

The original Ontario scheme permitted release of identifying information only if a birth parent and an adult adoptee entered their names on the Adoption Disclosure Register and there was a "match". Further under the original scheme, the consent of the adoptive parents was required for the disclosure of identifying information, even though the adoptee had reached adulthood. The requirement for the consent of adoptive parents was a significant hurdle for some while very few adoptive parents refused to consent; many adoptees were reluctant to seek their adoptive parents' consent because they did not want their search to be interpreted as rejection of the adoptive family. After considerable debate, the Ontario legislation deleted the requirement for the consent of adoptive parents, leaving the disclosure of identifying information essentially an issue between the adoptee and birth family members. The new scheme came into effect in 1988, and provides that there ordinarily will only be a release of identifying information if an adult adoptee and a birth parent (or a birth grandparent or sibling) register and there is a "match". The new Ontario scheme requires that if an adoptee has registered but the birth parent has not, there must be a "discrete and reasonable search" to contact that person and ask whether the birth parents will consent to having their identity revealed.

The revised Ontario legislation also permits release without the consent of birth parents, if, in the opinion of the Registrar at the Adoption Disclosure Register, the health, safety or welfare of a person requires such disclosure. Further, the disclosure of identifying information may be refused if it is believed that this might "result in serious physical or emotional harm to any person", though the refusal may be appealed to an independent Board.

Once identifying information is disclosed, the parties are free to arrange a meeting, though the child protection authorities have the responsibility to provide counselling to all concerned before the information is disclosed. While the

Ontario legislative scheme is the most comprehensive in Canada,[59] a number of other provinces, including Manitoba and British Columbia, have established somewhat similar adoption registers.

In the absence of express legislative provision, most courts have been careful to guard the confidentiality of the birth family when asked by an adopted child to open court records related to the adoption. Typical is a decision of the Ontario Court of Appeal in 1983, refusing a 55-year-old woman the right to inspect documents related to her adoption, on the basis that her curiosity about her origins was not important enough either to outweigh the rights of the other parties to the adoption to confidentiality, or to jeopardize the province's interest in maintaining the integrity of its adoption system by preventing such access, except through the mechanism of the Provincial Adoption Disclosure Register. The Court also ruled that Ontario's statutory provision preventing the adoptee's inspection of adoption documents did not violate the adoptee's rights under the *Canadian Charter of Rights and Freedoms.*[60]

The best interests of the child governs a court decision to grant a birth parent's application for an order that an adoption file be opened for inspection. In the absence of evidence addressing the impact of such opening on the adopted child, the court does not assume that the adopted child will benefit.

In a recent Ontario case,[61] the court considered not only the birth mother's desire to make contact with her child, but also the fact that her child was now of university age, and might have had no curiosity about his natural mother, in which case any inquiry or communication could come to him as "brutal surprise."[62] The child welfare agency had provided the natural mother with a detailed and positive report, containing non-identifying information that ought to have allayed her concerns about her son's welfare and his adoptive family. The natural mother had also registered with the Provincial Adoption Disclosure Registry, and if the applicant's adopted son developed any curiosity about his roots and his natural mother, he would be free to register also, at which time a meeting could be arranged. In the court's opinion, that was the extent of the remedy available to the birth parent.

SURROGATE MOTHERHOOD

A branch that has grown out of adoption law in the absence of any statutory law to address the issue is surrogate motherhood, although one can trace its roots to Old Testament times. The arrangement basically involves a woman agreeing

---

[59] Enacted by S.O. 1987, c. 4, s. 7; now found in the Ontario *Child and Family Services Act,* S.O. 1984, c. 55, ss. 157–158j.

[60] *Ferguson* v. *Director of Child Welfare, Minister of Community and Social Services* (1984), 36 R.F.L. (2d) 405 (Ont. S.C.A.D.) See also *Re Adoption of B.A.* (1981), 17 R.F.L. (2d) 140 (Man. Co. Ct).

[61] *Tyler* v. *District Court of Ontario* (1986), 1 R.F.L. (3d) 140 (Ont. Dist. Ct).

[62] *Ibid.* at 140.

to be artificially inseminated by a man who is not her husband and then, at the child's birth, relinquishing all parental rights and responsibilities to him and his wife through adoption. The problem is that most surrogate parenting arrangements involve financial compensation of the woman who has agreed to bear the child, and agreements that involve payment of a fee in exchange for a consent to an adoption or a placement for adoption are illegal under provincial adoption legislation. This strict control of payments made in connection with an adoption creates a legal barrier for surrogate parenting contracts in Canada, since such arrangements involve an application for adoption by the wife of the biological father with the consent of the biological mother.

Surrogate motherhood is morally and politically controversial. In 1985 the Ontario Law Reform Commission issued a report proposing that the government legalize the practice, but closely regulate it, with the courts required to scrutinize any agreements before they are given legal effect to ensure that they are not unconscionable.[63] The Ontario government has failed to act on this report, and in the fall of 1989 the federal government established a Royal Commission to study a range of issues related to developments in reproductive technology, including surrogate motherhood.

American states have had a variety of responses to surrogate motherhood. Some have declared the practice illegal, either as a result of legislation or judicial decision. In a few states, however, the practice is legal, and it is apparent that some Canadians are going to the United States to execute and perform surrogate motherhood contracts under the supervision of American lawyers.

CONCLUSION

The institution of adoption has evolved enormously over the years. In ancient Rome it was intended to provide acceptable heirs for those without biological offspring. In the late 19th century, statutory adoption schemes were established to promote the welfare of orphaned infants and children born out of wedlock, and treated them as if they were born to their adoptive parents.

In recent years there have been many more stepparent adoptions and private intermediaries have become increasingly involved in arranging adoptions. On the other hand, with better birth control and more unwed mothers keeping their children, there have been fewer newborn infants available for adoption and an increasing tendency for older children to be placed for adoption. These developments have caused a reassessment of some of the accepted practices and laws. There is more thought given to post-adoption access and disclosure of information, and more recognition of the legal rights of all those involved in the process.

The adoptive relationship does not always succeed. In particular, with the onset of adolescence, and the common questions and challenges of that stage of

---

[63] There is a growing body of literature on surrogate motherhood. See, e.g., Ontario Law Reform Commission, *Report on Human Artificial Reproduction and Related Matters* (Toronto: 1985); and E. Faulkner, "The Case of Baby M." (1989) 3 C.J.W.L. 239.

life, the relationship sometimes breaks down, and children are placed in the care of a protection agency. However, many families experience difficulties with adolescence, and all problems in an adoptive family should not be blamed on adoption alone.

If a child is emotionally and legally free to be adopted and the adoptive parents are truly ready for life-long commitment to the child, the adoption process is often the best possible option for a child who cannot be cared for by the natural family members. When the chemistry works, and when the legal rights of the parties have been properly respected, the benefits to a child of a loving, committed substitute family make this the best possible permanency plan that society can offer.

8

ABORIGINAL CHILD WELFARE IN CANADA

Judge Murray Sinclair, *Donna Phillips*[†] *and Nicholas Bala*[‡]

INTRODUCTION

Child welfare practices have been a major factor in the deterioration of aboriginal cultures in Canada, on par with the residential school policies and the laws promulgated by the federal Department of Indian and Northern Affairs prohibiting the native potlatch custom. Aboriginal people have shown justified concern about the deterioration of their families, communities, values and customs as a result of the child welfare policies of Canadian governments.

One of the most obvious indicators of the deterioration in aboriginal cultures is that aboriginal children have been taken into the child welfare system in disproportionately large numbers. In some provinces, the majority of child apprehensions involve aboriginal children. The magnitude of the problem is apparent when one considers that children make up over half of the current aboriginal population, and that the aboriginal population continues to increase at a much faster rate than that of the general population.[1] To understand the underlying causes for the severe problems affecting large numbers of aboriginal children, one must consider such factors as cultural conflict and jurisdictional disputes between governments, as well as poverty and other socioeconomic problems.

Available evidence indicates that many aboriginal children who have become involved with the child welfare system at an early age have gone on to spend time in multiple foster placements, and later in young offender institutions and the adult correctional system. Aboriginal groups have expressed deep concerns that the pattern of apprehensions inhibits the development of these children as future contributing members of aboriginal communities, and that it has negative

* Associate Chief Judge, Provincial Court, and Co-Commissioner, Public Inquiry into the Administration of Justice and Aboriginal People, Winnipeg, Manitoba; Canada's second aboriginal judge.

† Research Assistant, Canadian Research Institute for Law and the Family, Calgary, Alberta.

‡ Professor, Faculty of Law, Queen's University, Kingston, Ontario.

1 1986 Canada census.

implications for society in general. One aboriginal group asks: "Is the system conditioning our young for lives in institutions and not in society?"[2]

The cost of these trends to society, in both human and financial terms, is only now becoming apparent. Public awareness of the financial expense related to institutionalizing aboriginal people has increased, and many members of society are now well aware of the need to address the social problems created or exacerbated by nonaboriginal delivery of child welfare services to aboriginal people. Although some aboriginal communities have made significant strides in obtaining more control over the future of their children and communities, they have yet to obtain full control, free from federal and provincial government involvement.

In examining the situation of aboriginal children within Manitoba's justice system, Judge Kimelman stated:

> Children need protection to ensure that they are not removed from their families without substantial cause. It has been observed that social workers tend to make idealistic judgments about family functioning and may view situations as neglect where no actual harm is likely to occur.[3]

It is inevitable that child protection workers, whether they work in an urban, rural or reserve environment, will encounter cases involving aboriginal children. Social workers who are not informed of the aboriginal communities' struggle for control of child welfare services, or of the cultural, social, legal and historical dynamics involved, will be unable to adequately meet the test of providing for the best interests of the child. Further, they will be unable to provide proper support to the aboriginal communities which are expanding their role in the child welfare system. Unfortunately, research in the field is sparse, and there are relatively few resources to help child protection workers understand these complex issues.

In an attempt to provide some basic information on problems of aboriginal child welfare, this chapter will review historical developments in aboriginal child welfare, current cultural and legal issues, and present government responses.

HISTORICAL BACKGROUND

Assimilation

Understanding Canadian history from an aboriginal perspective enables an appreciation of the recent developments in aboriginal child welfare. Since the earliest contact between Canada's aboriginal people and European settlers, there have been conflicting values concerning family relationships and child-rearing. Initially, those differences were not problematic, as there was little social interac-

---

[2] Swampy Cree submission to the Public Inquiry into the Administration of Justice and Aboriginal People of Manitoba. The Pas, Manitoba, (17 January 1989) at 14.

[3] E.C. Kimelman, Chairman, *No Quiet Place: Review Committee on Indian and Métis Adoptions and Placements* (Manitoba: Manitoba Community Services, 1985) at 45.

tion between the two sides. However, soon after their arrival, the European colonists thought it would benefit all concerned if aboriginal people conformed to child-rearing practices more in keeping with the colonists' views, values and beliefs.

The religious missionaries were the first to attempt to change Canada's aboriginal population, with a particular emphasis on conversion to Christianity, as part of a worldwide effort.[4] Initially, interaction between colonists and aboriginal people was mutually beneficial, and in many ways the aboriginal people controlled their own cultural and economic development. For example, they used annual payments from settlers for land to develop their agricultural and other resources. However, there was a gradual and growing emphasis on assimilation by missionaries and settlers. This shift in attitudes had devastating effects on aboriginal cultures:

> Part of the reason for this change in attitude lay ... in the Indians' diminishing utility as Indians. As the 19th century progressed, Indians were becoming less valued for their original cultural attributes, whether as partners in the fur trade or as military allies. Settlement assumed priority. This new paternalistic, one-sided relationship received its legal justification in the *British North America Act*, which ... took away Indians' independent status by making them wards of the federal government. As consolidated in the *Indian Acts* of 1876 and 1880, Indian self-government was abolished, and finance and all social services, including education, were placed under federal control. Lands reserved for Indians' use were to be managed on their behalf until such time as individual Indians enfranchised themselves or became sufficiently "civilized" to be allowed a measure of self-government.[5]

The commitment to assimilation was reflected in the policies initiated in the 19th century by Canadian governments to educate aboriginal children in the ways of the "white man." Many of the treaty negotiations which occurred after Confederation contain references by the government treaty commissioners to promote this objective. The residential school system of the late 19th and 20th centuries clearly demonstrated the belief of governments and the dominant society that assimilation through education of young aboriginal children was necessary and was to be achieved by removing the children from the influence of their parents and community.

Aboriginal children were taken to residential schools, removing them from the influences of their traditional culture and way of life, as well as from their parents and communities. They were invariably forbidden to speak their own languages or practice any of their customs, which were generally considered to be uncivilized.

---

[4] The history of missionary activity is recounted in J.W. Grant, *Moon of Wintertime: Missionaries and the Indians of Canada in Encounter Since 1534* (Toronto: University of Toronto Press, 1984).

[5] J. Barman, Y. Hebert and D. McCaskill, eds, *Indian Education in Canada: The Legacy*, vol. 1 (Vancouver: University of British Columbia Press, 1986) at 4.

Preference was given to the creation of large industrial residential schools located away from reserves and, a few years later, to boarding schools nearer reserves for younger children. There, attendance would be ensured, and all aspects of life, from dress to use of English language to behaviour, would be carefully regulated. Curriculum was to be limited to basic education combined with half-day practical training in agriculture, the crafts, or household duties in order to prepare pupils for their expected future existence on the lower fringes of the dominant society.[6]

Many aboriginal parents appeared to cooperate with the placing of their children in residential schools, seeing it as beneficial to have their children educated in nonaboriginal schools. Indeed, available evidence suggests that with some of the treaties, the "schoolhouse" clauses were requested by the Indians and not simply imposed by the government negotiators. This, however, does not imply that there was a willingness for the parents to surrender custody of their children, but only that they wanted their children to be educated.

Indian children, understandably, did not always cooperate. It became necessary to facilitate the return of children who ran away from residential schools. Regulations were enacted which removed the authority of Indian parents over their children while they were in residential schools. Although no law was ever enacted to support the practice, Indian parents were required to seek and obtain passes from their local Indian agent to leave the reserve. Passes were not easily obtained, and if parents wished to travel from their reserve to see their child at one of the residential schools, passes were often denied, especially if the visit was not taking place during an established school holiday.

It is now clear that such removal of children from their families and communities was often a highly destructive emotional experience, and that the devaluation of the children's culture and heritage which occurred in such institutions had a very negative effect on their self-esteem. Further, at some residential schools, there were devastating patterns of physical and sexual abuse. Disease in the residential schools was also a problem:

> Insufficient care was exercised in the admission of children to the schools. The well-known predisposition of Indians to tuberculosis resulted in a very large percentage of deaths among the pupils. They were housed in buildings not carefully designed for school purposes, and these buildings became infected and dangerous to the inmates. It is quite within the mark to say that fifty percent of the children who passed through these schools did not live to benefit from the education which they had received therein.[7]

The residential school system was phased out through the 1950s and 1960s. Day schools were then established for the Indian children, but many of the poor conditions continued:

---

[6] *Ibid.* at 6.

[7] D. C. Scott in D. Purich, *Our Land: Native Rights in Canada* (Toronto: James Lorimer, 1986) at 134.

[The] ... conditions meant that many Indian people viewed education as a negative experience in their lives and avoided educational opportunities. Worse still, they did little to encourage their children, and probably discouraged them in pursuing educational opportunities. The price which Canadian society is paying for this poor education is readily visible today.[8]

Also during the 1950s and 1960s, the number of aboriginal families moving from reserves to find employment and educational opportunities increased. These families were faced with the stresses of entering a foreign, urban culture as well as a loss of community support. Many aboriginal children in urban settings were, and still are, considered by child welfare authorities to be neglected.

Life for a child on a Reserve or in a native community is described as one of safety, love, adventure, and freedom. A child feels, and is welcome in any home and may join any family for a meal. A mother is not concerned if a child does not return home for a meal or even to sleep. The mother knows that some family is willingly providing for the child. This pattern is one that causes native parents grief when they move into urban centers because the reality is that urban life is different and dangerous. A mother who does not immediately report her child as missing is viewed as neglectful by the urban agencies.[9]

In the late 1960s and early 1970s, the number of aboriginal children that were thought to need protection by child welfare authorities increased significantly. These children were usually apprehended and placed in nonaboriginal foster or group homes. Thus, even though the residential school system faded away, aboriginal people continued to be dominated by the push towards assimilation. In fact, many aboriginal people view the child welfare system as a vehicle for cultural genocide, since it has typically given "little weight to the values, lifestyle and laws" of the aboriginal people in Canada, and because it has imposed on them the "standards, cultural values, laws and systems" of the dominant society.[10]

CULTURAL ISSUES

Philosophy of Life

Aboriginal people are attempting to gain control of the child welfare programs which affect their lives. To understand the reasons for this and the complexity of the cultural issues involved, one must consider the world view common to all Indian cultures. This spiritual world view assumes that all aborigi-

---

[8]   *Ibid.*

[9]   E.C. Kimelman, *supra*, note 3 at 163.

[10]   B. Morse, "Native Indian and Métis Children in Canada: Victims of the Child Welfare System" in Verma & Bagley, eds, *Race Relations and Cultural Differences* (London: Croom Helm, 1984) at 31.

nal people have a relationship with the land, and that they must accommodate to it, displaying an attitude of respect. All customs stem from this philosophy.

Many nonaboriginal people erroneously believe that the traditions, values and beliefs of Indian cultures have completely disappeared. Although aboriginal cultures have undergone changes of a contemporary nature, their identity as separate peoples continues to be an important part of the lives of Canada's aboriginal population.

> Today's Indian cultures are not aboriginal cultures. Many earlier sources of economic existence are gone (although traditional economic pursuits such as hunting, fishing, and trapping are still viable ways of earning a living in many northern Indian communities). Much is being lost because of the assimilation pressures of government policy and the innovations of modern technology. Some Indian languages are on the verge of extinction. Many Indians have adopted Christianity and no longer practice their sacred ways. As well many institutions of larger society have replaced aboriginal institutions. In dress, housing, employment, and other external aspects of culture, Indian peoples are becoming almost indistinguishable from other Canadians.

> But to conclude, as did the authors of the cultural assimilationist educational policy, that Indians would eventually disappear as a distinctive cultural group would be a serious mistake. Indians have not assimilated. Their identity as separate people—with a vision of reality and destiny and of themselves and their world—remains an essential feature of their lives.[11]

Child-Rearing

The fundamentally different world views between aboriginal and nonaboriginal people have resulted in cultural conflict. While there are many different aboriginal tribes in Canada, each with a distinctive language and culture, there are striking similarities, including similar philosophies and practices. The aboriginal philosophy that humans are a part of, and must sustain, the delicate balance in the universe is contrary to most Caucasian religions which consider humans to be superior to all other forms of life. These opposing philosophies create basic differences between aboriginal and Caucasian child-rearing practices.

There are critical differences between the child-rearing practices of aboriginal peoples and those who are of European background.[12] One difference is that, generally, aboriginal parents respect their child's individuality and allow the child great freedom to develop naturally, whereas nonaboriginal parents direct and control their children. Another is that aboriginal children are socialized in a different way than nonaboriginal children, learning through example to display feelings only at appropriate times and in private, for the public display of emotion is considered to be a source of discomfort to the viewer. This emotional self-control has often been mistaken for indifference by nonaboriginal people.

---

[11] J. Barman, Y. Hebert, & D. McCaskill, eds, *Indian Education in Canada: The Challenge*, vol. 2 (Vancouver: University of British Columbia Press, 1986) at 156.

[12] R. Andres, "The Apprehension of Native Children" (April 1981), 4 *Ontario Indian*.

An aboriginal child may be cared for by several households of an extended family with the natural parents' understanding that the child would receive the same love and care which they would provide. This contrasts with the non-aboriginal emphasis on the nuclear family as the basic unit of child care provision.

A key difference in discipline is the use of teasing in many tribal groups to shame and humour a child into good behaviour. This is often interpreted as psychological abuse by those unfamiliar with aboriginal ways. Also, since aboriginal children are considered by their elders to be at one with nature, they are allowed great freedom to search for enlightenment. The directive approach of nonaboriginal schools conflicts with this nondirective approach, and many aboriginal children have difficulty achieving goals set in the formal Canadian classroom, causing them to become discouraged with school. Children caught between aboriginal and nonaboriginal customs and expectations such as these are often confused and find it extremely difficult to conform to either.

A Child's Right to Aboriginal Culture

Much attention has recently been given to the confusion and identity crises experienced by young aboriginal children who have been apprehended and placed in nonaboriginal homes. It is now believed that these emotional problems will, at least in part, be addressed by keeping children within their own communities and culture. Bands in several Canadian jurisdictions now administer their own child welfare services, placing children in homes of other band members, thus decreasing the need for nonaboriginal foster homes. The intergovernmental agreements making this possible will be discussed later in this chapter.

Courts are now more likely to consider the importance of exposing children to their own native culture. Courts will sometimes allow access to the parents, with temporary or permanent custody to the Minister or agency, to ensure an apprehended child has continued exposure to that culture.[13] Canadian courts have also started to recognize the importance of cultural and religious heritage as a factor in dealing with child protection applications, although it many not always be decisive.

Further, the courts and legislatures have also begun to recognize the status of Indian bands and communities to participate in protection proceedings. In *Tom* v. *The Children's Aid Society of Winnipeg*[14] the Court of Appeal of Manitoba held that customary law does not give a band standing to apply for guardianship of a

---

[13] See, e.g., *McNeil* v. *Superintendent of Family and Child Services*, [1983] 3 C.N.L.R. 41 (B.C.C.A.).

[14] [1982] 1 C.N.L.R. 170, [1982] 2 W.W.R. 212 (Man. C.A.).

child, but in *Re C. and V.C.*[15] a British Columbia court held that an individual who is a Band member may apply for custody, with the support of the Band, if this is necessary to keep children in the community. Courts have gone even further where a band has established a child care agency. In provinces like Manitoba and Ontario, legislation gives such agencies legal standing to intervene in cases involving children who are band members; there are also judicial decisions in the absence of legislation that have had this effect.[16]

Although courts seem to place increasing emphasis on the aboriginal child's right to his or her culture, other considerations are still often given a higher priority in determining the best interests of the child. The complexity of this issue was apparent in *Racine* v. *Woods*[17], which involved an aboriginal child who was placed in a foster home shortly after her birth. When the native mother attempted to reclaim her child, the foster parents refused to return her to the mother. The mother, three years later, made a second attempt to have the child returned. The foster parents subsequently applied for an adoption order which was granted, and the trial judge dispensed with parental consent to the adoption because of the mother's previous "abandonment" of the baby. The adoption was later set aside by the Manitoba Court of Appeal, which voiced concern that adoption would have greatly effected the child's exposure to her heritage, and determined that the trial judge had erred in concluding the baby had been abandoned. The Supreme Court of Canada overturned this appellate decision, ruling that the importance of exposing children to their cultural background decreases as the time spent with caregivers outside their community increases and relationships to nonaboriginal caregivers are strengthened.

Other cases involving the rights of natural aboriginal parents versus long-term caregivers and prospective adoptive parents have tended to also favour the prospective adoptive parents, emphasizing the bond already established and the potential trauma of separation, and de-emphasizing the importance of the child's cultural heritage.[18]

---

[15] (1982), [1983] 3 C.N.L.R. 58, 40 B.C.L.R. 234 (B.C. Prov. Ct).

[16] *Pitzel and Pitzel* v. *Children's Aid Society of Winnipeg*, [1984] 4 C.N.L.R. 41, [1984] 5 W.W.R. 474 (Man. Q.B.). This decision predated the enactment of the present Manitoba statute in 1985.

[17] (1983), [1984] 1 C.N.L.R. 161, (1983), [1984] 1 W.W.R. 1 (S.C.C.). For a critique of *Racine* v. *Woods* and a provocative discussion of many of the issues in this chapter, see P. Monture, "A Vicious Circle: Child Welfare and the First Nations" (1989), 3 C.J.W.L. 1–17.

[18] See, e.g., *Natural Parents* v. *Superintendent of Child Welfare* (1975), 60 D.L.R. (3d) 148; (1975), [1976] 1 W.W.R. 699 (S.C.C.); and *King* v. *Low* [1985] 1 S.C.R. 87, 44 R.F.L. (2d) 113 (S.C.C.).

Court decisions not to return aboriginal children to their natural families have been based upon various considerations. In one case it was found that the need for cultural awareness was met by the foster family, which was granted an adoption order.[19] In another, the reserve was found to be lacking the necessary resources to deal with a child's developmental problems and special needs,[20] and in yet another, the court concluded that the reserve did not have the proper medical and educational facilities for the child, so the natural parents were deprived of custody.[21] Although there has been more judicial recognition of the importance of aboriginal children's cultural identity, many aboriginals and commentators believe this factor has not been weighed heavily enough by the courts.

Customary Law

Until recently, the legal system has failed to recognize in child welfare matters the importance of aboriginal customs and traditions. Of particular importance is the idea that the child is a member of a total community, not just a member of a single nuclear family. A number of aboriginal customs, such as extended family parenting, stem from this. Many aboriginal people feel that the courts do not give enough recognition to specific customs and laws such as these.

Adoption is one aboriginal custom which has, uniquely, been recognized by Canadian courts since the 1960s.[22] One aspect of aboriginal custom adoption is that the children do not lose contact with their natural parents, and as Judge Kimelman stated:

> The raising of children is seen as a communal responsibility with the immediate and extended family carrying the primary responsibility for a specific child. In addition to the input of grandparents, aunts, uncles, and older siblings, the parents, it is understood, may select a specific person to assume a special role in a child's life. This person will oversee the child's development, teach necessary skills, and maintain a lifelong relationship with the child.

> Adoption in native communities does not only apply to children. A family may adopt a grandparent. A child may adopt an uncle or an aunt. A man may adopt another as a brother and each will assume all the rights and responsibilities of a natural brother to each other's wife, children, and relatives.[23]

---

[19] *Wilson* v. *Young* (1983), [1984] 2 C.N.L.R. 185, 28 Sask. R. 287.

[20] *Supra*, note 13.

[21] *S.A.L. and G.I.L.* v. *Legal Aid Manitoba* (1982), [1983] 1 C.N.L.R. 157, [1982] 6 W.W.R. 260 (Alta C.A.).

[22] See *Re Katie's Adoption Petition* (1962), 38 W.W.R. 100 (NWT); and *Re Beaulieu's Petition* (1969), 67 W.W.R. 669 (N.W.T.).

[23] *Supra*, note 3 at 163.

In one Ontario case, the court recognized the importance of customary aboriginal adoption and decided to place two sisters with relatives on the Grassy Narrows reserve where the natural mother also lived; this was contrary to the protection agency's plan that the children be adopted by a family on another reserve. In making the decision to place the children on the same reserve as their mother, Judge Andrews observed:

> [this placement] ... will be in accord with the tribal tradition of "custom adoption" by reason of blood relationship. There is no evidence to indicate whether or not a subsequent legal adoption will offer any particular benefit to the children.[24]

This case is also significant because it reflects Ontario's new legislation requiring the consideration of cultural factors when placing aboriginal children for adoption.[25]

The court in *Re Tagornak*[26] held that customary adoption is recognized not only on the basis of case law but also as a right under s. 35(1) of the *Constitution Act, 1982*, which states:

> The existing aboriginal and treaty rights of the aboriginal peoples of Canada are hereby recognized and affirmed.

For many aboriginal people, customary aboriginal adoption is preferable to statutory adoption schemes as it permits the natural parents to know where their child has been placed, and it emphasizes and recognizes the importance of maintaining the child's cultural ties.

It is interesting to note that many of the recent developments in adoption law in Canada and other countries have been in the direction of a more open adoption process, moves which have brought statutory adoption closer to aboriginal custom. More disclosure of information and post-adoption access are examples, and some authors have advocated steps to further open the adoption process.[27]

Standard of Care

It has been argued that aboriginal people should decide what constitutes neglect within their own community[28] and that the evaluation of aboriginal parent-

---

[24] *Re D.L.S. and D.M.S.; J.T.K. and L.S.* v. *Kenora-Patricia C.F.S.*, [1985] W.D.F.L. 934 (Ont. Prov. Ct-Fam. Div.).

[25] See, e.g., *Child and Family Services Act*, S.O. 1984, c. 55, s. 37(4), which specifically requires courts to consider "the importance ... of the uniqueness of Indian and native culture, heritage and traditions, of preserving the child's cultural identity," as a factor in a child's "best interests;" see also s. 191 that recognizes "customary care."

[26] (1983), 50 A.R. 237 (N.W.T.S.C.).

[27] See, e.g., L. Caplan, "A Reporter at Large: An Open Adoption, Part I" (21 May 1990) The New Yorker 40, and "Part II" (28 May 1990) The New Yorker 73, for a description of how open adoption functions.

[28] T. Sullivan, "Native Children in Treatment: Clinical, Social and Cultural Issues" (1983), 1 Journal of Child Care 75 at 87.

ing by nonaboriginal people does not usually take into account the different value systems, customs and community characteristics. A fairly common charge by nonaboriginal protection workers is that aboriginal children are "neglected." This may reflect a worker's negative view of both the permissive aboriginal parenting style, which allows children to explore and learn from their environment, and care being provided frequently by extended family members, often for extended periods of time.

Though the concept of neglect has not yet been defined by aboriginal people for aboriginal people, a number of more sensitive court decisions in Canada have ruled that different standards of care should be applied to parents in rural aboriginal communities than those which are applied to nonaboriginal, middle-class communities.

In *Re E.C.D.M.*[29] the court applied standards to an aboriginal group that differed from those of white middle-class society. In this case, a 24-year-old single mother residing in a rural Cree community in Northern Saskatchewan opposed a permanent wardship application for her 2-year-old child. Judge Moxley outlined some community differences to be taken into account. These included: cultural differences such as an extended family concept and nonintervention in child-rearing; acquired community habits such as widespread drinking; and conditions forced on the community such as a high level of unemployment and dependence upon government assistance. These differences formed the basis of a secondary standard which was then applied to the case.

In another Saskatchewan case, an aboriginal mother was successful in appealing the permanent wardship of her 3-year-old child. After the child was initially found to be in need of protection, the mother successfully completed treatment for her alcohol addiction and established another home separate from the people with whom she had previously associated. Judge Johnson considered community standards of care:

> What is basic in this kind of problem is the right and need of the child to be raised, if possible, by its natural mother in its natural environment and its own cultural surroundings. Although the standard of living provided by that mother and the care given to the child may not be considered acceptable by others, nevertheless if those standards conform to those considered average in the particular class or group to which the parent(s) belong, the court ought not to interfere.[30]

This important issue was also considered in *Director of Child Welfare* v. *B.B.*, where standards other than those of the broader nonaboriginal society were applied by the trial court considering whether two aboriginal siblings were in need of protection. The trial judge held the 18-month-old twins were no longer in need of protection and were to be returned to their mother. The mother had never

---

[29] (1980), 17 R.F.L. (2d) 274 (Sask. Prov. Ct); see also the discussion of this case in Chapter 4.

[30] *Mooswa et al.* v. *Minister of Social Services for the Province of Saskatchewan* (1976), 30 R.F.L. 101 at 102 (Sask. Q.B.).

had custody of these children. She was living in a four-room house with another 5-year-old child, her 65-year-old mother, her sister, and her sister's two young children. The three adults received social assistance, and all were non-status Indians living on the outskirts of a reservation. Alcohol abuse in the home was evident. In deciding the twins were not in need of protection, Martin Prov. J. stated:

> I have carefully reviewed the evidence and while I find that the B. condition, and I refer to the extended family at Easterville, deplorable by standards which I take to be the norm for middle class white society, I cannot find proof, on balance, of the kind required that would allow me to say that B.B. should be denied the return of her children.

> I find that none of the incidents referred to or the living conditions reported are so far out of the ordinary, for Easterville, that I can say that the children would probably be at risk if returned to the mother.[31]

The trial decision was appealed by the protection agency, and overturned by the Manitoba Court of Appeal, with Monnin C.J.M. stating:

> That there is poverty in the area is not denied but poverty and the customs of the inhabitants of Easterville are not the issue. The sole issue is what is in the best interests of the twins ...

> I do not accept as sound the principle enunciated by the trial judge that there are certain standards or norms which are acceptable for Easterville but unacceptable for the rest of the province. Economic conditions may differ but there is only one standard of care to be considered and applied whether the infants reside or whether the household is situated in Easterville, The Pas, Churchill, Brandon, Crescentwood, Tuxedo, West Kildonan or the Core area. In my opinion, the type of household in the case before us cannot provide the simple and essential elements of life since all three adults have shown themselves to be irresponsible where the other children are concerned and regularly over-indulge in alcohol.[32]

The decision of the Manitoba Court of Appeal was appealed to the Supreme Court of Canada. The Supreme Court rejected the approach of the Court of Appeal to the issue of the appropriate standard of care and ordered a new trial. Sopinka J. stated:

> Although we do not agree with the test applied by the majority of the Court of Appeal, we agree with their conclusion that the children are in need of protection pursuant to s. 17(b)(i). We are of the opinion, however, that the Court of Appeal failed to adequately consider the alternatives in s. 38 of the Act, and in addition, we have been told of evidence that indicates a change of circumstances have occurred. Accordingly, we would refer the matter back to the trial

---

[31] *Director of Child Welfare* v. *B.B.* (1988), 14 R.F.L. (3d) 113 at 115 (Man. C.A.).

[32] *Ibid.* at 114.

judge to consider what order is now appropriate under s. 38. The children are to remain temporary wards pending further order.[33]

This case is a good example of the child welfare dilemma faced by aboriginal people. It is encouraging that the Supreme Court of Canada appears to recognize the inappropriateness of automatically applying the standards of the dominant society to aboriginal peoples. Increasingly, aboriginal communities are demanding that their own values and standards be applied when decisions are made concerning their children.

JURISDICTIONAL RESPONSIBILITY

Background

Since the establishment of Canada in 1867, legislation regarding aboriginal people has been the responsibility of the federal Parliament, while child welfare matters have fallen under provincial jurisdiction. Prior to the 1950s it was rare for provincial child welfare services to be offered on Indian reserves. Children considered to be in need of protection were apprehended by Indian agents and either placed with another family on the reserve or sent to residential schools.[34]

While s. 91(24) of the *Constitution Act* gives the federal government legislative authority over "Indians and lands reserved for Indians,"[35] the federal government is not obligated to provide services under s. 91(24) of the *Constitution Act* or the *Indian Act*. Although Parliament has the jurisdiction to legislate on aboriginal child welfare, it has chosen not to do so.

The *Indian Act* was amended in 1951 to include a section clarifying the extent to which provincial legislation applies to aboriginal people. Section 88 states:

> Subject to the terms of any treaty and any other Act of the Parliament of Canada, all laws of general application from time to time in force in any province are applicable to and in respect of Indians in that province, except to the extent that such laws are inconsistent with this Act and except to the extent that such laws make provision for any matter for which provision is made by or under this Act.[36]

Because the *Indian Act* contains no reference to child protection, this section implicitly requires that provincial child protection laws and services extend to aboriginal children, both on- and off-reserve. However, in the 1950s and 1960s, there was little federal effort to provide financial assistance to the provinces to

---

[33] *B.B.* v *Director of Child and Family Services* (1989), 62 Man. R. (2d) 233 at 234 (S.C.C.), [1989] W.D.F.L. 967. The trial judge subsequently returned the children to parental care; at last report that decision was again being appealed by the agency.

[34] J.A. MacDonald, "The Spallumcheen Indian Band By-Law and its Potential Impact on Native Indian Child Welfare Policy in British Columbia" (1983) 1 Can. J. Fam. L. 75 at 77.

[35] *Constitution Act, 1982*, being Schedule B. of the *Canada Act 1982* (U.K.), 1982, c. 11, s. 91(24).

[36] *Indian Act*, R.S.C. 1970, c. I–6, s. 88.

pay for aboriginal child welfare services, and provincial governments were reluctant to extend provincial services to Indian reserves, primarily for financial reasons.

More recently the federal government has recognized that it has some obligation for assuring that child protection services are provided to aboriginal communities. Thus, it has begun to reimburse some of the provinces, and also funds some Indian bands under child welfare agreements. However, the federal government continues to disclaim full constitutional and legal responsibility for aboriginal child welfare issues.

The result of this prolonged jurisdictional dispute is that the quantity and quality of child welfare services provided to aboriginal children on reserves across Canada has varied greatly, depending upon the government agreements that have existed. Some provinces provide child protection services to aboriginal children living on reserves, on the condition that the province is compensated by the federal government. Other provinces, it would seem primarily because of this jurisdictional concern, have provided very limited services, for example, only in "life-or-death" situations. The result is that some aboriginal families in need of family support services are not provided with even basic services, and difficult situations worsen until they become life-threatening and children have to be removed.

Court Decisions

The Supreme Court of Canada addressed the question of whether Indians were subject to the provisions of provincial child welfare legislation in *Natural Parents* v. *Superintendent of Child Welfare*.[37] It was argued by the parents of an Indian child being placed under care by the provincial Superintendent of Child Welfare of British Columbia that the provincial legislation was not applicable to them for several reasons, including the argument that they were subject to federal jurisdiction and not provincial child welfare laws. The Supreme Court ruled that s. 88 of the *Indian Act* made provincial legislation applicable to Indians, as long as it was not in conflict with federal legislation, with any regulation issued under federal legislation, with any band bylaw issued under the *Indian Act*, or with any treaty between Indians and the Crown. The Manitoba Court of Appeal in *Nelson* v. *Children's Aid Society of Eastern Manitoba*[38] also held that by virtue of s. 88 of the *Indian Act* the provincial child protection legislation applied to status Indians as a law of "general application" not in conflict with any treaty or Act of Parliament.

In Manitoba, as with several other provinces, the historical position of the provincial government has been that Indians were the legal and fiscal responsibility of the federal government, and that the province had no responsibility to

---

[37]　(1975), 60 D.L.R. (3d) 148 (S.C.C.).

[38]　[1975] 5 W.W.R. 45 (Man. C.A.).

provide services to aboriginal people living on reserves. Where child welfare was concerned, this meant in the past that unless the federal government agreed to reimburse the province financially, Manitoba would not extend the same social services to Indians which it provided to other Manitobans. Just as importantly, it would not pay private agencies for services they wished to provide to reserve residents. Since all child welfare agencies in Manitoba were dependent on the province for their funding, Manitoba's political and legal position swung considerable weight.

The provincial justification was based partly on the province's interpretation of s. 91(24) of the *Constitution Act* as well as appearing responsive to the concerns of those of Manitoba's aboriginal leaders who had stated that they were opposed to provincial interference in their affairs. Yet, provincially mandated child protection workers were often confronted with information about circumstances which normally justified a child protection agency intervening and providing services to a child living on a reserve.

As it does today, Manitoba's legislation at the time required any worker who was aware of a child being in need of protection to apprehend that child and take them before a court. The dilemma created by the provincial policy soon became apparent, and the province softened its position, authorizing provincial child protection workers to intervene in "life-or-death" situations. The workers were, however, directed to refrain from providing any other services to the family, such as counselling and referral. These preventive and less intrusive services were regularly available to nonaboriginal families for the purpose of assisting them in their crises, preventing family breakups or helping parents regain the custody of their children.

Judge Graeme Garson of the Manitoba Provincial Court was confronted with a case in 1978 which arose directly from this policy.[39] The mother was known to be experiencing considerable coping problems which often resulted in her children being neglected. Evidence showed that counselling and other forms of assistance were needed, but were not provided to her because of the provincial policy. Although he granted a permanent order of guardianship, Judge Garson held that the Manitoba government's denial of preventive support services to residents of Indian reserves was discriminatory and illegal. He found that under s. 88 of the *Indian Act*, provincial legislation of general application applied to Indians and that child welfare services should be provided to status Indians on the same basis and criteria as to other residents of the province.

The case sent a mild shock wave through the government, which thought it was on safe ground in the position it took. The provincial government, which did not want to provide such services without federal fiscal input, and Indian leaders, who did not want the province involved at all, were forced to recognize that if their respective positions were going to be protected, it would be through some

---

[39] *Director of Child Welfare* v. *B.* (1978), [1979] 6 W.W.R. 229 (Man. Prov. Ct).

form of negotiated resolution. The courts were indicating that an unequal provision of services to Indian people would not be tolerated.

GOVERNMENT RESPONSES

Bilateral and Tripartite Agreements

Generally, bilateral and tripartite agreements have become the most common methods of addressing jurisdictional disputes over the provision of Indian child welfare services. Bilateral agreements generally provide that the federal government will pay the cost of services to be provided by the provinces or by Indian bands to Indian people.

Most tripartite agreements between the Indian, provincial and federal governments are established under existing provincial child welfare legislation. Under these agreements the province usually agrees to address the needs of aboriginal children and communities by assisting in the establishment and mandating of aboriginal child welfare agencies under provincial legislation. The federal government provides full or partial financial assistance for these agencies. Such agreements have been signed in some provinces.

Under a tripartite agreement, the provincial laws governing child welfare services are followed both on and off the reserves. Aboriginal people may be given authority to administer the laws, but do not have the jurisdiction to enforce their own laws or customs. However, they are at least able to put their own interpretation on the provincial laws, thereby incorporating aboriginal values, beliefs and customs in the provision of child welfare services to aboriginal children.

Although bilateral and trilateral agreements address the jurisdictional difficulties and help alleviate some of the problems, they do not permit aboriginal people to define how their lives and the lives of their children are to be governed and controlled. For tripartite agreements to be successful they need to be accepted by the people they are intended to govern. Although it is possible for the federal and provincial governments to delegate their respective jurisdictions and powers to the Indian bands, without financial control such measures are seen by some as a temporary approach.

Tripartite agreements seem to be only an interim solution. With the requirement that provincial legislation govern the administration of aboriginal child welfare matters, there is little or no recognition of customary law. Indian bands which have signed such agreements have generally done so because they felt it was the quickest way to obtain needed services for their children.

Provincial Responses

There is tremendous disparity in the quantity and quality of social services provided to aboriginal children from province to province. To profile the wide variation of these governmental responses to the aboriginal child welfare problem, an overview of the situations in Alberta, British Columbia, Manitoba, Ontario and Saskatchewan is provided here.

Alberta

Alberta's *Child Welfare Act* requires that if a child is an Indian band member and lives on a reserve, the band must be consulted before application is made for orders of supervision or guardianship. Also, any person adopting an Indian child must ensure the maintenance of the child's rights as an Indian and must inform the child of his or her status as an Indian.[40]

In Alberta there are two tripartite agreements in existence. The Blackfoot Social Services Agreement is thought to be the oldest tripartite child care agreement in Canada, since it was negotiated in the early 1970s between the Band, the provincial Department of Family and Social Services and the federal Department of Indian and Northern Affairs. It requires the federal government to reimburse the Band for all costs related to the provision of child care services to Band members and the provincial government to provide an employee (at the Band's cost) authorized to invoke the statutory provisions of the province's *Child Welfare Act*. A similar agreement exists with the Lesser Slave Lake Indian Regional Council and a child welfare bylaw is presently being developed by four bands in the Hobbema area to cover band members.

British Columbia—The Spallumcheen Band Bylaw

The enactment of band bylaws increases the level of self-determination by Indian governments, and provides Indian people with the authority to legislate and provide appropriate child welfare services with less interference from provincial and federal governments. This solution better permits bands to consider customary laws and practices in child welfare matters.

At the present time there is only one fully functional Indian child welfare program in British Columbia, run by the Spallumcheen Band.[41] In 1980 the newly enacted *Family and Child Services Act* of British Columbia contained a clause which required the court to serve the Band of which the child is a member with Notice of the Hearing before dealing with the child. Except for that provision, the British Columbia legislation was, and still is, similar in most respects to other provincial legislation in that it pays no particular regard to aboriginal people as a special group. In October 1980, the Spallumcheen Band, residing in the Okanagan Valley, took direct action against the Ministry of Human Resources. To that point, 150 children had been removed from their reserve since 1960. All of those children had been placed in non-Indian off-reserve homes. Since the Band population was 300, the removal of 150 children had a dramatic effect upon the community's population and sense of future.

---

[40] S.A. 1984, c. C–8.1, s. 73.

[41] See J.A. MacDonald, "The Spallumcheen Indian Band By-Law and its Potential Impact on Native Indian Child Welfare Policy in British Columbia" (1983) 1 Can. J. Fam. L. 75 at 77.

On Thanksgiving Day 1980, Chief Wayne Christian of the Spallumcheen Band organized an "Indian Child Caravan" which converged on the home of the provincial Minister of Human Resources. Prior to that date, the Band had enacted its own Child Care Bylaw which had been presented to the Minister. Following the protest, the Minister of Human Resources signed an agreement with the Band, recognizing the Band's bylaw and agreeing to work with the Band for the return of Band children to the reserve. The federal government later signed an agreement to provide funding to support these services.

The bylaw gives the Spallumcheen Band exclusive jurisdiction over any proceeding involving the removal of a child from a Band family. The Band Council is responsible for administering the provisions of the bylaw and when a Band child is in need of protection, the chief and Council and every person authorized by them are empowered to remove the child from the home and take the child into care. As legal guardians, the chief and Council are responsible for the child's placement in a suitable home. Their decision is guided by Band custom and, in the case of an older child, the child's wishes. The child's family is given assistance and placements occur in the following order of preference: (a) with the parent(s); (b) with a member of the child's extended family living on the reserve; (c) with a member of the child's extended family living on another reserve; (d) with a member of the child's extended family living off-reserve; (e) with an Indian family living on a reserve; and, (f) with an Indian family living off-reserve. For a child to be placed in the home of a non-Indian living off the reserve it must be the only alternative with the best interests of the child as the deciding factor in every case.

The Band Council's decision can be reviewed by the entire Band, if requested by a Band member, parent, Indian guardian, or member of the child's extended family. The child, child's parent, Indian guardian, or an extended family member may apply to the Band Council for the child's return or transfer to the home of another Indian guardian, with the decision reviewable by the entire Band.

The Spallumcheen Band asserts the authority for its bylaw in s. 81 of the *Indian Act* which provides *inter alia*:

> The council of a band may make bylaws not inconsistent with this Act ... for any or all of the following purposes, namely:
>
> > (a) to provide for the health of residents on the reserve ... ;
> >
> > (d) the prevention of disorderly conduct and nuisances; ...
> >
> > (g) with respect to any matter arising out of or ancillary to the exercise of powers under this section.[42]

Indian band bylaws, properly enacted, would clearly supplant provincial child welfare legislation because of s. 88 of the *Indian Act*.

Indian bands have generally not utilized the bylaw-making powers available to them under the *Indian Act* and it is unlikely that any more such bylaws will be enacted. Bylaws enacted under the *Indian Act* would give Indian people some

---

[42] *Indian Act*, R.S.C. 1985, c. I–5, s. 81.

control over their lives and their children and perhaps alleviate some of the problems, but most bands do not have the necessary resources that go with the responsibility of taking such control.

In addition, the bylaw power of s. 81 does not explicitly give bands the power to make bylaws regarding child welfare, and the federal government has recently indicated that it will disallow any more of these bylaw arrangements.[43]

Manitoba

During the 1980s, three master tripartite agreements were signed by the federal, provincial and Indian organizations (the Four Nations Confederacy, the Manitoba Keewatinowi Okimakinak Inc., and the Brotherhood of Indian Nations) in Manitoba. There are several subsidiary agreements to these master agreements, allowing child protection services to be provided by aboriginally administered agencies on many reserves. In 1981–82, Manitoba Indian bands provided only 53,576 days of care to aboriginal children (15% of the total days of care provided to aboriginal children). Over a 4-year period this increased to 221,482 days (86% of total days of care provided to aboriginal children).[44]

Indian bands have the objective of complete control over their child welfare services and policies, as part of their goal of Indian self-government. Manitoba's tripartite agreements require services to be provided by Indian agencies in accordance with provincial legislation and, from the Indian viewpoint, were signed solely as interim measures until the long-term goal of complete Indian responsibility for child welfare matters is achieved. The Manitoba agreements recognize that the responsibility for the development of on-reserve child welfare services lies with the Indian bands that, with provincial recognition, establish Indian child welfare agencies. All funding comes from the federal government.

The situation in Manitoba's child welfare system has become increasingly complex as aboriginal and nonaboriginal agencies must determine which agency has jurisdiction over a particular child. This sometimes results in the need for a court appearance to transfer jurisdiction to the appropriate agency.[45]

---

[43] The federal Minister of Indian and Northern Affairs has the power to disallow such a bylaw by virtue of s. 82 of the *Indian Act.*

[44] Department of Indian and Northern Affairs, *Indian Child and Family Services in Canada: Final Report* (Ottawa, 1987).

[45] In May 1990, Madame Justice Cheryl Davidson of the Manitoba Court of Queen's Bench (Family Division) rendered the first decision which attempted to answer the jurisdictional question of Manitoba's Indian child welfare agencies. She held that an Indian child welfare agency in Manitoba is legally restricted to provide services within the geographical boundaries of those reserves listed in the Regulation establishing the agency: *Northwest Child and Family Services Agency* v. *T. (S.J.) and D. (C.)* (7 May 1990), Winnipeg Center 88–01–02570 (Man. Q.B.-Fam. Div.) [unreported]. The case is being considered for appeal by the Indian agency.

Ontario

Ontario legislation also recognizes the rights of aboriginal children and communities in its child welfare laws. Its *Child and Family Services Act* sets out the most complete provincial legislative scheme for the protection of aboriginal children.[46] These provisions clearly allow bands and native communities more involvement in the administration of child welfare programs.

First, the Act makes reference to both Indian and native people, with "Indian" having the same definition as in the *Indian Act*, and "native person" being defined as a person who is a member of a native community but not a band member.[47] This allows the legislation to be applied to all aboriginal people, whether they live on a reserve or not, provided they belong to a "native community," as designated by the Minister of Community and Social Services. Non-status Indians and Métis can be brought within the definition of "native communities" by the Minister, though this has not yet occurred.

Second, provision is made in the Act for an agency to be designated by a band or a native community as a native child and family service authority, with responsibility for providing child welfare services to that community.[48] There are now three native-run child welfare agencies in northern Ontario, with responsibility for some or all aspects of child welfare for the Indian populations within the geographical areas they serve. In areas where non-native-run agencies are still providing services to native communities, the agencies must regularly consult with these communities about services provided, including the apprehension and placement of children in residential care, and in some localities native groups are providing some services on a contract basis to the nonaboriginal child protection agencies.

The Declaration of Principles of Ontario's *Child and Family Services Act* states that:

> Indian and native people should be entitled to provide, wherever possible, their own child and family services, and that all services to Indian and native children and families should be provided in a manner that recognizes their culture, heritage and traditions and the concept of the extended family.[49]

Further, specific provisions require that an agency or court making a determination in the best interests of an aboriginal child must take into consideration the importance of preserving the child's heritage and cultural identity. This emphasis on the preservation of cultural identity and contact is operationalized in various ways. If a protection application is commenced under the Act in connection with

---

[46] See E.F. Carasco, "Canadian Native Children: Have Child Welfare Laws Broken the Circle?" (1986) 5 Can. J. Fam. L. 109 at 133.

[47] *Child and Family Services Act*, S.O. 1984, c. 55, ss. 3(15)(20).

[48] *Ibid.*, s. 194.

[49] *Ibid.*, s. 1(f).

a native child, a representative of the child's community is to be notified and is entitled to participate in the court proceedings.[50] This allows native communities to be involved in planning for their children, and may result in children who have left a native community and are living in a large urban center being returned to their community under a child protection order.

When an Ontario court is considering what type of order to make in regard to a child who has been found to be in need of protection, unless there is substantial reason for placing the child elsewhere, the judge is required to place the child in the following order: (a) with a member of the child's extended family; (b) with a member of the child's band or native community; or, (c) with another Indian or native family.[51] If an Indian or native child is to be placed for adoption, the society or agency must give the child's band or native community 30 days notice of this intention.[52] This is to allow aboriginal communities to have input in the decision-making about the adoption of their children, and make representations about culturally appropriate placements.

Several pilot projects have been implemented under the new legislation, which is continually being monitored.

Saskatchewan

There are presently no tripartite or bilateral child welfare agreements in Saskatchewan. The provincial government provides all apprehensions and protection services to aboriginal children on-reserve on an emergency basis, but only when the safety of the child is in immediate jeopardy. Off-reserve services to aboriginal children and families are provided in the same way as they are to nonaboriginal families. As in Manitoba prior to the 1980s, the Saskatchewan government maintains that the federal government has complete responsibility for the welfare of aboriginal children on the reserves, and that the provincial Department of Social Services will intervene only if the federal Department of Indian and Northern Affairs refuses, or if the federal Department is unable to provide appropriate services and a Band Council requests such services from the provincial government.

United States

Broad federal child protection legislation for aboriginal children has been enacted in the United States. By virtue of the *Indian Child Welfare Act*[53], the United States government has recognized the importance of providing culturally appropriate child welfare services.

---

[50] *Ibid.*, s. 39 (1)(4).

[51] *Ibid.*, s. 53(5).

[52] *Ibid.*, s. 134(3).

[53] (1978), 25 U.S.C. para. 1901 *et seq.* For a description, see Davies, "Implementing The *Indian Child Welfare Act*," (July 1982) Clearing House Review 179.

The Act recognizes shortcomings in the dominant society's system for dealing with aboriginal children, and the deleterious effects of its imposition on aboriginal people. Its enactment reflected the following:

1. an alarmingly high percentage of Indian families have been broken up by their children's removal and placement in non-Indian homes;

2. state agencies have often failed to recognize cultural and social standards prevailing in Indian communities and families; and,

3. the federal Bureau of Indian Affairs has often failed to fulfill its responsibility to Indian tribes by failing to advocate effectively with state governments and with non-native agencies and by failing to seek funding necessary for Indian tribes to fulfill effectively their responsibilities to their children.

Under this Act, American tribes are vested with jurisdiction in child protection proceedings involving aboriginal children living on reserves. Aboriginal people and tribal courts have the authority to decide whether an aboriginal child will be removed from his or her family and community; American state courts and governments are required to respect these decisions.

Tribes in the United States also have the power to intervene in court cases dealing with Indian children living off-reservation who may be subject to foster care placements or termination of parental rights. In these courts there is preference for placement with the extended family or in an aboriginal community. Funds for services and the administration of tribal courts are provided by the federal Bureau of Indian Affairs.

MÉTIS CHILDREN

The term "Métis" historically applied to individuals of mixed aboriginal and French ancestry who settled in Manitoba and other parts of Western Canada, but is now used more loosely to refer to those of mixed aboriginal and white ancestry. The Métis were not legally regarded as "status Indians" governed by the *Indian Act*. Physiologically and culturally the Métis share some of the characteristics of Indians, but they have a unique culture, with distinctive social, economic and political institutions. It is significant that when the *Canadian Charter of Rights and Freedoms* came into force in 1982, s. 35 explicitly recognized that the "aboriginal peoples of Canada includes the ... Métis" and "recognized and affirmed" their "existing aboriginal rights." It is, however, unclear exactly what rights the Métis peoples have, and this will have to be resolved through political negotiations or by the courts.

In terms of child welfare, provincial governments historically treated Métis and other non-status Indians[54] as part of the general population. There are, for example, no statistics on the number of Métis and non-status Indian children in

---

[54] "Non-status Indians" refers to those of Indian ancestry, or mixed Indian and white ancestry, who have lost the legal status of Indians and hence are no longer governed by the *Indian Act*.

care of the protection authorities, and very few studies have been done of their special problems. It is, however, clear that Métis children and families have faced problems similar to those of other aboriginal groups. They have been disproportionately taken into care and have often not received appropriate services. The plight of Métis children received national attention following the 1984 death of Richard Cardinal, a Métis youth who moved through many foster placements. He committed suicide in a state of despair, but left behind a moving journal of his experiences.

No province has legislation that explicitly recognizes the unique nature of child welfare problems facing Métis communities, though the statues in Alberta, Manitoba and Ontario stipulate that a judge making a decision about the "best interests" of a child is required to take account of the child's "cultural and linguistic heritage."

Métis organizations have been advocating the establishment of their own child welfare agencies to deal with children and families in their communities, but none have been set up. However, governments are slowly beginning to recognize the needs and rights of the Métis, and special programs for Métis children have been established in Manitoba, Alberta and Saskatchewan, with government funding and community involvement.

CONCLUSION

The dominant nonaboriginal society has not responded adequately to the problems of aboriginal children and communities. Assimilationist and culturally insensitive policies have often harmed these children and their communities. This is not to say that Canada's aboriginal people do not face enormous problems with their children and family structures. Alcoholism, spousal battering, and child sexual abuse are very serious problems in many aboriginal families and communities, and must be addressed. Many aboriginal adults were themselves brought up in residential schools and lack appropriate role models for being nurturing parents.

The problems of providing appropriate child welfare services for aboriginal children will defy a single, quick solution. Different communities have different strengths and problems. The challenges facing isolated northern communities, where aboriginal languages are still spoken, are different from those faced by aboriginal people who have moved to large urban settings in southern Canada.

An important step will be for nonaboriginal professionals who work with aboriginal children and families to be better-trained and more sensitive to the culture, heritage and values of Canada's aboriginal people, and to recognize their unique strengths and challenges. The professionals involved include social workers, child care workers, teachers, doctors, nurses, police officers, lawyers and judges. As much as possible, the education should be provided by aboriginal people to others.

Another important measure will be the increased recruitment and training of aboriginal people to work with their communities and help them solve their problems. This process must involve the school system, as well as post-second-ary institutions. In particular, various professional schools and colleges must be more aggressive in their recruitment of aboriginal individuals, and more sensitive of them once enrolled. Agencies and institutions must also change their hiring and employment practices. While some services should be provided by profes-sionals and paraprofessionals, there is also an important place for volunteers and lay persons in aboriginal communities, to serve in such roles as counsellors, foster parents, support persons and youth leaders.

There must also be changes in our policies and laws, and in the manner in which services are provided to aboriginal communities.

Such changes have been occurring and aboriginal people are slowly gaining control over services provided to their communities, though it is apparent that some communities are more willing and able to do so than others. Legislation has been amended in provinces such as Ontario, Alberta and Manitoba to make it more responsive to the needs of aboriginal children, and tripartite agreements have also given some aboriginal communities more control over child welfare matters.

Many aboriginal people, however, feel that these measures are not adequate. They feel that it is not sufficient that the federal and provincial governments should be delegating responsibilities to aboriginal communities, but rather be-lieve that they should have responsibility for their own children and should enact their own child welfare codes. The federal Parliament clearly has the constitu-tional authority to permit Indian bands to enact their own child welfare laws, but it has thus far failed to act. Some aboriginal groups are advocating such action or asserting that responsibility for the provision of child welfare services should be granted to aboriginal communities as part of broader moves towards aboriginal self-government.

It is apparent that the objective of full control of child welfare will take considerable time to achieve, and in the interim sensitizing and educating non-aboriginal agencies and professionals, and recruiting more aboriginal profession-als will be vitally important. It is also critically important that the dominant nonaboriginal society learn from its aboriginal people, for in many ways the holistic, naturalistic values and philosophies of Canada's aboriginal people may be more sensitive and appropriate than those of the dominant society.

9

THE LAWYER'S ROLE

INTRODUCTION

Jennifer A. Blishen[*]

Over the past decade child protection in Canada has become an increasingly sophisticated, complex and legalistic process. Current Canadian child protection legislation has increasingly mirrored society's focus on protection of individual civil rights. Although the protection of children remains paramount, the integrity and the rights of the family unit are to be respected and maintained whenever possible. This orientation, reflected in the *Canadian Charter of Rights and Freedoms*, has resulted in a more adversarial approach to child protection.

An increase in government-funded Legal Aid Plans has resulted in low-income parents more readily obtaining legal representation in child protection matters. While the right to legal representation is accepted, it can be argued that greater ready access to Legal Aid has resulted in more numerous and protracted court proceedings. "I'll fight to the end because I have nothing to lose" is not an uncommon attitude among some parents. There have also been increasing efforts to provide legal representation for children.

In some provinces the courts dealing with child protection issues have become "paper courts," requiring more sophisticated, detailed affidavit evidence, statements of fact and trial briefs. This paperwork is not within the customary expertise of the social worker. Legal advice and assistance in preparing such documentation is crucial.

Child protection agencies have also become more complex, with larger bureaucracies, more professional staff and more complicated policies and procedures. Legal advice is required in the formulation of such policies and procedures at the early stages and during implementation in order to avoid legal pitfalls.

---

[*] Senior Counsel, The Children's Aid Society of Ottawa-Carleton, Ottawa, Ontario.

A: REPRESENTING CHILDREN

*Susan G. Himel**

The notion of legal representation for children is relatively new in the Canadian child protection system. While the late 19th century witnessed changes in the rights afforded to children, the sense of children as equal participants in a legal proceeding is recent.

Child Representation in Ontario

The most extensive program of child representation in Canada was established in Ontario, following two reports of the Attorney General's Committee on Representation of Children in the late 1970s.[1] As a result, an amendment to Ontario's *Child Welfare Act* created statutory provisions for independent representation and set forth the criteria to be considered by a judge in determining whether legal representation was needed.[2]

The Child Representation Programme of the Office of the Official Guardian for Ontario became operational in February 1980. By appointing staff lawyers and private practitioners to a special panel, representation of more than 20,000 children has been provided.[3] The *Child and Family Services Act*, which replaced the *Child Welfare Act*, incorporates similar provision for independent representation of children in protection proceedings.[4]

While this program was established in Ontario, somewhat different schemes for child representation evolved in other provinces. However, the overall effect of the experiences has resulted in the emergence of general agreement on the special nature of child representation:

- lawyers representing children have a different type of clientele than lawyers representing adults;
- lawyers representing children require special expertise to do the job well; and,

---

[*] Deputy Offical Guardian (Personal Rights), Ministry of the Attorney General, Toronto, Ontario.

[1] Ontario Ministry of the Attorney General, "Report of the Committee on the Representation of Children in the Provincial Court (Family Division)" (1977), 29 R.F.L. 134; Ontario Ministry of the Attorney General, "Second Report of the Attorney General's Committee on the Representation of Children" (1978), 7 R.F.L. (2d) 1.

[2] R.S.O. 1980, c. 66, s. 20.

[3] Statistics of the Office of the Official Guardian, Ontario, 1989.

[4] S.O. 1984, c. 55, s. 38.

- most lawyers representing children appear to view their role as not merely a "mouthpiece" for their clients, but believe that they should have a special model of representation, bearing in mind the vulnerability of their child clients.

The Role of Child's Counsel

As a result of Canadian experience, three different approaches to the representation for children have developed: the advocate, the guardian, and the *amicus curiae*. In the traditional advocate role, the lawyer protects and advances the interests of the child client and, if the child is capable of expressing wishes, the lawyer advances those views. The lawyer acting as guardian for the child becomes an investigator, a counsel and a guardian of the best interests of the child, in which case the wishes of the child would be one factor considered. In the *amicus curiae* (friend of the court) model, counsel is appointed by the court to assist the court in its consideration of the best interests of the child and counsel owes allegiance and responsibility ultimately to the court.

In April 1980, the Professional Conduct Committee of the Law Society of Upper Canada formed a Subcommittee to study the relationship between the lawyer and child in a child welfare proceeding. This Subcommittee recommended that lawyers representing children adopt the traditional "solicitor-client approach," rather than the "guardianship type of representation," at least in situations where the child has capacity to instruct a lawyer.[5] The issue of the capacity of the child to instruct counsel must be determined by the individual lawyer in the particular circumstances of the case. The Subcommittee did not recommend any changes to the Rules of Professional Conduct, nor was it prepared to offer specific direction on the appropriate representational stance of the child's lawyer.

The role of child's counsel has evolved with little guidance from the legislature or professional bodies. Ontario's statute simply provides for the availability of "legal representation" for the child in circumstances where the court considers it "desirable to protect the interests of the child."[6] The statute sets out criteria for the court to consider when deciding whether to order representation, such as: if the agency proposes to remove the child from the parent's care and there are differing views between the child and the parents, or the child and the agency; if the child is in care and no parent appears before the court; if it is alleged the child is in need of protection by reason of physical harm, sexual abuse, or emotional abuse; or, if the child is not permitted to be present at the hearing (which would include children under 12 who are usually excluded and those 12 and older who may be excluded by court order if they would be emotionally harmed by being present). In practice, Ontario courts will usually direct repre-

---

[5] *Report of the Law Society of Upper Canada Subcommittee on Representation of Children* (Toronto: Law Society of Upper Canada, 1980). The Law Society of Upper Canada is the professional governing body for lawyers in Ontario.

[6] *Child and Family Services Act*, S.O. 1984, c. 55, s. 38.

sentation for the child in any case for which the agency, parents or an interested party requests it. If a child contacts the court or agency to request counsel, this will invariably be provided. In most contested child protection cases in Ontario there is now a lawyer for the child. In practice, arrangements for representation may be made without a court order.

The Ontario legislation does not comment on the representational stance of the child's legal representative. Two leading cases in the area provide different viewpoints on the role of child's counsel. In the case of *Re W.*, Judge Abella held that the court should not dictate to a child's lawyer the role of the lawyer in the proceeding. However, certain guidelines were offered. The judge was of the view that the lawyer for a child is no different than the lawyer for any other party, stating that "He or she is there to represent the client by protecting the client's interests and carrying out the client's instruction ... "[7] Judge Abella commented that there must be flexibility in the role of the lawyer, depending on the ability of the child to instruct counsel and where capacity is lacking, protecting the client's interests by ensuring that the evidence before the court is complete and accurate.

In the case of *Re C.*, Judge Karswick allowed counsel for the children to convey the views and preferences of the children, as well as provide his own view of what was in the best interests of the children:

> It can be acknowledged that the views and preferences of a child are not necessarily the determining factor in deciding the issue of custody but simply one important element among a number of others that have to be considered in resolving the crucial issue. When one considers the fundamental importance of this issue of custody for both the family and the community I do not think that the court can, nor should it, direct the child's counsel to take a strict adversarial role and act as a "mouthpiece," blindly advocating a view, preference or instructions which confound or shock his professional opinion of what is in the best interest of the child. It makes eminently good sense to have counsel take an active, real and positive role in the social context of the Family Court and, as officers of this Court, assume the obligation to adduce all relevant and material evidence on the issue of what is in the best interest of the child and when called upon, to express a professional and responsible view of what that disposition should be.[8]

In a recent decision, counsel for an 11-year-old girl outlined the views of the child to the court, but due to the child's ambivalence and situation, also advanced a position based upon her own assessment of the best interests of the child. The judge, Nasmith P.C.J., was critical of that approach and commented:

> I have some concerns, as I have expressed before, about the idea of the child's lawyer (especially where the child is approaching 12 years of age) taking any position other than the traditional position of a lawyer taking instructions and

---

[7]   *Re W.* (1980), 13 R.F.L. 380 at 382 (Ont. Prov. Ct - Fam. Div.).

[8]   *Re C.* (1980), 14 R.F.L. (2d) 21 at 25–26 (Ont. Prov. Ct - Fam. Div.).

acting pursuant to the stated wishes of the client. The maternalism involved in [the child's lawyer's] approach, I think, as a general matter, is problematic insofar as it deprives the child of a direct mouthpiece and involves the lawyer in taking a role in assessing all of the evidence and then making a decision as to what is considered to be in the best interests of the child.[9]

It is noteworthy that the approach suggested by Judge Nasmith to representing children does not take into account the various emotional factors which may affect the expressed wishes of a child in a protection case. If conveying the stated wishes of the child was the sole role of child's counsel, surely such information could be more easily brought to the court's attention by a variety of other means.

The question of the appropriate role is probably the most difficult issue for lawyers representing children. To offer assistance to lawyers providing such services under the auspices of the Official Guardian's Office in Ontario, guidelines have been formulated. These are not directives, as counsel for the child is the independent representative for the child and is not acting on behalf of the Official Guardian. The guidelines reflect a combination of the approaches suggested by the courts in the early decisions discussed above, as well as the approach of the Subcommittee of the Law Society. Where the child lacks the capacity to instruct a lawyer, counsel should adopt a "best interests approach" to representation, putting forward counsel's own view as to the best disposition. Where the child is able to express views and preferences, those views must be communicated to the court. Those views should be the basis of the position of counsel, *unless* the wishes of the child would result in the child being placed in a situation of peril. In that event, counsel should convey those wishes to the court, but should also present evidence which would assist the court in formulating a disposition in the best interests of the child.

Counsel for the child often faces argument from the protection agency or the parents that they advocate for the best interests of the child and that, therefore, a lawyer for a child is unnecessary. The experience of lawyers representing children shows otherwise. The experience of the Ontario Child Representation Programme show that the child's counsel has frequently assisted in narrowing issues and converting contested cases to matters resolved on consent. Lawyers representing children can play a unique role in narrowing issues and serving as informal mediators. One of the reasons for this success is that lawyers for children are seen as independent and without a particular stance to which they must adhere.

For example, in one case when sexual abuse allegations were made and there was complete denial by the alleged perpetrator, there appeared to be no middle ground. The role of the child's counsel in informal pre-trials was to support a plan for the protection of the child through therapy and supervision. This involved encouraging the parents and the agency to both make certain concessions, leading to a settlement that was in the best interests of the child, without going to trial. Counsel for the other parties did not have the same ability to effect such

---

[9] *C.A.S. of Metropolitan Toronto* v. *Duke K. and Mary K.* (1989), 2 Ont. Fam. L.R. 111 at 111–12, 13 A.C.W.S. (3d) 277 (Ont. Prov. Ct - Fam. Div.).

resolution because they were perceived as having a vested interest and lacking objectivity. The effect of a negotiated result on the administration of justice, the family and, in particular the child, cannot be underestimated.

Lawyers for children have an important role in ensuring that all relevant evidence is placed before the court. While the other parties in a proceeding may not be prepared to produce reports or information unfavourable to their client's position, child's counsel may call all evidence that would assist the court in its determination of the best interests of the child. Counsel for the child may present information about the child and on behalf of the child, while avoiding the trauma of having the child called as a witness and being subject to cross-examination by lawyers for the agency and parents. In a recent case of a lengthy protection trial involving, amongst other things, allegations of sexual abuse, counsel for the child was successful in obtaining orders to quash subpoenas initiated by the parent's counsel that required the children to testify.[10] Child's counsel had an important role in demonstrating that emotional harm would result if the child was required to testify, yet was able to ensure that all relevant evidence about the children was before the court. In fact, numerous videotapes of statements made by the children to their therapist were available to the court.

Child protection agencies are obliged to apprehend children in high risk situations, yet try to preserve the integrity of the family. These helper and enforcer roles are often in conflict. Lawyers representing children are not encumbered by this conflict. In one case involving physical abuse allegations[11], the agency sought to terminate its involvement because of the therapist's view that the parents had made a substantial effort to involve themselves in therapy, and should therefore be "rewarded" by the agency's withdrawal from the case. Child's counsel adamantly opposed such termination and recommended continued supervision for a period, so the child would be monitored until he would be able to articulate his views sufficiently to offer some protection to himself. The parties eventually acceded to the position of counsel for the child; the case demonstrates the difficulty faced by the agency in performing both the helper and enforcer functions.

In several Canadian jurisdictions, child welfare laws have been moving toward less intervention by protection agencies, the preservation of the family unit and the least restrictive alternative as a model of assisting families. Thus, the child protection agency may feel obliged to seek a temporary wardship order rather than a permanent order in order to allow parents an opportunity to improve their situation. While this is clearly preferable from the parents' perspective, consideration must also be given to the effect of lengthy delays on young children. A lawyer for the child is not encumbered in the same way as the agency

---

[10] *Children's Aid Society of Hamilton-Wentworth* v. *D.C., H.C. and M.R.* (30 March 1987), (Unified Fam. Ct) [unreported], Beckett J.

[11] *In the matter of Children's Aid Society of Metropolitan Toronto* v. *C.J. and J.B.* (1986), (Prov. Ct - Fam. Div.) [unreported].

and may have a key role in expediting the case so permanent wardship and adoption can occur at the earliest opportunity, in situations where the parental history is not promising and no progress is being made toward returning the child without significant risk.

Finally, lawyers representing children with capacity to provide instructions often advocate the wishes of the child. It is the agency's mandate to protect children in accordance with the statutory provision. The position of the agency may conflict with the child's wishes. Agencies are not able to advocate the best interests and wishes of the child simultaneously. Lawyers representing children can perform an advocacy role, presenting the child's wishes in the courtroom, and can play an important role by informing the child of developments and major decisions affecting the child's life.

For all of these reasons, independent legal representation of children has become an appealing concept.

Confidentiality

The issue of determining which stance to adopt while representing a child is unique to the child's counsel, whereas many other dilemmas of dealing with children at risk are similar for lawyers and mental health professionals. In many protection cases children have difficulty forming relationships and developing a sense of confidence in adults, whether these adults are there to assist children or not. Over time and with effort, an important relationship may be created with a social worker, lawyer, doctor or teacher. When children communicate confidential information to a trusted adult, a number of dilemmas emerge. The professional is interested in helping the child and therefore protecting the child from risk. However, the child often recognizes the ramifications of the professional divulging information received from the child to the court, parents or other professionals.

For most professionals, their decision is straightforward. All Canadian provinces have child abuse reporting laws. The professional who has reasonable grounds to suspect that a child is suffering or may have suffered abuse is required to report. This obligation applies even though the information reported may be confidential or privileged. However, the duty to report does not override solicitor-client privilege. Thus, the child's lawyer may have important but confidential information and not be obliged to disclose this to the court or a protection agency. How does the lawyer handle this? If the lawyer divulges information against the child's instructions, the solicitor-client relationship may be damaged forever.

Many lawyers are prepared to decide by considering which approach is least detrimental to the child. The lawyer representing the child wants to prevent ongoing abuse and protect the child from such risk. The Rules of Professional

Conduct permit the disclosure of confidential information in order to prevent the commission of a future crime, though they do not require such a disclosure.[12] For example, if a girl provides her lawyer with confidential information on what is occurring in the home, and yet instructs counsel that she wishes to return home and would live with her father despite the fact that he is sexually abusing her, the lawyer may breach the confidence in order to prevent ongoing sexual assault of the child but is not ethically obliged to do so. While disclosing the information may ultimately assist the child, the child may feel betrayed by the disclosure. In practice, generally the best approach for child's counsel is to encourage the child to disclose to qualified protection experts, and seek the input of the child protection authorities in offering the child and the family whatever assistance is available.

A child who makes revelations of abuse confidentially to a lawyer, typically is implicitly making a request for help. However, many abused children feel ambivalent or guilty, and are reluctant to make this request directly.

Are Children's Lawyers Really Necessary?

It is sometimes suggested that resources, limited as they are in the child protection area, should be utilized to prevent and treat child abuse rather than to involve yet another lawyer in the court process. It has also been suggested that lawyers are ill-equipped to deal with children who are victims of abuse and neglect. These criticisms are shortsighted. Lawyers representing children have an important role in the court process which will determine essential issues affecting the child. Lawyers can learn to become better equipped to deal with a specialized clientele. There is no doubt that ongoing training of lawyers is essential to maintain knowledge and expertise in this very specialized field, and lawyers representing children are generally committed to continuing education in order to serve their very exceptional clientele better.

Child's counsel is also usually eager to receive assistance and input from experts who can provide the necessary factual and opinion evidence to assist in the case. For this reason, lawyers representing children often adopt the multidisciplinary approach to child representation, drawing on the expertise of various professionals when formulating a position. Each discipline can benefit from the input of the other, and no one professional can provide all the answers to this grave problem.

It is sometimes difficult for other professionals involved in the child protection system to accept the role of child's counsel, especially if counsel is advocating a result which the social worker, medical doctor or other expert may consider contrary to the best interests of the child. However, if all the professionals

---

[12] Law Society of Upper Canada, *Rules of Professional Conduct* (Toronto: Law Society of Upper Canada, 1987) Rule 4, Commentary 11.

assisting children in this difficult process are prepared to accept that each has a unique role to play, a mutual understanding of respective roles will emerge.

Child Representation in Various Provinces

There is substantial variation in how legal representation is provided for children in different Canadian jurisdictions. Unfortunately, it is not available through a formalized scheme in all provinces. In Ontario, the program has existed for almost 10 years and is administered through the Office of the Official Guardian and a specially selected panel of lawyers who are appointed because of their experience and interest in representation of children. They are required to participate in continuing education programs offered from time to time.

In British Columbia, there is provision under the *Family Relations Act* for the provincial Attorney General to appoint a "family advocate" to act as counsel for the interests and welfare of the child in certain legal proceedings, including child protection and adoption cases.[13] Representation can be provided through the services of a lawyer employed by the Ministry of the Attorney General or by private counsel paid by the Ministry. In practice, there is rarely legal representation for a child in protection proceedings in British Columbia. The Superintendent of Family and Child Services is presumed to operate with reference to the child's best interests and hence representation for the child is regarded as unnecessary. In special cases, however, legal representation has been ordered, particularly where the child is old enough to express views. In one case a 12-year-old was suffering from leukemia and required a blood transfusion.[14] The child was apprehended because of the parents' failure to allow such treatment. The court felt it was appropriate to have the family advocate provide separate legal representation for the child.

In Alberta, there has been considerable controversy over the representation of children. In 1985, the province created the Office of the Children's Guardian. While the Director of Child Welfare retained responsibility for the provision of child protection services, including the presentation of cases in court, the Children's Guardian was given legal "guardianship" over children in care. The Children's Guardian could also participate in protection proceedings and was expected to have a broad advocacy function for children in care. There was considerable confusion over the role of the Children's Guardian, and in a couple of highly publicized cases the position of the Guardian was contrary to the

---

[13] R.S.B.C. 1979, c. 121, s. 2; See F. Maczko, "Some Problems with Acting for Children" (1978) 2 Can. J. Fam. L. 267, which describes the British Columbia model of "Family Advocate" representation.

[14] *In the matter of Sarah Joy M.* (3 November 1988), (B.C. Prov. Ct) [unreported], Auxler P.C.J.

wishes of the child. In one case, the judge indicated that a child had a constitutional right to independent legal representation separate from that of the Children's Guardian, as the proceedings threatened her "liberty and security of the person."[15] There were a number of cases in which the Alberta Legal Aid Plan ensured that children in child welfare cases had their own lawyers.[16]

As a result of the controversy and court challenges, new legislation has been enacted in Alberta to clarify and circumscribe the authority of the renamed Children's Advocate and to specify that the Office is intended to "represent the rights, interests, and viewpoints of children."[17] Experience with the ambiguity in the role of counsel for children in Ontario suggests that the new Alberta statute may not have resolved all of the uncertainty, as there may be a conflict between rights, interests and viewpoints.

In Saskatchewan, there is no separate child representation program for protection cases as the Ministry of Social Services is viewed as being responsible for protecting the best interests of the child.

In Manitoba, *The Child and Family Services Act*, provides:

> In the case of a child, a judge ... may order that legal counsel be appointed to represent the interests of the child and, if the child is 12 years of age or older, may order that the child have the right to instruct the legal counsel.[18]

The statute further sets forth factors affecting the need for counsel for the child.

In the Province of Québec, the *Youth Protection Act* requires that the court inform the parents and the child of their right to be represented by a lawyer and further provides:

> Where the court establishes that the interests of the child are opposed to those of his parents, it must see that an advocate is specifically assigned to the defence of the child and that he does not act, at the same time, as counsel or attorney for the parents.[19]

In Québec, the Legal Aid system has staff lawyers who specialize in the representation of children in protection cases and other youth related matters.

---

[15] *Tschritter* v. *Children's Guardian* (1989), 19 R.F.L. (3d) 1 (Alta C.A.); see also *N.P.P.* v. *Regional Children's Guardian* (1988), 14 R.F.L. (3d) 55 (Alta Q.B.).

[16] The Alberta *Child Welfare Act*, S.A. 1984, c. C–8.1, s. 78 allows a judge to "direct that the child be represented by a lawyer" if the child, the Director of Child Welfare or a parent requests it and the court is satisfied that the "interests or views of the child would not be otherwise adequately represented."

[17] *Child Welfare Amendment Act of 1988*, S.A. 1988, c. 15, s. 2.1(3)(c).

[18] R.S.M. 1987, c. C80, s. 34(2).

[19] R.S.Q. 1977, c. P–34.1, s. 80.

In New Brunswick, the *Family Services Act* allows for the appointment of counsel for the child in protection cases and custody or access disputes through the Attorney General's office.[20]

In Newfoundland, there is no separate system of representation for children in protection cases. Counsel has been appointed in exceptional cases.[21] A similar situation exists in Nova Scotia, where separate representation has been provided on an infrequent basis by order of the court.

In Prince Edward Island, there is no separate child representation program. As in Saskatchewan, the Ministry of Health and Social Services is regarded as responsible for protecting the best interests of the child.

In the North West Territories there is no program of independent representation, although the court has directed that legal counsel be appointed in exceptional cases. The lawyer is selected through the legal aid panel and is paid through the Social Services Ministry.

Conclusion: The Complex Role of Children's Lawyers

It is apparent that there is enormous variation in the availability of counsel for children in different Canadian provinces. In discussing the possible models of representation, reference was made to the *amicus curiae* role, the traditional advocate role and the guardian role. In some cases, a blending of the three models of representation may occur. McHale discusses the appropriate role for a lawyer representing children in protection cases:

> It is submitted that a major factor in the role confusion often experienced by counsel representing children is the tacit expectation that a single role should cover all aspects of their duties. The lawyer's proper role as representative of the child involves in fact a variety of roles. While the desire for a single, invariable role is understandable, the unique nature of litigation involving children does not allow exclusive adherence to any one of the above mentioned orientations if the child's best interests are to be realized. Determination of the proper role in a given case is achieved only after considering the kind of proceeding, the state of proceeding, the needs of the child represented and the capacity of the child to express his own wishes to counsel.[22]

To deal with the complex issues involving the role of child's counsel, lawyers should receive continuing education and training, including input from other

---

[20] S.N.B. 1980, c. F–2.2, s. 7.

[21] In *Beson* v. *Director of Child Welfare* (1982), 30 R.F.L. (2d) 438 (S.C.C.) the Supreme Court of Canada appointed counsel to represent a child in a dispute between prospective adoptive parents and child welfare authorities; the decision under appeal was from Newfoundland.

[22] M.J.J. McHale, "The Proper Role of the Lawyer as Legal Representative of the Child" (1980) 18 Alta L. Rev. 216 at 220.

disciplines.[23] Knowledge of childhood stages of development is essential for the lawyer who must assess the capacity of the child to instruct counsel and formulate a position accordingly.[24]

The lawyer's role in the representation of children in protection cases is both challenging and dynamic. A flexible approach to the model of representation and the formulation of representational stance is essential. To ensure that the notion of separate representation for children continues, it is important that lawyers be exposed to special ongoing training with a multidisciplinary approach in order to achieve high quality independent representation for the child client.

B: REPRESENTING PARENTS

Judge Mary Jane Hatton[*]

The multifaceted role of a lawyer as advocate, investigator and social worker is clearly demonstrated in the representation of parents in child protection proceedings. It is not sufficient for the lawyer simply to show up in court and serve as the "mouthpiece" of the parents. The preparation and presentation of the parents' case requires the doggedness of a detective, the compassion and resilience of a social worker and the eloquence of an advocate. Child protection cases are not routine cases; they do not deal in such tangibles as commercial transactions or the enforcement of contracts. They reflect and define some of the most fundamental values of our society, such as the power of the state, parental autonomy, the needs and rights of individuals within the family unit and the protection and nurturing of society's children.

Personal Framework for Practice

Many lawyers avoid representing parents in child protection proceedings. Some find this area of work depressing, as one must deal with issues such as physical abuse, sexual abuse, parental neglect and traumatized children. Not only do lawyers find these matters distressing, but they may be unable or unwilling to deal with clients who come from multi-problem backgrounds. Many parents struggle daily with chronic poverty, family violence, employment difficulties, intellectual limitations and serious emotional problems. A lawyer doing child protection work must not only cope with the legal ramifications of a case, but

---

[*] Provincial Court (Family Division), Toronto, Ontario. This chapter was written before Judge Hatton's appointment to the Bench; it reflects her views as a privately practicing lawyer.

[23] G.M. Thomson, "Eliminating Role Confusion in the Child's Lawyer: The Ontario Experience" (1983) 4 Can. J. Fam. L. 125 at 150.

[24] S. Ramsey, "Representation of the Child in Protection Proceedings: The Determination of Decision-Making Capacity" (Fall 1983) 17 Fam. L.Q. 287 at 320.

also with difficult and needy clients. The demands made by the client on the lawyer's personal and professional resources are sometimes onerous. For these reasons, many lawyers prefer less emotionally draining areas of law. For those lawyers who do enter the fray of child protection proceedings, it is important to develop a framework with which to approach this type of case. My own framework consists of three overriding principles. First, I believe that in the majority of child protection proceedings there is a systemic bias against parents by other participants in the process. There is an assumption that, if the protection agency has become involved in a family's life, there must be good reason. The assumption implies that these parents cannot properly care for their children without some form of state intervention. The lawyer for the parents must approach each case from the viewpoint that state intervention is not required in a family's life, unless proven on credible evidence and after every opportunity has been given to the parents to care for their children without state and court involvement.

Second, most parents in child protection proceedings face overwhelming obstacles in their day-to-day lives. It is helpful for me when dealing with a difficult client to ask myself how I would cope with the life situations that my clients face, such as an abusive background, single parenthood or violent marital strife. If I can recognize my clients' strengths, it is less overwhelming to deal with those aspects of their lifestyles and personalities that might seem sordid or distasteful.

Third, I remind myself that to have a child removed from a parent's care is one of the most devastating experiences a person can ever face. The lawyer's role is to make certain that state intervention is absolutely necessary and that no alternatives exist. I prefer to view child protection cases not as depressing, but as demanding of one's skills as an advocate and of one's personal resources for compassion and understanding.

Investigation of the Agency's Case

The first task for the parents' lawyer is a thorough investigation of the agency's case as early as possible in the proceeding. There are numerous advantages to conducting a thorough investigation. First, the parents' lawyer becomes fully apprised of the concerns of the agency and can discuss these issues in detail with the client. Second, if certain facts can be agreed upon, the contentious issues can be clearly identified and extraneous issues eliminated. Third, counsel can assess the weaknesses of the agency's case; this information can be used constructively to advocate the parents' position.

The information required by the lawyer includes: (a) copies of court documents and the chronology of the legal proceedings, the history of the agency's involvement with the family, including the source and reason for the initial referral, and the frequency, purpose and outcome of all contacts by agency personnel with the parent and the child; (b) a list of the resources within the agency or in the community with which the parent or child has had contact; (c) copies of assessments, reports, homestudies, case conference notes, records and other relevant documents in the possession of the agency; (d) information regarding similar documents available from other agencies or persons; (e) the allegations and concerns of the agency with respect to the client's parenting of the child; (f) information regarding any concurrent criminal proceedings; (g) the criminal record of the parent; and (h) the recommendations of the agency and the reasons for those recommendations.

The easiest way for the parents' lawyer to obtain disclosure is to arrange a meeting with the agency worker or lawyer. The parents' lawyer will seek the opportunity to review the workers' notes and recordings on the case and to interview the agency representatives. If voluntary disclosure is not forthcoming, in most jurisdictions counsel can bring a motion for disclosure before a judge, and request that the agency disclose the material facts and evidence upon which it will rely at the hearing. It is also necessary for the lawyer to obtain disclosure from any other parties, such as guardians or relatives.[25]

Conducting an Independent Investigation

In some instances, it is necessary for the parents' counsel to conduct an investigation independent from that of the agency. This occurs if the lawyer believes that the state's investigation is incomplete or seriously flawed, and the agency is unwilling to reopen it. The difficulty for the parents' lawyer is that the clients usually do not have the financial resources to conduct a thorough investigation. If a client is on a Legal Aid certificate, it is usually difficult for the lawyer to obtain the necessary authorization from the Legal Aid authorities to pay for an independent investigation. There are situations that demand further investigation by the parents and their lawyer. For example, individuals such as relatives, babysitters and other caretakers may not have been interviewed, and their input may be crucial to counteract allegations against the parents. In sexual or physical abuse cases, the agency often obtains a medical or psychiatric assessment. This diagnosis can be unfair, unduly biased against a parent or simply incomplete. It may be incumbent on the parents' lawyer to arrange for a second opinion and for any further consultations with medical personnel that are required.

In situations where further investigation is required, or obvious discrepancies and inaccuracies appear in the agency's investigation, counsel for a parent is obligated to rectify the shortcomings in appropriate ways. The parents' lawyer can advise the agency of the problems and request that the agency utilize its resources to remedy the problems. For tactical reasons, particularly in cases where a trial seems inevitable, the parents' lawyer may not want to advise the agency of the deficiencies of its case. If the agency's position can be successfully challenged and weakened at trial, then the parents' case may be strengthened. The contrary view is that a settlement may be effected earlier if there is full

---

[25] While in some jurisdictions, children may be considered parties to a protection proceeding, they are not obliged to disclose their case prior to or during a hearing.

disclosure by parents' counsel at the outset as to the incompleteness and weaknesses of the agency's position.

If the agency is unable or unwilling to reopen the investigation, a separate one should be arranged. The following approaches may be considered by the parents' lawyer:

1. Retain an expert to conduct an assessment. This could include hiring a social worker to conduct a study in the parents' home, having a team of professionals assess the family members and their interactions, or obtaining an independent psychiatric evaluation of a parent with alleged mental health problems.

2. Interview those persons previously omitted from the agency investigation, such as access supervisors, daycare providers, school teachers, relatives or friends.

3. In physical abuse or neglect cases, obtain all medical information regarding the family. This includes speaking to the family doctor and specialists who have examined the parents or children, and obtaining copies of all hospital records to note the observations of nurses, social workers and other hospital personnel. A second medical opinion should be obtained with respect to injuries and their cause. The lawyer should also explore differing medical opinions, and perhaps arrange to meet the doctors to review their findings.

4. In sexual abuse cases, the lawyer may refer the client for psychological and other relevant testing, such as phallometric testing or polygraphs. An expert's interpretation of a child's statement or contradictory statement made by the child to other persons may be obtained. If there are serious concerns about the child's credibility, the lawyer may also arrange a psychiatric consultation.

5. All community resources which have assisted the parent or child should be contacted for their observations with respect to parenting issues.

Formulating the Client's Plan

The third task of the parents' lawyer is to respond to allegations of the child protection agency by formulating a realistic and reasonable plan with the client. As a lawyer, I have found this part of the process most difficult. It is very tempting to sit in one's office and formulate an exhaustive and exhausting list of tasks for the client to perform in order to obtain the return of a child. We all have views of what clients should or should not do. However, many clients do not have the personal resources we might wish. Many parents suffer from difficulties such as health problems, mental instability, emotional fragility, poverty and immigrant adjustment problems. The lawyer must avoid the belief that he or she can save clients from all adversities. The lawyer must be clear-sighted about the client's abilities and limitations, and must work with the parent to formulate a realistic plan.

Many lawyers have little experience with the cultural and socioeconomic problems of child protection clients. Many of the clients are transient, isolated within their communities or experience feelings of powerlessness and hopelessness. Some have psychological or social problems, such as drug addiction, mental illness or developmental handicaps. Other clients are simply unable to follow even uncomplicated instructions or fulfill realistic expectations. These problems have the potential to alienate the client from the lawyer or the lawyer from the client, as each has different expectations of what can or should be done.

The lawyer must tread carefully with the client in formulating a parenting plan. The lawyer must remain sympathetic to the client's plight and, at the same time, point out valid concerns of the agency and the legal issues to be faced in the court proceeding. The lawyer must confront the client with parenting problems, while offering support and encouragement to help the client overcome them. In many cases the parents will find it difficult to trust an authority figure, including their own lawyer. The parent may see the lawyer as part of the overall system. If the lawyer is unduly harsh or judgmental, the client will lose confidence in the lawyer as an ally and advocate. However, if the lawyer minimizes concerns or fails to discuss detrimental evidence, the parent will not make necessary changes or be sufficiently apprised of the seriousness of the case.

I have found the best approach is to advise the parent in a factual manner of the evidence, and of findings of fact a judge will likely make. I explore with clients their version of events and allegations, including positive aspects of the evidence. Even if the evidence is fairly overwhelming against the parent, it is important to suggest changes in their behaviour that could counteract the agency's concerns.

It is difficult when a client refuses to acknowledge parenting problems or minimizes the impact of their behaviour on a child. The client who continually denies wrongdoing or inadequacies is not usually open to counselling, assessment or suggestions of different ways to parent. The most the lawyer can do in these situations is point out the strengths of the agency's case and advise the client of the likely result if certain problems are not alleviated.

Many parents will make promises and resolutions to do things differently if the child is returned home. Past experience may have demonstrated to the lawyer that such good intentions often are not realized. The lawyer should encourage the client to be realistic about what can be accomplished and to set goals that are not recipes for failure.[26] The plan should be simple, but sufficiently detailed and comprehensive so that all agency concerns are addressed in some way.

The parenting plan should address the following issues:

1. If the parent is seeking the child's return, all aspects of day-to-day care should be presented. This includes information about accommodations,

---

[26] Relatively little has been written for lawyers on dealing with parents in protection cases. However, for a good discussion, see R. Groves, "Lawyers, Psychologists and Psychological Evidence in Protection Hearings " (1980) 5 Queen's L.J. 241 at 252–54.

amenities available in the neighbourhood, the availability of schools, the parents' employment, child care and babysitting arrangements, the availability of relatives and friends as caretakers, and information about a spouse or partner with whom the parent is living.

2. In those cases where there are valid concerns about a parent, specific proposals must be provided for alleviating or eliminating those problems. For example, if a parent is an alcoholic or drug abuser, the client should attend a self-help group, psychiatric counselling or a specialized treatment program for addicts. Similarly, if mental health issues are raised, the parent should begin a program of therapy recommended by a competent professional. The parent should enroll in these programs at the earliest possible time and be able to provide evidence of progress at the trial.

3. If the issue is that the child needs treatment, the parent must propose a plan whereby treatment will be provided.

4. Sometimes the dispute centres on the question of a parent's access to a child. The parent's recommendation on access should propose the frequency, duration and location of the visits, the transportation arrangements and the degree and method of supervision, if any. If the contact is to take place in the parent's home, the parent should propose specific routines and activities and describe how they will benefit the child.

5. The parent should focus on short- and long-term goals with respect to the child. For example, a parent may not be ready to have a child returned home because the parent has unsuitable accommodation. In this case, the parent should propose a scheme of regular frequent visits with the child over a specified period, and the return of the child when accommodation has been secured.

6. It is crucial that the lawyer connect the client with community resources and supports. These are often community agencies with a different mandate and function from the protection authorities. The community agencies may have more supportive relationships with the parents. As previously stated, many clients are simply overwhelmed by numerous problems. Some of these problems can be addressed through the use of other resources, such as after-school programs for the children, babysitters to provide relief for a single parent or supportive groups in the community.

Child protection proceedings are a massive invasion by the state into the most private and intimate aspects of a person's life. Most clients resent this invasion and have trouble coping with the demands of so many people, including social workers, lawyers, assessors and community resources. All plans formulated by the parent in conjunction with the lawyer should balance the state's mandate to safeguard the well-being of a child with preserving the parents' sense of privacy. A plan that does not recognize the fundamental need of a parent for dignity, self-respect and privacy is doomed to failure.

Advocating the Client's Position

The fourth task of the lawyer is that of advocacy. Vigorously advocating and defending the parents' position is not confined to the trial; it is also an integral part of the negotiations and interim hearings.

Obtaining instructions from the client can be problematic. In certain cases, a client will present a position that the lawyer knows will not be accepted by the court and that may be harmful to the client's case. Although the lawyer will attempt to influence or modify those instructions, it is ultimately the parents' case, not the lawyer's. If the lawyer feels psychologically or morally incapable of advocating the client's plan, the lawyer should withdraw from the case and suggest that the clients either retain other counsel or represent themselves.

Advocating the client's position involves protecting the client's interests at all stages of the proceedings. For example, if there is an ongoing conflict between a client and a case worker, the lawyer may request that all further communication between the two be through counsel. This curtails the ability of the agency to gather further negative evidence against the client. However, this stance may backfire on the parent, if the parent is seen as uncooperative, evasive and uncommunicative. In addition, the agency may not be able to fully assess the parents' plan.

The lawyer must keep the parent apprised of the evidence as it is collected and discuss with the client ways to counteract negative evidence and bring out positive evidence.

Good advocacy includes attempting to obtain a reasonable settlement of the case without protracted litigation. A meeting of all the parties and their counsel should take place early in the proceeding, no later than at the conclusion of the preliminary investigations. The purpose of a settlement meeting is to clarify each party's position and to explore possible areas of agreement and compromise. In less serious cases, it may be possible for parents' counsel to negotiate a voluntary service contract between the parent and the agency, on the condition that the court application be withdrawn. Even when agreement cannot be reached on all the contentious issues, the areas of disagreement can be more clearly delineated and the trial shortened and simplified.

An independent assessment of all the parties is another useful tool for settlement. If the parties can agree to have a professional assessment done by a particular expert, they should also define in advance the issues to be addressed in the assessment, the background information to be provided to the assessor, the persons to be interviewed and the scope of the assessment. The recommendations of the assessor may be instrumental in achieving a settlement among the parties or, if the case goes to trial, may be highly influential in the litigation.

An assessment is not always helpful to the parents' position. If the lawyer has misgivings about the benefits of an assessment, the lawyer should advise the client of those misgivings. If the parents are determined to go to trial in the face of overwhelming evidence against them, an assessment will only add greater weight to the agency's position and will be unlikely to procure a settlement.

A recent development across Canada is the use of mediation in some child protection matters. Under the guidance of a trained mediator, the parties, including the agency, try to effect a settlement. The mediator's role is to act as a neutral facilitator. A lawyer acting for a parent might consider this option provided the mediator is skilled in redressing any power imbalances between the parties. However, the agency is unlikely to agree to mediation if they have strong concerns about the risk to the child of having a continuing relationship with the parents.

In many jurisdictions, there will be a pre-trial conference in an effort to settle cases or to shorten the final hearing by narrowing issues. At the "pre-trial," each party will advise a judge of the witnesses to be called, each witness's evidence, documentary evidence and of the position to be put forth. Pre-trials can be particularly useful for a parent's lawyer. If the pre-trial judge can be persuaded of the merits of the parents' position, this can influence the other parties to settle the case. Alternatively, the input of the judge at the pre-trial stage might convince the parent not to oppose the agency's plan.

The trial itself presents a number of strategic options to the parents' lawyer. The tactical approach taken by the lawyer depends on the parents' position, the strengths and weaknesses of each party's case, the credibility of the parent as a witness, the availability of corroborating witnesses and the strategies of the other lawyers.

At the commencement of the trial, the parents' counsel will generally state the parents' position. This brief opening statement should summarize the allegations that are admitted, the issues in dispute and the parents' plan. This strategy directs the judge's attention to the contentious areas; the judge will also be aware of the parents' recommendation as the agency evidence unfolds.

An obvious strategy for the parents' lawyer is to cross-examine the witnesses called by the agency and by any other parties. Several methods can be used, such as testing the reliability of observations, posing other possible explanations for the events described, pointing out evidence that contradicts the witness's testimony, drawing out biases and preconceptions from the witness or attacking the witness's credibility. Another approach on cross-examination is to question the thoroughness of the social worker's investigation, the even-handedness of the worker's approach to the parent, and the range of services offered to the client.

In some cases, it may be unlikely that the impact of a witness's testimony can be lessened on cross-examination. In these situations, it is better not to cross-examine the agency's witnesses but, rather, the lawyer for the parents will attempt to rebut the witness's evidence through the parents' testimony or with the evidence of other witnesses called on behalf of the parent.

The lawyer can choose not to call the parent to testify. This tactic poses significant risks, as the judge will not have the opportunity to assess the parents' credibility and sincerity, nor will the judge be able to hear the details of their plan for the child directly from the parents.

At the conclusion of the hearing, the parents' counsel should make submissions emphasizing those aspects of the parents' plan which address the agency's protection concerns. The lawyer's goal is to persuade the court that the client's position is a reasonable and realistic response to the identified problems and that the agency's recommendations are unnecessarily drastic or intrusive.

Conclusion

In a decision-making process which so profoundly affects the lives of children and families, it is reassuring to see parents being represented by a diligent, energetic and committed lawyer. In my experience, the representation of parents in child protection proceedings is the most demanding yet the most rewarding area of family law. The "odds" are usually against your client. The client may be difficult, defensive and emotionally demanding. There will often be very significant social, cultural and educational differences between yourself and your clients. In some cases the alleged behaviour of your client toward his or her child may be repulsive to you; in other cases the invasive actions of the state may offend your notions of family autonomy and personal privacy and integrity.

The challenge of representing parents in child protection cases lies in balancing all these considerations, while remaining mindful of the primary function—that is, advocating the client's position.

C: REPRESENTING THE AGENCY

Jennifer A. Blishen[*]

Given the high profile of child protection litigation over the past decade, it is easy to understand why child protection agencies increasingly need access to lawyers for legal advice and representation.

The practice of agencies having a court worker for legal representation developed in the days when judges dealing with child protection matters were often not legally trained, parents rarely had lawyers, and child representation was unheard of. The court worker was generally an experienced social worker who, through a combination of interest, talent or necessity, would assume the role of agency representative in protection proceedings. Although still used by some agencies, the role of the court worker in child protection has rapidly diminished in recent years, since even the most routine matters require the specialized skills of a lawyer.

---

[*] Senior Counsel, The Children's Aid Society of Ottawa-Carleton, Ottawa, Ontario.

Models for Representation

Child protection agencies must now consider how to best provide legal representation. In Canada, types of protection services for children vary, as do the legal services to support them.

The legal services of child protection agencies are usually based on one of the following models:

- a court worker (not a lawyer) who routinely presents cases on behalf of the child protection agency, usually with help from a lawyer on difficult, contested matters;
- a lawyer in private practice who is retained by the agency on a standing or on a case-by-case basis;
- a staff lawyer within the child protection agency (in-house counsel);
- a government lawyer (attached either to the Ministry that deals with the provision of child protection services or to the provincial Ministry of the Attorney General); or,
- some combination of the above.

Most agencies, particularly in Ontario and Québec, now opt for the in-house counsel mode of legal representation. This is often precipitated by the escalating costs of retaining outside counsel. If annual legal bills are between $50,000 and $100,000, an agency should consider hiring a lawyer. Some of the arguments in favour of having staff lawyers are as follows:

1. There is a reduced cost to the agency for legal fees.

2. In-house lawyers are readily available for ongoing case consultation and planning. Using lawyers for case planning can prevent disruption of plans which fail to accord with legal requirements or realities.

3. In-house counsel are able to gain an understanding of the organizational, social, economic and political aspects of day-to-day functioning within the agency. They also become sensitized to and appreciative of the clinical aspects of the service. However, staff lawyers must never assume the role of social worker or become so immersed in bureaucratic considerations that they lose objectivity in making legal decisions. An agency hires a lawyer for legal representation and advice on the law, not to provide social work services.

4. Staff lawyers can practice preventive law by providing advice on the development of procedures and policies, and by anticipating legal pitfalls or errors. Lawyers can propose alternative measures to avoid the possibility of illegality. The provision of training programs for agency staff on legal issues and evidentiary considerations can also serve as a form of preventive law.

5. Experienced staff lawyers, who are familiar with the relevant legislation and with Ministry and agency policies and procedures, are well-equipped to make material contributions to the formulation of new government policy and legislation. This should be encouraged.

While there are benefits to having staff lawyers, there are also difficulties associated with their use. Compared to incomes in private practice, salaries for child protection staff lawyers are generally modest, especially in the case of experienced counsel. Similarly, ongoing career prospects or options within child protection make it difficult to attract experienced counsel. Common resources to law firms such as modern office equipment, a law library, and well-trained support staff, are rarely found in child protection agencies. Because of these factors, there is a tendency to hire younger, less-experienced lawyers who often leave after a few years, just as they are gaining some expertise. As a result, staff lawyers in the protection field sometimes lack experience and a broad base of expertise.

Many of the problems associated with retaining experienced staff lawyers also make it difficult to keep experienced child protection workers. Many child protection cases, especially those of a high profile or controversial nature, proceed to trial. It is unfortunate that child protection agencies are not more frequently represented by skilled, experienced counsel with appropriate administrative supports.

An agency may need to retain specialized counsel to deal with issues outside the day-to-day expertise of their staff lawyers. For example, specialized knowledge in the area of labour relations may occasionally be required by a child protection agency, especially if staff is unionized.

The Role of the Agency Lawyer in Child Protection Cases

If a case is involved in the court process, the agency's lawyer should assist the caseworker in the management of day-to-day issues, such as parental access and obtaining medical reports and assessments. The lawyer should become involved in a contested case at an early stage, to provide ongoing advice and direction. A team approach is generally the most effective method of preparing a case for court.

Social workers in child protection are sometimes dismayed to find that agency counsel do not perform their functions in the same manner as a lawyer would in acting for a private client. At times it appears that caseworkers would be most satisfied if the agency's lawyer served as simply the agency's "mouthpiece" before the court. While in the course of all civil cases, a lawyer's conduct is governed by a duty to the court, to the standards of the profession and to the public, the paramount duty in the traditional civil case is to the client.[27] This duty was clearly articulated in an 1820 English case.

> An advocate, by the sacred duty which he owes his client, knows in the discharge of that office, but one person in the world, that client and none other.

---

[27] W.B. Williston & R.J. Rolls, *The Conduct of an Action* (Toronto: Butterworths, 1982) at 180.

To save the client by all expedient means—to protect that client at all hazards and costs to all others, and amongst others to himself—is the highest and most unquestioned of his duties; and he must not regard the alarm, the suffering, the torment, the destruction, which he may bring upon any other.[28]

Child protection cases, however, are different from other civil cases; in particular, they do not deal with disputes between two private individuals. Child protection agencies serve as an arm of the state, intervening in families to protect children and promote their interests and well-being. It has been suggested that a child protection agency is "appointed by the community to act in matters to protect the interests of children."[29] Their lawyers, therefore, are acting on behalf of society and their duty must correspond to that role. The role of agency counsel is thus not the same as that of a lawyer for a private litigant.

A lawyer for a private litigant is ethically obliged to not knowingly put false evidence before a court, but does not have an obligation to bring forward evidence unfavourable to the position of his or her client. As a public functionary, the lawyer for the child protection agency has a broader role. The agency lawyer should disclose its case to the parties prior to court and should present to the court all relevant, credible evidence. No relevant evidence should be suppressed in order to "win" the case.

Presentation and Disclosure of Evidence

A lawyer representing a child protection agency is responsible for presenting a collective agency viewpoint to the court. This collective viewpoint is often reached only after numerous consultations between the caseworker, supervisor and, sometimes, the agency director. It can include input from other agency resource workers and even outside personnel, such as psychologists, doctors, public health nurses and homemakers. With such a large number of individuals involved, there can be disagreement about the ultimate position to be taken by the agency. These ongoing internal debates are healthy and normal, and reflect the very controversy which makes a contested hearing before the court legitimate.

A question arises about the duty of the agency's lawyer: should the fact that there are potential witnesses, who may be agency employees, whose evidence and opinions may not be supportive of the agency's position be disclosed to the court or other parties? It is this author's opinion that the child protection lawyer has a primary duty to present the evidence that is necessary to successfully put the issues before the court. To fail to bring forward important witnesses simply because their evidence or opinions do not support the agency's position would not be in the interests of justice, and would be a breach of the duty of counsel for

---

[28] *Ibid.* at 180.

[29] *Re Helmes* (1976), 13 O.R. (2d) 4, 28 R.F.L. 380 (Ont. Div. Ct).

a protection agency to the court. Child protection cases are extremely serious and determine the future of a child; all relevant evidence must be heard by the judge.

Child protection has become an increasingly adversarial process and it is sometimes difficult for agency counsel to maintain a balanced approach. The very nature of cases, such as those involving physical or sexual abuse, may be so repugnant to agency counsel that they wish to take a traditional adversarial approach. However, to let personal feelings interfere with professional judgment would be inappropriate. Careful recruitment of counsel and training as to their duty to the court, along with the experience gained in presenting cases before the court, can lessen or alleviate these difficulties.

It is important to note that the duty to present all relevant evidence must be tempered by an obligation to minimize the length of the hearing, if possible. Most courts encourage counsel to narrow the issues and to reduce the volume of evidence whenever possible, through the use of pre-trial conferences and disclosure.

In civil litigation there is usually a requirement for full and complete disclosure of evidence to avoid surprises at trial and to enable cases to be evaluated and tried on their true merits.[30] In child protection, full and complete disclosure is also the rule. However, there may be exceptions and often delicate judgment calls are required in the release of information, especially if it includes the identity of informants who fear retaliation, the identity or whereabouts of foster parents or potential adoptive parents, or information that may result in harm to a client or third party if released. The timing of disclosure may also be important. For example, in a child sexual abuse case, disclosure of the allegations to the alleged perpetrators or their counsel prior to police questioning may badly undermine the police investigation.

The child protection lawyer may find guidance with respect to the presentation of evidence and disclosure by examining the role of the Crown attorney in a criminal case. The Canadian Bar Association's *Code of Professional Conduct* sets out the ethical standard for the special role of a prosecutor in a criminal case:

> When engaged as a prosecutor, the lawyer's prime duty is not to seek a conviction but to present before the trial court all available, credible evidence relevant to the alleged crime in order that justice may be done through a fair trial upon the merits. The prosecutor exercises a public function involving much discretion and power and must act fairly and dispassionately. The prosecutor should ... make timely disclosure to the accused or defence counsel (or to the court if the accused is not represented) of all relevant facts and known

---

[30] E.A. Cherniak, "The Ethics of Advocacy" (1985) 19 L. Soc. Gaz. 145. See also Chapter 3 of this book concerning pre-trial conferences and disclosure.

witnesses, whether tending to show guilt or innocence, or that would affect the punishment of the accused.[31]

Thus the duty of the Crown is not to "win" the case or to obtain a conviction but to see that justice is done by presenting all relevant evidence. As Justice Rand of the Supreme Court of Canada stated in 1954:

> It cannot be over-emphasized that the purpose of a criminal prosecution is not to obtain a conviction, it is to lay before the jury what the Crown considers to be credible evidence relevant to what is alleged to be a crime. Counsel have a duty to see that all available legal proof of the facts is presented: it should be done firmly and pressed to its legitimate strength but it must also be done fairly. The role of prosecutor excludes any notion of winning or losing; his function is a matter of public duty than [sic] which in civil life there can be none charged with greater personal responsibility. It is to be efficiently performed with ingrained sense of the dignity, the seriousness and the justness of judicial proceedings.[32]

There are some who argue that the role of child protection lawyers should be no different than that of a privately retained advocate acting on instructions to further their clients' interests. Others, including this author, see the role of the child protection lawyer as most closely analogous to that of the Crown attorney, with the corresponding public duty.

If a similar guideline was drafted for the role of a child protection lawyer it might read as follows:

> When engaged as counsel for a child protection agency, the lawyer's prime duty is not to seek the order requested by the child protection agency, but to present before the trial court all available, credible evidence relevant to the application, in order that the protection and best interests of the child can be achieved through a fair trial upon the merits.

Of course, this does not mean that the lawyer for the agency has a strictly neutral stance in the proceedings. The agency's lawyer has a particular obligation to assure that evidence supporting its position is placed before the court in a logical and coherent fashion. Further, the lawyer will ensure that the evidence placed before the court by the other parties is fully tested by cross-examination, and where appropriate by calling rebuttal evidence. In practice, tactical considerations often cause agency lawyers to be a little less aggressive in cross-examining parents than a lawyer for the parents may be with protection workers. The weakness of the parents' case is often apparent without the necessity of engaging in a humiliating cross-examination with the purpose of emphasizing their inadequacies. Further, such tactics may needlessly jeopardize the prospects for continuing to work with the parents after the court hearing. However, in appropriate

---

[31] Canadian Bar Association, *Code of Professional Conduct*, (Ottawa: Canadian Bar Association, 1988) at 37. In *Children's Aid Society of Durham Region and W.* (1990) 72 O.R. (2d) 711 (Ont. Prov. Ct. - Fam. Div.) Webster Prov. J. expressed "doubts" about the position of a child protection agency that argued that it was not obliged to present evidence of a police officer "that ... was not of benefit to their case."

[32] *Boucher* v. *the Queen* (1954), [1955] S.C.R. 16 at 23–24.

situations, agency counsel can be aggressive by supporting the position of the agency, ensuring that its witnesses are not improperly questioned, and by challenging the evidence of the other parties.

Lawyer and Social Worker Roles

While it is important for a lawyer to remain objective and separate legal functions from casework functions, in some cases it may sometimes seem that the casework function has been usurped by the lawyer. In hotly contested cases, the legal advisor will not only decide what evidence to present to the court and be involved in providing disclosure, but should also be consulted on an ongoing basis by the caseworker regarding such issues as: obtaining medical, psychological and other assessments; the scope of services to be offered; and, access to the parents. Handling the everyday aspects of the case may be subjected to close legal scrutiny if a case goes to court, so advice from agency counsel is therefore crucial.

On the other hand, in straightforward cases which proceed to court with the consent of the parents, or without their active opposition, caseworkers are often expected to perform certain quasi-legal, court-related tasks. Service of documents, drafting of some court documentation and disclosure may be handled by the caseworker. When a matter is contested, the lawyer and caseworker should consult and allocate the tasks between them.

Providing Legal Advice

The lawyer is sometimes called in on the eve of the court hearing, when positions are entrenched and emotions are running high. In a system where the agency uses a court worker until the last minute and then retains outside counsel, or where the assignment of cases is shared among a number of lawyers and made close to the court date, problems are inevitable. Wherever possible, a lawyer should be assigned to a contested case at the early stages and should be available to provide advice on an ongoing basis. This is most easily achieved with in-house counsel. The lawyer and caseworker should work as a team to effectively prepare the case for court. The lawyer is able to perform a number of ongoing functions:

1. At the outset, an assessment of the relative strengths and weaknesses of the case from the legal point of view can be provided.

2. The lawyer can provide the caseworker with some indication of how the case is likely to fare before the court.

3. The caseworker can be assisted in examining how the other parties might view the proposed plan. The personalities and styles of the lawyers for other parties can be taken into consideration.

4. Concrete suggestions can be provided regarding case management, for example, obtaining assessments and providing resources, with a view to future court activity.

5. Advice can be provided regarding settlement proposals. The lawyer can provide advice based upon a number of factors including the strength of the evidence, particular knowledge of the judge's response to similar cases, any perceived errors in the management of the case, or the risk that the agency might be ordered to pay the legal costs of the parents.

6. When a trial appears unavoidable, direction can be provided in preparing for court and presenting evidence.

Costs in Child Protection Proceedings

In ordinary civil cases, costs are usually awarded; this means that the unsuccessful party is required to compensate the successful party for much of the cost of monies spent on legal fees and disbursements. The compensation is usually partial. However, the courts have traditionally viewed child protection as a very different form of litigation:

> Protection agencies are not ordinary litigants. They should not be penalized in attempting to carry out their statutory mandate under the child protection legislation. The adversarial concept of winning or losing does not apply very well to protection cases and, more important, ... it would be generally undesirable for a protection agency to have to be concerned about the cost implications of a course of action that they otherwise believed was in the child's best interests. This makes sense to me if good faith and due diligence and reason have been exercised by the agency.[33]

Therefore, although the court has jurisdiction to order costs, they are usually only ordered against a child protection agency in exceptional circumstances, where the court believes there has been indefensible conduct on the part of the agency.

In a 1981 Ontario Family Court decision, Judge Felstiner reviewed four cases where costs were awarded against a Children's Aid Society and concluded that "the award of costs in these four cases was based on a malfeasance or error by a Children's Aid Society." He went on to state that "the Society should not be penalized for attempting to carry out its statutory purpose of "protecting children where necessary" according to its best judgment, unless the Society acted in some indefensible way."[34]

Costs have also been awarded in cases where the court perceives an abuse of process on the part of the Children's Aid Society. In a 1987 case, the court

---

[33] *M.W.* v. *Catholic Children's Aid Society of Metro Toronto* (4 March 1986), York C184/85 (Ont. Fam. Ct), Nasmith P.C.J.; leave to appeal issue of costs refused, (27 March 1986), York (Ont. Dist. Ct) [unreported] Haley Dist. J.

[34] *Re Y Infants (No.2)* (1981), 3 F.L.R.R. 180, 7 A.C.W.S. (2d) 412 (Ont. Prov. Ct - Fam. Div.) [unreported].

indicated that "an attempt to relitigate an issue on substantially the same facts, whether or not an appeal or judicial review was sought before a higher tribunal, constitutes an abuse of process."[35]

In recent years, courts have awarded costs against child protection agencies in cases where the handling of a matter in the court by a child protection agency is seen as overzealous or insensitive to the rights of the other parties.[36] An Ontario lawyer points out that overzealousness on the part of Children's Aid Society has met the "exceptional circumstances" test in older cases as well. In the 1915 case of *Re Wardle*, the court awarded costs against the agency for acting "overzealously and without sufficient investigation into the facts or proper regard to the wishes of the parents and the conditions at their home."[37] Protracted trials resulting from hearing unnecessary witnesses, failure to call witnesses with relevant evidence or inadequate disclosure might also lead a court to consider an order of costs against the child protection agency.

The courts have begun using costs not only to comment upon the conduct of child protection cases while they are before the court, but also to evaluate the management of cases long before they reach the courtroom door. For example, failure to conduct a thorough and continuing investigation before trial has resulted in costs being awarded against the Children's Aid Society.[38]

In a 1987 Ontario decision, a trial judge awarded costs against the Children's Aid Society after a lengthy trial. The test he applied in awarding costs was: "Would the Society be perceived by ordinary persons as having acted fairly?" In giving reasons for judgment, the judge articulated a number of duties which he felt the Society had breached in handling the case:

1. to conduct a thorough investigation before acting;

2. to work with the police in conducting an investigation into allegations of sexual abuse;

3. to consider alternative measures for protection of children before proceeding to court;

---

[35] *Helen Louise H. & Francis Bernard H.* v. *Catholic Children's Aid Society of Metro Toronto* (30 July 1987), York D1241/87 (Ont. Fam. Ct), James P.C.J.

[36] *Re D.H. (An Infant)* (13 April 1982), Peel 2315/81 (Ont. Fam. Ct), Dunn P.C.J.

[37] D.W. Phillips, "Costs in Child Protection and Abuse Cases" (1988) 3 Can. Fam. L.Q. 71 at 74.

[38] *Re Catholic C.A.S. and Pamela M.* (1982), 36 O.R. (2d) 451 (Ont. Prov. Ct—Fam. Div.), per Nasmith P.C.J., revd. on merits (1983), 44 O.R. (2d) 375.

4. to treat the parents fairly and equally and with as much dignity as possible;

5. to continue the Society's investigation up until the time of final determination in a vigorous, professional manner;

6. to reassess the Society's position as more information becomes available; and,

7. to ensure the Society's workers are skilled in the performance of their roles.[39]

These duties should guide the conduct and case presentation of all child protection agencies.

It should be noted that parents may also have costs awarded against them based on the same exceptional circumstances test,[40] though judges are most reluctant to add "insult to injury" and only award costs against parents in the rarest of cases.

Conclusion

As we enter the 1990s, our society is increasingly focusing on the needs and interests of its children. Courts and tribunals must make difficult decisions and recommendations which not only affect the future lives of children, but also respect the autonomy and integrity of the family unit.

Child protection has become increasingly complex, sophisticated and legalistic, making it easy to understand why the role of the child protection lawyer has become more important. Providing ongoing legal advice in case management and planning, providing disclosure, marshalling and presenting evidence, assisting with settlement negotiations and providing general legal guidance to the agency are all significant aspects of the role of agency lawyers. To be a lawyer dealing with the protection and best interests of children is to fulfill an important and increasingly challenging function.

---

[39] *D.B.* v. *Children's Aid Society of Durham Region* (1987), 20 C.P.C. (2d) 61 at 66–73 (Ont. Prov. Ct - Fam. Div.).

[40] Costs were awarded against the parents in *Children's Aid Society of Ottawa-Carleton* v. *Zuliema & Anthony F.* (16 January 1987), Ottawa-Carleton 761/85 (Ont. Prov. Ct - Fam. Div.), Sheffield P.C.J.; *R.S.* v. *Children's Aid Society of Sudbury & Manitoulin* (23 April 1987), Sudbury 745/81 (Ont. Prov. Ct - Fam. Div.), Cousineau P.C.J.

10

ABUSE AND NEGLECT ALLEGATIONS IN CHILD CUSTODY AND PROTECTION CASES

Mary-Jo Maur Raycroft[*]

INTRODUCTION

If the parents of a child separate or divorce, or if they have never lived together, an arrangement must be made for the custody (or care) of the child. There will usually also be an arrangement for access, that is, visits between the child and the noncustodial parent. Custody and access issues may be the subject of an informal arrangement between the parents, a formal written agreement or a court order which can be made with or without the consent of the parents. All Canadian provinces and territories have legislation governing custody applications, and the federal *Divorce Act* has similar provisions. These statutes stipulate that custody and access disputes are to be decided on the basis of the "best interests" of the child, and also provide that a person who is not a biological parent may seek custody at any time.[1]

Sometimes during a court application for custody or access, an allegation of abuse or neglect will be made. If this happens, it is likely the local child protection agency will become involved, especially if the allegation is of sexual abuse. The period following a separation is often one of tremendous instability for one or both parents. Investigations of allegations of abuse in the context of custody and access disputes can be extremely difficult, and may be rendered more difficult by the atmosphere of mistrust and hostility. Allegations and counter-allegations may fly, leaving the protection worker to decide whether the evidence supports or refutes those allegations.

If allegations of abuse are made in the context of parental separation, the case can be particularly stressful for everyone: parents, children, lawyers, protection workers and the judge. The inherent difficulties of these cases may have encouraged child protection agencies to avoid getting involved in custody and access

---

[*] Lawyer in private practice, Kingston, Ontario. This chapter is extracted from the author's LL.M. thesis.

[1] *Divorce Act*, 1985, S.C. 1986, c. 4, s. 16(1); in Ontario, for example, *Children's Law Reform Act*, S.O. 1982, c. 20, s. 21 states that "A parent of a child or any other person may apply to a court for an order respecting custody ... "

cases, even if there has been an abuse allegation. However, failing to investigate an allegation of abuse simply because the case arises in the context of a custody or access dispute can have dire consequences for the child, and may subject the agency and worker to possible civil liability if harm comes to the child.

DEFINITION OF TERMS

It is useful to understand some of the terms used frequently by matrimonial lawyers and others involved in custody and access disputes.

Custody

A person having custody of a child may make all decisions regarding the child, including those related to the child's education, health, religion and day-to-day schedule, without having to obtain the consent of a parent without custody rights. An important feature of custody is that, regardless of the order or agreement made, it can never be permanently binding. Any interested person may apply for custody of, or access to, a child at any time, although existing orders and agreements should be honoured until they are formally varied.

Access

Access is the right to visit a child who is not in one's custody. It means the noncustodial parent, or sometimes another relative such as a grandparent, may visit with the child, usually at regular intervals for specified periods of time. A typical access arrangement may allow visits every second weekend and half of holiday periods, though arrangements for more or less access are also common. If the parents are able to communicate effectively, access orders or agreements may simply provide for "reasonable access", meaning the parents arrange access visits suitable for themselves and the children, varying the arrangements according to their needs.

Access usually includes the right to receive information from the appropriate agencies about the education, health and welfare of the child. This means a person with access may contact professionals involved with a child, such as teachers and doctors, and is entitled to obtain the same reports from these professionals as the custodial parent.

In some situations, particularly those with a well-substantiated allegation of sexual abuse, access may be supervised. This is usually pursuant to a court order, and means the visits between the person with access and the child must be supervised by some other person or organization. The supervising person may be another relative, such as a grandparent, or may even be the custodial parent. Supervision is sometimes provided by an outside agency, such as the Salvation Army.

Joint Custody

Joint custody is a nebulous term which generally means that the parents of a child will share parenting duties. The parents or court may fashion any reasonable arrangement that involves sharing of parental responsibility. The child may live with one parent most of the time, in which case the child is said to have a primary residence, and visit with the other; alternatively, the child may live with each parent for roughly equal periods of time, moving regularly from one residence to another. Decision-making responsibilities may be divided in a variety of ways or shared by both parents.

Joint custody is usually appropriate only when the parents are able to put aside other differences and concentrate on the children without any unnecessary argument. It is seldom, if ever, appropriate in situations where there are any substantiated allegations of abuse.

Joint custody used to be arranged only with the parents' agreement, and a judge would never impose joint custody on separated or divorced parents. Now that more fathers participate in their children's upbringing, some judges order joint custody despite the objections of either or both parents.[2]

Interim and Final Custody Orders

The crucial decision of interim custody often must be made close to the outset of custody litigation. If the custody application is contested, the child will usually live with one of the parents until a final custody determination is made.

At the time of initial separation one or both parents usually brings a motion for interim custody. In other words, they ask the court to decide who will have care of the child until the trial. Interim applications of this kind are generally resolved relatively quickly, and oral evidence is seldom heard by the court. Instead, the judge's decision is based on sworn written statements (affidavits) from the parents and any other individual whose evidence may be important.

It is difficult for the parent not awarded interim custody, as custody litigation often stretches out for months or even years. The longer a child remains with one parent and has no major problems, the more likely that a judge (and assessing mental health professionals) will decide that the child should remain permanently in the custody of that parent. Since the judge is usually loathe to disrupt a child's situation without good reasons, the decision on an interim hearing can have a tremendous impact upon the outcome of a final hearing.

The decision of interim custody is even more critical than usual in cases where a parent is alleged to have committed child sexual abuse. In these cases, at the interim hearing the lawyers will try to present at least a summary of all evidence usually heard at a final hearing. This is to substantiate or discredit the allegation of abuse. If an allegation of abuse is made and a judge has reasonable

---

[2]   See *Alfoldi* v. *Bard* (1989), 20 R.F.L. (3d) 290 (Ont. Dist. Ct).

grounds to believe it is true, it is likely that at the interim stage that parent will be denied access, or will only have supervised access.

After a trial, a judge will make a final order concerning custody and access. However, this type of order is never truly final, and if there is a change in circumstances which affects the child's best interests, the order may be varied.

Assessments

The court often benefits from the assistance of a mental health professional in deciding where a child is best placed. In custody and access litigation the court often orders an assessment to be conducted by a qualified person, and then reported to the court. Assessments may be prepared at the request of one party, who retains the assessor, or at the request of both parties, in which case they jointly select an assessor. An assessment may also be ordered by the court, in which case the assessment might be done by a court-affiliated clinic or by an assessor appointed by the judge, often acting with the consent of the parties.

Similar assessments may be ordered under child protection legislation. Although the purposes of child protection litigation and custody litigation differ, both types of assessment are similar. Assessments are very useful, and frequently are the basis of a negotiated settlement between the parties. They are also influential if case goes to trial, though the courts have indicated that they are not obliged to follow the recommendations in an assessment.

These assessments and the resulting reports may be completed by psychiatrists, psychologists or social workers concerning the suitability of the parties as parents, or as persons potentially having access to a child. The person who prepares the report may be called as a witness at an eventual trial, and subjected to examination in court.

In most custody and access disputes, the assessment will focus on the custody and access arrangement that, in the assessor's opinion, is in the best interests of the child. However, as discussed below, if there is an allegation of abuse, the assessment process may be more complex and will tend to focus on the veracity of the allegation.

Child Representation

As discussed in Chapter 9, it is routine in several Canadian jurisdictions for the child to be represented independently of the parents in child protection cases. It is less common for a child in custody or access proceedings to be legally represented, unless there is some indication that the child's interests need to be independently represented.

Best Interests of the Child

The test used by the court in custody or access litigation is whether the arrangement proposed is in the "best interests of the child."[3] This test is applied across North America. The test must be vague in order to permit the court and the parents to come to a resolution which will suit each individual child. It generally means that a court must consider factors such as: the ties a child may have to one parent or the other; the child's preferences; the length of time a child has been in one parent's custody; and the ability, both emotional and financial, of the competing parents to raise the child. As can be imagined, the criteria for determining what is best for a child are diverse. The judge must listen to all of the evidence, then decide what is best for the child, not what will make the parents, or even the child, happy.

Even though the best interests test is vague, at times it is relatively easy to determine its application. Clearly, if a parent with custody is found by a court to be abusing a child, it would not be in the child's interests to remain with that parent. If a noncustodial parent has been abusing the child, a court would have to decide whether it is in the child's best interests to continue to have visits with that parent, and if so, under what conditions. If access continues in such situations, it would almost always be supervised, at least for a period of time.

Child in Need of Protection

Child protection legislation has a different purpose than custody legislation. The function of child protection agencies is to protect children from harm, but to interfere only when it is clearly necessary. Accordingly, agencies are usually permitted to intervene only if the child has, in fact, been harmed, or if there is a substantial risk that such harm is likely to result if the child remains in the home.

Therefore, the issue in a child protection case is different from that in custody litigation. In a child protection case, the question is: Will this child be at risk of harm if left with the parent or parents? By contrast, in a custody contest the question is: Where is it in the child's best interests to live? In child protection litigation, a court is largely restricted to choosing between a natural parent and the state or its appointed caregivers.[4] In custody litigation, a court may choose to

---

[3] The term "best interests of the child" is also used in some child protection statutes. When used in the custody or access context, the court will decide what it considers to be "best" for the child. There is no onus in favour of either parent. In the child protection context, if a child is found to be in need of protection, there is still a general presumption that the child should remain with the natural parents, under the supervision of the agency, and there is an onus on the agency to establish that it is in the "best interests" of a child to be removed from parental care and to justify the agency's intrusion into the family.

[4] There are some jurisdictions, such as Ontario, where protection legislation allows a court to order that a child live with a person other than the parent who had custody, subject to supervision by the protection agency. However, these orders require a finding that the child is in need of protection (i.e., that the child is likely to be harmed by the parent). See *Child and Family Services Act*, S.O. 1984, c. 55, s. 53(1).

leave children where they are, have them live with a different parent, or impose joint custody.

When a custody or access order conflicts with the order of a court in child protection proceedings, the child protection order prevails, since the court has an overriding duty to protect children.

FALSE ALLEGATIONS OF SEXUAL ABUSE

It is generally accepted in mental health circles that young children rarely lie about incidents of sexual abuse, although parents involved in a custody or access dispute will sometimes initiate what turns out to be a false report of child sexual abuse.[5] Further, young children may be pressured by a parent into supporting a false allegation, or may become confused as to what really occurred as a result of repeated or highly suggestive questioning by a parent.

It is important to point out that most "false" reports are not maliciously motivated. However, some may be intentionally false; for example, a parent may knowingly provide false information to gain an advantage over the other parent. The motivation for a parent to fabricate an incident of sexual abuse where there is a contested custody or access action is obvious.

In other cases, there may be a legitimate misunderstanding of the other parent's actions toward a child. There are cases in which the atmosphere of mistrust, a common element in many separations, results in one parent misinterpreting what may be innocent actions by the other parent, and alleging sexual abuse. In yet others, an accusing parent may be suffering from a mental or emotional disturbance which may cause a false report. The point, for those involved in investigating and litigating such cases, is that the incidence of false reports, regardless of their cause, is higher in cases where there is a custody or access dispute.[6]

Despite these factors, studies suggesting a higher incidence of false reports in custody and access cases should not cause anyone to dismiss a child's allegation of sexual abuse simply because it arises in the context of a custody or access dispute.

---

[5] See, e.g., M. Mian et al., "Review of 125 Children 6 Years of Age and Under Who Were Sexually Abused" (1986) 10 Child Abuse and Neglect 223.

[6] D. Jones, "Reliable and Fictitious Accounts of Sexual Abuse to Children" (1987) 2 Journal of Interpersonal Violence 27; N. Bala and J. Anweiller, "Allegations of Sexual Abuse in a Parental Custody Case: Smokescreen or Fire?" (1987) 2 Can. Fam. L. Q. 343.

While the studies to date do demonstrate a higher incidence of false allegations in the context of parental separation, it is apparent that even in this situation there are many true allegations. The difficult job of investigators and the courts is to distinguish the true from the false. Further, the research studies should be considered cautiously since they have involved small clinical samples and may not be true for the population at large.[7]

Commentators point out that the existence of a custody or access dispute may actually precipitate sexual abuse of a child. After separation the parent without custody (usually the father) may feel lonely and may find the innocent affection of a young child irresistible.[8] There also may be situations in which it is only after a separation has occurred that a child will feel that incidents of abuse can be safely revealed, as the offending parent is out of the home.

Therefore, an allegation made by a child or a parent during a custody or access dispute should be treated with the same caution, seriousness and thoroughness that an allegation arising at any other time would. Due to the existence of the custody or access dispute, careful examination of the parents will be required. The investigation should ensure that the allegation is not spiteful, based on a misunderstanding borne out of the couple's mistrust, or the result of a mental or emotional disturbance in the reporting parent. The investigator requires great sensitivity in interviewing the child.

THE COURT PROCESS

Investigation

If an allegation of abuse, sexual or otherwise, arises in the course of a custody or access dispute, there may be a number of investigations carried out simultaneously. The child protection agency may initiate an investigation using one of its workers; the police may be investigating potential criminal charges; and one or both parents may have started investigating the problem using independently retained experts.

Results of multiple simultaneous investigations can be chaotic at worst and unproductive at best. It can be upsetting and confusing for the child if there are several interviews by different professionals. Many child protection agencies in Canada have established child abuse protocols, which are guidelines for child

---

[7] F. Sink, "Studies of True and False Allegations: a Critical Review," in *American Bar Association Benchbook on Child Sexual Abuse Allegations in Custody Disputes* (Washington, D.C.: American Bar Association, 1987); and D. Finkelhor, *Designing New Studies: A Sourcebook on Child Sexual Abuse* (Beverly Hills: Sage Publications, 1986).

[8] M. Mian et al., *supra*, note 5.; M.L. Fassel, "Some Considerations on the Issue of Child Sexual Abuse Allegations in Custody Disputes" (Address to the Federation of Law Societies Program on Family Law, July 1988) [unpublished]; and K. MacFarlane, "Child Sexual Abuse Allegations in Divorce Proceedings," *Sexual Abuse of Young Children* (New York: The Guileford Press, 1986) c. 7.

protection workers, police investigators and others on how to investigate an allegation of sexual abuse. Most protocols agree in principle that the interviews are to be conducted sensitively and that the questioning is to be as unbiased as possible. Most protocols also emphasize the importance of minimizing the number of interviews to which a child is subjected. However, differences arise in the actual methods used by various investigators to establish the veracity of an allegation.

For example, in some places the protocol requires that the initial interview of a child be conducted by a protection worker, whereas in other locales the police officer may conduct the first interview, or a police officer and protection worker may perform this task together. In some places, the initial interview is videotaped or audiotaped, and in others it is not. The differences can be important and may dramatically affect the outcome.

It should be appreciated that even after a thorough investigation, a protection worker, police officer or mental health professional may be uncertain about whether abuse truly occurred. The conclusion of an investigation may range from certainty that abuse occurred to certainty that it did not. Sometimes the findings will fall between the extremes, with investigators only having a probability-based belief, or even frankly acknowledging that the investigation is inconclusive. Criminal prosecution will be undertaken only in cases where there is a very high degree of certainty. Protection agencies will be reluctant to bring an application based on concerns about abuse if they are truly uncertain about what has occurred. A parental custody or access case, however, may proceed in the face of considerable uncertainty, with the abuse allegations forming only part of the total case.

Concurrent Child Protection and Child Custody Proceedings

Depending upon the outcome of the investigation, the agency may need to decide whether to play a role in the court process. An agency may decide it is necessary to bring forward a protection application immediately. Alternatively, if the custody or access proceedings are resolved in a manner which protects the child, the agency may decide it is not necessary to bring a protection application before the court. It is also possible that a social worker from the protection agency may testify as a witness in custody or access hearings; this can occur whether or not the agency chooses to be a party to the custody or access application or to bring its own protection application. If a protection application is commenced, the parents may discontinue the custody or access proceedings to await the outcome of the protection proceeding.

In those cases where there are reasons for having a protection application at the same time as a custody or access application, the case law and, in some situations, the legislation and rules of civil procedure generally require that the proceedings be dealt with separately. For example, if the custody dispute takes place pursuant to the federal *Divorce Act*, it will be heard in a superior court by a federally-appointed judge, whereas the child protection application must be decided in the Family Court by a provincially-appointed judge.[9] On the other hand, if the child custody proceeding is initiated under provincial legislation in the provincial Family Court, there is no rule preventing the two applications from being heard at the same time. However, some judges feel there are valid legal reasons for not hearing the two matters simultaneously.[10] If both proceedings are held in the same court, they will usually be held in succession; there are generally valid legal and practical reasons for holding the child protection application first.

A finding by a court that a child is in need of protection must override any custody order made in favour of a person found to have caused harm, or threatened harm, to the child.[11] Therefore, it normally stands to reason that a child protection hearing should proceed before a custody trial. If the court hears the protection application and decides there is no substantial risk of harm to the child in remaining where he or she is, then the custody application can continue.

Legal reasons for hearing the two types of application separately are generally compelling. The agency must first prove to a judge that a child is in need of protection and then must prove that certain actions should be taken as a result of this finding. In a child protection application, a parent need only take a reactive stance. It need not be shown that it is in the child's best interests to remain in the home, only that the child is not at risk of harm. In custody litigation, the parent alleging abuse must prove it, and each parent must show, on balance of probabilities, that their proposals for custody are in the child's best interests. The kinds of evidence that would be used in the two types of application differ because of these different legal burdens. This could create substantial confusion if both cases are dealt with together.

In practice, the problem of multiple proceedings can often be resolved without the need for two trials. The focus in both proceedings remains on the child and the child's needs. Once an agency is involved, there will usually be negotiations between both parents and their lawyers, the agency and perhaps the child's lawyer. Both cases will only proceed to a hearing if no reasonable solution can be found and agreed upon by the parties. Often, as noted above, the agency will not proceed with a protection application if it is satisfied that the allegations of

---

9   This assumes the province in question does not have a Unified Family Court. In some provinces, Unified Family Courts have been established to hear all types of family law cases. Such courts can and do hear custody applications under the *Divorce Act, 1985*, S.C. 1986, c. 4, as well as child protection matters under provincial legislation.

10 See e.g. *Children's Aid Society of Belleville, Hastings & Trenton* v. *H.* (1984), 27 A.C.W.S. (2d) 158 (Ont. Fam. Ct).

11 This will be so even if the custody order is made by a superior court and the protection order by a provincial court. As a general rule, an order of a superior court on the same issue overrides that of a provincial court, but a custody hearing is not on the same issue as a child protection hearing because the legal tests are different and the litigation in each case proceeds under different statutes. The order placing the child under the protection of the state agency takes priority.

abuse will be explored in the parental custody or access trial. Occasionally the agency will request to be a party to the parental dispute to ensure that its concerns are addressed, though this may be opposed by a parent as inappropriate intervention in a private dispute.

Assessments

Psycho-social assessments are usually important pieces of evidence in both custody or access disputes and in child protection applications, and many clinicians perform assessments for both types of cases. If there are simultaneous protection and custody proceedings, one might assume that a single assessment could be done to save time and resources. In some cases this may be a good idea, but the purpose of the investigation in a custody or access case is different than in a child protection application. The assessing clinician would have to be given clear guidance from the court or the parties' counsel to ensure that the interests of the parents, the agency and the child do not become blurred.[12]

In many cases, an agency proceeds to gather information from competent experts who have previously assessed the child or the parents and can prove its case without a formal, court-ordered assessment. In such cases, there might later be a court-ordered assessment to assist in determining what long-term placement options are best for a child, and not whether, in the short-term, the child is in need of immediate protection.

Sexual Behaviour Testing

The results of sexual behaviour testing may be employed as evidence either in custody and access disputes or in child protection cases. Phallometric testing is used to measure a man's sexual response to photographs of people, including children, in various sexual and non-sexual positions, by monitoring minute physiological responses of the penis through use of electrodes.

It is difficult to interpret the results of phallometric testing, and professionals admit to its potential inaccuracy. In one study with known child sexual abusers,

---

[12] In Ontario, the use of a single assessment for both custody or access and child protection purposes can have unfortunate results for the parent against whom the allegation of abuse is made. If an assessment is ordered under the *Child and Family Services Act*, S.O. 1984, c. 55, in the course of a child protection application, s. 50 requires that the court first make a finding that the child is in need of protection. If the parent who has been alleged to have abused the child consents to the assessment under this Act, this may constitute an admission that the child is in need of protection.

the rate of false negative results reached 50%. That is, 50% of a group of individuals known to be abusers were given phallometric tests which indicated they were not likely to have sexually abused children. There are, however, relatively few false positives;[13] that is, if a man's responses indicate that he is sexually stimulated by pictures of young children, it is very likely that he is an abuser.

In many cases, an accused father will submit to testing voluntarily.[14] Even though in theory the onus of proof is on the person or agency making the allegation, the alleged abuser is wise to gather evidence that may exonerate him. Although a negative result on a sexual behaviour test may not be conclusive, it can influence the conclusion of an investigator or the court that the allegations are false. Similarly, it can be helpful for a man accused of abuse to take a polygraph test. While the test results are generally not admissible in court, they can influence an investigator and support a decision not to proceed with a criminal prosecution or protection application.

Problems for the Legal Profession

The adversarial nature of custody or access proceedings in which allegations of abuse have been made sometimes compounds the difficulties inherent in this situation. Counsel for a mother accusing a father of child sexual abuse during a custody or access dispute may feel a professional duty to exhaust every piece of potential evidence, no matter how distasteful or emotionally difficult this is. Counsel for the accused father may respond by making an allegation of inappropriate behaviour against the mother or her new partner or by alleging that the accusation is a reflection of the mother's psychologically unbalanced state. The potential for this type of testimony to permanently damage parental and parent-child relationships is great.

Judges have, perhaps, the most difficult task of all. In many cases, there will be no hard (or physical) evidence of the abuse, nor will there be eyewitnesses, other than the child victim. A judge may be given: (a) conflicting testimony, from one parent that the abuse occurred and from the other that it did not; (b) inconclusive sexual behaviour testing results; and, (c) an assessment which can neither verify nor dismiss the allegation of abuse. The judge will then be asked to decide whether the abuse occurred and, if so, what should be done about it. In such situations, some judges provide an evaluation period and make a long interim

---

[13] This insight was taken from a letter to the author from Dr. Howard Barbaree, one of the directors of the Kingston Sexual Behaviour Clinic. The Clinic is one of few places in Canada conducting this type of investigation.

[14] Although the issue does not appear to have been litigated, it may be unconstitutional to order a man to submit to such intrusive testing. However, Ontario's *Courts of Justice Act*, S.O. 1984, c. 11, s. 118, permits a court to order a medical examination of a party if the party's physical or mental condition is "in question" and the examination would be relevant to a "material issue." This might include sexual behaviour testing in a case where sexual abuse of a child was at issue.

order for supervision of a parent's care (in the case of a child protection application) or for supervised access (in the case of a custody or access dispute). At the end of the interim period, the matter may be reviewed by the court.

Sometimes a judge will be unable to find that abuse has occurred, but nevertheless makes a determination, based on the "best interests" of the child, to deny the alleged abuser custody or even access. There may be cases in which the "suspicions" of the judge do not merit a finding of abuse, but nevertheless influence the final outcome. However, there are cases where the judge determines that the allegation of sexual abuse was not proven on the balance of probabilities, and makes a final order for regular unsupervised access or even custody to the accused parent.[15] The outcome will depend largely on the judge's view as to whether there is enough evidence to conclude there is, in fact, sexual abuse occurring. Judges are not consistent about what evidence justifies a conclusion of sexual abuse in the absence of physical proof.

One might assume judges would be more conservative on interim applications than at final hearings, and would order supervised access, or perhaps even a cessation of access, until the matter is heard at a full trial. In fact, it appears that decisions on interim applications are as unpredictable as they are at the end of a full trial.[16]

---

[15] The author has read at least one assessment in which a mother accused a father of sexual abuse and the assessing psychiatrist felt the accusation was malicious, so recommended awarding custody to the father even after a long period of interim custody to the mother.

[16] See e.g. *S. v. S.* [1987] W.D.F.L. 897 (Ont. S.C.), in which the judge decided that, even though an assessment report was inconclusive, he had to restrict access in order to "err on the side of excess caution" and protect the child; and, by contrast, in the decision of the same judge in *Stuart* v. *Stuart* (1985), 32 A.C.W.S. (2d) 53, there were similar facts; however, he felt that the "wife had not proven allegations of abuse to a degree that would require remedial action from this court ... " Both applications were interim.

11

CRIMINAL PROSECUTIONS FOR ABUSE AND NEGLECT

Shelley Hallett[*]

INTRODUCTION

Some situations involving parental abuse or neglect may constitute the basis for prosecution under the *Criminal Code*.[1] It is a criminal offence to fail to provide a child with "necessities of life," to use force against a child which is not "reasonable" and for the "purposes of correction," or to sexually abuse a child. A criminal prosecution is theoretically distinct from the protection process, though both processes may proceed simultaneously, and there may be a relationship between them. The essential purposes of a criminal prosecution are the protection of society generally, and the social denunciation and punishment of offenders. The criminal law serves as a social symbol and its enforcement is generally accepted as having a deterrent effect on offenders. Rehabilitation is an important but secondary objective. The protection process, on the other hand, is intended to intervene in the lives of families to directly protect the child, removing the child from parental care if necessary and, if possible, assisting the parents to improve the quality of parental care they provide.

In a criminal case, the onus is on the prosecution to prove its case beyond a reasonable doubt; this constitutes the highest legal standard of proof. Criminal proceedings employ strict rules of evidence and provide the accused with a full set of procedural protections under the *Canadian Charter of Rights and Freedoms*.[2] For example, in a criminal case it is usually necessary for the child victim of alleged abuse to testify in court and be available for cross-examination. It is somewhat easier to prove abuse or neglect in a civil case, such as in a child protection hearing. The agency is only obliged to prove its case according to the lower civil standard of proof, on the balance of probabilities. In civil cases, the rules of evidence are not as strict and the *Charter* has only limited applicability.

---

[*]   Court Reform Task Force, Ontario Ministry of the Attorney General, Toronto, Ontario.

[1]   R.S.C. 1985, c. C–46.

[2]   Part I of the *Constitution Act, 1982*, being Schedule B of the *Canada Act 1982 (U.K.)*, 1982, c. 11 [hereinafter *Charter*].

As a result, there may be an acquittal in criminal court or no criminal prosecution at all, while a finding of abuse could be made in the protection case.

Police are responsible for criminal investigations, while the Crown attorney is responsible for presenting a criminal case in court. There are sometimes disagreements between the child protection agency on one hand, and the police and Crown attorney on the other, about how a child abuse incident should be handled. Sometimes the protection agency has a concern about the potential detrimental effect of a prosecution upon the parents or their relationship with the child, resulting in the agency's reluctance to support a criminal prosecution. Alternatively, the police may be unwilling to press criminal charges in a case where the protection agency thinks such a prosecution would be appropriate. Recently there has been an effort to improve the relationship between child protection agencies and those responsible for criminal prosecutions by developing protocols to govern joint investigations and responsibilities.

In many localities there are still no protocols to guide joint investigations and involvement by police and protection agencies, yet many complications can arise if a protection case and criminal prosecution proceed simultaneously. There is no established rule about which case should be resolved first. From the child's perspective, early resolution may be more desirable, since a permanent or long-term placement could then be arranged. On the other hand, a parent may argue that a long-term placement decision cannot be made until the parent's future is resolved in the criminal case. Further, parents may feel disadvantaged if the protection case is dealt with first, since they may feel tactically compelled to testify in the protection case; if they do not testify, the judge may be very reluctant to allow the child to remain in their care. However, in a criminal case, the parent has a constitutional right to remain silent and is not obliged to testify.

Until recently, criminal prosecutions for abuse or neglect were relatively rare. However, these prosecutions are becoming more common as more cases of sexual abuse arise. Many abuse cases involve parents, but others are charged as well. In Canada, a large number of charges have recently been laid against teachers, priests and others for abusing their positions of trust by sexually exploiting children.

Criminal prosecutions for sexual abuse have been facilitated by changes in the laws respecting sexual offences against children which came into effect in January, 1988 (Bill C–15).[3] These offences are unique because they are child-specific: only children can be the victims of these crimes. Convictions appear on a criminal record and signal the offender as a likely child molester.

It should be noted that the federal Parliament has jurisdiction for enacting criminal law and procedure (e.g., the *Criminal Code* is federal legislation) while child protection law is a provincial responsibility. Responsibility for police and the prosecution of criminal cases, such as those involving child abuse and neglect, also rests with the provincial governments.

---

[3] *An Act to Amend the Criminal Code and the Canada Evidence Act*, S.C. 1987, c. 24.

Child protection hearings are discussed extensively elsewhere in this book. This chapter focuses on the process and issues relating to criminal prosecutions in cases of child abuse and neglect.

COMMENCING A CRIMINAL PROSECUTION

Any person may go before a justice of the peace (a lower-level judicial officer) to commence a criminal prosecution against another individual by swearing out an information. The informant must swear before the justice of the peace that he or she has reasonable and probable grounds to believe that the accused person has committed a specific offence.

Informations charging criminal offences are most frequently laid by police officers. They must believe that an offence has taken place. While this does not mean that the officer must have direct knowledge that an offence has been committed, the officer's reasons must go beyond mere speculation. This requirement guards against the arbitrary use of police power.

The police officer usually establishes reasonable and probable grounds to believe that an offence has been committed following an investigation, unless the officer has actually found the offender committing the offence. The investigation may last several days or even months, or for only a few minutes. Usually, the victim of the alleged offence will be one of the first persons to whom the officer will speak during the investigation. Items that may have been used in the course of the offence (e.g., weapons), or that otherwise support the story of the victim and other witnesses (e.g., blood-stained clothing or an item left at the scene by the offender), will be collected during the officer's investigation and kept as exhibits for later use at trial.

The requirement that an informant believe on reasonable and probable grounds that an offence has been committed is sometimes problematic in the context of sexual offences against children. Many victims of such offences are very young; thus they are at a disadvantage in expressing themselves in a convincing way to an investigating police officer. Although most police officers are now aware of the need for special sensitivity while interviewing child victims of abuse, many still have not received extensive training concerning this process. Further, the offences are rarely committed in the presence of other credible witnesses and physical evidence of sexual abuse often cannot be found. The younger the child in such circumstances, the more the investigating police officer may face a dilemma in proceeding with a charge. Investigators in this situation must be particularly thorough, exploring all avenues that may disclose evidence supportive of the child victim's complaint. Such avenues generally include discussions with the child's parents or caregivers, the child's family doctor, experts in child development, other children who are and have been in contact with the alleged offender and, certainly, the accused.

No investigation based solely upon an interview with the alleged child victim is complete. In cases involving allegations of abuse, the decision not to lay a charge can only be justified following a full investigation.

The investigation often includes speaking with the person suspected of the offence. Sometimes, after interviewing a suspect, the police will decide not to lay a charge. Under the *Charter*, when police interview an individual charged with an offence, they are obliged to ensure that the person is aware of the right to consult a lawyer prior to making a statement. An individual is under no obligation to make a statement to the police and has the right to remain silent.

JUDICIAL INTERIM RELEASE (BAIL) HEARINGS

When the police believe that someone has committed an offence, they have the authority to arrest that person. This involves taking the accused into custody and confining that person to the police station or another detention facility. For many offences, including those involving the abuse or neglect of children, the police have limited discretion to release the person shortly after arrest and without a court appearance, provided he or she signs a written document promising to come to court on a specified date. The document may be either an appearance notice, a promise to appear, or a recognizance. However, the police cannot impose conditions on the accused as part of the release. For example, the police cannot require the accused to stay away from the alleged victim pending trial. A court may, however, impose conditions upon the accused who is held in detention and released following a bail hearing.

When accused persons are arrested and detained in custody by the police, they must be taken before a justice of the peace or provincial court judge within 24 hours, or as soon as possible, for a bail hearing, to determine whether they should be detained in custody pending trial. At a bail hearing the court must decide whether the accused should be released from custody before the trial and, if so, under what conditions.

In cases involving an allegation of child abuse, the public interest usually requires arrest and detention of the accused until a bail hearing is held. Release by the police is rarely appropriate; the risk of the accused seeking out the child for the purpose of intimidation or repetition of the offence is too great, particularly as no conditions can be attached to the release that would serve to protect the child or other children who may be at risk from that offender.

The bail hearing usually takes place at the courthouse or police station. At the bail hearing the Crown attorney is required to show cause why the accused should be detained in custody until trial, or released into the community after conditions of release are set.[4] Often, the Crown attorney proceeds to show cause by reading the allegations of the offence to the court. If the accused does not consent to the allegations being read to the court, or when the Crown attorney

---

[4] In most bail hearings, the onus is on the Crown to show that detention of the accused is justified. However, in specific situations (e.g., when the accused is charged with one indictable offence while already out on bail on another one, or is charged with an offence relating to his failure to appear in court or abide by bail conditions) the onus shifts to the detained accused to show cause why he or she should *not* be detained. This reverse onus makes it more difficult for an accused to be released from custody.

prefers to do so, witnesses for the Crown may be called to testify about the case. In this event, the police officer involved in the case is usually called by the Crown. In addition to the allegations pertaining to the offence, the Crown attorney generally provides details about the accused's address, employment, marital and family status, previous criminal convictions, current outstanding charges and other bail releases.

The strict rules of evidence that apply at a trial do not apply at the bail hearing. Rather, the judge " ... may receive and base his decision upon evidence considered credible or trustworthy by him in the circumstances of each case."[5] Thus, the police officer may give evidence not only as to what the officer personally observed during the investigation, but also about anticipated testimony in the case, including what a child or other witness have told the officer. This is preferable to calling the child to testify at the bail hearing, which would expose the child to an unnecessary and undesirable courtroom appearance. The defence may also call witnesses at the bail hearing. The accused may testify, but is not required to do so. At a bail hearing, the accused may not be questioned about the charges.[6]

There are only two considerations for the judge deciding whether to grant bail. The first is whether it is necessary to detain the accused in order to ensure their attendance at trial to answer to the charges. If detention is not necessary on that basis, the court goes on to consider whether it is necessary to detain the accused in order to protect the public, including the victim, having regard to all circumstances surrounding the alleged offence and offender. These should include consideration of whether there is a "substantial likelihood" that the accused will commit another criminal offence or interfere with the administration of justice (e.g., by intimidating witnesses) upon being released.[7]

If the court decides it is not necessary for the accused to be detained, they will be released upon signing an undertaking or a recognizance, with or without conditions. A recognizance is more onerous for the accused, as it also requires an amount of money to be paid by the accused if they fail to appear for court or does not comply with a condition imposed by the court. The amount of money for which the accused may be liable is determined by the court and appears on the face of the recognizance. In addition, the court may require that an accused have a surety before being released on a recognizance. A surety is a person, usually a friend or relative, who guarantees payment of the money if the accused does not come to court for the trial or breaches bail conditions. The surety or sureties who offer to be responsible for the accused are named in the recogni-

---

[5] *Criminal Code*, R.S.C. 1985, c. C–46, s. 518(1)(e).

[6] Other defense witnesses at the bail hearing may be asked questions relating to the offence, including the whereabouts of the accused at the time of its commission. The Crown attorney is entitled to cross-examine all witnesses whom the defence calls at the bail hearing, just as the accused or his or her lawyer may cross-examine all Crown witnesses.

[7] *Supra*, note 5, s. 515(10)(b).

zance. The court may also stipulate that the accused or the surety deposit cash or pledge other valuable security (e.g., Canada Savings bonds or a lien on property such as a house) as a condition of the accused's release.

In a criminal case involving an allegation of child abuse, where an accused is not detained at the bail hearing, a suitable form of release would typically be a recognizance in the form of a substantial amount of money with a surety and a prohibition from communicating with the child victim or visiting the place where the child is living or going to school. In cases of extrafamilial abuse, prudent conditions would be regularly reporting to the police, staying away from public playgrounds, schoolyards and swimming pools, and not associating with children under a certain age. Abstaining from alcohol and consulting a family doctor to take prescribed treatment may also be appropriate conditions if the accused acknowledges an illness.[8]

GUILTY PLEA

At any appearance in court, even at the bail hearing, the accused is entitled to enter a guilty plea. A guilty plea dispenses with the necessity of having a trial at which all of the witnesses would be required to testify.

When the accused indicates to the court the desire to plead guilty, the clerk of the court stands up and formally reads the charge or arraigns the accused from the information that the police officer has filed with the court. During arraignment, the clerk must ask the accused whether he or she pleads guilty or not guilty. Upon the accused's plea of guilty the clerk records the plea on the information.

The Crown attorney is then called upon to read the facts of the case to the court from a summary that has been prepared by the investigating police officer. At this point the accused or his or her lawyer may wish to modify or qualify some of the facts alleged by the Crown.[9] If the accused denies an essential element of the offence (e.g., the intention to touch a child's genitals for a sexual purpose, claiming that the touching was accidental), the judge is obliged to strike the guilty plea and order a trial.

On most guilty pleas, the facts read into the record by the Crown attorney are accepted with little modification by the defence. The judge makes a formal

---

[8] The police officer who prepares the bail hearing documentation to be used by the Crown attorney should recommend to the Crown conditions to be followed by the accused in the event of his release on bail. These recommended conditions should be dictated by the circumstances disclosed by the case investigation. Such recommendations guide the Crown and the court in setting the terms of release and are most effective when the officer consults with the protection worker on the case.

[9] The Crown attorney may agree to some modification of the facts read in support of the charge, particularly if they relate to less important features of the case. However, the Crown will not accede to a proposed variation of the factual summary if a disputed fact should be considered by the judge in imposing an appropriate sentence. If the Crown attorney declines to modify the summary, the accused may be allowed to change the plea to "not guilty" and the case is adjourned to a later date for trial. Alternatively, the case may be put over to another court day to enable the Crown to call evidence only to prove the disputed fact.

finding of the accused's guilt. The trial stage of the criminal proceeding is then over and the sentence hearing takes place. Sentencing may occur on the same day as the finding of guilt or may be adjourned by the court to another day to allow a pre-sentence report to be prepared or witnesses to be called for the purpose of the sentencing hearing.

PLEA BARGAINING

Prior to entering a guilty plea or going through with a trial, the accused may wish to know what sentence the Crown will recommend to the judge if a guilty plea is entered. Saving the community the cost of a trial, and the witnesses the trauma or inconvenience of testifying, are recognized by judges as having the potential to reduce the sentence that would ordinarily be imposed after a full trial. An accused may wish to know whether the Crown attorney will agree to a variation of the offence synopsis to be read to the court on the basis that the brief prepared by the police contains some inaccurate information or allegations that could not be proven upon a trial. The defence might also wish to know whether the Crown attorney will accept a guilty plea to one or two of several offences or to a less serious charge than the one faced by the accused.

These matters are commonly discussed out of court by the Crown attorney and the accused's lawyer. Such discussions are popularly termed "plea bargaining", but are more correctly referred to as "plea negotiations" or "plea discussions". Plea discussions play an essential and practical role in the criminal justice system. Often both lawyers will be able to agree that after a trial on the existing evidence the accused would likely be found guilty of a certain offence and not guilty of others. They might also agree as to what sentence is appropriate in view of the law that must be applied to the facts of the case. The Crown attorney may then undertake to recommend this sentence if the accused pleads guilty. While the sentencing judge is not bound by the plea discussions, judges generally accept recommendations made jointly by lawyers for the accused and Crown after such discussions.

Plea discussions can result in tremendous savings of the time, effort and cost that normally would be expended on a criminal trial. The accused becomes certain of the charges upon which he or she will be convicted and the sentence that is likely to be imparted and may also have the sentence reduced in consideration of the guilty plea. The Crown enjoys the benefit of a certain conviction. This is significant as every trial involves a risk of acquittal, which may present danger to the community as a guilty party goes free. Witnesses are spared the inconvenience and stress of testifying, which may be particularly important in cases involving children or intrafamilial abuse.

Sometimes plea bargaining will occur just before a trial is scheduled to commence. Thus a child and other witnesses may be at the court and ready to testify only to find that the case has been resolved.

DISCLOSURE

An accused is entitled to obtain disclosure of the Crown's case prior to any trial to allow the accused to properly prepare a defence, or decide whether to enter into plea discussions with the Crown. Disclosure is usually provided to the accused's lawyer by the Crown attorney, and consists of written summaries of each witness's evidence, a copy of any statement the accused has given to the police, and the results of scientific analysis of the exhibits seized by the police.[10]

THE PRELIMINARY INQUIRY

When an accused faces an indictable offence[11] he or she may elect (i.e., choose) a trial in a superior court rather than the provincial court. This entitles the accused to a preliminary inquiry, typically conducted by a judge in the provincial court.

This hearing usually takes place within a few months of the laying of the information. The Crown must call evidence at this hearing to show that the case against the accused is sufficient to warrant putting the accused through a trial. The preliminary inquiry also serves the purpose of giving the accused more knowledge of the Crown's case and of helping to decide whether to enter a guilty plea without a trial.[12] The preliminary inquiry resembles a trial and the same rules of evidence apply; however, the defence rarely calls any witnesses.

---

[10] Disclosure practices in Crown attorneys' offices vary across Canada. While some Crown attorneys are extremely protective of the privacy of Crown witnesses and will not provide addresses or even last names of witnesses to the defence, others feel obliged to give out personal information concerning the victim if they are persuaded that it may be important to the accused's defence. A witness' history of mental illness or prior sexual victimization by another offender may have an important connection to the case and the Crown attorney may feel ethically bound to reveal such background information to the defence.

[11] Offences are categorized as indictable, summary or hybrid. Indictable offences are more serious and have greater penalties. An accused person charged with an indictable offence is generally afforded extra procedural protections, such as the right to a preliminary inquiry and a jury trial. Summary offences are considered less serious, have lesser maximum penalties (typically a maximum of 6 months in prison and/or a $2,000 fine) and are resolved by a more expeditious procedure. Hybrid offences afford the Crown a choice (or election) as to whether to proceed summarily or by indictment. Most offences involving allegations of child abuse or neglect are hybrid.

[12] The advantages of a preliminary inquiry to the defence are clear. Defence counsel will use this opportunity to ask the child a wide range of questions about the case, even on marginally relevant issues. A transcript of the child's testimony will be available later at the trial. If the child's answers to the same questions are different at trial, the child may appear inconsistent and therefore unreliable on the main issue, such as the sexual assault. Witnesses should therefore be prepared for a preliminary inquiry as if it were a trial. If they do not know how to answer certain questions, they should be encouraged ahead of time to say so rather than guess at possibly wrong answers.

Often the Crown is able to satisfy the test of sufficiency after calling one or two witnesses, generally making the preliminary inquiry much shorter than a trial. However, in most cases involving offences of physical and sexual abuse against children it is necessary for the Crown to call the child victim to testify at the preliminary inquiry and make the child available for cross-examination by defence counsel. Thus, if a case goes to trial, a victim of abuse may have to testify twice.

If the test of sufficiency is met or the defence waives the right to a preliminary inquiry, the presiding judge will commit the case for trial in the higher court, often in another building. The case may not come to trial for several months or even a year or more, depending on the pending caseload in the particular jurisdiction.[13] If the Crown's evidence does not meet the test of sufficiency at the preliminary inquiry, the accused is discharged and is free to go.

TRIAL

The basic procedure followed in a trial is the same whether it is held before a jury, a judge alone in superior court or in provincial court. The trial commences with the accused being arraigned and advising the court of his "not guilty" plea. In a jury trial the Crown attorney then addresses the jury and proceeds to call and question witnesses. As questioning of each witness is completed by Crown counsel, the accused's counsel has the right to cross-examine that witness. After all witnesses for the Crown have been examined and cross-examined, the Crown closes its case.

One of the most important functions of the Crown attorney is to introduce in court the evidence gathered by the police showing that an accused person has committed the offence with which he is charged. This must be done fairly and impartially. In a criminal trial the onus is always on the Crown to prove the guilt of the accused beyond a reasonable doubt. If it becomes clear that a charge against an accused cannot be proven because of insufficient evidence, the Crown attorney is duty-bound to withdraw that charge.[14]

When the Crown's case is closed, the defence must decide whether the accused will testify and whether to call other witnesses to testify. The accused is not required by law to testify or to call any other witnesses. If the accused opts to testify or the defence calls other witnesses on its behalf, the same questioning pattern is followed in reverse; that is, after each defence witness is questioned by the lawyer for the accused, Crown counsel is afforded the opportunity of cross-

---

[13] This illustrates another clear advantage of the preliminary inquiry to the defence: the time it affords the accused to put off the trial and commencement of the sentence. Some accused put this time to good use by engaging in a treatment program, finding a job, or giving up drugs or alcohol, all of which puts them in a better light at the time of sentence.

[14] An essential pre-trial duty of the Crown attorney is to advise the police whether the police have enough evidence to prove a proposed charge according to the highest standard of proof (beyond a reasonable doubt). Sometimes, after consultation with the Crown, police officers may decide not to lay a charge. This also explains why charges are sometimes withdrawn before a trial.

examining the witness. After the case for the defence is completed, the Crown may exercise the right to call more witnesses to reply to evidence called by the defence.

When all of the witnesses have testified, counsel for the Crown and the defence summarize the evidence and present their arguments on the applicable law to the presiding judge. If there is a jury, both lawyers address their comments on the evidence to the jury and, after hearing legal argument from counsel, the judge instructs the jury in the law. In a jury trial, the jurors are the ultimate "triers of fact", responsible for deciding whether to convict or acquit. Any verdict must be unanimous; if it is not there is said to be a "hung jury" and there will ordinarily have to be another trial. If there is no jury, the judge alone is responsible for deciding all issues of fact and law.

EVIDENCE

The process of giving testimony by witnesses through questioning by the Crown and defence counsel is governed by strict rules of evidence applied by the judge throughout the trial. One source of the rules of evidence is legislation, as in the federal *Canada Evidence Act*,[15] which applies to criminal trials. Evidence law also comes from precedents set by English and Canadian judges and applied over many years (and even centuries) to cases with similar fact situations. This type of law is known as common law, as distinguished from statutory law, like the *Canada Evidence Act*. The *Charter of Rights* may also have a role in determining what evidence is admissible; evidence obtained in violation of the accused's rights under the *Charter* may be excluded if receiving it would "bring the administration of justice into disrepute."

Rules of evidence are based on notions of fairness and are intended to ensure that an accused person receives a just trial, based on reliable proof. For example, although an accused may be perceived as depraved or eccentric, the rules of evidence ordinarily prohibit the introduction of examples of bad character as proof of a criminal charge. In law, such evidence is not considered trustworthy enough to show that the accused committed a certain offence on a specific date. Admission of such evidence could also be very unfair; the judge or jury might find accused persons guilty simply because they are thought to be bad persons and not necessarily because they committed the offence.[16]

---

[15] R.S.C. 1985, c. C–5.

[16] The courts have recognized that there are circumstances in which the probative value of evidence of prior, similar acts exceeds any prejudice to the accused and will admit evidence of "similar" occurrences. This can be especially important in child sexual abuse cases where it may buttress the credibility of a child or rebut the suggestion that touching was "innocent in purpose". See *R. v. L.E.D.*, [1989] 2 S.C.R. 111; see also "*R. v. C.R.B.*" Lawyers Weekly (4 May 1990) full text 1002–019.

Similarly, the requirements of fairness and reliability explain why the rules of evidence generally exclude hearsay testimony from a criminal trial. Hearsay evidence consists of information that another person has told the witness. The introduction of hearsay does not allow for the cross-examination of the person who made the statement and is therefore considered less reliable than a statement made in court.

Evidence law allows experts to be called to give opinions on subjects beyond the general knowledge of the trier of fact (the judge or jury). The party who is proposing to call an expert must establish to the judge's satisfaction that the witness has the proper credentials to qualify as an expert. In the context of child physical and sexual abuse, opinion evidence is usually given by medical doctors, psychiatrists, psychologists and sometimes social workers who have developed a special expertise. Unequivocal physical evidence rarely exists in sexual abuse cases; thus, there is an increasing tendency to call experts to confirm the offence by assessing the psychological condition of the child. Such evidence may explain why disclosure of abuse was delayed or a child recants when the defence argues that the incident was fabricated. While the defence may argue in a conventional fashion that a child who recants or delays in disclosing an incident of abuse is probably fabricating, expert evidence may explain that such behaviour is actually consistent with the offence having been committed. However, the use of experts to support allegations of abuse in a criminal trial remains controversial, and the law regarding the admissibility of this type of evidence remains unsettled. Both the hearsay rule and expert evidence are more fully discussed in Chapter 13.

Section 16 of the *Canada Evidence Act* sets out the conditions under which children may give evidence in court. The threshold for receiving children's evidence has been substantially lowered since the 1988 amendment to this section by Bill C–15. If the child understands the nature of the oath he or she may testify under oath. However, even without understanding the nature of an oath, the child will be able to testify if the judge is satisfied that the child is able to communicate the evidence and can simply promise to tell the truth. This is a new, more realistic standard that many young victims can meet, in contrast to the previous test, which tended to focus more on the somewhat arcane issue of the child's understanding of the nature of the oath.

Evidentiary Innovations in Child Sexual Abuse Cases

A provision in the *Criminal Code* allows a judge to clear a courtroom of observers where it is in the interest of the proper administration of justice.[17] Prosecutors commonly invoke this section in cases involving sexual offences against child victims who must testify. Another provision in the same section of

---

[17] *Supra*, note 5, s. 486(1). Clearing the court "in the interest of ... the proper administration of justice" has been held to be justified in cases where a witness may need the reassurance of the exclusion of the public in order to testify fully and candidly.

the *Code* allows the court to ban publication or broadcast of the identity, or information that could disclose the identity, of the victim or witness in trials of most sexual offences.

One new provision introduced by Bill C–15 allows for the child victim to testify in front of a screen that blocks the child's view of the accused.[18] Alternatively, a judge may allow the child victim to testify from outside the courtroom by means of closed-circuit television, provided the judge, jury, and accused can see the child testifying and the accused can communicate with his lawyer while watching the testimony.[19] Before either of these methods can be employed the law requires that the judge make a finding that their use " ... is necessary to obtain a full and candid account ... "[20] of the alleged offence from the victim. This is usually established by hearing evidence from someone close to the child, perhaps a parent or social worker, concerning the child's inhibitions about testifying in open court without these aids.

Another new provision allows a videotape of a child witness describing an alleged sexual offence to be shown in court as evidence.[21] The videotape must have been made within a "reasonable time" of the commission of the alleged offence. Even with a videotape, the child must still testify in person at the proceedings for the purpose of adopting the contents of the videotape and being available for cross-examination.

The 1988 amendments to the *Criminal Code*, brought in by Bill C–15, create greater potential for facilitating the introduction of children's evidence in these cases. However, courts throughout the country are still deciding the constitutionality of some of these provisions and it may be some time before the degree to which they may be implemented becomes clear.

SENTENCING

The judge who presides at the trial must sentence an accused who is found guilty. Prior to imposing sentence the judge hears representations on behalf of the accused and the Crown as to what would be a fitting sentence. Sentences found by appeal courts to be appropriate for offences committed in similar situations may also be presented to the judge by both counsel to provide guidance as to the appropriate sentence to be imposed.

Sentencing submissions on behalf of the offender generally inform the court about the person's age, marital and family status, employment, and educational and social background. Defence counsel may wish to show that the offence was out of character for the offender by calling witnesses to testify about ordinarily

---

[18] *Ibid.* s. 486(2.1).

[19] *Ibid.*, s. 486(2.2).

[20] *Ibid.*, s. 486(2.1).

[21] *Ibid.*, s. 715.1.

good character and worthwhile activities in the community. The offender may wish to express remorse for the offence or to proffer, through counsel, some explanation for it. The accused's lawyer will attempt to highlight those circumstances of the offence which mitigate its seriousness (e.g., refraining from violence or lack of premeditation). Medical or other professional reports may be tendered by the defence to show the steps toward rehabilitation taken by the offender since the commission of the offence (e.g., engaging in therapy or a drug treatment program).

At sentencing the Crown attorney formally introduces the criminal record of the offender. The Crown may also tender a victim impact statement showing the effect of the offence on the victim, or may call oral testimony to this effect. The Crown attorney expresses the community's views on the seriousness of the offence, highlighting aggravating features that may call for a severe sentence, often considered the best way to protect society. Frequently, in more serious cases, a probation officer will prepare a pre-sentence report for the court to provide information about the offender's background and prospects for rehabilitation.

A judge sentencing an abuser has considerable discretion. The maximum statutory penalty is very rarely imposed.[22] In abuse cases there is a definite tendency to impose a jail term, which may range from a few weeks to several years.

Many judges are concerned that offenders receive appropriate treatment and recognize that the possibilities for treatment in prison are limited, though not nonexistent. In some situations, a judge will impose a probation period, invariably with a condition that the abuser undergo treatment. A probation period may be imposed, either instead of imprisonment, or to follow a prison sentence not exceeding 2 years.

The court is more likely to impose a longer sentence if a sexual abuse case involves a breach of trust (e.g., abuse by a teacher or parent), violence or threats of violence, multiple victims, a repeat offender, abuse continuing over a long period of time, or more serious abuse (e.g., intercourse as opposed to fondling through clothes).[23] Amenability of an abuser to treatment and an expression of remorse may lead to a less severe sentence.

---

[22] This is reserved for the most serious example of an offence committed by the worst offender, a theoretical case situation rarely acknowledged in reality by any sentencing judge.

[23] For cases establishing some of the principles of sentencing, see *R. v. Nye* (1988), 27 O.A.C. 136 (Ont. C.A.), in which an abuser with a prior record of sex offences against children received 6 months imprisonment followed by 3 years probation for fondling a 13-year-old girl. In *R. v. Owens* (1986), 33 C.C.C. (3d) 275 (Ont. C.A.), a male teacher received 3 months imprisonment followed by 2 years probation for fondling young male students.

One particularly difficult issue that sometimes arises in intrafamilial cases is when the victim of abuse asks to testify at the sentencing hearing to request leniency. This may reflect guilt or familial pressure, as well as genuine sentiment on the victim's part. Although judges are doubtless moved by these appeals, they have indicated that the wishes of the victim cannot be determinative. It is recognized that if the courts were to place much weight on the views of the victim, there would be even more pressure on children to request leniency for abusive parents. As the Alberta Court of Appeal observed:

> We cannot ... save the denunciatory sentence only for cases where families are not to be restored ... if we did so, the offender could hold the family hostage to feelings of pity or guilt ... if we lighten the sentence because a child victim "forgives" her father, we are threatening the child that if she will not forgive her father we will condemn him to prison. This is not right.[24]

---

[24] *R.* v. *T.*; *R.* v. *S.* (1983), 46 A.R. 87 at 91 (Alta C.A.) In this sentencing appeal, the court ordered a man imprisoned for 2 years less a day, followed by 2 years probation, despite his willingness to undergo treatment and his victim's request for leniency. The man was convicted of sexually abusing his daughter over a lengthy period of time, with numerous sexual acts, including intercourse. On the same occasion the Alberta Court of Appeal affirmed a suspended sentence for a man who fondled his daughter on a single incident, because the man expressed remorse and had undergone treatment.

PREPARING CHILDREN FOR TESTIFYING IN COURT

*Wendy Harvey**

INTRODUCTION

Reports of child abuse, particularly sexual abuse, have increased enormously in recent years, and children are more frequently called upon to be witnesses in court. In protection proceedings and parental custody or access disputes, judges usually make a finding that abuse has occurred based on the evidence of witnesses other than the child who is the subject of the proceeding.[1] However, in criminal cases involving allegations of sexual abuse, it is almost always necessary for the child to be a witness for there to be a successful prosecution.

In 1988, the criminal law was amended to facilitate the giving of evidence by children.[2] It is now possible for children to testify, whether or not they understand the nature of an oath. They must only have the "ability to communicate" and the capacity to "promise to tell the truth." However, it is critically important that children, especially young children, be adequately prepared for testifying in court, so that they can communicate effectively and not be unduly traumatized by the experience.

Preparation of a child for the court experience is important whatever the nature of the proceeding, but it is especially crucial for the criminal prosecution. Most of the professional literature on the subject of preparing children to testify focuses on the criminal setting, for this is the forum in which they most frequently are witnesses. Further, it is the most adversarial setting in which a child may appear, and the area in which there is the most potential for hostile or

---

* Crown Counsel, Ministry of the Attorney General, Vancouver, British Columbia.

[1] See, e.g., *D.R.H.* v. *Superintendent of Family and Child Services* (1984), 41 R.F.L. (2d) 337 (B.C.C.A.).

[2] Bill C–15, in effect January 1, 1988. For a description of the new laws, see Stewart & Bala, *Understanding Criminal Prosecutions for Child Sexual Abuse: Bill C–15 and the Criminal Code*, (Toronto: Institute for the Prevention of Child Abuse, 1988).

abusive questioning. This chapter is intended to serve as an introduction for those who may be involved in preparing child victims of abuse to testify in court.[3]

DYNAMICS OF THE CHILD SEXUAL ASSAULT PROSECUTION

More child witnesses are now testifying in criminal court than ever before in the history of Canadian law. This is primarily due to the recent awareness of child sexual assault and the growing number of reports of abuse. In most of these cases, there are two people who actually witnessed the act: the perpetrator and the child victim. If there is a trial, the child and the adult may give different versions of what occurred. Although other witnesses may testify during the criminal trial, it is often the child witness that stands between the accused and the door to freedom. This means the child is vulnerable to the defence counsel's attempts to discredit the child, either through cross-examination or by calling other witnesses. While the Crown attorney and judge have a role in protecting the child from improper questioning, it must be appreciated that a central focus of a criminal trial in our society is the protection of the legal rights of the accused, and the defence has considerable scope in how it conducts its case.

A child needs to be supported through the experience of testifying to encourage unfettered communication. Support means preparation before the testimony, accompanying the child to court for the testimony and skilled questioning by the Crown attorney. Those who prepare children for court should understand the dynamics of a child sexual assault trial, and be able to anticipate the child's fears and questions. Some of the procedural and evidentiary features of the criminal courts that children have difficulty understanding are embedded in the very foundation of our judicial system.

Fundamental principles of criminal law are designed to guarantee freedom and justice in our society, and to protect the rights of the accused. However, the system sometimes appears to be stacked against child witnesses and the credibility of their statements. Children often express quizzical confusion about the following:

- Why is the accused presumed innocent until proven guilty?
- Why must the Crown prove the case beyond a reasonable doubt?
- Why does the accused have the right to remain silent? In other words, why do the victims have to go through all the rigours of investigation and trial as if they are not believed, when it appears the accused doesn't have to say anything?

In our system many allegations of sexual assault go unprosecuted and many others that go to court result in acquittals, despite the allegations of the child. It is

---

[3] See also W. Harvey & A. Watson-Russel, *So You Have To Go to Court* (Toronto: Butterworths, 1986), which is written for professionals to read to children who will be going to court.

not uncommon for the trier of fact to find the accused not guilty, without the accused having to call evidence or testify. This is because the prosecution must prove the case beyond a reasonable doubt. If the defence can demonstrate weaknesses in the child's allegations, the prosecution has not fulfilled its onus.

If the Crown has difficulty in prosecuting its case, the defence may not call evidence and the accused may decide not to testify and run the risk of having his own credibility challenged, particularly if he has a criminal record of any sort.[*] In the event the accused does testify, it is not a contest between the accused and the child because of the strict onus on the prosecution. Even if there are inadequacies in the accused's testimony, if there are also difficulties in that of the child, the prosecution has not fulfilled its onus and there may be an acquittal.

Children are presumed incompetent as witnesses, and their evidence is considered fraught with frailties. When children take the stand, unlike an adult, they must undergo an inquiry to satisfy the judge that they are competent. In the event they are permitted to testify under oath, despite Parliament's recent attempts to legislate away corroboration requirements, some judges still sometimes warn the jury on the frailties of children's evidence.

The system is designed to guarantee the accused's rights, and not to provide children safety and comfort in the courtroom. Only recently have large-scale attempts been made to enhance the accessibility of children to the criminal courts, and not without loud voices of dissension which say the child advocates have gone too far towards a blueprint of conviction for those accused.

There are common themes raised by the defence counsel to discredit a child's allegation of sexual abuse. In the course of the trial, the child is often asked extremely embarrassing and emotionally evocative questions, sometimes far beyond the coping ability of a child. Some recurrent themes raised by defence counsel include:

1. The complaint was made after a long delay from the time the event is said to have occurred, which suggests falsehood. The defence may argue that if this abuse occurred, one would anticipate early disclosure. That there were many people in the child's life whom she loved and trusted, and to whom one would anticipate she would tell, adds weight to this position. That the child still associated herself with the accused during the period of alleged abuse, gave him gifts or acted affectionately towards him, may also add weight to the argument.[4]

---

[*] (In this chapter the accused will be referred to by the masculine pronoun, because although some child sexual abusers are female, the vast majority are male. The victims will be referred to by the female pronoun, though a significant portion of victims of child sexual abuse are boys.)

[4] Recent cases have held that the Crown can call expert witnesses in a child sexual abuse prosecution to explain the delay in disclosure or the phenomenon of recantation. See *R*. v. *F.E.J.* (1990), 74 C.R. (3d) 269 (Ont. C.A.).

2. The complainant made up this allegation for her own reasons (revenge, anger, seeking attention, confusion), and once the investigation started she felt compelled to stick to her story. Her therapists, the investigators, the prosecutor and other persons involved have contributed to her fabrication by continually supporting her rather than challenging her "lie".

3. Because the child's situation has improved since her complaint (i.e., moving to a new home with more material goods and more attention) she is not prepared to recant the story.

4. The child is convinced by overzealous investigators and prosecutors that this happened. She starts by acting or saying something which makes people suspicious. The interviewers put words in her mind and mouth which sound like an allegation. They teach her the proper names of the sex organs and the names for sexual activity. In therapy the child is taught to hate the accused and that he is a bad man. The child is young and vulnerable and moves with the flow to please these new authoritarian and obliging persons in her life.

5. Once one child spoke of abuse, friends and school mates followed suit because they wanted the attention too or really thought hysterically that they were abused too. The investigators and parents contributed to the similarities in their complaints by not keeping them separate and by discussing details in their presence.

6. If there is a confession by the accused, it may be explained as simply an attempt to gain entry to the therapeutic system and avoid the criminal process, as the product of inappropriate coercion or guilt-inducing questioning by investigators, or in an intrafamilial case as prompted by a desire to satisfy a condition imposed by protection authorities as a term of access to the child.

The defence attempts to demonstrate these types of themes and create a reasonable doubt by cross-examination of the Crown witnesses. For example, a victim assistance person might be asked, "You say you saw the complainant 10 times before trial and often spoke to her about her complaint. I suggest that during those times you added your thoughts in your own words to anything she might have been saying. And isn't it true that at times many children would meet together and share their experiences with details similar to what we heard today?"

Although there are many avenues to challenge the child's allegations, an important focus of the accused is typically through the cross-examination of the child. It is often not difficult for the accused to discredit a child witness. Children in many places in Canada are testifying 1 to 2 years or more after the actual assault, about incidents evoking fear, confusion and misunderstanding. The court forum is not only foreign to them, but is not designed to accommodate their needs. Many of the adult participants are ignorant of child development issues and the dynamics of abuse or, alternatively, feel the fundamental principles of criminal law supersede any considerations for the child.

Also, historically, the criminal law has pronounced a bias against children as credible witnesses. Therefore, not only must the prosecution prove the case beyond a reasonable doubt, but within a context where children are presumed to be carriers of falsehood.[5] On the witness stand, once the child has narrated the allegation, the cross-examination by defence, although in theory designed to elicit truth from adults, often serves as a technique to confuse and intimidate the young child. She may be shown gifts and cards which she gave to the accused in the past, asked about her personal diary or sexual contact she has had with other children or be accused of lying, often using long convoluted questions, at times specifically designed to confuse. As Dr. J. Yuille describes: [6]

> One only needs to witness a single instance of the cross-examination of a child witness to realize that the procedure is ill suited to children. It is easy to confuse a young child with the use of age-inappropriate language, long and circuitous questions, and a confrontational style. The adversarial system creates as many problems as it solves in the area of child sexual abuse.

Dr. Yuille summarizes some of the literature on child witnesses.

> A number of studies have indicated that younger children are susceptible to suggestion, although the extent of this susceptibility has been debated. However, a recent review of procedures that prosecutors and defence lawyers can employ when examining and cross-examining children demonstrates that in the courtroom suggestibility is a real issue. Myers provides a number of examples of how children can be confused and misled by a defence attorney in order to cause doubt in the victim's testimony. For example, he suggests confusing the child by asking questions following more than one train of thought at a time and changing the temporal order of the events.

From what we know of the dynamics of child abuse and disclosure, a complaint by a child of sexual abuse is clearly not easy to make, it is difficult to assess, and within the contest of the Canadian criminal justice system it is often difficult to prove. The challenge is to accommodate child victims in our courts without harming them. The challenge is to do this while providing the ultimate protection for the child, which is maintaining an objectivity that doesn't put the support process itself into suspicion and the weight of the complaint into jeopardy.

In this context, good standards of practice by those involved from the beginning in the investigation and prosecution, as well as in any concurrent child protection proceedings, can assist the child complainant to make her complaint from a strengthened position.

The child's position is strengthened if:

---

[5]   See N. Bala, "Double Victims: Child Sexual Abuse and the Criminal Justice System in Canada" (1990) forthcoming 15(1) Queen's L.J.

[6]   J. Yuille, *Expert Evidence by Psychologists: Sometime Problematic and Often Premature* (Vancouver: 1989) at 190.

1. There is confirming evidence to the child's complaint, the most helpful being the confession of the accused, but also medical evidence or even physical evidence, like a semen sample or clothing.

2. All those in contact with the child have been not only supportive and well intentioned, but also skilled and conscious of contamination issues.

3. The child herself is thoroughly but properly prepared to face the rigors of the criminal process by individuals who understand the system and are not afraid of it.

THE CHILD WITNESS' STATUS IN COURT

A person's status in the criminal court room determines the extent to which one can address the judge and be heard on matters that affect the unfolding of the prosecution. Both the prosecuting and defence lawyers have status to address the judge, with the Crown addressing matters on behalf of the state and the defence on behalf of the accused. If the accused is unrepresented, he still has status and may address the court and make applications on his behalf without prejudicing his right to remain silent (i.e., to not give evidence as a witness).

A witness generally does not have the legal status to address the court about the governing of the trial, except for such matters as requesting a drink of water or seeking a recess to go to the bathroom. A complainant (victim of the alleged offence) or a lawyer acting on her behalf, may also request a ban, under s. 486(3) of the *Criminal Code,*[7] on the publication of information that would identify her. However, the child has no status to ask the court to receive a videotape of a prior statement under s. 715.1 of the *Code*, or to permit testimony via closed circuit television under s. 486(2.1); such requests can only be made by the Crown attorney.

The accused and his interests are represented in court, but the child witness has no true representation. Practically speaking, in most instances it appears the Crown attorney is representing the child and her interests, because the prosecution is better served if the child is well prepared and protected. However, there may be circumstances where the duty of the Crown attorney as an officer of the court overrides any practical benefit to protect the child. The Crown attorney is, for example, obliged to disclose to the lawyer for the accused prior to the trial the evidence which the prosecution will be putting before the court; the Crown must also disclose evidence the police have discovered that supports acquittal. The accused has no comparable duty of disclosure.

The *Code of Conduct* of the Canadian Bar Association establishes the following duties for a prosecutor:

> When engaged as a prosecutor, the lawyer's prime duty is not to seek a conviction, but to present before the trial court all available credible evidence relevant to the alleged crime in order that justice may be done through a fair trial upon the merits. The prosecutor exercises a public function involving much

---

[7] *Criminal Code*, R.S.C. 1985, c. C–46.

discretion and power and must act fairly and dispassionately. The prosecutor should not do anything that might prevent the accused from being represented by counsel or communicating with counsel ... and, to the extent required by law and accepted practice, should make timely disclosure to the accused or defence counsel of all relevant facts and known witnesses, whether tending to show guilt or innocence, or that would affect the punishment of the accused.[8]

Thus, even if the Crown attorney is sensitive and experienced in handling child sexual abuse cases, there will be times when it seems that the child is not directly represented in the court, whereas the accused may have an aggressive lawyer, consistently advocating to protect his interests. These problems will be exacerbated if, as is sometimes the case, the Crown attorney lacks experience or sensitivity with this type of case, or has not had an opportunity to meet the child before court and adequately prepare for the trial.

PRINCIPLES OF TRIAL PREPARATION

Practitioners preparing children for court, whether police, social workers or lawyers, must not be naive to the process and the effect that their contact with the child may have on the evaluation of the child's credibility. In other words, what may be innocent gestures—such as giving the child a candy to comfort her into testifying, going repeatedly over her disclosure or speaking disparagingly of the accused—may provide the ammunition required by the defence to build up the reasonable doubt theme described earlier in this chapter. Equally, those who prepare children must evaluate their own feelings about the effectiveness of the system because fear, cynicism, dismay or intimidation may be unwittingly communicated to the child.

Those dealing with children who will be going to court should adopt a general attitude which balances the important principles of the system. This guides one's decision-making concerning the daily routines.

First, professionals must recognize the need to maintain a balance between the importance of protecting the rights of the accused and those of the children. Such a balance sends messages and information to the child consistent with the likely outcomes of the process stages. The system recognizes the balances and outcomes reflect this. Thus it is not helpful or appropriate to raise expectations that everything in the criminal process will succeed according to the needs and wants of the child.

Second, the practitioner should constantly balance three goals in preparing the child for court. By doing so, one can support the child through the process, while conducting oneself with integrity and skill. The following should be sought:

1. minimal repeated trauma to the child by the investigative and court process;

2. eliciting valid information from the child; and,

3. maintaining the integrity of the preparation process.

---

[8]   *Code of Conduct* (Ottawa: Canadian Bar Association, 1988) at 37.

WHO PREPARES THE CHILD FOR COURT

There are situations in which it is very important that a particular person is, or is not, involved in preparing a child for court. In some cases the defence will cast aspersions on a child's testimony because a particular person was involved in court preparation. There may be suggestions that the person preparing the child had improper motives or engaged in improper conduct. For example, if a case includes an allegation of abuse in the context of a parental custody dispute, it is inappropriate to have the non-offending parent involved in preparing the child for court. On the other hand, as between several professionals, such as police, child protection workers, or other social workers, it may not be significant that one or another is involved, as long as those preparing the child for court have sensitivity, understanding and knowledge.

There are a wide variety of agencies and individuals participating in the preparation of children. The respective roles differ from province to province, city to city. and agency to agency. Children are prepared by police, social workers, therapists, Crown attorneys, victim assistance workers, child care workers, volunteers, parents and others. It seems to have been acknowledged that preparation is required and different individuals and agencies are taking part to ensure it happens.

A preparation that consists of repeated discussion of the assault may be looked upon suspiciously. Some therapists, for example, spend hours of sessions going over and providing insights about the abuse with the child. Often, despite the validity of the complaint, this results in the child sounding like a psychology scholar by court day, which may negatively affect her credibility. A therapist might consider not discussing the details of the activity with the child prior to court but, rather, focus on other therapeutic issues such as self-esteem or relationships. Equally, documenting the process would enable a therapist to defend the techniques used if suggestions of contamination are made. Having a video-tape of the child's own description of the abuse, made prior to the commencement of therapy, may also serve to dispel arguments that the therapist improperly influenced the child.

Ideally for a prosecutor the fewer people the child has discussed the events with before the trial, the better. An increased number of conversations increase the types of reaction to the child's allegations and therefore leaves room for suggestions of contamination.

If the Crown attorney is involved in an extensive review of the evidence with the child prior to court, it is preferable to have another person present during the interview. This may prevent the Crown attorney from being called as a witness to testify about pre-trial conversations, as the other person can be a witness, if this is necessary to dispel suggestions of inappropriate preparation or contamination. A person who is called as a witness cannot also be a prosecutor in the same case.

If individuals other than the Crown attorney are preparing the child for court, they should include the Crown as part of the preparation. The prosecutor will then be able to function better in court having assessed what helps a particular child communicate well in court and what she is going to say. Crown attorneys with experience in this area always want to meet with the child in advance, if only to establish a rapport, and often want to play a role in reviewing the evidence that the child will give. Some Crown attorneys want to be the only ones to review the child's testimony with the child before the trial, though even these lawyers acknowledge the crucial role that others can play in terms of preparing the child for the experience of testifying and providing emotional support during and after court.

DEVELOPING A SYSTEM FOR CHILD WITNESS PREPARATION

The criminal justice context demands a systemized approach to preparing children and their families for the court process and testifying. A systemized approach, properly developed and administered, encourages a consistency not always present if preparation is done on an ad hoc basis, even by well-intentioned individuals. Proper development of a system of preparation requires a consideration of many factors: cost effectiveness, standards, accountability, efficiency, training, continuing education, balancing the child's needs with the demands of the criminal justice system and with the demands of the individuals in it, the mandate of the organization providing the service (e.g., advocacy or informing and supporting the child), and philosophy.

Preparation should be done by individuals who are familiar with current research relating to child witnesses and sexual abuse, case law, the demands of the criminal justice system, as well the needs of the child witness. A structured program for preparation will likely address efficiency and cost effectiveness issues. Efficiency is particularly important in preparing children in a rural community or in communities isolated from courthouses and current information.

Those involved in the trial process, such as the police and the judiciary, should be familiar with, and trust, the preparation methods used. Even if defence lawyers attack the process, preparation must take place. It is important to familiarize all professionals involved in the criminal justice system with the process despite the turnover and differing attitudes and energy levels of persons involved.

The preparation program may be police, community, mental health, social services or prosecution based, depending on the protocols, personality, needs and structure of a given community and its members. Although the Crown attorney plays an essential role in the preparation of a child, other professionals typically constitute the core of the non-testimony preparation.

A standardized approach may be administered at different degrees or levels. For example, individuals in a small community may draft a protocol designing the roles of different agencies and how they interrelate in the preparation process. However, the development of a curriculum which is available to any organization may be carried out for a larger geographic area.

A system of preparation should include the following:

1. A step-by-step procedure for imparting knowledge to children and other care-givers about:

   (a) the criminal justice system in general;

   (b) what the child and family might expect of different stages in the process.

2. A procedure for designing strategies around:

   (a) the child's needs related to court and the coping mechanisms that work best with different types of children;

   (b) liaison with the police and Crown attorney assigned to the case to encourage dovetailed preparation;

   (c) the child's current and future support network and how it might be included in the preparation.

3. Materials for each child and caregiver which might include:

   (a) a record keeping method for the child's preparation;

   (b) a list of fears written by the child;

   (c) a children's book on the court process;

   (d) a parent's guide to the court process;

   (e) videotapes for children and parents on the expected process.

The effectiveness of court preparation is enhanced with concurrent policies providing guidelines for police, child protection, Crown attorneys, court services and corrections.

SAMPLE PREPARATION

It is generally preferable to have a series of preparation meetings with the child held over a number of days. The following topics could be included.

Day One: Introduction

- Explain the purpose of preparation.
- Outline the course content.
- Have the child keep a journal (in which she can write down any questions for the Crown and document the events of the course).
- Receive information of the child's existing impressions of court.
- Introduce the courtroom and its participants.
- Use audiovisual products to introduce the criminal process.
- Give the child material for home reading.
- Invite the child to write down questions for next day.
- Complete the questionnaire on scheduling preferences.

Day Two: **More on court**

- Engage in, or see a video of, a court role play. For the role play use situations unrelated to the case at hand (e.g., Goldilocks story, stolen pop bottles, broken window and so forth).

Day Three: **Practical matters**

With the child, go through a checklist of the practical matters that should be addressed, including:

- Without inducing fear in the child, hear what the child's fears and apprehensions are around testifying and respond to those fears.
- Make arrangements for the child to meet the prosecutor if it has not already been done. The prosecutor may attend this session or the worker may visit the Crown's office with the child. Develop a protocol for this that is consistent with the needs of the community.

Day Four: **Preparing the evidence**

This can be done in stages and may take several visits. It should be done by the lawyer who is taking the case through court and may include the following:

- Have the child recount the event from memory.
- Give the child an opportunity to read or view previous testimony or statements.
- Discuss how these matters will be treated in court.
- Communicate to the child questions that will be asked and invite her to find her own words to answer the questions.
- Demonstrate some techniques commonly used in court by lawyers in their questioning.
- Inform the child that there may be many questions not covered during the preparation and help her develop coping mechanisms for any situation in court.

Preparing for court procedure

- Prepare the child for each stage of her testimony. (e.g., what it means when the defence counsel picks up the typed version of her statement and asks her to identify it).
- Develop methods to deal with all contingencies (e.g., tears, if the child stops talking, objections or going to the bathroom).
- Find out what the child's apprehensions are and offer legal solutions (e.g., the possibility of a screen, closed circuit television or exclusion of the public from court).
- Go into the courtroom in advance and make sure everything is ready for the child as planned.

Day Five: **After court**

- The witness often requires a debriefing session once court is over.

An acknowledgement letter or certificate of participation can go a long way in assisting the young child during this period of withdrawal and healing. For some children it may be appropriate to give a "hero badge" or some other symbol of participation.

ROLE OF CROWN COUNSEL IN COURT PREPARATION

There is a continuing discussion in Canada over the appropriate role of non-lawyers in preparing children for court, and there should always be consultation with the Crown attorney before establishing a protocol. It is the writer's opinion that the Crown attorney should always be the one who reviews the evidence with the child. Other issues which some feel should be left to a lawyer are:

General

- right to a fair trial
- presumption of innocence
- court jurisdiction

Procedure

- charging the accused
- purpose of a preliminary hearing
- trial by jury and trial by judge alone
- implications for the witnesses of trials in different settings
- cross-examination by defence counsel

Court Preparation

- the role of Crown attorney
- the role of the witnesses
- the role of the defence lawyer
- the role of the judge
- where child waits before testifying
- who will wait with the child
- how the child will know when to come into the courtroom
- how to signal a desire to use the bathroom

The main concern expressed by Crown counsel when non-lawyers prepare child witnesses for court is that legal information imparted to the witnesses may not be correct, or may be presented in a way that could later cast aspersion on the witnesses' credibility. As stated above, individual communities are encouraged to benefit from the establishment of an interagency protocol on child witness preparation.

RULES OF EVIDENCE AND PREPARING FOR COURT

D.A. Rollie Thompson[*]

THE COURTROOM FROM THE WITNESS'S PERSPECTIVE

"What you see depends upon where you sit." That just about sums it up for participants in the trial process. The counsels sit at their respective tables, looking at the judge and, to one side, the witness. The judge sits up at the front, surveying the assembled parties and their lawyers, taking notes and swivelling towards the witness from time to time. Both perspectives are well-discussed in the literature on child protection and in the chapters of this book.

But what if you are a witness? You are called in from the waiting room when your number comes up. As the courtroom door opens for you, the room generally falls silent. You walk to the witness stand, with all eyes on you. Bible in hand, you take the oath, swearing to "tell the truth, the whole truth and nothing but the truth, so help me God." You sit down, give your name (spelling it if it's anything but "Smith") and the questions begin. Lawyers' questions—times, dates, places, who did what when, who said what—details, details, details, often beyond the perception or memory of the average Nobel prize winner. Then cross-examination—more questions, only now delivered with an edge in the lawyer's voice, pushing, probing, pulling, twisting, making the simple complex and the complex simple. Then the judge questions you, the lawyers get one last kick, and at last you get out of that chair. Now you get to walk back to that courtroom door, only this time no one is watching. They're finished with you.

It may not quite be Franz Kafka, but neither is it a day at the beach. This chapter will focus on the witness's perspective of the proceedings—across the table in the lawyer's office before court, in the waiting room outside Family Court and from the witness stand in the courtroom.

First, I will address the rights and obligations of a witness in child protection proceedings. Second, I will set out the basics of witness preparation for court, primarily what you are entitled to expect from the lawyer calling you. Third, the fundamentals of witness examination in the courtroom are presented. Fourth, I will discuss the cardinal principles of evidence law. Fifth, I will isolate a few of

---

[*] Associate Professor, Dalhousie Law School, Halifax, Nova Scotia.

the most important rules of evidence for a witness in protection proceedings: opinion evidence, hearsay, past parenting evidence and privilege. In conclusion, I will make a few observations on evidence law in protection cases. Throughout I will focus on the relationships between lawyers and witnesses, which reflect an odd mix of law, trial practice and etiquette.[1]

WHAT TO DO AFTER THE SUBPOENA IS SERVED: YOUR RIGHTS AND OBLIGATIONS

Your career as a witness in any particular case will typically begin with a telephone call from one of the lawyers in the case. In this section, I will take you from that first call to the arrival of the subpoena, and your resulting obligations and rights as a witness.

Dealing With Lawyers

That First Contact

Except for agency workers, most witnesses will first come into contact with a lawyer in a protection case with a telephone call, more or less out of the blue, from one of the lawyers, whether agency counsel, counsel for one or both parents or counsel for the child. From the beginning of this first conversation, a witness is entitled to know the lawyer's name, his or her firm, whom the lawyer represents and the particular proceeding in question. If the lawyer shows the poor manners of not introducing these particulars, the prospective witness should insist upon obtaining these details before any discussion takes place.

Generally speaking, witnesses have no obligation to discuss the details of their potential evidence with any counsel. Subject to confidentiality requirements, a witness may talk or not talk to the lawyer or limit the matters discussed. The witness controls the agenda at this early stage—you can stop the conversation at any time, refuse to answer certain questions, limit your answers or postpone discussion.

A professional witness will invariably have to be concerned with confidentiality, according to either the canons of the profession or the policies of the institution within which he or she works. A written release from the professional's client may be necessary, although some will be satisfied with prior verbal approval from the client or simply a familiarity with the client's lawyer.

Agency workers may face a different set of obligations in dealing with counsel for the parents or child. Unlike other witnesses, the agency worker in my view bears a general obligation of disclosure to opposing counsel, subject to agency policies and statutory requirements. Like agency counsel, an agency

---

[1] Obviously, the agency worker will have a different relationship with agency counsel, one much more long-term and complex in nature than that of a non-agency witness. At this point I will focus solely upon the role of the agency worker as witness, although even here there are some significant differences. In the text, I will distinguish between "agency workers" and "non-agency witnesses."

worker should have an affirmative obligation to make full disclosure to counsel for other parties, subject to claims of privilege and accepted local procedures.

No Property in a Witness

Technically, no counsel has property in a witness. The mere fact that one counsel has contacted a witness first or even subpoenaed a witness, does not mean that the witness is barred from speaking to counsel for other parties. Again, subject to confidentiality restrictions, you are free to talk as much or as little as you wish. However, it should be pointed out that if you are a professional person, your unjustified refusal to discuss a case with a lawyer may be brought out at trial as adversely affecting your credibility, especially if you only talked to the lawyer for one side.

In one case where I acted for the parents, a worker for a family support agency was subpoenaed to testify by the agency. Between the time I spoke to the witness and her subsequent testimony at trial, the worker had changed her views on the parents' amenability to supervision and rehabilitation. Unfortunately, the worker was under the false impression that she could not talk to me after she received her subpoena from the agency, causing both myself and my clients to be surprised at her change of heart on the stand. That worker was perfectly free to approach me, as parents' counsel, prior to court and tell me of her changed views.

Getting to Court: A Subpoena

Some witnesses will be quite content to attend court without a subpoena. Most lawyers, however, will have a subpoena served upon you. There are a number of reasons for the use of subpoenas. First, if a witness has not been subpoenaed and does not attend as expected, the lawyer may be denied an adjournment to locate and call the witness. Second, many witnesses will require a subpoena to obtain time off work. Third, most professionals should and do require a subpoena, to protect themselves on matters of confidentiality. Fourth, some willing witnesses may want a subpoena, since it allows them to say "I had no option" after the fact to the parents. Finally, some witnesses simply will not attend without a subpoena, and some not even then.

What is a subpoena? Briefly stated, a subpoena (or a summons in some jurisdictions) amounts to an order from the court requiring you to attend court to be a witness at a stated place and time. Failure to obey a properly served subpoena can result in the issuance of a warrant for the arrest, detention and delivery of the witness to the court by the police.

Generally, a subpoena must be served upon the witness personally, along with any required witness fees. Apart from some special situations, no particular advance notice that a subpoena will be served is required, although common courtesy and a desire for a happy witness generally ensures that lawyers will provide adequate advance notice.

The subpoena will specify the place, date, time and proceeding in which you are to testify. It may require only that you personally attend, or it may go further and require that you bring with you documents or files relevant to the proceeding. If the latter direction is found in the body of the subpoena, then you must attend along with those documents or files.

As a matter of courtesy, most lawyers will provide you with the details of the timing of your attendance. If you are concerned about scheduling, then you should bring this to the attention of the lawyer calling you. Professionals with busy schedules can often be called first thing in the morning or the afternoon to ensure minimum disruption. But, in the end, unless you have a specific understanding with the lawyer calling you about the time of your appearance, the subpoena rules and you must attend as directed, even if it forces you to rearrange your appointment book.

If you attend at court and the matter is adjourned, then you may be called into the courtroom and directed to return at a specified date, which has the same operative effect as the subpoena proper.

Talking About the Case: Exclusion Orders

Protection proceedings are generally closed to the public, with only the parties and their counsel present, subject to statutory provisions respecting publicity and attendance of others in the courtroom. Witnesses are generally left outside in the waiting room until it is time to testify. Formal exclusion orders are often not made, although that is the implicit effect of the closed courtroom.

In addition to ensuring the privacy of proceedings, exclusion orders serve a number of important purposes: to avoid collusion amongst witnesses; to prevent the possibility of perjury; to avert the inevitable influence of one witness's testimony upon others, conscious or unconscious; and to deny witnesses the benefit of watching the cross-examination of other witnesses so that a witness cannot anticipate his or her own cross-examination.

Where witnesses are excluded, the judge or counsel should explain the effect of the order to witnesses to guide their conduct outside the courtroom. First, one witness is not allowed to talk to other witnesses about the contents of their prospective testimony. Second, a witness leaving the courtroom is not to disclose the testimony given or questions asked to other witnesses waiting outside. Third, only after a witness is off the stand and has been released from any possibility of being recalled can that witness converse about his or her evidence with another witness, and then only if that person is similarly finished. It is worth noting that lawyers are also bound by exclusion orders, once made, such that a lawyer may not disclose the substance of courtroom testimony to a prospective witness. Of course, prior to court, a witness is free to discuss the contents of his or her own prospective testimony with a lawyer, as part of the preparation process.

Generally, when a witness has finished testifying, counsel will indicate whether there is any further need for a witness to remain available to be recalled to the stand. If counsel fail to express any such need, but equally fail to release the witness from further attendance, the witness is entitled to request such a release from the judge and, if there is no objection from counsel, the witness will be free to go.

PREPARING FOR COURT: THE WITNESS'S RIGHT TO ADEQUATE PREPARATION

The Witness's Right, The Lawyer's Obligation

The lawyer who calls you as a witness is expected to give you proper preparation for court, as a matter of professional courtesy and sound trial practice. Preparation practices vary considerably amongst lawyers, depending upon the time available, the courtroom experience of the witness and the importance of the witness to the case. Witnesses can, and should, insist upon proper preparation from the lawyer calling them. A lawyer's failure to do so doesn't excuse the witness from testifying, but it can certainly affect the quality and cogency of the testimony.

Even if time constraints are tight, as with interim hearings or last-minute arrangements, a witness is entitled to some minimum steps, even in the hallway outside the courtroom before the hearing begins. The 5-minute-manager version of preparation should include the following basics from the lawyer: an explanation of what the hearing is about, what the major issues are, what your testimony is needed to prove, and a very rough outline of the topics to be covered.

The Basics of Witness Preparation

Usually a witness will have had at least one meeting, if not more, with the lawyer who is calling the witness, including a review of any relevant documents or files. The witness preparation interview should take place before the hearing, well enough in advance to resolve any problems, but not so early that the witness may forget the instructions.

It is important for witnesses to appreciate that there is nothing wrong with reviewing their testimony with the lawyer calling them. It is an acknowledged and necessary part of trial preparation; judges and opposing lawyers know that it takes place. There is no reason to hide or to be embarrassed in the courtroom about prior consultations with the lawyer. If asked whether the lawyer calling you has discussed your testimony with you, the question should be answered with a simple "yes", if this occurred.

There are ethical rules governing a lawyer's preparation of a witness, but you should let the lawyer worry about those. Simply put, a lawyer preparing a witness is entitled to instruct the witness about the methods, techniques and proprieties of testifying, but is not permitted to tell the witness what to say. Preparation focuses on *how* to testify. As an example, I once had a witness in a case who was a retired member of the Navy, but when asked in my office what he had previously done for a living, he answered, "I was a member of the Canadian Armed

Forces, Maritime Command." I told him, "No you weren't, you were in the Navy," to make the point that there was no need to use stilted, formal language and that his everyday way of speaking was good enough in court.

In preparing a witness, I generally begin with the minimum described above. First, it is essential that an individual witness appreciate what the case is about and what the central issues are, including the positions of the parties. Only then can a witness grasp why I am asking my questions and why opposing counsel will be pursuing their lines of cross-examination. Then I go on to explain the role played by this particular witness: what their testimony is intended to prove and how they fit into my theory of the case. Many lawyers fail to provide this sort of information, treating the witness as just a cog in the machine. In my opinion, a witness is entitled to this information, since the witness is more than just a receptacle of a fixed supply of testimony, and is, in fact, a participant in the process. Should a lawyer fail to supply this larger context, the witness should ask questions to elicit this information.

The witness preparation interview then proceeds to the nuts and bolts of direct examination, sometimes called examination-in-chief. During direct examination, the examining lawyer is generally not permitted to lead the witness; that is, ask questions which suggest the desired answer. This means the questions must be open-ended in form. It is thus essential that the witness understand the matters sought by these formal, studiously neutral questions. That understanding is obtained by the lawyer taking the witness through the complete intended direct examination, at least once, or more often if necessary.

On this dry run, the lawyer and the witness essentially negotiate the form and content of the witness's testimony. If the lawyer presents a question that is unclear, the witness should ask that the proposed question be reformulated. If the witness does not understand the rationale for any question, the lawyer should explain the point of the question. If matters are left out, then the witness should ask why and explain why he or she thinks it is sufficiently important to be included. In some areas, it may be necessary for the witness to indicate the limits of first-hand knowledge to settle whether a question and answer will serve any useful purpose. In matters of opinion, you may feel there are limits to the opinions you are prepared to express and those limits should be clearly defined for the lawyer. By the time this process is complete, the direct examination should flow smoothly, with comfortable transitions from one topic to another and questions that the witness understands and can answer.

While preparation is necessary, your direct examination should not appear stilted or rehearsed. To avoid this, I tend to vary the structure and sequence of my questioning on each run through the direct examination.

If exhibits are to be introduced through the witness, typically documents from the witness's file, I walk the witness through the formal process of proving or authenticating the exhibit as it will take place in the courtroom. It is vital that the witness have copies of any exhibits and read them carefully before the hearing date. If a witness intends to "refresh memory" from notes or a file, I take the witness through the rote questions required for the court to grant permission to do so. More on this later.

For expert witnesses giving opinion evidence, it is critical that the lawyer and the witness have a common understanding of the precise phrasing and scope of questions eliciting opinions. Here the expert witness must be much more active in the preparation process, firmly establishing the permissible parameters of the questions and ensuring accurate and precise language.

Proper preparation should cover not only direct examination, but also the cross-examination by opposing counsel. All witnesses should be subjected to some sample cross-examination, for a couple of reasons. First, there are always weaknesses in direct testimony and the witness should be prepared to meet those weaknesses, which will be probed by opposing counsel. Second, cross-examining lawyers use a traditional collection of techniques. The lawyer calling you should, through a sample cross-examination, demonstrate those techniques and assist the witness in finding methods of responding to them. Some simple examples include attempting to turn a minor inconsistency into a major one, forcing the witness to qualify strong statements, confusing the witness, limiting the witness's ability to qualify answers and leading the witness into "traps."

The lawyer should also explain that, on occasion, one or other of the lawyers will object to a question or answer. Once a lawyer rises to object, the witness should immediately stop talking. The lawyers will then argue about whether a question is permissible or certain testimony is admissible and the judge will rule whether the question can be answered or the testimony continued. Once the judge has made a ruling, then the witness will be told whether or not to proceed with the answer. Whether an objection is sustained or overruled should not be taken by the witness as a reflection on the quality of the testimony—it's a matter of legalities, for the lawyers and the judge.

Lastly, the lawyer should give you some guidance on the basics of courtroom layout and practice, such as where the witness stand is, where the lawyers sit and how to address the judge. In this pre-hearing interview, it is vital that the witness raise any questions, fears or concerns about testifying or the testimony to be given. Once you take the stand, the lawyer calling you is no longer able to help you on these points.

Some Pointers for Witnesses

As part of witness preparation, most lawyers will run through a standard list of do's and don't's. Some even put the list in writing for the prospective witness to review. Here is a sample of some of the instructions I offer to witnesses:

1. *Tell the Truth.* Honesty *is* the best policy. Honesty means being accurate, not venturing beyond what you know and not backing off from what you do know.

2. *Listen to the Question.* And answer the question that is asked. Answer that question and no more. If your lawyer wants more information from

you, he or she will ask another question. If the other lawyers want more information from you, let them ask another question.

3. *Take Your Time.* Testifying is not a quiz show. Think before you answer. If you need more time to think, tell the court that you need a moment to think about the matter.

4. *Don't Guess.* If you don't know, say "I don't know." If you can't remember, say "I can't remember." No one can know or remember everything—judges realize that too.

5. *If You Don't Understand the Question, Say So.* If you don't understand the question, especially in cross-examination, ask the lawyer to repeat or rephrase the question. It is up to the lawyers to ask understandable questions—you're just a witness.

6. *Speak Up.* Answer questions clearly and firmly. Say "yes" or "no," because the court reporter or tape recorder can't record a nod or a shake of the head.

7. *Be As Precise As You Can Be, But No More.* No one remembers every detail. If you can give an exact date, time or distance, fine. But if you can't, do your best while making clear that you are approximating.

8. *Never Say Never, Never Say Always.* Beware of answering any question by saying "I never do this" or "I always do that." The other lawyer may well find some occasion when you did otherwise.

9. *If You Make a Mistake, Admit It.* If you slip up while testifying, correct yourself as soon as possible. We all sometimes make mistakes.

10. *Be Polite and Serious.* Simple courtesy to others in the courtroom always makes a good impression. And the courtroom is no place for jokes and wisecracks.

11. *Don't Argue With the Other Lawyer.* Just answer the questions in cross-examination. Don't argue with the other lawyer—the lawyer will always win the argument, not because he or she is smarter, but because the lawyers get to ask the questions.

12. *Don't Lose Your Temper.* Opposing lawyers try to aggravate you. Don't give them the satisfaction of losing your temper. If you lose your temper, you may say dumb things that will come back to haunt you.

13. *Don't Ramble or Volunteer Information.* In cross-examination, answer the question, then stop. Don't ramble on just to fill the silence in the courtroom. It's up to the other lawyer to think up the next question. Don't volunteer information.

14. *If You're Certain, Don't Back Down.* Cross-examining lawyers will try to make you qualify yourself. If you are sure of what you saw or heard, stick to your guns in cross-examination.

15. *When You Want to Make a Point, Look at the Judge.* In the end, it is the judge who has to decide the case. That's the person you have to convince,

so don't forget to look at the judge, rather than the lawyers asking you the questions.

Besides running you through these do's and don't's, the lawyer should also address any particular problems that you have exhibited in your preparation interview. Each of us has annoying habits, tics or nervous behaviours which detract from our testimonial abilities—everything from pulling one ear to inappropriate smiling to fiddling with some article of clothing or whatever. It is better that the witness be embarrassed in the privacy of the lawyer's office than in the public forum of a courtroom.

THE BASICS OF WITNESS EXAMINATION: A PRIMER FOR WITNESSES

By definition, lawyers are comfortable with the formalities and rituals of courtrooms. After all, that's where litigation lawyers spend much of their lives. Not so for the witness, especially the inexperienced witness. In this section, I will outline the basics of the examination of a witness, providing some pointers along the way.

The Basic Structure of a Witness Examination

There is a well-defined pattern to the short (sometimes longer) life of a witness on the stand in the courtroom. After you are called to the front of the courtroom, the clerk will place the Bible in your right hand and recite the standard oath.[2] The precise form of the oath varies, depending upon local practice, but it will run something like this: "Do you swear that the evidence to be given by you to the court touching the matters in question between the parties shall be the truth, the whole truth and nothing but the truth, so help you God?" To which you reply, "I do."

With the oath out of the way, you take the witness chair. The lawyer who has called you will then begin the direct examination, usually with some basic identifying information: your name, address, occupation, position, etc. If your name poses any difficulties at all, you will be asked to spell your name for the court record.

The direct examination by the lawyer will consist of non-leading or open-ended questions, as was reviewed in the preparation interview. Once the direct is complete, the examining lawyer will sit down. At this point, the judge will turn to the opposing lawyer (or one of them if there is more than one) and ask for cross-examination. Cross-examination consists of a series of leading questions or, better, leading statements. No longer will the questions take the form, "Where were you at 5 o'clock that day?" but instead, "At 5 o'clock, you were at the home of Mrs. Smith, weren't you?"

---

[2] If for any reason you object to taking the oath on the Bible, or a similar Holy Book like the Torah or Koran, you may choose to affirm; i.e., to give a solemn affirmation that you will tell the truth, in a form similar to the oath, but without reference to God.

Once the cross-examining lawyer is finished, the lawyer calling you will be asked for any redirect (i.e., any further questions arising from the cross-examination). There may or may not be any redirect.

At this point, the judge may choose to ask you a number of questions, which may or may not be leading. After the judge is finished, he or she will afford the lawyers an opportunity to ask further questions, the lawyer calling you first and then the cross-examining lawyer(s). Now you're finished and the judge will tell you that you may leave the witness stand.

Direct Examination

With the benefit of proper preparation, your direct examination should be relatively straight-forward, following the sequence of topics and questions now familiar from the earlier session(s) with the lawyer. By the time you take the stand, you should be comfortable with the awkward form of open-ended questions on direct.

The purpose of direct examination is to lay out for the court what this witness knows that is of relevance to the issues in the case. First, it is critical for the lawyer to create a record, to place into evidence that information which is necessary to the lawyer's theory of the case; that is, the intended argument as to why his or her client should succeed. Second, the testimony should be organized and elicited in a way which is as persuasive to the court as possible. To be persuasive, the testimony must be clearly and logically developed and the witness must be credible—the first of these is largely in the hands of the lawyer, but the second is largely determined by the background and demeanour of the witness.

During direct examination, opposing counsel may object to a question asked by examining counsel or to some part of your answer. Later in this chapter, I will deal in greater detail with objections based upon the most important rules of evidence: hearsay, opinion and privilege. Here I will only briefly recount the most common objections raised on direct examination.

1. *Improper Leading.* A leading question can take one of two forms. Best known is a question which suggests the answer the questioner desires. Less common, but equally objectionable, is a question which provides factual detail which could and should originate from the witness.[3] In the first case, the concern is improper suggestion to the witness and, in the second, that of improper ratification by the witness. Both attempt to ensure that the court hears the evidence as told freely and in his or her own words by the witness.

There is no absolute rule against leading questions. The rule only bars improper leading. It is permissible for counsel to lead in a variety of situations: introductory matters; matters not in dispute; authenticating or

---

[3]   On these and other issues of the form of questions on direct and cross-examination, see M.P. Denbeaux & D.M. Risinger, "Questioning Questions: Objections to Form in the Interrogation of Witnesses" (1979) 33 Arkansas L. Rev. 439.

proving exhibits; sometimes where the material is extremely complicated; to contradict a specific statement of another witness; to elicit testimony from a witness of limited abilities; to supply detail omitted by the
witness out of forgetfulness or impaired memory; or to correct obvious
misstatements of a witness. Determining whether a question is leading or
not, how much leading may take place and when it becomes characterized as improper leading are left to the discretion of the trial judge,
usually brought into play by an objection from one of the lawyers.

If a judge concludes that a question involves improper leading, then
one of three steps can be taken: (a) most commonly, the question is
disallowed and the lawyer is asked to rephrase the question; (b) counsel
is admonished by the judge, typically where the leading is the product of
incompetence or bad intent; or, (c) in rare cases, the judge will disallow
the question and, because of the seriously suggestive nature of the question on important matters, not allow the question to be restated. Most
importantly, any answer to a question after improper leading may be
given less weight in the judge's later assessment of the witness's testimony.

For the witness, it is important to realize that improper leading is a sin
committed by lawyers. The witness is a mere bystander in the fray, bearing no responsibility for the judge's anger or frustration. Your job is to
wait until the fuss is over and answer the next question.

2. *Hearsay.* Sometimes a question will explicitly seek hearsay and sometimes the witness will inadvertently introduce hearsay in the answer. The
witness should be instructed in preparation about the hearsay rule to
avoid objections of this kind. Hearsay is an out-of-court statement (usually by someone other than the witness on the stand) offered to prove the
truth of the matters asserted in the statement. I will address the hearsay
rule and its exceptions below.

3. *Opinion.* If a witness is not qualified as an expert witness (and thus
entitled to give opinion evidence), then there are limits upon the witness
giving testimony in the form of opinions, as opposed to matters of fact.
More on this later.

4. *Unresponsive.* The witness is required to answer the questions put on
direct and then stop. If the witness fails to answer the question directly or
answers and then rambles, an objection may be made. In this case, it is
the fault of the witness and the witness may even be instructed on how to
answer questions, with varying degrees of restraint, by the presiding
judge.

There is an endless variety of potential objections during direct examination,
of which only the most common are listed here. The vast majority of objections
on direct reflect poor preparation of the witness by counsel or poor self-prepara-

tion by counsel. Some objections reflect battles amongst lawyers over evidentiary matters of little direct concern to the witness.[4]

Refreshing Memory: Using Notes

Most professional witnesses will bring their notes or file concerning the child or parents to the stand. When you deal with many individuals in the course of your work, it is difficult, if not impossible, to testify to the details without aid of your notes. You should have discussed the use of your notes in advance with the lawyer calling you.

If you wish to consult your notes to testify, the lawyer will typically take you through a rote series of leading questions: "Do you have with you your notes concerning your meetings with Mrs. Smith? And were those notes made by you at or near the time of the matters noted? Do you wish to consult those notes in giving your testimony today?"[5] At this point, the judge will generally look to the opposing lawyer and ask if he or she has any objections, after which the court will generally grant permission to employ the notes in testifying.

A few points about notes. First, it is not necessary to exhaust your memory before being permitted to look at your notes. It is sufficient that you can give a fuller and more accurate account of the facts with the aid of the notes.

Second, once you use the notes to refresh your memory, opposing counsel will generally be permitted to inspect *all* your notes or your *whole* file prior to cross-examination, not just the parts you relied upon in direct examination. In effect, this means that everything in your file or notes can conceivably become fair game for cross-examination. Accordingly, it is essential that the lawyer calling you be familiar with the full file (assuming no confidentiality problems) and, more important, that you as a witness review the full contents of your file or notes before taking the stand. In my experience, some professionals are surprised to learn that the opposing lawyer is free to root through the notes, especially as such notes in protection cases often contain damaging confidential information about the parties.

In taking notes, especially where a proceeding can reasonably be anticipated or is already under way, the professional should be aware of what can happen to those notes in the courtroom. Many such witnesses find themselves on the horns of a dilemma. If you take careful notes, then lawyers will pick through the details for those most useful to their case. Yet if you fail to keep adequate notes, your credibility will be attacked based upon your largely unaided memory. Moreover, it is in the nature of note-taking to be selective—to note only the important or the

---

[4] In some instances, as in matters of opinion or privilege, the lawyer calling you should be aware of the problem in advance and warn you of the impending battle, precisely to avoid misinterpretation by the witness.

[5] Despite the form of these rote questions, a witness may refresh his or her memory from notes made later or even made by another person, so long as the notes act "as a trigger for [the witness's] memory:" *R.* v. *Bengert (No. 5)* (1978), 15 C.R. (3d) 21 (B.C.S.C.) at 23, affirmed (1980), 15 C.R. (3d) 114 (B.C.C.A.) at 160–63.

unusual. For example, if the professional supervised a parental visit, an uneventful visit may only result in a note, "Parent visited today for two hours," while an eventful visit will cause much more detailed note-taking, exposing the witness to allegations of bias or at least unfair selectivity. I believe it is a wise course for witnesses to attempt to maintain consistent note-taking, with sufficient detail of all encounters, to avoid such allegations.

Once granted permission to use notes, it is vital that the witness not merely read the notes, but truly use them as intended, namely to trigger or refresh memory. The notes should be an aid, not a crutch. Further, care should be taken to recount all the circumstances of a given encounter as revealed in the notes. Opposing counsel is entitled to inspect the notes and any conscious or unconscious editing on the stand will offer a prime target for cross-examination.

Cross-Examination

The cross-examiner generally has three purposes: (a) to obtain statements, especially admissions, of fact useful to his or her case; (b) to test and discredit the story of the witness by exposing inconsistencies, gaps or errors; and (c) to discredit or impeach the basic credibility of the witness. This is not an easy task for the lawyer, despite your recollections of old Perry Mason shows, as most witnesses do their best to tell the truth on direct and all witnesses are on their guard for cross-examination.

Cross-examining lawyers attempt to control the witness, to draw out from the witness only what they want. Some lawyers seek to control the witness through bluster, raised voice and intimidation. Often the most effective lawyers are the quiet, courteous and determined ones, who control your answers through a steady stream of carefully planned questions that do not disclose their purpose.

The cross-examiner's major tool for control is the leading question or statement. Or, more particularly, a series of simple, clear statements to which you tend to reply "yes" or "no." For example, where an agency worker on direct characterizes a mother's behaviour with her child during a supervised visit at the agency as "uncertain," "distant" and "unemotional," the mother's counsel might pursue the following cross-examination:

Q. This was the first visit for the mother since the apprehension, wasn't it?

A. Yes.

Q. In fact, wasn't it the first time she had ever been inside the agency offices?

A. Yes.

Q. You were present in the room throughout the visit?

A. No, I would leave the room for a few minutes at a time.

Q. For the first half-hour, you were in the room the whole time, isn't that correct?

A. Yes.

Q. And naturally you were watching both mother and child carefully, weren't you?

A. Yes.

Q. And Mrs. Smith knew you were watching her carefully, didn't she?

A. I suppose so.

Q. Yourself, you weren't sure what to expect on this visit, right?

A. I had some idea, but no, I wasn't entirely sure.

Q. You wanted to make sure things went smoothly, didn't you?

A. Yes.

Q. So you were very careful in what you said and what you did?

A. Yes.

Q. You remained calm and professional throughout, I assume?

A. Yes, that's correct.

Note the form of the cross-examination questions—short, pointed statements, a little bit at a time, leaving little room for editorial comment. Also noteworthy is the cross-examiner's focus, not upon the mother, but upon the worker's own reactions. If continued in this vein, the cross-examination will succeed in conveying the tense, unfamiliar atmosphere, neutralizing the worker's statements on direct and laying the groundwork for a few comments in closing argument, all without ever once confronting the worker openly on the issues.

Fortunately or unfortunately, depending upon your perspective, skillful cross-examinations are relatively rare, especially in child protection cases. More common are unskilled, repetitive, awkward and ineffectual cross-examinations.

Improper Forms of Cross-Examination

Generally speaking, the lawyer who calls you as a witness is responsible for objecting to improper cross-examination. Accepting that objections must be made strategically to avoid an appearance of obstructionism, many lawyers subscribe to the philosophy that it is best to let the witness fend for himself or herself, to show that they can manage on their own. Because cross-examination focuses, not only on the facts of the case, but also on the credibility of the testimony and the witness, the courts will generally give wide latitude to the cross-examiner in the form and content of cross-examination.

Cross-examination does have its limits, although not always policed with vigour by lawyers and judges, and often not apparent to the witness on the stand. Here I want to focus upon improper forms of questions in cross-examination, for two reasons: first, to prepare you for what will surely come your way in cross-examination; and, second, to assist you as a witness when the lawyers don't offer much help. In this list, I will identify the problems by the traditional phraseology of objections to improper questions.

1. *Too General.* A witness is entitled to proper notice of the intended subject matter of the question. In effect, you are entitled to a sufficiently specific question to know what the examiner is after. For example, if you are asked: "How would you describe your relationship with the child's mother?" it is perfectly proper for you to reply, "In what respect?" or "What particular aspect of the relationship are you asking about?" Where a prior inconsistent statement may be involved, the questioner would have to be more specific than this; For example "Did you ever tell anybody anything different from your testimony today concerning this episode?"

2. *Irrelevant.* While a wider compass is permitted in cross-examination, clearly irrelevant questions are not permitted. In a protection case, if you were asked whether you were a member of the Socialist Social Workers Club, it is unlikely that your political views would possess any relevance to the facts in issue, including your credibility.[6] If there is any question as to the relevance of a cross-examination question, yet no objection is forthcoming from a lawyer, the witness may ask the judge whether the question is relevant and must be answered. The judge may require cross-examining counsel to explain the relevance of the question. But, if the judge rules the question relevant, you must answer the question. Should you continue to refuse to answer after the judge's ruling, you can be found in contempt of court.

3. *Seeking Inadmissible Evidence.* Just as during direct examination, a question asked in cross-examination may seek to elicit evidence that would contradict one of the rules of evidence, such as inadmissible hearsay, opinion or privileged information. Except for privilege, such problems should be left to the lawyers or the judge.

4. *Ambiguous.* The questions in cross-examination should be clear and reasonably specific. If you don't understand the question, you are entitled to say, "I don't understand the question," and then it is up to the lawyer to rephrase the question so that you can understand it. Some questions may appear intelligible, but the ambiguity comes with the answer. Consider this question to an eyewitness: "Are you sure there is no possibility you were mistaken?" A simple "yes" might mean, "yes, I am sure" or "yes, there is a possibility I was mistaken."

5. *Compound Questions.* A compound or multiple question is one which contains more than one question. In cross-examination, such compounding is particularly dangerous because the witness is pressed to ratify, through a single answer, more than one leading statement. For example, the question "Did you then go to the home of the parents and interview both parents and the child?" contains five separate factual inquiries. A

---

6   Just such a question of a witness, whether he was a Marxist-Leninist, was ruled irrelevant in a picket-line assault case in *R. v. Fields* (1986), 53 C.R. (3d) 260 (Ont. C.A.).

"yes" answer ratifies them all, while a "no" answer could deny one or all of them. The witness is entitled to have questions asked one at a time.

6. *Misstates the Evidence.* The cross-examiner may, intentionally or unintentionally, misstate the evidence of another witness or your own evidence. If this occurs with your evidence and the lawyer calling you does not object, you should be quick to correct the misstatement.

7. *False Choice, Misleading.* Some questions are truly trick questions, in that they contain a false choice or a false dichotomy between two non-exhaustive alternatives. Take the classic although now disreputable question, "Have you stopped beating your wife?" or if you prefer, "Have you ceased being an alcoholic?" Whether you answer "yes" or "no," you implicitly ratify the underlying assumption and any reluctance to answer makes you appear less than frank.[7] Few witnesses will have the presence of mind to address and deny the hidden assumption by saying "I have never beaten my wife" or "I have never been an alcoholic."

A less obvious form of false choice arises from a particularly improper form of cross-examination, one roundly condemned by the courts (including the Supreme Court of Canada), but one still ever-present in courtrooms. Where an inconsistency is revealed between an answer of one witness and the evidence of another witness, the lawyer then asks, "Are you suggesting that witness A is lying?" There are many possible explanations for differing accounts, only one of which is that one or the other must be lying—a classic false choice. Not dissimilar is another gambit, where a witness acknowledges an inconsistency between an answer in cross-examination and a previous answer (on direct or in some pre-hearing statement), namely the question: "Well, which one is the truth?" or "So were you telling the truth then or are you telling the truth now?" Again, this presumes that only one of the two statements is the truth and excludes any other possible explanation for the inconsistency.

8. *Argumentative.* These are usually rhetorical questions, not really intended to be answered, and represent little more than an attempt by the lawyer to make part of his or her closing argument during cross-examination. Akin to this form of impropriety is editorializing upon your answers by the cross-examining lawyer, a more subtle but effective means to the same end. Leave these complaints to the lawyers.

9. *Badgering.* The Americans have a nice objection to this, termed "asked and answered." A cross-examiner is allowed to be persistent, to come back at the same point in different ways, in the hope of dislodging the witness from a previous answer. At some stage, persistence passes to redundancy, then on to badgering or full-scale arguing with the witness.

---

[7] *Supra*, note 3 at 478–81, for an excellent analysis of trick questions.

Somewhere between redundancy and badgering, the court usually loses patience and allows a well-timed objection.

10. *Let the Witness Finish the Answer*. Believe it or not, the most common objection in cross-examination is the failure of examining counsel to allow the witness to answer the question. Cross-examination is a battle for control, between lawyer and witness. Many lawyers attempt to exert control by cutting off an answer, after the desired "yes" or "no" answer. Most judges, with or without objection, will allow the witness to finish the answer, as long as the witness has been reasonably pointed and brief in previous answers.

The natural tendency of most witnesses, including experts, is to respond to a leading question in cross-examination with "yes, but ....," then moving on to the qualifications upon the "yes" or "no." Any pause or breath between "yes" and "but" will provide the opening for the skilled cross-examiner to ask the next question, without appearing discourteous or unfair. Witnesses should work at avoiding this natural tendency, and try to let their answers take the form of "Insofar as (qualifying remarks), yes," putting the qualification first and forcing the cross-examiner to wait for the "yes" or "no" at the end.

Cross-Examination on Previous Inconsistent Statements

None of us are ever perfectly consistent over time in our statements about a set of events or conditions. Especially in protection cases, witnesses will often have a long association with a family and the children, through ups and downs, through periods of support and periods of criticism. This creates fertile ground for previous inconsistent statements, the fodder of cross-examiners.

What can a cross-examiner do with a previous inconsistent statement? The lawyer is permitted to question you about the general subject matter of the prior statement, without disclosing to you his or her intention to employ the statement. After extracting inconsistent statements from you on cross-examination, the lawyer may then direct you to your previous written or oral statement.

Once confronted with the inconsistent statement, as a witness, you have three choices. First, you can adopt the prior statement, admitting its correctness and acknowledging the error of your current testimony. Second, you can admit making the prior statement, but seek to explain away the inconsistency, either in cross-examination or later on redirect. For example, it may be that you were in error earlier and, after an opportunity to reflect, you have changed your mind. Third, you can deny having made the earlier statement. If you do, however, the cross-examining lawyer will be allowed to call evidence from some other witness to prove you made the earlier statement. The judge will then be left to decide whether the earlier statement was, in fact, made.

Lawyers use previous inconsistent statements to cast doubt on a witness's credibility. Such statements can be drawn from a variety of sources: other witnesses to whom you may have spoken earlier, letters, notes in your file, other documents authored by you, previous affidavits or testimony in this or another proceeding. For this reason, before testifying, you should review your file carefully, both on your own and with the lawyer calling you as a witness.

Redirect Examination

After cross-examination is over, the lawyer calling you will be permitted an opportunity to conduct a redirect examination. Redirect is limited to new matters arising from the cross-examination, either to clarify or to further develop answers given on cross. Where no damage has been done in cross-examination, lawyers will generally not conduct any redirect.

THE CARDINAL PRINCIPLES OF EVIDENCE LAW

From the witness chair, legal arguments over the admissibility of evidence appear to be arcane disputes, largely engaged in by lawyers to keep damaging or prejudicial evidence out of the record. In fact, the law of evidence starts from a basic premise of admissibility unless some clear rule of evidence requires exclusion of evidence. Further, there is a tendency for the parties, especially in a protection proceeding, to implicitly or explicitly consent to admission of evidence that may be technically inadmissible; in such situations judges rarely object to the admission of evidence that the parties are prepared to have admitted. When evidence objections are raised, however, the arguments will focus upon the so-called exclusionary rules, the variety of exceptions to the rule of admissibility. Here I will outline some of the general precepts of evidence law, before discussing the most important exclusionary rules.

All Relevant Evidence Is Admissible

The first principle of evidence law is that all relevant evidence is admissible. Relevant evidence means "evidence having any tendency to make the existence of any fact that is of consequence to the determination of the [proceeding] more probable or less probable than it would be without the evidence."[8]

There are two components to relevance. First, any evidence offered must bear upon a fact in issue; that is, a fact which is of consequence to the litigation. Whether a fact is in issue is determined by the substantive law in the field and, within that substantive law, by the matters in dispute between the particular parties. For example, if the parent in a protection case concedes that the child is in need of protection, then the facts remaining in issue will relate solely to disposition. The second component is the more familiar meaning of relevance: the probative value of the evidence offered in relation to some fact in issue. That

---

[8]   This definition is drawn from the American Federal Rules of Evidence, Rule 401, reproduced in E.M. Cleary, ed., *McCormick on Evidence*, 3rd ed. (St. Paul: West Publishing Co., 1984) at 542.

relationship has little or nothing to do with law, but is simply a matter of logic, experience and common sense.

Ultimately, the issue of relevance is a matter for the trial judge to determine. Given the multiplicity of issues in protection cases and the vague standards for finding and disposition, the limits of relevance in protection cases tend to be widely drawn and sometimes difficult to discern.

Direct and Circumstantial Evidence

A distinction is sometimes drawn between direct and circumstantial evidence, with some undertone that the latter is less weighty evidence. Direct evidence consists of the testimony of an eyewitness to a specific event, for example, a person sitting in the family home when a parent physically assaults a child. Circumstantial evidence consists of evidence of facts which provide the basis for an inference that the event occurred, for example, evidence of a doctor that a child had suffered repeated serious injuries consistent only with the intentional application of force.

One should not presume that direct evidence of necessity possesses greater value than circumstantial evidence. Staying with the abuse example, compare the cogency of the doctor's circumstantial evidence of abuse with a parent's direct evidence that the child suffered the injury by falling off a tricycle. The former circumstantial evidence will generally be preferred if the child's injuries are inconsistent with the parent's explanation. Circumstantial evidence from a credible witness is often more telling than direct evidence from a witness whose credibility is in issue.

Exclusionary Rules: Hearsay, Opinion, and Privilege

Evidence law starts from the premise that relevant evidence is admissible; that is, it may be placed before the judge for consideration in reaching a decision. Over the years, evidence law has developed a variety of rules which serve to exclude evidence from consideration by the judge. In protection proceedings, those most commonly employed would be the rule excluding hearsay, the rule limiting opinion evidence, the rules of privilege and rules respecting evidence of past parenting. Each of these will be explored in greater detail below. If the judge rules that an item of evidence offends against one of these rules, then the evidence will be excluded; that is, the judge will not hear the evidence and it cannot form the basis of the court's ultimate decision.

Admissibility and Weight

Most evidence arguments relate to admissibility, (i.e., whether the judge can hear and consider the evidence at all). But even if evidence is ruled admissible during the trial, that is not the end of the matter. After all the evidence has been heard, the lawyers will argue in their closing submissions over the weight to be given to individual items of evidence.

When we speak of the weight of the evidence, we are merely talking about the probative value of the evidence. For example, a note made by a nurse on a hospital chart may be ruled admissible as hearsay that comes in under the exception for business records, but the note may be sufficiently ambiguous that, without the more detailed explanation of that same nurse on the witness stand, the court may conclude that the note deserves little or no weight in proving the matter in issue, for example, the matter of the mother's treatment of the child immediately after birth.

The weight accorded to any item of evidence is finally a matter for the trial judge, when he or she makes the necessary factual findings to determine the appropriate disposition or whether the child is in need of protection.

Credibility

A central issue in most cases, especially protection cases, is the credibility of the witnesses. In determining what weight to give to testimony heard during the trial, the judge will have to determine credibility (i.e., who to believe on any given issue). The credibility of a witness is a function of the court's assessment of a witness's testimonial factors (i.e., personal knowledge based on perception, ability to perceive the event testified about, experiential capacity, memory, ability to communicate verbally and sincerity).[9]

The assessment of credibility is one of the most difficult tasks facing a trial judge, who must rely primarily upon what the witness said in testimony as well as how the witness said it. A judge may occasionally find a witness simply not credible at all. More commonly, the judge will be left to sift through the testimony, accepting bits and pieces, preferring the evidence of one witness over that of another on a specific issue or event. In protection cases, precisely because the issues concern human relationships and characteristics, credibility is crucial to the fact-finding process. For this reason, protection appeals are rarely successful; as appeal courts defer to the immense advantage of the trial judge in seeing the witnesses in person and observing their demeanour on the stand.

Application of Evidence Rules in Protection Cases

Despite the fixed sound of the phrase "rules of evidence", evidence law is applied with varying degrees of rigour depending upon the legal setting. Any person who has attended both a criminal trial for sexual abuse of a child and a child protection hearing in Family Court devoted to the same incidents will notice the different approach.

The rules of evidence are applied most stringently in criminal prosecutions, largely out of a concern for fairness focused on the accused. The limits of relevance are more tightly drawn and the exclusionary rules policed with greater care. Rules of evidence are relaxed somewhat in civil proceedings, where the

---

[9]   S.A. Schiff, *Evidence in the Litigation Process*, vol. 1, 3d ed. (Toronto: Carswell, 1988) at 200–02.

interests of the parties are more evenly balanced. Within the civil sphere, family law cases tend to display an even more relaxed attitude towards evidence rules, notably in cases involving children. Where children are involved, the inherent vagueness of the "best interests" test renders the limits of relevance even harder to draw and there are strong tendencies for judges to admit more hearsay and opinion.

Protection proceedings sit uncomfortably within this spectrum in the application of evidence rules. As such cases must fundamentally focus on the welfare of the child, there are strong pressures to relax the rules of evidence, as in private custody cases. But, at the same time, protection proceedings involve a clash between the state and the individual, much like criminal matters, with the state agency bringing the parents and child before the court and seeking court-sanctioned intervention in the family. An order of permanent wardship (i.e., a permanent severing of the parent-child tie) is amongst the most serious steps that a society can take outside the criminal sphere. The seriousness of the issues and the gravity of the consequences drive courts toward a special concern for accuracy in fact-finding and for fairness to the parents and child.

These pressures upon protection courts have led to some inconsistency and uncertainty in evidence rulings, depending upon the individual judge's perception of the appropriate model to apply.[10] At this point, I want to caution the reader: beware, the evidence law described in some parts of this chapter may or may not reflect your own experience in the particular courtrooms in your jurisdiction.

OPINION EVIDENCE

Facts and Opinions

Evidence law distinguishes between facts and opinions. Witnesses testify as to facts based upon their personal knowledge, leaving it up to the judge to draw inferences from those facts. Any inference or conclusion drawn from those observed facts is characterized as opinion. There are two broad exceptions to this rule.

First, in matters calling for special skill or knowledge, a properly qualified expert will be permitted to range beyond first-hand knowledge of facts and offer opinions, providing inferences which the judge is unable to draw on account of the technical nature of the facts. Second, because of the often difficult and artificial distinction between fact and opinion, a lay witness (i.e., one not qualified as an expert) may be permitted to testify in the form of an opinion if the witness is in this way able to express more accurately the facts perceived.

---

[10] I have developed these points in greater detail in a two-part article: "Taking Children *and* Facts Seriously: Evidence Law in Child Protection Proceedings - Part I" (1988), 7 Can. J. Fam. L. 11 and "Part II" (1989), 7 Can. J. Fam. L. 223. Much of the remainder of this chapter draws heavily from this earlier article. Those with a desire to read further on these matters—with the benefit of excessive legal citation—can refer to this two-part article.

Protection cases pose many problems in the application of these opinion rules because of the inherently interpretive nature of most evidence of child-rearing, parent-child interaction, child behaviour and parental conduct. When does an observation of fact become opinion? How much expertise must a witness demonstrate before being allowed to venture more complex opinions? What are the boundaries of the varying forms of expertise of witnesses called in protection cases?

Qualifying as an Expert

Before being allowed to give opinion evidence, an expert must first be qualified by reason of sufficient skill, knowledge and experience in the pertinent field. The witness's qualifications are established in an initial stage of testimony, technically called a "voir dire," to determine the admissibility of the expert opinion evidence.

Like any other part of a direct examination, the lawyer calling the expert should have run through the intended questions on the voir dire with the witness in the preparation interview. At the hearing, the lawyer will pose a straightforward series of questions pertaining to the expert witness's education, training, professional designations, publications, work experience and previous instances of acceptance by other courts as an expert—in effect, your curriculum vitae. It is not only proper, but advisable, that the lawyer lead the witness through this information, in order to avoid the appearance that the expert is blowing his or her own horn. In fact, a simple and effective way of proving qualifications is for the lawyer to introduce the witness's curriculum vitae as an exhibit, followed by questioning to highlight the relevant portions.

After counsel has completed the direct examination regarding qualifications, opposing counsel will have the opportunity to cross-examine on qualifications. In many instances, opposing counsel will concede the expert's qualifications (i.e., the admissibility of the expert opinion). If there is a question as to the witness's qualifications or the scope of the witness's permissible opinions, then counsel will argue the issue and the judge will rule on the issues. A typical ruling might be: "I find Ms. Jones qualified to give opinion evidence as an expert social worker" or, where more specialized issues are involved, the court might add: "… and, more particularly, on the basis of her extensive practical experience and specialized training, to give expert evidence in respect of sexual abuse of children." Once the judge has ruled, the remainder of the witness's direct examination will take place. Even if there has been no challenge to the admissibility of the expert's opinions, opposing counsel will later cross-examine with a view to attacking the weight to be given to the opinions subsequently expressed.

The test for expert qualification is skill or expertise, not how that skill has been acquired, whether by education, training or experience. Hence, a social worker with 15 years of front-line experience in the field of child protection may qualify just as does a younger social worker with less experience but extensive education and training. In my own experience, being practical people, judges are inclined to prefer experience over academic education.

A recent Ontario case, *C.C.A.S. of Hamilton-Wentworth* v. *J.C.S.*,[11] points up some of the difficulties which can be encountered. The agency social worker had completed 1 year of a B.S.W. program, followed by a 2-year diploma in social services from a community college. After 2 years as a family enrichment worker, she had spent 8 months as a children's services worker, with some brief job-oriented training courses during that time, characterized as "superficial" by the trial judge. The case in question was in fact one of her first, starting shortly after her employment with the agency. Agency counsel sought to qualify her as an expert witness to render opinions on the issues of the best interests of the child, the appropriate disposition and the mother's parenting skills.

Judge Steinberg described the skills required to express these opinions as " … assessment skills not unlike those normally attributed to experienced psychologists and psychiatrists and senior experienced social workers."[12] First, the judge noted the worker's training was practical rather than theoretical. Second, the worker did not display the requisite work experience. The worker's experience was "very limited" and some of her experience was acquired from this very case, one of the first assigned to her.

For purposes of expert evidence, the individual worker's inexperience was not saved by the fact that she worked within a team at the agency, nor by the outstanding rating she received from her supervisor. As the court pointed out, the worker's "first-class potential" would have to be realized through future experience before she would be allowed to give expert opinion evidence. Based on this ruling, admittedly more strict than those commonly found in protection decisions, cases handled by inexperienced workers would require the active involvement of more senior agency workers or others who would qualify as expert witnesses.

The second half of the qualification equation is concerned with the nature of the opinions to be expressed. The more complex and specialized the subject matter of the opinions, the more demanding the court will be as to the witness's qualifications.

The Expert's Opinions

Once qualified, an expert is liberated from the strict requirements for most witnesses that their testimony is based upon and devoted solely to first-hand observations of fact. In arriving at an opinion, an expert need not be so confined. The expert witness can draw upon varied sources of information in forming the opinions, such as first-hand observation, interviews, institutional records, other expert reports, texts, scientific literature, personal research and past professional

---

[11] (1986), 9 C.P.C. (2d) 265 (Ont. Unif. Fam. Ct).

[12] *Ibid.* at 270.

experience in the field. In addition to being entitled to draw upon such information, the expert must detail the information upon which his or her opinion is based.

Inevitably, a substantial portion of that information base will consist of hearsay (i.e., out-of-court statements made by others to the expert to prove the matters asserted). Although it may be hearsay, an expert is allowed to state it in court for the purpose of identifying the basis of the opinion. It will be up to the lawyer calling the expert to ensure that those facts that form the basis of the opinion are properly proved through other witnesses and properly admissible evidence in order to underpin and support the expert's opinion.

A few comments about testifying on direct and cross-examination for experts are relevant here. First, experts must employ sophisticated, sometimes arcane, language to express their opinions accurately. Once a technical term is used, it should be explained in non-technical, accessible language. Further, jargon should be avoided where humanly possible. I once had a psychiatrist describe my parent client as "an episodic recreational user of soft drugs," which he then explained, at my insistence, to mean: "That's like being a social drinker." Second, as mentioned earlier, in respect of direct examination, experts should be quite specific about the limits and content of the opinions they are prepared to express on the stand. In my experience, experts have a tendency to express broader opinions in a private interview, when they aren't thinking of testifying (unlike lawyers, who always think in such terms), opinions which go further than they are prepared to defend on the stand. Further, lawyers usually have in mind the opinion they want for purposes of their case and often try to push and pull the opinion into that desired box. The expert must resist and, to avert difficulties on the stand, even negotiate the very phrasing of critical questions.

Expert witnesses should be aware of the cross-examining lawyer's techniques to attack opinions expressed on direct. First, the brave or foolhardy lawyer may attempt to take the expert head-on in his or her field of expertise, employing texts, articles and other opinions to challenge the very formation of the opinion. In this type of cross-examination the expert has the upper hand against all but the most disciplined and knowledgeable lawyers. The expert witness need only become more detailed and specific about his or her knowledge in the field and the cross-examiner will often be forced to back off.

Another approach is to probe the expert's methods and sources. In assessments, for example, the cross-examiner will delve into the length and quality of interviews, the detail of note-taking, the adequacy of information, the range and quality of third-party sources explored, alternative hypotheses considered and rejected, matters included and excluded from the expert's report and direct testimony. In an imperfect world, with limited time and resources, few experts will achieve the perfection sought by the cross-examiner, thus opening up possible lines of methodological attack.

Third, the cross-examiner can accept the factual assumptions of the expert and attempt to offer an alternative interpretation (more favourable to the lawyer's client) than that put forward by the expert. In doing so, the lawyer is given the considerable advantage of choosing the field of the debate and confining the expert to answering in those areas. The expert must review his or her opinions for such weaknesses of interpretation and canvass the possible alternatives, preferably in conjunction with preparation by the lawyer calling the expert.

Fourth, and most common and effective, the cross-examiner will draw out factual errors and omissions on the one hand and supply new or additional facts on the other. By this technique, the lawyer seeks to undermine the opinion at its factual base, a field of endeavour where lawyers feel more comfortable. Typically, a series of such cross-examination questions will conclude with "Had you been aware of fact X, would that have altered your opinion?"

Opinion from Non-Expert Witnesses

As mentioned above, there is a second exception to the opinion rule, that of lay or non-expert opinion. The mere fact that a witness is not qualified as an expert does not bar the witness from occasionally testifying in the form of opinion. In my experience, courts in protection cases are prepared to allow considerable leeway for opinions, given the highly interpretive nature of much factual evidence about child-rearing and human behaviour.

A non-expert witness may express an opinion on matters requiring no special skill, where the facts perceived by the witness and the inferences from them are so closely associated that the opinion amounts to no more than a compendious statement of facts. While this covers a fair bit of ground in protection cases, there remain some important limits upon this lay opinion exception.

First, the witness may only testify to personal observations of the parent and child. Unlike an expert, a lay witness may not draw upon second-hand or hearsay sources in forming or expressing an opinion.

Second, this exception is intended only to allow the witness more accurately to express the facts perceived. It is not a licence to offer free-standing, expert-like opinions. The opinion must be tied specifically to observed events, to the more concrete, detailed and specific end of the opinion spectrum. Thus, the non-expert witness should not phrase an answer in general terms, such as: "Mrs. Smith fails to discipline her child in age-appropriate fashion," but in more concrete, factual terms, such as: "Mrs. Smith would slap her 10-month-old for minor misbehaviour like picking up a dangerous object, rather than simply removing the object from the child and saying 'no' in a firm voice."

Third, precisely because these opinions require nothing more than ordinary experience and no specialized knowledge, no preference should be given to the opinion of a non-expert social worker or official than to that of any other ordinary person, like a neighbour. All adults with a modicum of life experience should be treated similarly in the area of lay opinion, with credibility determined not by expertise but by the usual testimonial qualifications for factual matters.

Some Expert Issues: Syndromes, Sexual Abuse and Polygraphs

Before leaving the opinion rule, a few recurring issues from protection cases should be considered; issues where the law is sometimes unclear and the practice of individual judges varies widely.

First comes a special kind of expert evidence offered in abuse cases, that of battered child syndrome and battering parent syndrome. The former type of evidence is plainly admissible, assuming a properly qualified expert, as the pattern of old injuries to a child is used as circumstantial evidence of intentional rather than accidental injury. Overlapping with this admissible evidence, however, is the second sort of syndrome evidence, where an expert seeks to match this parent's characteristics with a clinical profile of the battering parent. This syndrome evidence is offered either to prove who in the past abused the child or to prove the likelihood of abuse in future.

Some Canadian courts blithely admit this evidence, while others express serious misgivings about its use.[13] At a minimum, such syndrome or profile evidence should only be admissible through a highly-trained specialized professional capable of explaining the limits and value of such evidence.

The second type of expert evidence relates to child sexual abuse dynamics and credibility. Expert evidence of this kind can be classified into a variety of general categories: (a) evidence about the dynamics of child sexual abuse disclosure, including delayed disclosure, accommodation and recantation; (b) evidence of behavioural symptoms that can accompany sexual abuse; (c) evidence of factors that affect the reliability of the child's disclosures; and, (d) evidence of whether this child is telling the truth. Criminal courts have uniformly rejected category (d), doubted the admissibility of category (c), and traditionally been deeply suspicious of categories (a) and (b) although they have recently shown much more flexibility in deciding whether to admit this type of evidence.[14]

Protection courts appear to have admitted all four categories of expert evidence, with only the occasional felt need to justify allowing category (d). In most instances, the expert offering the opinion of the child's truthfulness is the same expert who has interviewed and assessed the child and, pursuant to the emerging child sexual abuse hearsay exception, has relayed the child's statements of abuse to the court. In effect, the court is relying upon the expert's assessment of the child's credibility, as the child may not be taking the stand, and hence an opinion on the child's credibility may be admissible in a civil protection proceeding.

---

[13] Compare *C.A.S. of Halifax* v. *Lake* (1981), 45 N.S.R. (2d) 361 (S.C.A.D.) (birthdate apprehension with predictive evidence of abuse offered by beginning psychiatric resident with no background in field, admitted) with *Re Chrysler* (1978), 5 R.F.L. (2d) 50 (Ont. Prov. Ct - Fam. Div.) (agency nurse-practitioner attempting to offer such evidence, with some criticism from Karswick, P.C.J.).

[14] See *R.* v. *F.E.J.* (1990), 74 C.R. (3d) 269 (Ont. C.A.) (psychologist and social worker permitted to testify that a child's recantation of prior allegations of abuse against her father was consistent with behaviour of other abused children); *R.* v. *Lavallee*, [1990] S.C.J. No. 36 (psychiatrist permitted to testify about battered wife syndrome; woman acquitted of murder charge on basis of self-defence).

In my opinion, experts and counsel calling them should do their best to elicit evidence as to the child's credibility in the more detailed, concrete form of category (c), rather than the bald and more objectionable category (d). So long as the parent denies the sexual abuse and expressly arguing or implying that the child is coached, exaggerating, fabricating or fantasizing, then categories (a), (b) and (c) are plainly admissible in protection proceedings, precisely to counter the impeachment of the child's credibility.

What about polygraph evidence? Typically, defence counsel have attempted to lead polygraph evidence respecting the alleged perpetrator, in order to shore up the parent's denials of sexual abuse, and to counter the child's allegations and the expert evidence offered in support of those allegations. Prior to 1987, judges were divided on the admissibility of polygraph evidence.

The issue has now been clearly resolved. In 1987, the Supreme Court of Canada ruled in a criminal case that " ... the polygraph has no place in the judicial process where it is employed as a tool to determine or to test the credibility of witnesses."[15] That holding has been explicitly and, I believe correctly, extended into protection proceedings to bar such evidence in a sexual abuse case: C.C.A.S. of Metro Toronto v. Janet S. and Angus M.[16] Consistent with this holding, there should be no reference made at all in the courtroom to polygraphs, a parent's agreement or refusal to take such a test, or the results of the test though investigators may continue to use them.

THE HEARSAY RULE AND ITS EXCEPTIONS

What Is Hearsay?

You are a witness on the stand. In a perfectly natural, neutral answer to a question, you say something like: "I arrived at the hospital and nurse X told me that there was a ruckus on the seventh floor where some parents were trying to take their child out of the hospital contrary to doctor's orders." Somewhere after "nurse X told me ...," depending upon reflexes and alertness, the opposing lawyer bounds to his or her feet uttering the dreaded words, "Objection, Your Honour, HEARSAY! " What is going on here, you may ask?

First, your answer may or may not constitute hearsay. To be hearsay, two elements are needed. First, an out-of-court statement. That is satisfied, as you are repeating what nurse X said—nurse X is not here on the stand testifying, you are. Second, the statement must be offered to prove the truth of the matters asserted. What is the matter asserted? Here it is everything after "nurse X told me." But is it being offered to prove that? That is the crux of the hearsay rule. If you are

---

[15] R. v. Beland and Phillips (1987), 60 C.R. (3d) 1 at 42, McIntyre J.

[16] [1988] W.D.F.L. 86 (Ont. Prov. Ct - Fam. Div.).

offering the statement only to explain why you in turn went immediately to the seventh floor, technically it is not hearsay. It would be hearsay if you were offering nurse X's statement to prove that the parents were in fact removing the child contrary to doctor's orders. In practice, most judges would prefer that the witness avoid any hearsay dangers, by simply testifying, "After I spoke to nurse X, I went immediately to the seventh floor," without disclosing the details of the nurse's statement.

A statement only infringes the hearsay rule when it is offered to prove the truth of the matter asserted. There are many occasions when a witness on the stand offers another person's statement for a non-hearsay purpose. The following would be relevant examples from protection cases that would not infringe the hearsay rule:

1. *"I asked Mrs. Smith to visit on Wednesday and she agreed to come that day."* Mrs. Smith's words are offered to prove her agreement, irrespective of truthfulness, and hence are admissible.

2. *"On Tuesday, Mrs. Smith telephoned and said she wouldn't be able to visit on Wednesday because of a doctor's appointment."* Again, no problem, as the statement is offered to prove it was made, not for its contents.

3. *"I received a call from Mrs. Smith's mother. She told me that her grandson had been beaten and I therefore attended at Mrs. Smith's home and apprehended the boy."* The grandmother's statement would be admissible to demonstrate the worker's reasonable and probable grounds for apprehension, but not to prove that the child had in fact been beaten.

4. *"Mrs. Smith called late Friday and said, 'Come quick. I need help. Billy's been hurt'."* The telephone statement is admissible, as the words are offered to prove the request and the awareness of harm to the child, rather than the assertion of any particular fact.

5. *"Mrs. Smith called late Friday and said, 'Come quick. I need help. My husband has beaten Billy up'."* This would be hearsay if it was offered to prove that Mr. Smith in fact had abused Billy and, in most instances, like the earlier hospital example, most courts would not allow it to be introduced, in the absence of some hearsay exception.

Critical to the determination of whether an out-of-court statement is hearsay is the purpose for which it is offered. If the statement is explicitly offered to prove the truth of the matter asserted, then it will be characterized as hearsay and therefore inadmissible unless it falls within an exception to the rule. Moreover, where a statement may be used for a hearsay or a non-hearsay purpose, courts will usually assess the importance of the non-hearsay purpose in determining its admissibility. In most instances, the court will admit the statement while noting its limited non-hearsay use, although occasionally the cautious judge will prefer to avoid hearing unnecessary hearsay on crucial matters in issue, as in example (5) above or the earlier hospital example.

Exceptions to the Hearsay Rule

Like all legal rules, the hearsay rule has its exceptions. In fact, some commentators suggest that the exceptions are sufficiently wide and numerous that they swamp the basic rule that hearsay is generally inadmissible. This can be confusing for witnesses—and even some lawyers and judges. The mere characterization of an out-of-court statement as hearsay is not the end of the matter. Once defined as hearsay, a statement may then find a home within one of the exceptions and, if so, is admissible in court to prove the truth of the matter asserted in the statement.

It is only possible to understand hearsay exceptions by understanding the rationale motivating exclusion of hearsay in the first place. What is so objectionable about hearsay evidence that we exclude it from courtrooms?

Here we go back to basics. Evidence at trial is presented by the oral testimony of witnesses, witnesses who testify under oath, who can be observed on the stand and who are subject to cross-examination by opposing counsel. By these methods, especially cross-examination, the parties and the court can assess the reliability of the testimony. Not so with a statement by an out-of-court declarant (i.e., the person making the statement)—that statement is made outside the courtroom, not under oath, with no direct opportunity to observe the witness's demeanour and with no opportunity to cross-examine when the statement was made. All of these safeguards are lost if a witness on the stand can repeat what someone else said, to prove the truth of the events asserted in that hearsay statement. Thus the hearsay rule is intended to further two important and related values in our judicial process: fairness, as parties should be afforded an opportunity to test evidence offered against them; and reliability, as courts should be able adequately to assess the probative value of the evidence which will be relied upon in reaching a decision.

Not surprisingly, then, exceptions to the hearsay rule are built around three requirements: necessity, reliability and fairness. Necessity means that, were it not for the exception, the evidence might be unavailable to the court. Faced with the choice between no evidence and less reliable hearsay evidence, the court will often admit the hearsay. A classic example would be statements of a person now deceased or otherwise unavailable to testify. Reliability means that there is some alternative assurance, other than cross-examination in the courtroom, that the out-of-court statement will be reasonably reliable. A prime example would be the exception for regularly kept business records, where the methods of record-keeping and business reliance on records offer a substitute test of trustworthiness. Finally, fairness incorporates both adequate notice to the opposing party of the hearsay statements to be used and some alternative method of testing hearsay reliability in the courtroom.

Hearsay exceptions have developed around these three characteristics in an interesting fashion. Over time, the law has developed classes or categories of hearsay statements which meet these requirements. Examples include business records, prior testimony and spontaneous statements. If a statement can be characterized as falling within a specified category of necessary, generally reliable statements, then it will be admitted into evidence. Apart from some statutory provision, our courts are not permitted to weigh the issues of necessity, reliability and fairness on a statement-by-statement basis, admitting this one and excluding that one, based upon individualized determinations of the hearsay dangers of misperception, faulty memory, inaccurate language or insincerity on the part of the out-of-court declarant. Courts must fit any particular statement into one or another of the judicially-recognized hearsay exceptions for a class of statements.

When hearsay objections are made in the courtroom, counsel will argue over whether a given statement does or does not fit into one of the exceptions, giving a certain air of abstraction to the debate. In truth, lawyers recognize and judges appreciate that the values of necessity, reliability and fairness underpin the discussion. In fact, some judges—in brief moments of candour—will admit that they can always find some fair way of admitting into evidence hearsay which is necessary and reliable, through use of the list of hearsay class exceptions.

In Canada, judges have a further technique for admitting hearsay, as the Supreme Court of Canada has ruled that judges are free to create and develop new hearsay class exceptions where warranted.[17] The most prominent example in recent years would be the evolving new hearsay exception in civil matters for a child's statements respecting sexual abuse, which I will address below.

Here I will only discuss the most important of the hearsay exceptions, those most frequently arising in child protection cases. Having laid out these exceptions, at the close of this section, I will briefly consider the present and future of the hearsay rule in protection cases.

Admissions by a Party

The single most important hearsay exception in protection cases is that of admissions by parents or other parties. To constitute hearsay admissible as an admission, the statement must be that of a party, typically a parent or guardian, and it must be offered by an opposing party *against* the party who made the statement.

Evidence scholars have long argued about the rationale for the admissions exception, as neither necessity (the party is usually available to testify) nor reliability (we don't care whether the party's statement is reliable) appear to ground this exception. Briefly stated, some notion of a party's responsibility for his or her statements within an adversary system of litigation seems to lie at the heart of this exception (i.e., "Anything you say may be used against you.").

Invariably, the parents in a protection case will have spoken to and consulted with a variety of professionals and other officials, both before and during the protection proceedings, such as agency social workers, social assistance workers, community health nurses, drug counsellors, police officers, doctors, hospital staff

---

[17] *Ares v. Venner*, [1970] S.C.R. 608, 14 D.L.R. (3d) 4.

and psychiatrists. Anything said by a parent to a witness called by agency counsel may be treated as an admission. An admission need not be an outright admission or confession of neglect or abuse, despite the term. It is enough that counsel for the agency—the opposing party—offers the statement in its case in chief, for whatever purpose.

Suppose you are a hospital social worker, called by the agency to give evidence in a protection case. The statements made by a parent during interviews constitute hearsay (i.e., out-of-court statements offered to prove the truth of the matters asserted) but may be treated as admissions. For example, if a parent states that he or she was abused as a child, that statement can come in under this exception to prove that the parent was in fact abused as a child. Of course, the parent is free to take the stand later to deny, clarify or explain that statement, thus leaving it for the court to resolve any questions of credibility or interpretation.

Given the private, often unwitnessed nature of much abuse and neglect, parental admissions will often make up much of the agency's case—to establish facts admitted, to lay the factual basis for expert opinion evidence and to afford the grounds for cross-examination of the parent's current testimony.

Parental admissions are treated differently in criminal prosecutions, where much more stringent conditions are applied to statements made to "persons in authority", such as police officers. Before an accused parent's confession to such a person can be admitted in a criminal court, the Crown must first prove beyond a reasonable doubt the statement is voluntary (i.e., that it was not obtained by inducements and was made with a full awareness of the consequences) and the court must be satisfied that the accused's *Charter* rights were not breached. Where criminal prosecution is likely, the interviewing of the alleged perpetrator is best left to the police, who can ensure that these criminal rules are satisfied.[18]

Business Records

Most provincial evidence statutes explicitly provide for the admissibility of business records or, more accurately, regularly kept records. What constitutes a business record? First, the record must be of an act, transaction, occurrence or event. Second, the record must have been made at the time of or shortly after the event recorded. Third, the record must have been made in the usual and ordinary course of business. Provided that the records meet these requirements, they can be introduced by anyone who made the record or even through a witness, such as a medical records librarian, who has official custody of the records.

This exception exists because many individuals within an institution, such as a hospital, record information over a period of time. The sheer cost and inconvenience of locating and calling all of them as witnesses generates the necessity to

---

[18] To some extent it will depend on the circumstances of a particular case to determine whether or not a child protection worker will be regarded as a "person in authority", and hence, in the context of a criminal prosecution, be required to satisfy the special rules to be able to testify about statements a parent made. However, if a criminal prosecution seems likely, it is usually best to leave the initial interview with a suspect to the police.

rely upon written records. As for reliability, institutions themselves rely upon these records for day-to-day operations and decision-making, providing some assurance that minimum standards of reliability in record-keeping are maintained.

The term "business records" may be misleading, as "business" is broadly defined to include "every kind of business, profession, occupation, calling, operation or activity, whether carried on for profit or otherwise," according to the statutes. Included in this broad range are hospitals, health clinics, doctors, drug rehabilitation centres, social assistance authorities, public housing authorities, psychologists and therapists. In some provinces, the records of child protection agencies have been held to fall within this exception.[19] The regularity with which the activities of the institution or individual are recorded provides the basis for the exception.

There are two important limits to the use of such records. First, records may not be used to prove opinions of the kind typically given by experts. For example, a hospital discharge summary, containing a doctor's diagnosis and opinion, may not be entered into evidence through this exception; the agency would have to call the doctor and subject his or her expert opinions to the rigours of cross-examination. Second, the statements entered in the records must be made by individuals operating under a "business duty". Records will often contain statements made by others and noted in the records by an agency worker or a hospital staff member. Not all such third-party statements will be admissible. Only those statements made by other persons who are themselves acting under a business duty to be careful about what they say are admissible, such as a statement made by one nurse to another nurse and recorded by the latter in the hospital records. By contrast, a statement made by a person outside of the institution's operations and thus not under any business duty, such as a statement to the nurse by a parent's relative, would not be admissible under this exception.

Judges tend to treat business records as inherently reliable, perhaps reflecting the court's preference for documentary evidence, especially if such documents were created before any court proceeding was anticipated. If a witness is subpoenaed to court with records, the records are usually entered as an exhibit, even though the witness subsequently uses the records to refresh his or her memory. In this case, the records themselves become evidence, along with the oral testimony of the witness. With increased record-keeping by institutions, professionals and officials, protection proceedings have become increasingly dominated by mounds of paper and bulging files.

---

[19] See, e.g., *Re Maloney* (1971), 12 R.F.L. 167 (N.S. Co. Ct). For a decision refusing to admit agency files as business records, see *L.T.H.* v. *C.A.S. Halifax* (1988), 16 R.F.L. (3d) 97 (N.S. Co. Ct.), rev'd on another point, 19 R.F.L. (3d) 171 (N.S.S.C.A.D).

Prior Testimony

Protection cases often involve families that have previously appeared in court for matters involving either this child or another child in the parent's care. Most provincial protection laws explicitly provide for admissibility of transcripts of testimony from prior protection proceedings, whether they involved this child or a child previously in a parent's care. Some statutes, like those of Ontario and Alberta, extend this exception even further to admit evidence from other trials, be they criminal or civil.

Consider the following example. Less than a year ago, a parent's first child was found in need of protection and was made a permanent ward based upon, say, a finding that the mother suffered from serious psychiatric disorders that interfered with her ability to parent. Now that parent has another child, who was apprehended shortly after birth for essentially the same reasons. The court hearing the second child's case may admit transcripts of the previous year's proceeding, in part or even in whole.

Again, necessity and reliability will be considered before the court decides whether to admit what is technically hearsay from the prior trial (i.e., statements not made in this court in this proceeding, but offered to prove the truth of the matters asserted in previous testimonies). Obvious necessity will be demonstrated if a witness who testified in the previous proceeding is currently unavailable. For the sake of convenience, the court may admit the previous testimony if recalling the witness is likely to serve little purpose. A classic example of reliable hearsay included in this exception is evidence previously given under oath and subjected to cross-examination by parent's counsel, who is often the same lawyer as in the current proceeding.

Statements by Children

In many instances, out-of-court statements by children will be admissible under one of two hearsay exceptions, thus allowing the court to hear the statements without the need to call the children as witnesses.

First, a child's spontaneous statement about abuse or neglect, made within some reasonable time after the events stated, will be admitted under the exception for spontaneous statements, sometimes called "part of the *res gestae*," a Latin phrase literally meaning "the thing being done." Necessity arises from the statement being made at or near the event and its reliability is found in its spontaneity, without an opportunity to fabricate or reflect upon the words spoken.

In a recent Ontario Court of Appeal decision, the Court was prepared to stretch the limits of this exception in a criminal sexual assault prosecution to admit into evidence a then 3½-year-old girl's description of sexual abuse by a family doctor, made half an hour after the events to her mother in the car at a shopping centre.[20] The court explicitly stated that delay in making a statement was less critical in the case of a young child, who would be unlikely to fabricate an incident of sexual abuse. Some courts have extended this exception to delays of a few hours, especially where the child makes the statement to the first available safe adult, such as a visiting social worker or a foster parent after a parental visit.[21]

A second hearsay exception used for children is that of statements concerning their current physical, mental or emotional state. As we have no other way of knowing a person's feelings (necessity) and most such statements are spontaneous or made for treatment purposes (reliability), they become admissible under this exception, as long as the statements describe a *current* condition. A child may say, "My bum hurts" or "I'm upset" or "I'm afraid of Daddy," and all of these out-of-court statements are admissible to prove the matters asserted. Considerable debate exists as to whether the *cause* of the condition is admissible under this exception (e.g., "I'm afraid of Daddy because he hit me hard last night"); however, most cases suggest it is not. A last point is worth noting: under this exception, a child's wishes may be placed in evidence, as the child's wishes or preferences reflect his or her mental or emotional state.

Children's Statements About Sexual Abuse

Increased awareness and reporting of sexual abuse and the difficulties of proof have driven Canadian courts dealing with civil cases to take a new approach to the out-of-court statements by a child victim of sexual abuse. Starting with the *D.R.H.* case, a child protection case in British Columbia in 1984,[22] and then in a number of other provinces,[23] many judges have recognized a new exception to the hearsay rule: under certain conditions, a witness can relate what a child said out of court about a situation of alleged sexual abuse, even if the child does not testify. Six years after the *D.R.H.* case, we can say that in a civil case a child's statements of sexual abuse will often be admitted in evidence through an adult witness, to prove the truth of the matters asserted (i.e., that sexual abuse did, in fact, occur). However, the exact nature of this newly evolving exception to the hearsay rule remains unclear, and some judges are still reluctant to admit this type of evidence. Further, it must be appreciated that, while this type of evidence is admissible, it is not necessarily conclusive proof of the fact that abuse occurred.

---

[20] *R.* v. *Khan* (1988), 27 O.A.C. 142, 42 C.C.C. (3d) 197 (Ont. C.A.).

[21] *R.* v. *Malette* (1988), 6 W.C.B. (2d) 341 (Ont. Dist. Ct) (7 hours elapsed before the 3-year-old child made her statement to her mother).

[22] *D.R.H.* v. *Superintendent of Family and Child Services* (1984), 41 R.F.L. (2d) 337 (B.C.C.A.). See also *J.D.K.* v. *S.A.K.* (1989), 20 R.F.L. (3d) 372 (B.C.S.C.).

[23] Alberta, Saskatchewan, Manitoba, Ontario, New Brunswick, Prince Edward Island, and Nova Scotia.

Again, necessity and reliability drive the new exception. The necessity is of two kinds: the difficulty of obtaining any other evidence of sexual abuse and the inability of the child to testify or the inadvisability of calling the child as a witness. Reliability stems from the court's prior assessment of the timing, content and circumstances of the statement, and the skills of the adult witness reporting the statements, as the reporting adult will serve as a substitute for the child and will, at least implicitly, be indicating a belief in the reliability of the child's statement.

The basis for this type of approach was emphasized in a Prince Edward Island child protection case involving allegations of sexual abuse of three siblings, aged 11, 9 and 5 years. The agency based its case largely on testimony by child care workers about statements made to them by the children. The Prince Edward Island Court of Appeal ruled the evidence inadmissible and ordered a new trial, but stated:

> If the child can not or for some valid reason does not testify about the facts asserted in the out-of-court statement and hearsay is excluded the court will be deprived of hearing what could be the most relevant of evidence. Faced with that situation, the court may admit the third party's evidence as proof of the facts contained in the child's statement, even though that evidence be hearsay, provided that, as groundwork for its admission, sufficient evidence is first led to establish the reliability of the out-of-court statement, and of the circumstances which establish the need to introduce the content of the child's statement through hearsay. In such cases, the court must always proceed with great caution both with regard to satisfying itself on the question of the reliability of the child's statements, as well as with respect to those circumstances which justify the need for the admissibility of the out-of-court statements.

> The problem with the hearsay evidence in the case at bar is that the trial judge received it without first hearing any evidence to justify receiving it on the basis of its necessity or reliability.[24]

Children's accounts have been accepted through doctors, psychologists, social workers, day care workers, school teachers, teacher's aides, police officers, foster parents, and even parents. Elsewhere I have suggested that the courts should employ a rule of preference as to the status of the in-court witness reporting the statements, starting with sexual abuse experts, followed by other experts with some training in the field, then to professionals generally, followed by independent third parties and lastly to persons employed by or related to either party.[25]

As we move up this ladder, we find witnesses with increasing skill and knowledge in the field, as well as an appreciation of the need for careful investigation and proper recording. There should be a reluctance to allow parents involved in a custody dispute to testify about hearsay statements of their children about such allegations; their lack of training and potential for bias raise concerns

---

[24] *W.M.* v. *Director of Child Welfare of Prince Edward Island* (1986), 3 R.F.L. (3d) 181 at 185 (P.E.I. C.A.).

[25] *Supra*, note 9, Part I at 67–70.

about the reliability of this type of evidence, and it can usually be introduced by a more neutral, better-trained investigator.

Judges in criminal cases take a much stricter approach to evidentiary issues, and have continued to refuse to allow a child's out-of-court statements about allegations of abuse to be admitted in evidence. However some flexibility has been shown, even in criminal prosecutions, especially if a statement is made soon after the alleged incident or is offered in addition to the child's testimony in order to refute suggestions of fabrication.[26] Recent amendments to the *Criminal Code* permit a videotape of the child being interviewed about allegations of sexual abuse to be admitted into evidence in a criminal trial, provided that the child testifies.[27]

In civil cases, especially child protection cases, the courts have been prepared to admit videotape, or audiotapes of a child's allegations of abuse, in those circumstances where the child's out-of-court statements are admissible under the new hearsay exception. Indeed, a video or audiotape may provide a more complete record than the oral testimony of the person who originally heard the statement.

General Purpose Statutory Hearsay Exceptions

The child protection statutes of Alberta and Ontario include what I call "general purpose hearsay exceptions,"[28] that is, broad discretion on the part of judges to admit hearsay evidence where necessary and reliable. Unlike the categories of exceptions discussed above, these statutory provisions appear to allow the court to admit hearsay on an item-by-item basis, subject to some prior demonstration of reliability and subject to appropriate conditions, such as notice, to maintain the basic fairness of the trial.

Judicial Attitudes Towards Hearsay in Protection Cases

In my view, the Alberta and Ontario protection statutes merely recognize explicitly what most protection courts do in practice. In protection cases, there are strong tendencies to relax and even ignore the hearsay rule, a tendency generally approved by higher courts.

Some judges characterize protection proceedings not as adversarial, but as more in the nature of an inquiry, where the court is less concerned about fairness to the adult parties and more concerned about hearing all relevant evidence, including hearsay, that might affect the child's future. At the other extreme are judges who firmly believe that the traditional adversarial process offers the best

---

[26] See, e.g., *R. v. Owens* (1986), 33 C.C.C. (3d) 275 (Ont. C.A.); and *R. v. Khan* (1988), 42 C.C.C. (3d) 197 (Ont. C.A.).

[27] R.S.C. 1985, c. C–46, s. 715.1.

[28] *Child Welfare Act*, S.A. 1984, c. C–8.1, s. 74(4); Ontario's *Child and Family Services Act*, S.O. 1984, c. 55, s. 46(2).

guarantees of a fully developed and reliable body of evidence upon which to base the court's decision. In between lie the majority of judges, who feel that hearsay rules can be relaxed while maintaining basic fairness towards the parties in protection cases. The trial judge has so much discretion to admit or exclude evidence that witnesses will find considerable variation amongst individual judges, even in adjacent courtrooms, in their approaches towards the hearsay rule.

EVIDENCE OF PAST PARENTING

Past parental behaviour towards *this* child, now the subject of a protection proceeding, is always admissible, even though it is often loosely and incorrectly described as "evidence of past parenting." Moreover, evidence of past parental conduct towards other children in their care is usually relevant to the full family history considered in determining the appropriate disposition order.

Here I use "evidence of past parenting" in a technical and limited sense, namely, evidence of past child-rearing practices or conduct on the part of the same parent in respect of a child in his or her care other than the child who is now the subject matter of the protection proceeding, where such evidence is offered to prove that *this* child is in need of protection.

C.A.S. of Winnipeg v. *Forth*[29] is a typical example. The parents' third child was apprehended at 5 months of age, after a series of unexplained minor injuries. The agency led evidence that the two older boys had been apprehended and made permanent wards 3 years earlier, after each boy had suffered serious injuries; one boy suffered remarkably similar injuries to the minor ones suffered by the third child. In effect, past parenting evidence was offered to prove not only intentional rather than accidental abuse, but also to demonstrate the probability of future abuse of the third child. The same principle holds in neglect cases, where the neglect stems from some underlying form of continuing parental incapacity, such as a mental disorder or handicap.

For past parenting evidence to be admissible on the issue of finding the child in need of protection, the courts should and sometimes do consider a number of factors, such as similarity of grounds for the finding, the amenability of causal factors to short-term change, the time that has elapsed and a change of parental partners. The greatest difficulties for use of past parenting evidence arise in cases of apprehension of a child at birth, where the past parenting evidence constitutes the whole basis of the agency case and thus may attract very careful scrutiny by the court.

---

[29] (1978), 1 R.F.L. (2d) 46 (Man. Prov. Ct - Fam. Div.).

PRIVILEGE

What is Privilege?

The rules of privilege provide a special basis for exclusion of evidence from the courtroom. Unlike the hearsay or opinion rules, which are primarily concerned with the reliability of evidence, privilege rules serve to exclude highly reliable evidence on the basis that other social values, outside the judicial process, are more important than truth-finding inside a courtroom.

Consider the following example. Outside the courtroom you see two lawyers, the agency counsel and the parents' lawyer, engaged in deep and obviously animated conversation. Snatches of comments waft across the hall, but you don't catch much of it. Probably the parents' counsel says, "Look, we're prepared to admit to the finding, if you're ready to agree to a supervision order with some stringent conditions," and the agency lawyer replies, "Our case for permanent wardship isn't the strongest, but we have concerns that I don't think we can satisfy by supervision." No resolution is reached and both lawyers go back into the courtroom. Despite potentially telling admissions from both sides, neither lawyer is free to adduce evidence of that hallway discussion, as their respective statements are privileged, being "without prejudice" negotiations with a view to settlement.

In my view, a sharp distinction can be made between two distinct kinds of privilege. First, there are a series of privileges that are carefully policed by the courts, most of which serve other important purposes within the legal process. This group would include: the privilege against self-incrimination of an accused person (i.e., the right to remain silent); the privilege of a witness not to have incriminating evidence used against him or her in later proceedings; solicitor-client privilege; the privilege for legal negotiations or efforts to settle; and, the privilege for informers.

The second category consists of a variety of privileges that are more frequently qualified or overridden in the interests of truth-finding, privileges that typically protect some social value or relationship extrinsic to legal processes: a variety of confidential and professional relationships; husband-wife privilege; and so-called Crown privilege or public interest immunity for such things as state secrets and Cabinet discussions.

In this short section, I will only discuss privileges of importance for witnesses on the stand in protection cases: claims of professional privilege for confidential communications, solicitor-client privilege and the privilege for informers.

Professional Privilege for Confidential Communications

Generally speaking, apart from confidential communications with one's lawyer, there is no absolute privilege for confidential communication between professionals and their clients or patients. Particularly in child protection and criminal cases, claims to professional privilege have been almost uniformly rejected in the case of doctor-patient, therapist-client and priest-penitent. Like it or not, when subpoenaed to court and asked questions pertaining to intimate, confidential information divulged by a person, the professional in a protection case must answer the questions and disclose the information.

Many professionals, especially those dealing with families and children, are surprised to learn that they must respond to such questions. Mere confidentiality between professional and client is not sufficient to ground a privilege (i.e., a right to refuse to answer such questions). Confidentiality may be essential to the relationship and may be assiduously observed by the professional in dealings with other third parties; however, once that professional takes the stand, it will be a rare case where a court will find that privilege at law exists.

Canadian courts have the authority to recognize and give effect to new categories of privilege for confidential communications, but four stringent criteria must be met: [30]

1. the communications must originate in confidence;
2. confidentiality must be essential to maintaining the relationship;
3. the relationship must be one which society feels should be sedulously fostered; and,
4. the injury caused to the relationship by disclosure must be greater than the benefit obtained by the proper disposal of litigation.

While many professional claims can meet the first three criteria, in the context of a child protection case, few claims are capable of passing the fourth, where benefit to truth-finding is balanced against injury to the professional relationship.

Consider a recent example, a criminal case involving charges of indecent assault, gross indecency and intercourse with a girl under 14. The accused claimed medical or therapist privilege for communications with a family clinic psychiatrist in the course of family therapy. The claim foundered on the fourth criterion, as the Ontario Court of Appeal held " ... the search for truth in the criminal process outweighs the need for family counselling, at least in cases of suspected child abuse."[31] The court ruled that detection and prevention of child abuse is more important than preserving the confidentiality of psychiatric counselling or encouraging patients to seek out psychiatric therapy.

It is difficult to imagine any instance where a protection court would hold that the fourth criterion could be met in the face of this overriding concern for the detection and prevention of child abuse and neglect. That said, it should be appreciated that denial of a legal privilege does not mean the professional will necessarily be forced to answer each and every question asked. The trial judge retains a residual discretion, as part of the more general judicial discretion to control the examination of witnesses and to determine sanctions for contempt.

---

[30] *Slavutych v. Baker*, [1976] 1 S.C.R. 254, 55 D.L.R. (3d) 224.

[31] *R. v. R.J.S.* (1985), 45 C.R. (3d) 161 at 162 (Ont. C.A.).

When a professional refuses to answer a particular question in the interests of preserving some important confidence, the trial judge will instruct the witness on the law of privilege and the realities of contempt of court. If the witness continues to refuse, a sympathetic judge may press examining counsel as to whether this particular answer is really crucial to the proceeding and many counsel will give in to this moral suasion. If counsel demands the answer, then the judge has no discretion to excuse the witness from answering. If the witness still refuses to answer, however, the court does have a discretion as to the appropriate sanction or penalty for the contempt, including no penalty. In my own experience, long before this point is reached, under the watchful eye of the judge, either witness or counsel will concede in this gambit of "privilege chicken." For professionals intent on preserving confidentiality, some careful thought about this inevitable scenario should precede any refusal to answer.

Solicitor-Client Privilege, Including Expert Reports

When we think of solicitor-client privilege, most think of *sotto voce* communications between a lawyer and client in the confines of the lawyer's office, an interview room or even a court hallway. For an agency social worker, it is important to remember that their communications with agency counsel may also be protected by this traditional notion of solicitor-client privilege.

Another branch of solicitor-client privilege is also important in protection cases. The lawyer's brief or work product (i.e., the notes and material in the lawyer's file) are also protected by the privilege, as it is critical that counsel be able to prepare the case without fear of interference. Included within this aspect of the privilege are communications and reports between expert and counsel with a view to litigation.

When counsel intends to call an expert, most rules of court require filing of an expert's report some time before trial. Until that point is reached, however, the expert's report will generally be privileged from production, so long as the primary purpose for which the report was prepared was to submit it to a legal adviser for advice and use in litigation. In practical terms, if the report is prepared on the specific request of counsel, after litigation has commenced, and is submitted directly to counsel, this dominant purpose test will generally be satisfied.

If there is more than one purpose that can be ascribed to the expert's report, for example, in a pre-existing or ongoing therapeutic or counselling relationship, courts may be quick to find that the dominant purpose test is not met and compel disclosure of the report to opposing parties, irrespective of its litigation purpose. For those slated to testify as expert witnesses, care should be taken in obtaining instructions and submission of reports, with proper advance advice and direction from counsel, to ensure a clear understanding of the procedures desired by the lawyer.

Privilege for Informers

There is clear common law authority that a state agency or its witness may not be compelled to disclose the identity of a person who provides information giving rise to an investigation.[32] This privilege is rationalized by the public interest in effective implementation of child protection laws and in the free flow of information to those officials charged with preventing and detecting child abuse and neglect.

There may be one small exception to this privilege where the identity of the informer is material to the parent's defence. In that rare case, almost invariably the agency will call the informer as a witness, thus avoiding the privilege issue.

COPING WITH EVIDENCE LAW: A LAWYER'S PLEA TO WITNESSES

For those not confused by a law degree, the foregoing rules of evidence will appear to be a series of unduly technical obstructions to any intelligent process of truth-finding. In part, this reflects the undue emphasis of traditional evidence law upon rules of exclusion; that is, when evidence should *not* be heard by the judge. In large measure, however, this appearance of obstructionism flows from the conflicting purposes within the legal process that our evidence law is intended to serve: reliability, fairness to the parties, trial efficiency and social values extrinsic to the trial process.

Rules of evidence and procedure together constitute a variety of laws often characterized as adjective law as opposed to substantive law. Substantive law consists of the legal rules and standards applicable to the resolution of the courtroom dispute. In the field of child protection, statutes and relevant judicial interpretations set out the criteria to be used in determining whether a child is in need of protection and what form of disposition is appropriate. Other chapters in this volume are devoted to the legal intricacies and underlying policies of this substantive law. The process of reaching those decisions is regulated by adjective law, rules of procedure and evidence applicable to protection proceedings. As a subsidiary form of law, adjective law must serve the larger substantive ends of protection law, namely, protecting children from harm, while also attempting to protect the family from unwarranted state intrusion.

Not only must evidence law in this field serve the intermediate ends of reliability, efficiency, fairness and extrinsic social values, but it must be adjusted to serve the larger goals of child protection law. Not surprisingly, then, evidence law as applied in protection cases varies from that found in criminal prosecutions for abuse or neglect or from that governing private custody disputes, as I explained earlier.

---

[32] *D. v. National Society for the Prevention of Cruelty to Children*, [1977] 1 All E.R. 589 (H.L.), approved by the Supreme Court of Canada in *Solicitor Gen. (Can.)* v. *Royal Commission of Inquiry into Confidentiality of Health Records in Ont.* (1981), 128 D.L.R. (3d) 193 at 221–24 & 226 and followed in *Re Infant* (1981), 32 B.C.L.R. 20 at 22 (S.C.).

Of necessity, evidence law in protection cases reflects the unique nature of these proceedings and the complex interests at stake, groping towards some middle ground between the stringent criminal approach and the very relaxed approach of private custody disputes. Also, because of the very broad language employed in the substantive law of child protection, judges trying such cases often find themselves navigating that middle ground without much clear guidance from the legislatures or the higher courts. Different judges will arrive at different accommodations of the competing purposes at play, leading to uncertain and inconsistent evidence rulings. In turn, this generates problems of predictability for lawyers preparing for trial and for witnesses prepared by those lawyers and testifying before those judges.

In effect, this amounts to a closing plea from a lawyer for tolerance and understanding from those who must, as witnesses, ultimately take the brunt of these legal difficulties. In this chapter, I have attempted to outline some of the basics of evidence law, recognizing that anyone who has been a witness will know that these rules are applied unevenly in real cases in real courtrooms. Some understanding of the rules should prove helpful, if only to know how far practice in this courtroom in front of this judge varies from the law as it is written.

For a witness, the best means of protection from the vagaries of evidence law and judicial interpretations thereof is proper and careful preparation in advance by the lawyer calling you. The first half of this chapter was therefore devoted to the rights of witnesses and the obligations of lawyers in that preparation process: dealing with lawyers, subpoenas, exclusion orders, the mechanics of preparation by lawyers, pointers for witnesses in testifying, the structure of witness examination and coping with cross-examination tactics.

Armed with this practical information and some basic appreciation of evidence law, a witness should be able to survive the experience of testifying in a child protection case, with a minimum of Kafkaesque trauma and some modicum of apparent (albeit misleading) assurance. It should then be possible for you as the witness to focus upon what you say in the courtroom, rather than whether you can say it (the rules of evidence) or how you say it (preparing for court).

14

CHILD PROTECTION PROCEEDINGS: SOME CONCLUDING THOUGHTS FROM THE BENCH

Judges play a key role in the child protection process. The expectation is that they will impartially decide the cases brought before them on the basis of the evidence presented and the governing legal principles. It is, however, clear that their beliefs, values, experiences and personalities affect how they perceive those who appear before them.

The attitude of the judge towards the child protection process will inevitably influence how procedural and substantive issues are resolved, as well as affecting the atmosphere in the courtroom. It is thus fitting to conclude this book with a collection of judicial perspectives on the child protection process.

It will be apparent from these contributions that there are significant differences between judges. In this regard, they are no different from the other professionals involved in the child protection process. Social workers, nurses, doctors, lawyers and ordinary citizens each have a unique attitude to the process.

While some may be concerned about the variation in judicial attitudes and the effect this may have on the outcome of cases, to others it simply reflects the fact that judging is a human activity. In any event, all those who appear in court or are interested in the proceedings should be aware of the effect of judicial attitudes on the process.

A: CHILD WELFARE HEARINGS FROM AN UNFAMILIAR PERSPECTIVE

Judge James P. Felstiner[*]

At a judicial training course in January 1989, the Family Court Judges of Ontario spent several days studying mediation practices with skilled trainers. One of the activities was for each judge to act in different roles in several simulated judicial mediation scenarios.

In one mock situation, I played the role of a young mother whose husband was a heavy drinker, and when drunk he was usually abusive to me. After one violent binge, which was especially frightening to our 18-month-old child, the police had taken my baby and placed him with the child protection agency.

The task for the judges was to engage in a mock mediation or pre-trial hearing to determine whether the conflict between my position (as the 20-year-old mother who emphatically wanted her child back) and the agency's could be resolved without a bitter, delayed and lengthy trial.

In this simulated pre-trial procedure (as in most real pre-trials), I, as the mother, was not to speak. Only the lawyers and the judge were to try to settle the conflict. I had accepted my lawyer's urgings to agree to this process, because I liked my lawyer and he had told me that the judge would listen to him fairly. He felt confident that the judge would recommend the return of my child. My lawyer told me he would have as much say as would the lawyer for the agency.

However, during the mock arguments, my lawyer made a number of statements without consulting me. I knew that he and I had prepared for the pre-trial for over an hour the day before, with my telling him about my situation. But I was not prepared for his ad-libbing as new or different slants came up, and sometimes he was not very accurate. He couldn't be; he had never been in my house and had never seen me with my kid.

My frustration with my lawyer not talking to me was small compared to my anger as I listened to the agency's lawyer misrepresent facts as I knew them. The agency's lawyer also attacked my character and belittled my strengths. And then in reply my lawyer would refer to this other lawyer as "my friend."[1] How could he be his friend if that man (the agency's lawyer) was trying to take my kid away? I thought the lawyer was to be *my* friend.

---

[*]   Provincial Court (Family Division), North York, Ontario.

[1]   Lawyers in court frequently refer to one another as "my friend" or "my learned friend." This ancient practice is based on notions of civility and of a common professional calling. However, in light of the confusion it causes clients, the use of this practice might usefully be reassessed.

I noticed that the agency's lawyer conferred frequently with the worker, who felt that I could not protect the child. But my lawyer only told me to let him handle the case and that I was not to interrupt. It did not seem to me that the sides were even. As a result, I interrupted the proceedings several times, and as my frustrations built up I shouted that the lawyer for the agency was a liar. But then, even my own lawyer told me to be quiet, and the judge said that if I did not keep quiet I would have to leave the pre-trial hearing.

By the end of this play-acting, I, the mother, felt powerless and helpless. The lawyer's and the judge's words were swirling back and forth. No one represented exactly what I wanted to say. Many of the statements did not match my perception of the situation which had led to my child being grabbed by the police.

I, the judge acting as a mother, came out of this training session with feelings of anger and helplessness which did not dissipate for several hours. And this had been an attempt at a mediation session, not a mock trial in which positions would have been even more extreme. During the hour or two that it took me to simmer down, I had other thoughts which might be similar to those of parents appearing in my court.

If I had not been granted interim custody of my child at that stage, the social worker (my enemy at the moment) would then have been telling me what *she* expected me to do in the interim to secure *her* approval for the return of my child. I thought that the judge would be the one to make that decision, not my social worker. I had the impression that I was not on an equal footing with the agency in this pre-trial proceeding. The worker for the agency was allowed to sit next to her lawyer, but I was sitting a row behind them and my lawyer.

I had heard the agency's lawyer suggest to the judge that I should return to live with my mother. The lawyer also recommended that I should not have any further contact with my husband, and the agency wanted me to seek a peace bond against him in the criminal courts. Did they ever think what my husband might do to me when he was next drunk if I dragged him to court? Why didn't my worker give me some realistic ideas as to how I could avoid my husband's anger and help him stop his damn drinking?

Why couldn't *I* decide what I had to do to take proper care of my child? What did they know about my mother's home except all the stories she told them about how stable her new common-law relationship was and how she loved her grandchild? Had they forgotten that the agency had taken me from her home twice when I was a kid? Why were they letting themselves be conned into thinking that she is now so competent, when she and her boyfriends made a mess of me and my brother?

With all these thoughts in my mind, I, the mother, was confused when I left that pre-trial hearing. I was also angry and felt very powerless. Everybody but me was going to decide not only what was going to happen to my child, but also what I had to do. It seemed to me that I, the mother, was losing or had lost all of my autonomy.

If this play-acting in a hotel room had been so powerful for me, as a judge acting the part of a young mother, how powerful must be the emotions of parents and children when they appear in our real courts? How many people in my court feel the way I had: powerless and helpless? The upset that I felt that day is not displayed as often in court as I would have expected. This is not to say that the parents involved in child protection proceedings do not display their emotions, for they do. But obviously the parties must be keeping some of their emotions in check.

One reason for the absence of more emotion in court may be that some parents who do not regain custody of their children silently understand and accept the need for wardship. It is almost never discussed in my presence, but how often do parents recognize that their children will be better off in either temporary or permanent care? My feeling as a judge is that some parents are prepared for, and not opposed to, permanent wardship. However, to maintain appearances in their neighbourhoods and with other family members, they may put up a good fight in court.

Returning to the mock pre-trial, one thought was especially strong in my mind both as the mother and as a judge: the relationship between the worker and the parent is complex and difficult. Considering the nature of the worker's role, it is surprising that conflicts are not far more evident in the courtroom. I believe it is a credit to the management of the agencies and the skills of the workers that more and worse acrimony and conflict do not exist. Yet obviously credit must also go to some parents.

Thinking as the mother in the mock pre-trial, I know that I would find it very difficult to like the worker who was trying to take my child away. If the agency had succeeded in convincing the judge that they should keep my child, how would I ever be able to talk to her again? I wonder if we, as judges, tend to ignore some of the very real problems existent in these situations.

It is significant that in my experience, the percentage of cases in which a child is found *not* to be in need of protection is minuscule. Most child welfare cases endure through a continuum of child growth and family development, or stagnation and destruction. There are few, if any, other types of litigation in which the combative parties must continue to relate to each other time and again for long periods of time after contested hearings.

I am constantly concerned about the effect of my decisions on parties before me. But how do judges learn of the aftermath of their decisions? In young offender matters, the legal system provides us with almost no knowledge of the results of our dispositions. I often feel that this would be comparable to surgeons not knowing the results of their operations.

Because child welfare cases are often of an ongoing nature, they afford us a better opportunity to be aware of the results of our judicial decisions. However, I feel that, occasionally, we judges ought to contemplate what might have happened if we had ruled differently.

Behind my desk I have a photograph of a happy, clean, smiling 12-year-old girl. Sarah gave it to me in August 1979 when I renewed her wardship for a second year. She had been in an excellent foster home and would stay for another year. This home encouraged and stimulated her in many ways that her own home could not. Sarah was severely hearing disabled, but in that first year had progressed rapidly in her speech skills. She was proud of her accomplishments. Sarah was adept at sign language, since her father and siblings were also deaf. Although she wanted to go home, Sarah, at 12 years of age, chose to remain in the foster home.

A year later Sarah and her family returned to court for the final decision as to whether she would be made a permanent ward and stay in the foster home or be returned to the care of her father. Sarah had continued to make remarkable gains, but with her older age she had seen more of her family and been subjected to their desires and pressures to have her home. I was conscious of jealousy on the part of her siblings. The hearing at this time was especially difficult and the decision equally so. In the end, I accepted Sarah's expressed wish to go home. This meant a return to a fractious family in a neighbourhood beset with problems. There was no school nearby for her speech therapy. I felt I had made the wrong decision, but it was one I had to make. Sarah had the right to go home, even if I thought that it was not in her very best interests.

A year later the agency applied to terminate supervision. Sarah, 14 years old, returned to court, dirty and pale, having lost ground with her speech abilities, and looking like a tired, angry and defeated 19-year-old. A return to her old foster home to regain the benefits she had derived was not possible and would not have been accepted by Sarah if it had been offered to her.

Supervision by the agency's worker had been insufficient to counter the negative aspects of Sarah's home and community. The supervision order was terminated and Sarah's case was closed. When I returned to my chambers I stared at Sarah's picture. The happy 12-year-old had lost the rest of her childhood. I wonder what Sarah would say today if asked if I had made the right decision when I ordered that she be returned home.

This was one of those special experiences in which a judge has a personal reaction to the results of his decisions. The happy decisions result in the judge obtaining brief glimpses of the joy parents and children may feel. The sad decisions also give the judge a momentary view of the reactions engendered in the family. I suspect, however, that all judges are generally unaware of what happens outside the courtroom after our decisions are made, yet I believe that this is knowledge which we should have. The experience of playing the role of a mother in a mock pre-trial hearing taught me far more about the realities of my court than I learn in many days of hearing cases.

B: LEGAL STRUCTURE IN CHILD PROTECTION PROCEEDINGS

Judge A. Peter Nasmith[*]

Judges do not receive much feedback, but I am told that I sit at the legalistic end of a spectrum of judicial labels. This has a pejorative ring for me in a setting where compassion and wisdom would be more commendable traits. My colleagues assure me that this label is only a reflection of my legal skills. I am not so sure about the skills and bemused by the label if it connotes an imbalance. Yet I must admit that legal structure has a high priority for me as a judge and I shall attempt to explain why that is so.

Training to be a trial lawyer, I spent 11 years in and around courtrooms before being appointed to the bench. I learned that basic principles of justice, among other things, limit the use of government power over individuals to situations where interference can be justified with reliable evidence.

One of the features of my judicial experience in protection cases has been a struggle to keep the hearings within a procedural paradigm, in which the fundamental principles of justice remain reasonably intact. The alternative is for the hearings to give way to unlimited discretion and arbitrariness, which lead, sooner or later, to injustice and abuse of power. A national newspaper cautions our citizens daily: "The subject who is truly loyal to the Chief Magistrate will neither advise nor submit to arbitrary measures."

For much of the 100 years that child protection laws have been evolving, fundamental procedural safeguards have been absent. Proper notification about the proceedings, scrutinizing the evidence that is admitted at the hearings, and the opportunity to confront and challenge the evidence of others and to question the bases of their opinions have not always been available.

It is not hard for me to understand why this is so. There is an unassailable premise that children's needs should be better served. In a sense, this harnesses a child-rescuing fantasy which can be used to rationalize either the neglect of justice or other forms of increased governmental power under such immaculate causes as eliminating the abuse of children.

Of course, most of us share the feelings about rescuing children. We bring to this mission our middle-class ideas about what is good for children. We are repulsed by the abuse, neglect and exploitation of children and we mourn the loss of a child's chance for a fulfilling life. We would all like to see a reduction in the ignorance and neglect in parenting by those who are usually themselves the victims of poor parenting. We see an educational and cultural problem in

---

[*]   Provincial Court (Family Division), Toronto, Ontario.

endless cycle. But one does not have to preside in protection court very long before realizing that clumsy and whimsical government intervention can be even more harmful to children than the abuse and neglect that is suspected or known.

The idea that middle-class values can be applied realistically to the poor and disadvantaged families that produce the majority of protection cases is only one of the myths enfolded in the child-rescuing fantasy. Numerous other myths abound, including the following:

1. Government intervention automatically improves a child's situation.
2. Tolerable standards of child care can be defined in other than vague and highly subjective terms.
3. Good treatment theories can be demonstrated scientifically as opposed to being esoteric ideas floating in and out of fashion.
4. Only the most serious cases are identified and absorb the resources. (The reality is that random identification occurs and once any case is reported, everyone is careful to cover against possible criticism—hence many trivial cases.)

Due to drug and alcohol addiction or other severe handicaps, some birth parents simply cannot raise children safely. There are many shocking and tragic cases of abuse, neglect and risk where court decisions are simplified by applying this cliché: "I don't know where the line is for tolerating risks to children, but I do know that, wherever it is, we are well over it in this case." In other words, in the extreme and obvious cases, there is no serious dispute about proof or the validity of any theory that the expert witness might rely on. The need for significant intervention virtually speaks for itself in some cases.

The majority of contested cases, however, occupy a huge, grey borderline area where the myths, middle-class values, reliability of the evidence and the validity of the expert theories about child-care choices are crucial to the decision to intervene. In these cases, legal rules and procedural safeguards are very important. In addition to the structure provided in the legislation and the decided cases, I keep the following, simple positions in mind:

1. If the applicant does not produce compelling evidence to show that it is better to have the child's placement changed, do not change it.
2. If the applicant does not produce compelling evidence to show which of the plans to protect the child is the least harmful, choose the least intrusive plan.

During my 13 years of judging, I have watched with some satisfaction as legal structure has been added to protection proceedings in Ontario. Legal structure has come in the form of: lawyers replacing lay persons to present the cases of protection agencies; lawyers representing the children and parents; better legal documentation, including pleadings in which the grounds of intervention are identified and the plans for intervention are spelled out; better organization, understanding and presentation of evidence; a rising consciousness about serving notice on necessary parties; and, most notably legislation which creates a fabric of basic principles to guide the courts and others in wielding the formidable powers of intervention.

Protection applications are set up to pit the state against the parents, but the proceedings are civil and not criminal in nature. Neither the presumption of innocence nor the right to remain silent are available to the parents. They are expected to respond to the state's protection concerns about their children even while the burden is on the state to prove the need for protection. Because the state as the applicant is so powerful, it is essential that parents and children have the facility to challenge the reliability of information that is being used. I can illustrate the point with a case that came before me. An infant had multiple bone lesions. The protection agency suspected the father of physical abuse. A team of "experts" from a large children's hospital confronted the father with their suspicions and his outrage served to confirm for them that he was violent and therefore guilty. The parents' lawyer struggled successfully for further medical investigation which eventually revealed that a rare bone disorder, not violence, was the likely cause of the lesions.

In my opinion, it is only when legal structure is guaranteed that we can hope for the success of mediation and reduced polarization between parents and the government in the future. In many cases, an atmosphere of cooperation and mutual problem-solving is likely to work better than court-imposed orders which often drive a wedge between the parents and the government. I am very optimistic about the benefits that mediation can bring to this area, but the effective use of mediation and pre-trial meetings will depend, once again, on a clear backdrop of legal structure. All parties must trust that the legal scales are balanced before they can work towards meaningful solutions in this delicate area.

One remarkable result of the infusion of law into protection proceedings in the 1970s and 1980s was that the traditional rules of evidence became exposed to a rather awkward period of review. The vital importance of the decisions in protection cases provided a good test of the original rationale for the rules of evidence. At times it looked as though we were going to have no rules of evidence at all for these cases. A draft of the *Canadian Uniform Evidence Code* suggested that the proposed Code should not apply to decisions involving children. In Ontario, a legislative provision was enacted[2] to confirm the admissibility of evidence of previous parenting, and this was taken by some judges as a direction to admit all hearsay evidence.[3] At the other end, there were legitimate concerns that courts would exclude highly relevant evidence because of a technical application of exclusionary hearsay rules.

---

[2]   *Child and Family Services Act*, S.O. 1984, c. 55, s. 46.

[3]   Hearsay evidence involves presenting to a court a perception made by someone outside of the courtroom which is tendered as true without the person who did the perceiving being available to be questioned or challenged as to its circumstances and meaning or the chance of error in the perception or the memory of it.

Most of the hearsay disputes in protection cases involve the admission of hospital and other institutional records and the admission of statements attributed to children but presented to the court through intermediaries. The rules of evidence seem to be surviving. For me, protection hearings are on the cutting edge of a progressive approach to hearsay evidence in civil cases that dovetails with the 1970 decision of the Supreme Court of Canada in *Ares* v. *Venner*,[4] and permits judicial discretion to expand exceptions to the rule excluding hearsay if there are grounds of necessity for doing so and circumstances tending to guarantee that the out-of-court source is reliable. Just how far the new exceptions will stretch remains to be seen, but at this point there is a trend towards admitting more hearsay, which in large part coincides with a desire to spare children from the trauma of testifying and to introduce institutional records of the family.

Methods to assist troubled families and programs for preventing child abuse and rehabilitating fractured families have not kept pace with the development of legal sophistication in the courts. Shrinking budgets and the resulting failure to attract enough creative and competent social workers and clinicians to the field is part of the reason for this. There are very few child welfare programs to deal effectively with older children who are runaways. It would be unwise, however, to turn legal structure on the one hand and effective protection field work on the other hand into an either/or dilemma, where the emphasis on justice is considered as an alternative to effective protection programming.

In early 1989, a child welfare seminar was held in Toronto for social workers and lawyers. A senior lawyer for a large protection agency and the director of another large agency publicly lamented the new emphasis on legal paperwork and its heavy bite on their budgets, and they yearned for the days when protection agencies had a freer reign in the courts. The implication was that field work is traded for legal work. I worry about this dichotomous thinking. Legal safeguards and good social work need not be mutually exclusive.

I have heard impressive testimony from experienced clinicians and social workers whose input has been helpful in clarifying the nature of the choices for a child. More often, witnesses are hampered by inexperience and the lack of reliable data to enable them to predict, with any persuasion, the best plan for a child's care.

While legal reforms in the child welfare area in the past decade have been impressive, they have not been sweeping. For example, in Ontario and elsewhere there remains an embarrassing government policy of falsifying statements of live birth following adoptions, as a relic of the ancient notion that all adoptions must be secret, and there has been a rather pathetic attempt to speed up cases by defining a number of biological fathers out of existence.

Between 1985 and 1989, I heard a series of lengthy trials turning on the apparent need to choose between terminating all birth family contact or preventing long-term foster parents from adopting and thereby increasing the perma-

---

[4]   [1970] S.C.R. 608, 14 D.L.R. (3d) 4.

nence and stability of the foster placement. The persisting idea that adoption must always foreclose any chance of birth family contact is evidence that sacred cows continue to stalk the adoption field, making adoption a less helpful choice than it would otherwise be and increasing the appearance of arbitrariness in the shaping of children's destinies.

There are other impediments to the reform of laws that govern child welfare decisions. Some courts will be reluctant to apply the *Canadian Charter of Rights and Freedoms*[5] to family law generally and child welfare law specifically. In a 1988 Ontario case, a trial judge carefully applied *Charter* principles in nullifying a definition of "parent" which excluded biological fathers who did not know they were the fathers. In leaving the impression that such people are irresponsible and therefore not worth the trouble of serving with any notices of proceedings concerning their children, the Divisional Court reversed the trial decision and supported the definition with a characterization of these people as "casual fornicators."[6] Another point, however, is that some of these unknowing biological fathers could well be important to their children quite apart from the duration of their relationship with the mother.

With time, the *Charter of Rights* could be helpful in reshaping the laws that govern child welfare and in clearing the way for a more democratic view of the best interests of children by removing some unnecessary obstructions such as: bureaucratic expediency, the unbalanced political accommodation of small but strong interest groups, paternalism, moralizing, stereotyping and mythology surrounding today's nuclear families and other archaic or overzealous forms of legislative or judicial generalizing.

To say that a judge in a protection proceeding has a special function unlike the traditional role of a judge in the adversary system is to understate a remarkable feature of child welfare hearings which is both interesting and controversial. Virtually all of the approved idiosyncrasies of the judge's role in protection cases are attributed to the fact that the issue is the welfare of a child whose fate should not depend on the vicissitudes of courtroom games. I have never fully understood why children's issues, by themselves, would revolutionize the adversary system. If we should change our system, it is not just because of children, but because we want the best fact-finding and the best decisions.

In any event, judges in protection cases are invited to become inquisitors and to ferret out evidence that the parties may have overlooked. We are supervisors of the case. Depending on the varying skills of counsel for protection agencies, we perform administrative and didactic functions while steering the case, making sure that the proper parties have been served and preventing a drift from adjournment to adjournment. To some extent, we also become self-styled experts on

---

[5] Part I of the *Constitution Act*, 1982, being Schedule B of the *Canada Act 1982* (U.K.), 1982, c. 11.

[6] *Ontario (Attorney General)* v. *Re Nevins, P.C.J.* (1988), 13 R.F.L. (3d) 113 at 119(Ont. Div. Ct).

child development theories through prolonged exposure to a myriad of theories, and to some extent we act as our own frame of reference for values and normalcy. We get right into the arena. While each of these tendencies to bias and over-involvement may be unavoidable, I think that they, too, further underline the need to provide for competent legal representation of the parties and to insist on a fair hearing where principles of justice are recognized.

Another major force in shaping the judge's novel role in protection cases comes from the hierarchy within the court system. The child welfare hearing has historically been the low rung on the court ladder. Family law as a subject has lacked prestige, and child welfare cases have ranked near the bottom of family law. Many of us feel that this is an ironic topsy-turvy of priorities. Protection hearings contain issues as profound and relevant to a healthy society as any issues in commercial or criminal cases and the procedural and evidential questions are as complex and demanding as in any other case, to say nothing of the substantive questions. Protection hearings should command the best facilities and support services: the more experienced and sophisticated social workers, the best lawyers, and the best, independent judges. Instead, protection cases are usually relegated to the grungiest court facilities, unskilled social workers, student lawyers cutting their teeth on their first cases, and judges whose salaries and other benefits are the lowest and who are sometimes mistaken for government functionaries who are expected to prop up the weaker components of the hearing.

We are blessed with some very good lawyers in these cases, and I have heard evidence from some enlightened and dedicated social workers and seen their remarkable accomplishments. There are certainly many intelligent clinicians who can give compelling opinion evidence. I regret that these are the exceptions that have tended to prove the general rule of mediocrity or worse in protection cases. Budgets need to be bolstered and priorities reviewed in order to erase the historical second-class syndrome that lingers here. In my opinion, there was marked improvement in the 1970s and 1980s, due mainly to progressive government policies and legal education. We may now be approaching another watershed as we enter the 1990s, when the direction will depend on funding and priorities. Second-class attention to the problems of families and children and the second-class features of the courts that deal with them will either be eliminated or reinforced. In the meantime, there are unusual pressures for judges to play a more active role than the appearance of objectivity can normally endure.

Accompanying the recent legalization of these protection proceedings has been the appointment of lawyers to the Family Courts as judges. If the standard of recruits is respectable, that can be attributed to the progressive spirit of reform within family law which began in the 1970s. There is also a missionary factor which helps to explain why good judges would stay in a second-rate court even when the vision of further meaningful reform fades. As with good social workers and good lawyers, I suppose it is sometimes possible for judges to rid themselves of elitist thinking, to forget about financial security and prestige, and to enjoy the truly rewarding and challenging human aspects of these critical child protection cases.

With some pleasure and relief, I can say that today when I walk into protection court, the improved legal structure frees me to worry less about procedural travesties and to concentrate more on being respectful to the parties, listening patiently and carefully to the evidence and attempting to be wise, compassionate and sensitive in my decisions.

C: REFLECTIONS AND EXPECTATIONS

*Judge Anne Russell**

Despite the best efforts of expert professionals in the field of child protection over the last century, effective remedies for aberrant human behaviour which contributes to child neglect and abuse continue to elude us. Fortunately, disillusion has not deterred continuing efforts to prevent and treat those problems. Every day our courts witness the perseverance and commitment of dedicated professionals who struggle to deal with human tragedy. Sometimes, the court process represents the end of a struggle to rehabilitate a family and a sense of failure and frustration prevails; at other times, the court process is just the beginning, and the optimism of child welfare workers and parents replenishes waning energies.

It is widely accepted that the Family Court is expected to act in the "best interests" of the child. That phrase itself is the subject of much dispute; it is so vague and subjective that it offers little real assistance to the judge. While the best interests principle is often touted, the best of family and social conditions is seldom achieved for a child who is the subject of a protection order.

The achievement of what is best for the child may be beyond the intellectual, emotional or financial resources of many families. The subjective nature of the principle may result in widely varying interpretations of what is best for the child. In applying the principle, courts are expected to make predictions based on unreliable indicators of human behaviour. The child's family may be unsound and unsafe, but the child's needs include the need to know and to belong to an intact family unit. The child's needs for a safe and secure environment must somehow be balanced with his or her needs for familial contact. This process involves balancing the present with the future, the known with the unknown, and the real with the intangible needs of the child.

---

*   Provincial Court (Family and Youth Divisions), Edmonton, Alberta.

The preservation of the family requires that caution be exercised to ensure that the best interests principle not be inappropriately applied. Sufficient cause must be demonstrated to warrant state intrusion. It was established very early in the common law of England that there must be some evidence of unfitness on the part of a parent before the courts would permit intrusion upon parental authority. While that principle has no application in cases of custody disputes between parents or others who have already established some significant relationship with the child, the principle does apply to cases where the child remains in the actual custody of the parent and the state tries to intervene. Before any level of intrusion will be permitted, the state must first show that significant family failure has occurred. It is only after such a failure has been established that the state can ask the court to consider what is in the best interests of the child. Even at this stage, caution must be exercised in the application of this principle.

The prognosis for children who are removed from their families is guarded, and though foster care or an adoptive placement may be of optimum quality, it may not be the panacea these children require. We are reminded daily of the unpredictability of human behaviour, the unreliability of our therapeutic resources to change it, and of the limited resources available in our society for rehabilitation.

It is essential that, when we do intervene in the life of a child, we not only be cautious, but also strive to be fair and just. When the social reform movement was in its infancy in the last century, Charles Dickens wrote, "In the little world in which children have their existence, whosoever brings them up, there is nothing so finely perceived and so finely felt as injustice." Injustices are also perceived and felt by the parents of the children we see in our courts. Though we cannot always ensure we are right in these matters, we can and must always ensure that we are fair. Fairness demands that parties be given adequate notice, a chance to participate in proceedings and reasons for decisions. It demands that they be treated with respect, courtesy, patience, tolerance and understanding. It demands that they be given an understanding of the process.

The court's role in child protection matters is unique. Judges are permitted to take a more active role in these proceedings. Judges may examine witnesses more freely than in other legal proceedings, and may even call their own witnesses, if certain important evidence is missing. The rules about hearsay evidence are relaxed to a limited extent. For example, the evidence of young children may be received without the necessity of the child testifying. However, not all hearsay evidence is admissible, even in these proceedings. Child welfare workers are often frustrated to discover that in their daily practice they are able to operate on a broader base of hearsay and untested information, which a court may wisely reject as unreliable.

Child welfare matters involve complex legal problems as well as social ones. It is essential that anyone working in the field of child protection develop an appreciation of, and respect for, the legal principles which must apply to the resolution of issues. The rules in these proceedings are not significantly different from those applied in other legal proceedings, except perhaps in respect of the use of hearsay evidence. These rules have been developed over centuries of experience and, while they may appear to frustrate and delay proceedings, they are the best protection we have to ensure the application of fairness and justice. As Felix Frankfurter, a great American jurist, stated: "The history of liberty has largely been the history of observance of procedural safeguards."[7]

Of course, judges are concerned with more than mere procedural issues. In child protection hearings, the paramount concern is the welfare of the child. The burden of the decision in these matters is heavy; it is the responsibility for the decision, and not the authority to make it, which is so keenly felt by the judge. However, the role of the judge in determining the future of a child is but one step in a continuum of decisions made for the child by society. Judicial decisions are not made in isolation. Nearly every child protection hearing involves the evidence of the child welfare worker and at least one expert.

The development of social science has resulted in a proliferation of experts and theories regarding human behaviour. While experts are often helpful, courts must not blindly embrace untested theory and too easily proffered opinion. It is the duty of the court to carefully weigh all evidence presented to it, including that of experts, to ensure that it is reasonably reliable.

While it is apparent that cross-examination often causes distress and discomfort to the witness, our law concerning the presentation and cross-examination of evidence is the best method we have yet produced to ascertain the truth and reliability of theories and assertions. The most effective and influential witnesses, expert or otherwise, are those whose objectivity, candour and integrity remain constant throughout the proceedings.

Anyone who applies his or her best efforts to making an application before a court in a child welfare matter suffers a sense of personal loss if the application is unsuccessful. Indeed, the application would not be legitimate if the applicant did not sincerely believe in the wisdom and prudence of its success. Professionalism, however, requires the maintenance of objectivity concerning the outcome of these applications. The child welfare authority successfully discharges its responsibility by commencing the application and presenting the best evidence. A denial of an application is not a shortcoming of the worker; these applications must not be viewed in "win" or "lose" terms.

The judge's perception of the evidence and the issues occurs from a different vantage point, and may not be in accord with that of the worker, who is in closer proximity to the source. While the judge's perception may not always be correct, it does have the advantage of a broader range of vision. In any event, responsibility for the decision ultimately rests with the judge.

On any day, in any Family Court in Canada, a multitude of human tragedies unfold; the average citizen likely has no concept of the extent of perversity in our midst, yet conscience and promoting social order demand that we endeavour to

---

[7] *McNabb* v. *United States* (1943), 318 US 332.

redress the conditions that create these tragedies. Quaint and uncommon attributes of fortitude and forbearance are needed by those engaged in this process. Social welfare is not a popular cause at this time; the economy, environment and control of drugs are more attractive political issues. Indeed, the focus on the economy and the deficit may be the nemesis of the social reform movement.

Some might question the temerity of social reformers who are committed to changing aberrant human behaviour where even God may appear to have failed. Some might question the audacity of reformers who presume to judge the standards of human behaviour. But none would question the duty of society to protect a child at risk. Human nature is such that we are compelled to intervene where parents are unwilling or unable to adequately respond to the child's needs. The issue is not whether children should be protected by the state, but rather when and how much protection should be provided.

It must be acknowledged that extensive social programs have failed to achieve the social harmony foreseen by the social reform movement in the last century. Crime has not been eliminated and families still fail.

Nevertheless, some changes have occurred. For example, society has acquired a begrudging acceptance of social responsibility. Our concept of the family has evolved. We have a new awareness and appreciation of diverse cultural values. We have greater respect for the rights of the individual. We have a healthy regard for the limitations of social science and of the economy to effect social change.

The survival of the family, the preservation of an economic base to support our massive social structures, the development of a global community and the schism between fundamentalists and progressives are all issues that will significantly affect the social programs of the 21st century. The demarcation of the boundaries of state intervention, the struggle to ensure fairness in the process of intervention, and the development of assessment and therapeutic resources will continue to be major issues in child protection proceedings. Undoubtedly, however, so long as society flourishes, many generations of children yet to come will require the protection of the state.

D: THE JUDGE'S ROLES AND RESPONSIBILITIES IN CHILD PROTECTION CASES

*Judge R. James Williams**

By training, judges are lawyers. Their expertise is, or should be, in the law. The primary responsibility of the judge lies within the trial process, a process that values fairness and rights and is, by tradition, adversarial. In family law, this adversarial approach is often criticized as exacerbating conflict rather than con-tributing constructively or creatively to its resolution.

In child protection proceedings, the trial process takes place in the shadow of a series of unique constraints and practical realities. These include the following:

- Unresolved conflicts exist between the rights of children, parents and the state.
- Child protection services, while therapeutic in philosophical orientation, often lack the resources to realize their goals.
- Parents and children are involuntary participants in the process.
- Families involved in child protection proceedings are often impover-ished.
- Trial decisions can become assessments of people, not acts.
- Decisions are both retrospective *and* prospective.
- There is uncertainty as to whether the trial process should be viewed as an inquiry whose purpose is to protect a child, or as a more traditional adversarial trial process.
- The termination of parental rights is a dramatic and emotional conse-quence that looms coercively in all child protection proceedings.

These factors combine to exaggerate the authority, discretion and impact of the judge. In family law, judges are less confined by precedent or legal rules than in other areas of law. Indeed, it is frequently said in family law that each case is *sui generis*, that is, unique.

Some social workers complain that the process is too legalistic, meaning too dominated by law and lawyers. Procedurally, law does and should dominate any trial process. Law has evolved a trial process that is based on fairness and accountability—elements that are essential to any child protection intervention.

---

* The Family Court for the Province of Nova Scotia, Dartmouth, Nova Scotia.

The trial process is decision-oriented and adjudicatory. What, then, are the issues to be decided in a child protection case?

Child protection proceedings are characterized by these recurring questions:[8]

- Did abuse or neglect occur?
- Where will the child live?
- What services will the family receive?
- When can state intervention begin or cease?
- Should parental rights be terminated?

While we can frame the questions in legal jargon, their answers are not found in legal abstractions. The issues and context of child protection are different from those in most other types of litigation. The issues involve judgments of people's needs, abilities and potential for change. They are measured against standards that are less than precisely stated in statutes.

In child protection, we do not ask the judge to be strictly adjudicatory, to merely decide whether parental rights should be terminated. Rather, we ask the judge and the legal process to proceed through a series of stages (e.g., finding in need of protection, supervision, and committal to care). The courts are statutorily mandated to be diagnostic (to determine whether there is a problem rendering the child in need of protection), coercively therapeutic (supervision) and adjudicatory (to decide the future of a child and family). Thus, there are three levels of intervention: identifying the problem through offering services, forcing the use of services and terminating parental rights. There is ongoing tension within and between cases, between the therapeutic and adjudicatory adversarial orientations. However, these orientations are not mutually exclusive; elements of both often co-exist.

The judge then, is an adjudicator with great authority and discretion overseeing a process that may be therapeutic or adversarial, but which must maintain what lawyers call due process. The legal process and its language are foreign to some of its major participants. The adjudicator is often separated culturally and economically from those who are judged. The issues being decided are fundamental to the very being of those before the court.

A former family court judge, George Thomson, said:

> In child protection matters, judges tend to display understandable uncertainty about the role or roles they are to assume, an uncertainty that is often shared by many of those that appear before the court ... The judge in a typical hearing may feel called upon to function as a decision-maker, symbolic representative of the authority of the state, an investigator, a parent and a therapist. An understanding of the complexity of the issues at hand may caution one against undue reliance on the efficacy of any one of the roles.[9]

---

[8] H.A. Davidson et al., *child Abuse and Neglect Litigation: A Manual for Judges* (Washington, D.C.: U.S. Dept. of Health and Human Services, 1981) at iii.

[9] G.M. Thomson, "Judging Judiciously in Child Protection Cases" in R.S. Abella and C. L'Heureux-Dubé, eds, *Family Law: Dimensions of Justice*, (Toronto: Butterworths, 1983) 213 at 215.

One might add translator and mediator to the roles mentioned by Thomson.

The caution provided by Thomson recognizes that between, and even within, individual situations before the court, judges may find themselves in different roles. There is, then, no one role for the judge. I would be skeptical about any restricted definition of the judge's role. I am more comfortable with the conceptualization of the judge having responsibilities, rather than a role. Responsibilities to what? I offer my own opinions:

1. *To the law.* Judges operate in a legal process that has evolved. Individuals have rights and obligations. The process should be continually explained and clarified to those before the court. Reasons should be given for decisions. The decisions and decision-making process must be accountable to the law. Without the law there is no accountability.

2. *To problem-solving.* The problems are human, family problems. They will continue in one form or another after the trial process is over. The judge should recognize that the adjudication process is not the only way to resolve problems. The judge can do this in at least two ways. First, by attempting to have the trial process facilitate, or at least not impede, problem-solving. Adequate early and complete disclosure is essential to any problem-solving. Other processes, for example mediation, can be seen as resources, as opposed to something foreign to the trial process. Second, by using or recognizing roles other than that of adjudicator. Pre-trials that are settlement oriented, or that bring focus to substantive rather than emotional issues, potentially enhance both problem-solving and the trial process itself. The judge who sees problem-solving in a broader context will help to blunt the polarization that results from the adversarial trial process. There are times, however, when that polarization is unavoidable or necessary.

3. *To decision-making.* Judges decide cases. In doing so, they should explain the rationales for their decisions; decisions should be given without undue delay; and the decisions must be based on evidence. The decisions impact upon the future of both child and family. My view is that the judge has a responsibility to control the trial process in order to ensure that there is evidence before the court upon which to base a decision. The decisions require the constant balancing of competing orientations (therapeutic vs. adversarial and adjudicatory vs. problem-solving), rights (of parent, child, and state) and obligations (of state to the parent, parent to the child, and state to the child). Decisions should address these issues.

4. *To the parents.* Parents are entitled to more than rights. They are entitled to dignity and respect, both personally and culturally. They must be not only listened to, but spoken to at a level that they understand. Problems, expectations and consequences should, where possible, be plainly and concretely identified. They should be given reasons for decisions.

5. *To the child welfare agency.* The decision-making process of a child welfare agency is both accountable to, and subject to, the scrutiny of the court. The court should recognize and be aware of the resources available to, and constraints upon, such agencies. Again, expectations should be stated explicitly. The social worker should be respected; it must be appreciated that either the same or another social worker will work with the family or the family's community again. The world does not end when the court hearing is over. The judge who needlessly denigrates the worker or agency undermines the likelihood of a parent working constructively with that agency in the future. As a result, the parent loses a potential resource. Conversely, the judge who fails to comment upon an agency practice that is viewed as inappropriate perpetuates that practice. Criticism should be professionally and constructively stated.

6. *To the child.* The child's needs, vulnerabilities, attachments, sense of time, uniqueness and rights must be maintained as the focus and rationale of child protection. Further, in appropriate cases, the views of the child must be taken into account.

7. *To the state.* Judges are authority figures. They set (within the confines of generally worded statutes) boundaries in child protection, defining the base level below which a child's level of care will not fall. In doing so, they must recognize individual rights and general standards within society.

8. *To themselves.* The foundation of responsible decision-making is knowledge. Areas of obvious applicability include the law, dispute resolution techniques, community resources, child development, psychology, communication skills and family dynamics. The institutional isolation of judges means that they must aggressively seek, expand and update knowledge and skills in these areas. Decisions, behaviour and actions should be regularly questioned, reviewed and learned from.

In the end, the judge's role is not unlike that of other professionals. At the core of any professional role is the ongoing responsibility to increase knowledge and self-awareness and to learn how we affect others.

For the judge in child protection proceedings, however, these responsibilities are exaggerated by institutional isolation, wide discretion, cultural and economic distance from those before him or her, authority, and the fact that decisions are often being made outside the judge's area of expertise—the law. It is the law that provides the child protection process, and ultimately the judge, with accountability. The integrity of the process depends upon the judge's grasp of the law and the trial process. The law is the foundation upon which the process ultimately rests. Judges must start there but should, in my view, go beyond this—seeking to extend their knowledge base and skills, being prepared to be creative and open to change and accepting the responsibility to be more than mere decision-makers.

TABLE OF CASES

TABLE OF STATUTES

PROVINCIAL

UNITED STATES

INDEX

66917